"Remarkable for its scope and acuity, impressively lucid and well informed, this book successfully locates Fanon in an established phenomenological tradition. In the process, it fundamentally alters the way we read the Martinican psychiatrist's *oeuvre*. Its succession of incisive and persuasive essays will quickly become a source for debate, elaboration, or contention."

— **Achille Mbembe**, *author of* Necropolitics

"After the post-Floyd summer of 2020, the global significance of race, racism, and ongoing anti-Blackness in particular has become impossible to deny, underlining the continuing, indeed enhanced, relevance of the imperishable texts of Frantz Fanon. This invaluable collection brings together new and classic analyses that should consolidate Fanon's stature both as a founder of 'critical' phenomenology and a pathbreaker in the theorization of an anti-essentialist, politically informed and socially contextualized, human psychology.

— **Charles Mills**, *author of* The Racial Contract *and* Black Rights/White Wrongs: The Critique of Racial Liberalism…?

"On a foray for love, theorists/psychologists edited this excellent collection, *Fanon, Phenomenology, and Psychology.* Anchored with a beautiful introduction, this book honors an ancestor who was and remains 'as much psychiatrist as revolutionary.' As we struggle for self-possession and protection from varied forms of lynching and disappearance, we can find respite here, and deep engagement with the language of struggle and liberation."

— **Joy James**, *editor of* Imprisoned Intellectuals *and author of* Seeking the Beloved Community

"Urgent, necessary, all-too-timely, *Fanon, Phenomenology, and Psychology* offers us not one but multiple Fanons for this contemporary moment. Within its pages we meet Fanon the psychiatrist, Fanon the phenomenologist, Fanon the freedom fighter and activist, Fanon the chronicler of colonialism, Fanon the diagnostician of racism, Fanon the theorist of time. The cumulative power and promise of the essays gathered here cannot be over-stated. This is just a dazzlingly exciting adventure in reading and thinking."

— **Ann Pellegrini**, *author of* Performance Anxieties: Staging Psychoanalysis, Staging Race

"This 'must read' volume, edited by three phenomenological psychologists, claims Frantz Fanon's right place at the gateway to critical and decolonial phenomenological psychologies. The book's chapters, written by world renowned Fanon scholars, make clear Fanon's importance for critiquing the whiteness of Eurocentric depth psychologies, while opening potential pathways to transdisciplinary psychologies of liberation that begin – as they must – with the racism that sustains coloniality."

– **Mary Watkins**, *author of* Mutual Accompaniment and the Creation of the Commons *and co-author of* Toward Psychologies of Liberation

"What more relevant text for our troubled times of racialised pandemic, Black Lives Matter mobilisations after the murder of George Floyd and the storming by White supremacists of Capitol Hill? In this volume, Fanon's contributions to and as phenomenology are explicated, assessed and shown to be unique and vital (in multiple senses). This bumper collection of new, specially written and classic papers on Fanon underscore why and how we need Fanon now, to think and rethink racialisation, embodiment and action."

– **Erica Burman**, *author of* Fanon, Education, Action: Fanon as Method

"Whether in the bottom of slave ships, the streets of North America, or within the context of a global Blackness, we are painfully aware of the indelible cries of Black bodies: 'I can't breathe!' That cry, that lament, speaks to an anti-Black world within which Frantz Fanon had higher hopes, where he desired to move with effortless grace and help to build the world together, but was constantly denied. Yet, Fanon knew that his racialized predicament, his deep alienation, was 'not an individual question.' *Fanon, Phenomenology, and Psychology*, interdisciplinary at its core, and at times even de-disciplinary, is a discursively diverse text that not only reminds us of the deep significance of Fanon's contestation of disciplinary purity or methodological fetishization, but it is a text that uncovers the persistent haunting reality of sociogenic anti-Black racism, where the Black body remains accused, where amputations and excisions are experienced, where the Black body is rendered 'an object among other objects,' where Black life continues to be disposable, fungible, and ungrievable. This critically engaging and urgent text that you hold, one that refuses to reduce the complexity of Fanon and his corpus to a singular conceptual orientation, and one that therefore recognizes the generativity of reading Fanon through multiple and overlapping frameworks, especially psychology and phenomenology, demonstrates the revolutionary force of Fanon's work for our contemporary mourning and his aspirations for a new humanism that refuses 'to accept the present as definitive.'"

– **George Yancy**, *author of* Backlash: What Happens When We Talk Honestly About Race in America

FANON, PHENOMENOLOGY, AND PSYCHOLOGY

Fanon, Phenomenology, and Psychology is the first edited collection dedicated to exploring the explicitly phenomenological foundations underlying Frantz Fanon's most important insights.

Featuring contributions from many of the world's leading scholars on Fanon, this volume foregrounds a series of crucial phenomenological topics – inclusive of the domains of experience, structure, embodiment, and temporality – pertaining to the analysis and interrogation of racism and anti-Blackness. Chapters highlight and expand Fanon's ongoing importance to the discipline of psychology while opening compelling new perspectives on psychopathology, decolonial praxis, racialized time, whiteness, Black subjectivity, the "racial ontologizing of the body," systematic structures of racism and resulting forms of trauma, Black Consciousness, and Africana phenomenology.

In an era characterized by resurgent forms of anti-Blackness and racism, this book is essential reading for students, scholars, and activists who remain inspired by Fanon's legacy.

Leswin Laubscher, PhD, is chair of the department of psychology at Duquesne University, Pittsburgh, and extraordinary professor in the department of psychology at the University of the Western Cape, South Africa. He is the author of the textbook *An Introduction to Psychology as a Human Science*.

Derek Hook, PhD, is associate professor of psychology at Duquesne University, Pittsburgh, and an extraordinary professor of psychology at the University of Pretoria, South Africa. He is the author of *Six Moments in Lacan*.

Miraj U. Desai, PhD, author of *Travel and Movement in Clinical Psychology: The World Outside the Clinic*, is on the faculty of the Yale Program for Recovery and Community Health.

THE PSYCHOLOGY AND THE OTHER BOOK SERIES

The *Psychology and the Other* Book Series highlights creative work at the intersections between psychology and the vast array of disciplines relevant to the human psyche. The interdisciplinary focus of this series brings psychology into conversation with continental philosophy, psychoanalysis, religious studies, anthropology, sociology, and social/critical theory. The cross-fertilization of theory and practice, encompassing such a range of perspectives, encourages the exploration of alternative paradigms and newly articulated vocabularies that speak to human identity, freedom, and suffering. Thus, we are encouraged to reimagine our encounters with difference, our notions of the "other," and what constitutes therapeutic modalities.

The study and practices of mental health practitioners, psychoanalysts, and scholars in the humanities will be sharpened, enhanced, and illuminated by these vibrant conversations, representing pluralistic methods of inquiry, including those typically identified as psychoanalytic, humanistic, qualitative, phenomenological, or existential.

Recent Series Titles Include:

Eros Crucified: Death, Desire, and the Divine in Psychoanalysis and Philosophy of Religion, 1ˢᵗ Edition,
By Matthew Clemente

Dante and the Other: A Phenomenology of Love, By Aaron B. Daniels

Beyond Clinical Dehumanisation toward the Other in Community Mental Health Care: Levinas, Wonder and Autoethnography, By Catherine A. Racine

Trust and Trauma: An Interdisciplinary Study in Human Nature, By Michael Oppenheim

Lacan and Race: Racism, Identity and Psychoanalytic Theory,
Edited by Sheldon George and Derek Hook

Self and Other in an Age of Uncertain Meaning: Communication and the Marriage of Minds,
By Timothy D. Stephen

Fanon, Phenomenology, and Psychology,
Edited by Leswin Laubscher, Derek Hook, and Miraj U. Desai

Madness in Experience and History: Merleau-Ponty's Phenomenology and Foucault's Archaeology,
By Hannah Lyn Venable

For a full list of titles in the series, please visit the Routledge
website at: https://www.routledge.com/Psychology-and-the-Other/book-series/PSYOTH

FANON, PHENOMENOLOGY, AND PSYCHOLOGY

Edited by
Leswin Laubscher, Derek Hook, and Miraj U. Desai

Routledge
Taylor & Francis Group

NEW YORK AND LONDON

First published 2022
by Routledge
605 Third Avenue, New York, NY 10158

and by Routledge
2 Park Square, Milton Park, Abingdon, Oxon, OX14 4RN

Routledge is an imprint of the Taylor & Francis Group, an informa business

Library of Congress Cataloging-in-Publication Data
Names: Laubscher, Leswin, editor. | Hook, Derek, editor. | Desai, Miraj,
editor.
Title: Fanon, phenomenology and psychology/edited by Leswin Laubscher,
Derek Hook and Miraj Desai.
Description: New York, NY: Routledge, 2022. |
Series: Psychology and the other | Includes bibliographical references.
Identifiers: LCCN 2021009986 (print) | LCCN 2021009987 (ebook) |
ISBN 9780367478766 (hardback) | ISBN 9780367471484 (paperback) |
ISBN 9781003037132 (ebook)
Subjects: LCSH: Fanon, Frantz, 1925-1961. | Phenomenological psychology. |
Phenomenology. | Psychology and philosophy. | Psychiatry–Philosophy.
Classification: LCC BF204.5 .F36 2022 (print) | LCC BF204.5 (ebook) |
DDC 150.19/2–dc23
LC record available at https://lccn.loc.gov/2021009986
LC ebook record available at https://lccn.loc.gov/2021009987

ISBN: 978-0-367-47876-6 (hbk)
ISBN: 978-0-367-47148-4 (pbk)
ISBN: 978-1-003-03713-2 (ebk)

DOI: 10.4324/9781003037132

Typeset in Baskerville
by Deanta Global Publishing Services, Chennai, India

By the manner of a life led, or the circumstances of a death suffered, a name can become an inspiration, an incantation to action and activism. But a name also conjures a singular individual, one we loved, who ate at our table, whose laughter remains in the echo of our hearts. By way of mourning and remembrance, we dedicate and bind this book to Antwon Rose II.

CONTENTS

CONTRIBUTORS

Sara Ahmed is an independent feminist scholar and writer. Her work is concerned with how power is experienced and challenged in everyday life and institutional cultures. She is currently completing a book entitled *Complaint!* for Duke University Press and has begun a new research project on common sense. Her previous publications include *What's The Use? On the Uses of Use* (2019), *Living a Feminist Life* (2017), *Willful Subjects* (2014), *On Being Included: Racism and Diversity in Institutional Life* (2012), *The Promise of Happiness* (2010), *Queer Phenomenology: Objects, Orientations, Others* (2006), *The Cultural Politics of Emotion* (2014, 2004), *Strange Encounters: Embodied Others in Post-Coloniality* (2000), and *Differences that Matter: Feminist Theory and Postmodernism* (1998).

Alia Al-Saji is associate professor of Philosophy at McGill University, in Montreal, Quebec. Her work brings together phenomenology, critical philosophy of race, and feminist theory, with an abiding interest in questions of time, affect, and racialization. Notable among her works, she is the author of "The Racialization of Muslim Veils" (*Philosophy and Social Criticism*, 2010), "Decolonizing Bergson" (*Beyond Bergson*, SUNY, 2019), and "Glued to the Image: A Critical Phenomenology of Racialization through Works of Art" (*Journal of Aesthetics and Art Criticism*, 2019). Al-Saji argues for the philosophical, political, and lived importance of affective hesitation, notably in "A Phenomenology of Hesitation" (*Living Alterities*, SUNY, 2014).

Robert Bernasconi is Edwin Erle Sparks Professor of Philosophy and African American Studies at Penn State University, in State College, Pennsylvania. He is the author of two books on Heidegger (*The Question of Language in Heidegger's History of Being* and *Heidegger in Question*) and one on Sartre (*How to Read Sartre*). He has written some twenty essays on Fanon, the most recent of which is "Frantz Fanon's Engagement with Phenomenology: Unlocking the Temporal Architecture of *Black Skin, White Masks*," which is forthcoming in *Research in Phenomenology* and which can be conceived as a sequel to the essay published in the present volume. In addition, he has published numerous essays in critical philosophy of race, and on Hegel, Levinas, and Derrida, among others. He is the editor of three journals: *Critical Philosophy of Race*, *Levinas Studies*, and *Eco-Ethica*.

Athena V. Colman is associate professor of Philosophy in the Faculty of Humanities at Brock University in St. Catharines, Ontario, where she is also core faculty on the program committee for the Centre for Women's and Gender Studies in the Faculty of Social Sciences. Her interests are transdisciplinary and include social and political thought through phenomenology, psychoanalysis, contemporary continental philosophy, and critical theory: the Frankfurt school. She lectures and supervises in Women's Studies, Dramatic Arts, Comparative Literatures and Arts, Organizational Behavior, Critical Disability Studies, Sociology, and Human Geography. Neither bookless nor catless, her publications are not as interesting as her students' but include work on Taoism, Hegel, Kristeva, Merleau-Ponty, Freud, Lacan, Fanon, Butler, and Irigaray. Her recent work contributes to the emerging field of transfeminism and focuses on the intersection of psychoanalysis and phenomenology in an effort to elaborate a morphological ontology of trans subjectivity.

Miraj U. Desai is on the faculty of the Program for Recovery and Community Health of the Yale School of Medicine, Department of Psychiatry, in New Haven, Connecticut. At Yale, he is also a member of the South Asian Studies Council, affiliated faculty in the Center on Climate Change and Health, and resident fellow of Pierson College. His book, *Travel and Movement in Clinical Psychology: The World Outside the Clinic*, draws on Zen Buddhism, phenomenology, Fanon, and nonviolent philosophy to explore the relations between mental health, oppression, and social justice. His most recent work examines institutional bias and racism. Dr. Desai has received funding from the National Institutes of Health, including for a participatory research project to address the social determinants of mental health, in partnership with local communities of color. He has received two Early Career Awards from the American Psychological Association, including from the Minority Fellowship Program, who noted his "outstanding scientific contributions and the application of this knowledge toward the improved mental and physical well-being of people of color."

Grant Farred's most recent publications include *Entre Nous: Between the World Cup and Me* (Duke University Press, 2019) and *The Burden of Over-Representation: Race, Sport and Philosophy* (Temple University Press, 2018). His monograph, *An Essay for Ezra: Racial Terror in America*, is forthcoming from the University of Minnesota Press (December 2021). Among his current projects-in-process are "Only A Black Athlete Can Save Us Now" (University of Minnesota Press) and "Mind of Blue: A Philosophy of Jazz" (Temple University Press).

Nigel C. Gibson is author of *Fanon: The Postcolonial Imagination* (Polity, 2003; Arabic translation, Arab Center for Research and Policy Studies, 2013) and *Fanonian Practices in South Africa: From Steve Biko to Abahlali baseMjondolo* (University of KwaZulu Natal and Palgrave, 2011), and he is the co-author, with Robert Beneduce, of *Frantz Fanon, Psychiatry and Politics* (Rowman and Littlefield and the University of Witwatersrand Press, 2017). He is currently working on an edited collection to be published by Daraja Press on the sixtieth anniversary of Fanon's *The Wretched of the Earth* in 2021. His two earlier edited collections on Fanon are *Rethinking Fanon: The Continuing Dialogue* (Humanity Books, 1999) and *Living Fanon: Global Perspectives* (Palgrave, 2011). He teaches at Emerson College in Boston, Massachusetts, and is honorary professor, UHURU, at the university currently known as Rhodes, in Makhanda (commonly known as Grahamstown), South Africa.

Lewis R. Gordon is professor of Philosophy at the University of Connecticut, in Storrs, Connecticut, and the current head of department. Among a wide range of interests, he has published extensively in the areas of Africana philosophy, existentialism, phenomenology, and the philosophy of the social, political, and cultural. His publications on Fanon are considered seminal works in the area, and include *Fanon and the Crisis of European Man* (Routledge, 1995) and *What Fanon Said* (Fordham University Press, 2015). Similarly, his works on existentialism, racism, and Africana philosophy are groundbreaking texts, examples of which are *Existentia Africana* (Routledge, 2000) and *Her Majesty's Other Children: Sketches of Racism from a Neocolonial Age* (Rowman & Littlefield, 1997), which won the Gustavus Myers Outstanding Book Award for the study of Human Rights in North America. Dr. Gordon has addressed audiences all over the globe, and has held honorary and courtesy appointments at several international universities, including in South Africa, Ireland, England, France, and Jamaica. His forthcoming book is *Freedom, Justice, and Decolonization* (Routledge, 2021).

Paget Henry is professor of Sociology and Africana Studies at Brown University, in Providence, Rhode Island, and works primarily in the fields of the political economy of Caribbean development and Caribbean philosophy. He is a founding member of the Caribbean Philosophical Association. Paget Henry is the author of four books, *Peripheral Capitalism and Underdevelopment in Antigua, Caliban's Reason: Introducing Afro-Caribbean Philosophy, Shouldering Antigua and Barbuda: The Life of V.C. Bird*, and *The Art of Mali Olatunji: Painterly Photography From Antigua and Barbuda*. He is also the editor of two journals: *The CLR James Journal*, the journal of the Caribbean Philosophical Association, and *The Antigua and Barbuda Review of Books*, the journal of the Antigua and Barbuda Studies Association.

Derek Hook is associate professor of Psychology at Duquesne University, in Pittsburgh, Pennsylvania, and an extraordinary professor of psychology at the University of Pretoria, South Africa. He is the author of *A Critical Psychology of the Colonial* (2011) and *Six Moments in Lacan* (2017). In addition to acting as a co-editor with Calum Neill on the Palgrave Lacan Series, he is also the editor of *Lie on Your Wounds: The Collected Prison Correspondence of Robert Mangaliso Sobukwe* and the co-editor (with Sheldon George) of *Lacan and Race* (2021). He maintains a YouTube channel with 50+ mini lectures on Lacanian Psychoanalysis.

Jean Khalfa is senior lecturer at the University of Cambridge, UK, where he specializes in the history of philosophy, modern literature (in particular contemporary poetry and writing in French from North Africa and the Caribbean), aesthetics, and anthropology. He is the editor of *What is Intelligence?* (CUP, 1994 and 1996); *Afrique du sud: le cap de bonne espérance* (with Chris Alden, Les Temps Modernes, 1995); *The New French Poetry, a Bilingual Anthology* (with David Kelley, Bloodaxe Books, 1996); *The Dialogue between Painting and Poetry* (Black Apollo Press, 2001); *An Introduction to the Philosophy of Gilles Deleuze* (Continuum, 2003); *Frantz Fanon*, a special issue of *Wasafiri* No 44 (Routledge, 2005); *Pour Frantz Fanon*, a special edition of *Les Temps Modernes*, No. 635–636 (Gallimard, 2006), and the first complete edition of Michel Foucault's *History of Madness* (Routledge, 2006 and 2009). His *Poetics of the Antilles: Poetry, History and Philosophy in the Writings of Perse, Césaire, Fanon and Glissant* was published in 2017 by Peter Lang, and his edition of Fanon's collected writings, *Écrits sur l'aliénation et la liberté* (Jean Khalfa and Robert Young, ed., La Découverte, 2015 and Hibr, Algiers, 2015; English translation: Bloomsbury, 2018), has been featured extensively in several radio and media outlets. Currently, Jean is working on a book on Fanon's *Les Damnés de la terre* (for Routledge) and a study of Foucault on insanity. He is the organizer of the Choiseul-Praslin Lectures and exhibitions, focusing on the relationship between poetry and image, and is a Chevalier dans l'Ordre des Palmes Académiques, an order of merit bestowed by the French Republic on distinguished academics.

Leswin Laubscher is associate professor and chair of the Department of Psychology at Duquesne University, in Pittsburgh, Pennsylvania. He counts teaching, research, and clinical experience as a psychologist in both the United States and South Africa. He has also held honorary and external appointments in addition to that at Duquesne, for example at the University of Stellenbosch in South Africa, and currently as extraordinary professor at the University of the Western Cape, South Africa. He is the co-editor of *The Qualitative Vision for Psychology* (2016) and author of *Introduction to Psychology as a Human Science* (2016) and several articles and chapters examining, particularly, the intersection of culture and psychology, Apartheid and psychology, and the importance of the philosophies of Jacques Derrida,

Emmanuel Levinas, and Frantz Fanon for psychology. He is currently finalizing a book on *Levinas and Psychology*, due for publication in late 2022.

Dilan Mahendran's early graduate career was focused on digital media literacy as a part of the Macarthur Foundation's Digital Youth Project (2007) where he conducted an ethnography of Hip Hop digital music production in the San Francisco Bay Area. During the end of Dilan's ethnographic work, he was keen on asking more fundamental questions about technology which led him to existential phenomenology and the Heideggerian critique of "modern technology." He completed his doctorate at the School of Information, UC Berkeley in 2011, focused on the phenomenological inquiry of race and computation. Today Dilan works as a research scientist focused on the social and ethical implications of distributed computing and machine learning.

Nelson Maldonado-Torres is director of the Rutgers Advanced Institute for Critical Caribbean Studies at Rutgers University, New Brunswick, New Jersey, where he also serves as chair of the program in Comparative Literature. He is also professor of Latino and Caribbean Studies and faculty affiliate in the Graduate Program in Women's, Gender, and Sexuality Studies in the same institution. Other relevant positions include co-chair of the Frantz Fanon Foundation, based in Paris, France, president emeritus of the Caribbean Philosophical Association (2008–2013), and distinguished visiting scholar of the Academy of Science of South Africa (2018–2019). His areas of expertise include Africana, Latinx, and Latin American philosophy, race and ethnic studies, decolonial thought, and theory and philosophy of religion. His publications include *Against War: Views from the Underside of Modernity* (2008), *La descolonización y el giro decolonial* (2011), and the co-edited books *Latin@s in the World-System: Decolonization Struggles in the 21st Century U.S. Empire* (2005), and *Decolonialidade e pensamento afrodiaspórico* [Decoloniality and Afro-diasporic thought] (2018). He has also published numerous articles and book chapters on different dimensions of decoloniality. His work involves collaborations with extra-academic organizations such as the Blackhouse Kollective in South Africa, Lazos America Unida in New Jersey, and the Colectiva Feminista en Construcción in Puerto Rico.

Helen Ngo is an honorary fellow at the School of Humanities and Social Sciences at Deakin University (Australia), having completed her PhD in Philosophy at SUNY Stony Brook, New York. She works at the intersection of phenomenology, critical philosophy of race, and feminist philosophy, and is broadly interested in questions of embodiment, place, intersubjectivity, and their political and ethical dimensions. Helen is author of *The Habits of Racism: A Phenomenology of Racism and Racialized Embodiment* (Lexington, 2017), and co-editor of *Philosophies of Difference: Nature, Racism, and Sexuate Difference* (Routledge, 2018). She has also published in journals such as *Philosophy and Social Criticism, Australian Feminist Law Journal*, and the *Journal of Intercultural Studies*.

Gayle Salamon is professor of English and the Program in Gender and Sexuality Studies at Princeton University, Princeton, New Jersey. Her research interests include phenomenology, feminist philosophy, Merleau-Ponty, queer and transgender theory, contemporary Continental philosophy, and disability studies. She is the author of *Assuming a Body: Transgender and Rhetorics of Materiality* (Columbia University Press, 2010), winner of the Lambda Literary Award in LGBT Studies. Her most recent book, *The Life and Death of Latisha King: A Critical*

Phenomenology of Transphobia (NYU Press, 2018), uses phenomenology to explore the case of Latisha King, a trans girl who was shot and killed in her Oxnard, California junior high school by a classmate. A co-edited volume with Gail Weiss and Ann Murphy, titled *Fifty Concepts for a Critical Phenomenology*, was published by Northwestern University Press in 2019. Dr. Salamon is currently at work on two projects: a manuscript on imagination and ethics in mid-century phenomenology, and a monograph exploring narrations of bodily pain and disability in contemporary memoir entitled *Painography: Metaphor and the Phenomenology of Chronic Pain.*

Lou Turner is clinical assistant professor in the Department of Urban and Regional Planning at the University of Illinois at Urbana-Champaign, Illinois, and former academic advisor and curriculum coordinator for the Department of African American Studies at the University of Illinois (2008–2017). Previously, he was assistant professor of Sociology, for 14 years, at North Central College, in Naperville, Illinois where he taught social theory, criminology, public policy, racial and ethnic relations, and urban sociology. He is co-author of *Frantz Fanon, Soweto and American Black Thought* (1978; 1986). A colleague of the late Hegelian-Marxist philosopher Raya Dunayevskaya, Lou Turner has written extensively on Fanonian, Marxian, and Hegelian dialectics. He has served as a councilor of the Hegel Society of America. With professor Helen Neville, Lou Turner recently co-edited a first-of-its-kind collection of writings for Routledge Press on Fanonian psychotherapeutic practices entitled, *Frantz Fanon's Psychotherapeutic Approaches to Clinical Work: Practicing Internationally with Marginalized Communities* (2020).

Jeremy Weate completed his PhD, *Phenomenology and Difference: The Body, Architecture and Race*, at Warwick University, UK, in 1998. He is the author of the best-selling book, *A Young Person's Guide to Philosophy*. Failing to become an academic, Weate fell into dotcom-era consulting in London, and then went on to spend over 17 years working as a consultant on natural resource governance, providing advice to governments, companies, and civil society organizations in over 20 countries. He spent 12 years living in Nigeria (2003–2015) and has visited over 60 countries, including Gabon in 2016, where he was initiated into Bwiti, which uses the psychedelic root iboga as sacrament. Jeremy's articles and academic papers have been published in *The Guardian, Christian Science Monitor, The Africa Report, Chimurenga, Research in African Literature, Philosophia Africana,* and *African Identities,* among other places. He is also co-founder of Cassava Republic, one of the leading publishing companies in Africa. He is currently CEO of the Vancouver-based Universal Ibogaine, which plans to turn the plant extract ibogaine into a medicine to treat addiction globally this decade. He continues to read Merleau-Ponty and to be inspired by the work of Frantz Fanon.

FOREWORD

Hospitality and Psychiatry: Just a Gut Feeling[1]

"You know, you only come to understand things through gut feeling" *[On ne comprend qu'avec ses tripes]*, Charles Geronimi

(Khalfa, 2018)

For over 70 years, Frantz Fanon's work has been praised and pilloried, in equal parts, for the audacity of his philosophical interventions and the passion of his political aspirations. Jean-Paul Sartre and Simone de Beauvoir celebrated him, Hannah Arendt disapproved of him, and across the world, for almost a century, Fanon's witness has inspired movements for liberation and justice. His legacy outlives both approbation and disapproval because Fanon's work engages with the urgent, even uncertain, task of the "time-at-hand." The time-at-hand frequently elides the slow and cumulative reflection of the *longue durée*; the time-at-hand is often represented in sudden, short measures of "moments," or "days" in an attempt to capture what Walter Benjamin calls the "graphicness" of the historical index: "Indeed to discover in the analysis of the small individual moment the crystal of the total event. And, therefore, to break with vulgar historical naturalism" (Benjamin, 1999, p. 461). For Fanon, as with Walter Benjamin, the "future" is not a political *prospect*; it is a political *project* that is proleptic, and as such, the future is "now," riskily and relentlessly "at hand," demanding decisions and judgments compelled by the urgencies of the incomplete and the unknown: "Each generation must discover its mission, fulfill it or betray it, in relative opacity" (Fanon, 2004, p. 145).

This crucial thought from *The Wretched of the Earth* – critical for any reading of the Fanonian *oeuvre* – sets a time-frame for the decolonizing project that departs from linear or evolutionary histories of nationalist progress. Fanon's appeal to a new global era of decolonization, sustained by the spirit of a "new humanism," is an invitation to live, to think, and to act, through the "relative opacity" of historical and territorial transitions that accompany the massive churn and change in the post-colonial world. Relative opacity isn't a species of psychoanalytic or phenomenological obscurantism; it is, ironically, a call to post-colonial political sobriety, a resistance to triumphalism and utopianism, an acknowledgment that time is always short in the service of grand designs.

The contributors to *Fanon, Phenomenology, and Psychology* are committed to the task of exploring the living conditions of "relative opacity" as they shape Fanon's frame of mind and impel his acts of interpretation and intervention. Phenomenology, psychiatry, and psychoanalysis are, in the main, inquiries that begin with the "opacities" of everyday life – projection, phobia, negation, phantasm, identification, objectification, inversion, anxiety, disavowal – in order to explore the ontological ambivalences and political struggles that ensue when the racial powers of colonial domination and denigration regulate the "psycho-affective" web (Fanon's term) (see Bhabha, 2004, p. xix) in which both colonizer and colonized are caught. It is the opacity of liminal conditions, their political iniquities and racial indignities, to which Fanon draws our attention, and it is those very "relative opacities" – "the anomalies of affect" in Fanon's (1994, p. 10) phrase – that drive the editors of this volume to engage with Fanon's proposition that "only a psychoanalytical interpretation of the black problem can lay bare the anomalies of affect that are responsible for the structure of the complex" (Fanon, 1994, p. 10).

What role do "anomalies of affect" play in the practice of Fanon's psychiatric project for a decolonizing "social therapy?" What are the productive uses of "relative opacity" in discovering the psychiatric mission of Fanon's generation? These questions came to me while I was reading Jean Khalfa's (2018) fine essay, "Fanon, Revolutionary Psychiatrist," and came upon an illuminating remark by Charles Geronimi about the practice of social therapy initiated by Fanon and his colleagues at Blida, committed to transforming the colonial culture of institutionalized psychiatric care. In his response to Khalfa, Geronimi speaks "from the gut":

> You know, you only come to understand things through gut feeling (*comprend qu'avec ses tripes*) … I had to show several things: that Algerian culture carried other values than colonial culture; that these structuring values ought to be taken on board confidently by those who bear them, that is, by Algerian patients or staff. To gain the support of the Algerian personnel, I had to arouse in them a feeling of revolt of the sort: 'We are just as able as the Europeans'. It was up to the Algerian staff to suggest the specific forms of sociability and incorporate them into the process of social therapy. That is what transpired.
>
> *(Geronimi, cited in Khalfa, 2018, p. 190)*

At this point, I was led by my gut – don't ask me why – to a passage in Fanon's (2018) essay, *Daily life in the douars*, that describes the culture of hospitality prevalent in the *douar*[2] with respect to the paradoxical figure of the "Muslim foreigner" (p. 380). The Muslim "foreigner" is a brother, immediately assimilable in the *douar* on the grounds of his shared faith and beliefs. But if the Muslim foreigner is a brother, he is also the Other.

> The case of the foreigner who arrives at the douar presents, it seems to us, interesting features that ought to be specified. Because he is Muslim, sustained by the same beliefs, an inheritor of the same faith, the foreigner is a brother … The hospitality reserved for him is always very generous … However, if the stranger is sacred and respectable, he is also the Other, one who comes from elsewhere, who has lived under other skies. This is why the presence of the traveler who gives himself defenseless to his host engenders a feeling of uneasiness: he represents the unknown, mystery. Even if he divulges his thoughts and opens up his heart directly, he cannot prevent anxiety from emerging all around him.
>
> *(Fanon, 2018, p. 380)*

On reading this passage I wondered whether the experimental attempt to socialize and humanize the segregated Muslim wards at Blida might have been inspired by this "other" Algerian structuring value, (in Geronimi's phrase) – the ethic of care and hospitality in the *douar*. The psychiatric patient, like the foreign brother, cannot prevent generating an affective and spatial anxiety around himself precisely because he *is* the uncanny brother; the brother as *foreigner*; the brother of an "other" mother-tongue. What makes the foreigner, or the traveler, a brother is his alterity – his condition of otherness – in a range of affective and circumstantial registers. He arrives at the *douar* quite unexpectedly and in "giv[ing] himself *defenseless*" to the host community he creates an aura of uneasiness about his person, and around himself. The shared faith entitles the Muslim foreigner to generous hospitality, but it does not protect him from being an object of anxiety: alterity, as Hannah Arendt (2003) once put it, is to have difference thrust into my Oneness. This uneasiness is not assuaged by the candor with which the foreign-brother shares his thoughts and tells his story. The anxious alterity that emerges around him because "he represents the unknown, the mystery" (Fanon, 2018, p. 380) is the affective condition that inspires the act of hospitality. Holding on to the moment of anxiety, and engaging with the risk of "relative opacity," are enabling rituals of acceptance and inclusion that welcome the foreigner-as-brother. Fanon continues:

If various systems of signals make him familiar to us, to all intents and purposes he represents a system of reference that escapes us ... He is, in a word, someone that must be treated with consideration, *because the power of his word, of his gaze is unknown, because he perhaps has some secret relation with these Other People.*

(Fanon, 2018, p. 380, emphasis added)

A system of reference that escapes us ... an unknown gaze ... the power of an unknown "foreign" word ... anxiety emerging all around ... Some secret relation: these are traces of "relative opacity" that give rise to the ethic of hospitality in the mission of Fanon's psychiatric social therapy. The avowal of a *secret* relation to "Other People" engenders a spirit of alterity – a social and ethical relationality (to oneself and others) premised on systems of signals that are proximate and familiar even as they brush against the grain of systems of reference that are "foreign" and unknown. The doubly embodied figure of the "brother/ foreigner" generates spatial anxiety and affective ambivalence within the community and identity of the *douar*: systemic signals of familiarity close the intimate circle of brotherhood and neighborhood; systemic references to foreignness that escape us – unknown gazes lived, and half-understood words learned, under other skies – break open the bonds of kinship and exceed the boundaries of sociability.

The ethic of hospitality, expressed in practices of care and consideration, works with, and through, the anxiety of alterity to achieve a "translational" psychiatric practice. Its aim is not simply to undermine the method of European techniques, but to establish a new model of institutional and professional agency amongst Algerian patients and staff. "I had to arouse in them a feeling of revolt of a sort: 'We are just as able as the Europeans,'" Geronimi states (cited in Khalfa, 2018, p. 190). "It was up to the Algerian staff to suggest the specific forms of sociability and incorporate them into the process of social therapy" (p. 190). Khalfa drives the point home:

The blueprint of a public mental health programme for a new country, which Fanon presented in his paper about the day-centre in Tunis, lays the groundwork for what was to be, under the name of *psychiatrie de secteur* (community psychiatry), a considerable transformation in Europe as well.

(Khalfa, 2018, p. 202)

Isn't there a kind of family resemblance between the defenseless psychiatric patient and the defenseless foreigner-as-brother? The ill patient's need for psychiatric hospitality is based on systems of reference that escape us: his distraught gaze is unknowable, as are his obscure words, and however sincere and open-hearted they might be, they never fail to generate anxiety and uneasiness amongst members of the *douar*. When Geronimi says "Psychiatry must be political," I ask myself, tentatively, whether psychiatry is a form of hospitality for the gaze we cannot decipher , or the language we cannot apprehend? The mode of psychiatric agency – "a feeling of revolt" – that Fanon and Geronimi initiate on the ward is an Algerian form of inclusive and egalitarian social therapy that bears a resemblance to the ethic of hospitality demonstrated in the care of foreigners-as-brothers in the douar *"whose limits and origin one is unaware of"* (Fanon, 2018, p. 380, emphasis added).

This last phrase from Fanon's (2018) essay on "the case of the foreigner who arrives at the douar" (p. 380), leads me, by the gut, to Fanon's arrival in Lyon. You know only too well the racial incident I'm talking about that took place on a crowded train. You've read it a hundred times at least, and each time it lifts off from the page and lands, like the owl of Minerva, in the very midst of our lives, whenever a person of color is assaulted on a street corner, a migrant is turned away at the border, or an undocumented child is lost to its parents. Or, to put it differently, wherever the "historical-racial schema" prevails and the "foreign-brother" or the "stranger-sister" fails to be treated with consideration, or is denied their right to hospitality, *"because the power of his/her word, of his/her gaze is unknown … and because his/her system of reference escapes us"* (Fanon, 2018, p. 380, emphasis added, "her" added). Here is that scene once again:

> "Look! a Negro! …
> Look! A Negro …
> *Maman*, look, a Negro; I'm scared! …"
> Disoriented, incapable of confronting the Other, the white man, who had no scruples about imprisoning me. I transported myself on that very day far, very far, from myself, and gave myself up as an object. What did this mean to me? Peeling, stripping my skin, causing a hemorrhage that left congealed black blood all over my body. Yet this reconsideration of myself, this thematization, was not my idea. I wanted quite simply to be a man among men. I would have liked to enter our world young and sleek, a world we could build together.
>
> *(Fanon, 2008, p. 92)*

Imprisoned by the racist gaze, the disoriented Fanon is barred from the encounter with the Other. He is eviscerated. The enabling anxiety of a relationship with Alterity – "in a word, someone that must be treated with consideration, *because the power of his word, of his gaze is unknown*" (Fanon, 2018, p. 380, emphasis added) – is denied him by the white gaze that chooses to flay the foreigner rather than offer him fealty. "Ontology does not allow us to understand the being of the black man, since it ignores the lived experience," Fanon (2018, p. 90) has famously written. Is the lived experience that ontology ignores something like the fundamental invocation, or invitation, offered by the ethic of hospitality to "be a man among men … to *enter* the world" (Fanon, 2018, p. 92, emphasis added)? Must the invitation to enter the realm of hospitality, which is the entryway to the world of humanity, be controlled by the barbarians at the gates, in our times as in Fanon's? Does the *psychiatrie de secteur* as lived out in the hospital provide us with a lesson in the politics of hospitality, once so flagrantly violated in the treatment of a Black foreigner on a train in Lyon: *"Maman*, the Negro's going to eat me" (Fanon, 2008, p. 93).

Does hospitality come before ontology?

This is just my gut feeling: *on ne comprend qu'avec ses tripes*.

Homi K. Bhabha

NOTES

1 My sincerest gratitude is extended to Paul Chouchana, who provided invaluable assistance in the preparation of this foreword.
2 A small North African village, traditionally tented.

REFERENCES

Arendt, H. (2003). Thinking and moral considerations. In J. Kohn (Ed.), *Responsibility and judgment* (pp. 159–189). New York: Schoken Books.

Benjamin, W. (1999). *The arcades project*. Cambridge, MA: Belknap Press.

Fanon, F. (2004). *The wretched of the Earth* (R. Philcox, Trans.). New York: Grove Press. (Original work published 1961)

Fanon, F. (2008). *Black skin, White masks* (R. Philcox, Trans.). New York: Grove Press. (Original work published 1952)

Fanon, F. (2018). Daily life in the douars. In J. Khalfa & R. J. C. Young (Eds.), *Alienation & freedom* (pp. 373–384). London: Bloomsbury. (Original work published 1954 or 1955)

Khalfa, J. (2018). Fanon, revolutionary psychiatrist. In J. Khalfa & R. J. C. Young (Eds.), *Alienation & freedom* (pp. 167–202). London: Bloomsbury.

ACKNOWLEDGMENTS

This book has been the outcome of many years of engagement with the work of Frantz Fanon. The editors wish to thank all the *students* who, having taken courses we have taught on Fanon, have helped us better understand Fanon's various – and often challenging – ideas and conceptualizations which, suffice it to say, have never been more crucial than today. A particular debt of gratitude goes to the *Department of Psychology at Duquesne University* whose longstanding tradition of Psychology as a Human Science has meant that Fanon's work is a necessary and integral – indeed, a canonical – part of the broader mission of a critical, progressive humanistic, and philosophically informed psychology. *Conor Sukhdeo* has provided invaluable editorial assistance and research support throughout the process of preparing the manuscript – we are much indebted to him. We are likewise appreciative of *Casey Lee*'s input and proof-reading assistance. *Marilyn Henline*'s help in coordinating various aspects of the project was also essential and much valued. A special note of thanks to *Kristine Blair*, Dean of the McAnulty College and Graduate School of Liberal Arts at Duquesne University, for her unstinting support of this initiative. We gratefully acknowledge receiving a National Endowment for the Humanities (NEH) Grant from her office which enabled us to fund this project. Finally, we also thank our respective *families* for their support, patience, and love as we labored away at this book.

Earlier versions of several of the book's chapters have been previously published, either as journal articles or as chapters in edited collections. Acknowledgments are due to the publishers, journals, and associated editors for permission to reproduce this material.

Sara Ahmed's chapter was previously published as:

Ahmed S. (2007). A phenomenology of whiteness. *Feminist Theory*, *8*(2), 149–168.

An earlier version of Alia Al-Saji's chapter was published as:

Al-Saji, A. (2013). Too late: Racialized time and the closure of the past. *Insights*, *6*(5), 1–13.

Robert Bernasconi's chapter was previously published as:

Bernasconi, R. (2019). Frantz Fanon and psychopathology: The progressive infrastructure of *Black Skin, White Masks*. In D. M. Goodman, E. R. Severson & H. Macdonald (Eds.), *Race, rage and resistance: Philosophy, psychology, and the perils of individualism* (pp. 34–45). London and New York: Routledge.

An earlier version of Miraj Desai's chapter was published as:

Desai, M. (2014). Psychology, the psychological, and critical praxis: A phenomenologist reads Frantz Fanon. *Theory & Psychology*, *24*(1), 58–75.

Grant Farred's chapter was previously published as:

Farred, G. (2012). To dwell for the postcolonial. *Journal of French and Francophone Philosophy – Revue de la philosophie française et de langue française*, *XX*(1), 75–86.

Lewis Gordon's chapter was previously published as:

Gordon, L. (2008). A phenomenology of Biko's Black consciousness. In A. Mngxitama, A. Alexander, & N. C. Gibson (Eds.), *Biko lives!* (pp. 83–94). London and New York: Palgrave.

Paget Henry's chapter was previously published as:

Henry, P. (2006). Africana phenomenology: Its philosophical implications. *World and Knowledges Otherwise*, Fall, 1–22.

An earlier version of Jean Khalfa's chapter was published as:

Khalfa, J. (2005). My body, this skin, this fire: Fanon on flesh. *Wasafiri*, *20*(44), 42–50.

An earlier version of Dilan Mahendran's chapter was published as:

Mahendran, D. (2007). The facticity of blackness: A non-conceptual approach to the study of race and racism in Fanon's and Merleau-Ponty's phenomenology. *Human Architecture: Journal of the Sociology of Self-Knowledge*, *5*(3), 191–203.

Nelson Maldonado-Torres' chapter was previously published as:

Maldonado-Torres, N. (2017). Frantz Fanon and the decolonial turn in psychology: From modern/colonial methods to the decolonial attitude. *South African Journal of Psychology*, *47*(4), 432–441.

An earlier version of Helen Ngo's chapter was published as:

Ngo, H. (2019). 'Get over it'? Racialized temporalities and bodily orientations in time. *Journal of Intercultural Studies*, *40*(2), 239–253.

Gayle Salamon's chapter was previously published as:

Salamon, G. (2006). 'The place where life hides away': Merleau-Ponty, Fanon, and the location of bodily being. *differences: A Journal of Feminist Studies*, *17*(2), 96–112.

Lou Turner's chapter was previously published as:

Turner, L. (2001). Frantz Fanon's phenomenology of Black mind. *Philosophy Today*, *45*, 99–104.

Jeremy Weate's chapter was previously published as:

Weate, J. (2001). Fanon, Merleau-Ponty and the difference of phenomenology. In R. Bernasconi (Ed.), *Race* (pp. 169–183). Oxford: Blackwell.

Leswin Laubscher, Derek Hook, and Miraj U. Desai

OF BODIES THAT MATTER

Fanon, Phenomenology, and Psychology

Leswin Laubscher, Derek Hook, and Miraj U. Desai

As we write here, and as we scramble to edit, collate, and organize the exemplary contributions to this book, protesters gather literally outside our windows or a few blocks from us to decry and denounce the murder of George Floyd in Minneapolis specifically, but also more broadly to announce and assert that "Black Lives Matter!" Or perhaps more accurately, that they *should* matter. It is a should and a shout that carries within it a political, juridical, social, economic, and ethical demand – a shout and a should desirous of that very "new humanism" and "restructuring (of) the world" that Frantz Fanon dreamt, described, and actively, passionately, made his regrettably short life's project.

Whereas we imagine the audience for this book having some familiarity with the life and writings of Frantz Fanon, we must also concede that to be a rather presumptuous and uneven fancy. How then, are we to introduce Fanon, or respond to the "who is Fanon" question, even (especially) if "only" by the license of a brief exordium. The tension for us is located between Heidegger responding to Aristotle's life as "He was born, he thought, he died. And all the rest is pure anecdote" (Dick & Kofman, 2002), on the one hand, and Derrida's reminder, with respect to the life of South African activist, Chris Hani, that "a man's life, as unique as his death, will always be more than a paradigm and something other than a symbol" (Derrida, 1994, p. xv). It seems to us that a referral to existing biographies [e.g. Caute (1970), Fanon, J. (2014), Gendzier (1973), Macey (2012)], as well as the chapters in this text (e.g. Nigel Gibson's), will have to be our route between the Scylla of a banal listing of biographical facts and dates and the impossible Charybdis that is our forging Fanon's signature, no matter how well or sincere the attempt. As for Fanon's work, we will similarly let the rest of this text accomplish the tasks of introduction and challenge for us. Hence, rather than attempting to tell who Fanon "is," we proceed here from who we are and have been by the gift of his life and work.

Those of us who have studied Fanon, and/or who have derived personal and academic inspiration from his work, have always known that his words and insights continued to be trenchantly relevant and appropriate to our world, one where people remain subjugated and relegated to the wretched and damned of the earth, where the specter of colonization and the challenges of decolonization hauntingly abide the present, and where Black bodies remain struck into the racist coin of hypervisibility and invisibility. As such it should perhaps not have been a surprise to notice, in the aftermath of George Floyd's killing, the quick, widespread, and popular reference and recourse to Fanon. A quote of Fanon's (albeit misquoted, and misattributed to the *Wretched of the Earth*), especially, took to social media in rather viral form: "When we revolt, it's not for a particular culture. We revolt, simply because, for many reasons, we can no longer breathe."[1] Podcasts, blogs, discussion boards, and even mainstream media brought Fanon into our present, and the explosion of anti-racist or Black Lives Matter reading lists – from those of *Oprah*, *Elle*, and *Good Housekeeping* (!) magazines, to the lists from "radical socialists" and "anarchists" – all index Fanon as essential reading (maybe it is also interpretatively telling that the *Wretched of the Earth* is the text most frequently listed, over and above *Black Skin, White Masks*. One wonders what cultural hermeneutic/dynamic underlies this reading preference[2]). "A decade after the United

DOI: 10.4324/9781003037132-101

States had *seemed* to some to turn the corner on racism by electing its first black president,"
Hudis writes, "the specter of Frantz Fanon has returned – with a vengeance" (2015, p. 1,
italics in original). Again, at some level, and given our longstanding and deeply held conviction, as scholars and readers of Fanon, that his voice needs to be heard more clearly and
widely than it has, indeed even that the world is in need of his voice, we were nonetheless
quite surprised at his seemingly sudden appearance on the popular scene, a gatecrashing
guest almost whom no one expected but whose force of presence demands the attention of
his entry. Tarrying with that surprise for a while longer, we also registered a certain anxiety, nestled between our desire and our reality, if not our experience as raced men: As much
as the world needs to hear Fanon, how ready is that world for the radical force of his voice?
By the experience of our Black, "ethnic," and "foreign" bodies, our worry was twofold:
That the world or at least this world we found ourselves in, was not ready, let alone willing,
or that, on the other hand, the sleight of hand was about to begin where the far-reaching
and revolutionary thrust of Fanon's thought would be banalized into superficial fortune
cookie wisdoms or social media profile quotes. We hope, sincerely, to be wrong – some
days it feels like this is a new moment, a different turning point, a time right and ripe for
his voice, even as we recognize that we've allowed that feeling, that hope, before, only for
it to leave us disappointed and frustrated. This book is also our small attempt, at the very
least within the arena of the academy, but hopefully also beyond, to check just such taming
designs.

But perhaps we are wrong altogether in assuming a gatecrashing Fanon, emerging
from "nowhere" all too suddenly, assuming in doing so an origin or beginning *ex nihilo*,
from nothing, on the one hand, or some priming "just right" historical moment that calls
and conjures up the figures appropriate to the moment, on the other. There may well be
other events, other places, other gatherings where he was always a longstanding and welcome guest, always an inspirational presence. In the jacket notes of David Caute's early
biography of Fanon, reference is made to the Chicago riots of 1967, and that "every brother
on a rooftop can quote Fanon" (Caute, 1970, jacket note). Perhaps we only take surprising
notice because this is a white and "mainstream" scene, now, forced to deal, beyond expectation or guess, with who shows up for dinner, or more appropriately, demands the seat that
was always theirs.

The truth of the matter is that, since his life and death, Fanon's words have not only
traveled powerfully across time and place, but also spoke "in different voices to different readers" (Silverman, 2005, p. 2). Under a heading aptly titled "Fanonian traveling",
Gibson writes that South African exiles to England, well steeped in Fanon's ideas, "especially the Black Consciousness Movement (BCM) ... set up office in London in the late
1970's" and brought Fanon "back" to Britain where, at the time, "Fanon was essentially
out of print" (Gibson, 1999, p. 12). Indeed, our own experiences attest to these statements of travel and voice quite tellingly. [3] More than 35 years ago, in South Africa of the
late 1970s and early 1980s – a past already longer than his life, we realize with a faintly
morbid start – Fanon's was an inspirational banner behind which Black students and anti-
Apartheid activists rallied the masses to take to the streets of a country wracked by political unrest and turmoil, and where the violent convulsions of the day were as much of birth
as death, of which we only presumed to know the difference. Which is also to say where
we conflated wishing and knowing – maybe the very structureless structure of revolution,
truth be told.

Reflecting on that first, and forever after, encounter with Fanon now, the text we read
most, or at least first, was *Black Skin, White Masks* – and in one of our experiences, in a

psychology class no less, accompanied as it was by Hussein Bulhan's groundbreaking *Frantz Fanon and the Psychology of Oppression* (1985), the first really deliberate and sustained examination of Fanon's psychological and psychiatric contributions.[4] Back then, Bulhan called psychology's neglect of Fanon "curious indeed," as Fanon "was first and foremost a psychiatrist by training and profession," and much of his writings "either had psychology as their major point of departure or they incorporated psychological dimensions to complement, illustrate, and concretize the macro-social experiences he sought to unveil and transform" (Bulhan, 1985, p. 6). Of course such neglect may be curious, but certainly not mysterious or even unexpected – Bulhan sets up this very challenge for a psychology allied with structural and racist privilege as opposed to a liberatory psychology of possibility and for the oppressed by the opening juxtaposing in his book of Hendrik Verwoerd, South African prime minister and architect of Apartheid, as well as a psychologist, against the figure of Frantz Fanon, freedom fighter and activist, as well as a psychiatrist. Indeed, having mentioned that we read Fanon in a psychology class, at university, this was also an Apartheid institution university, a Black university set apart for Black students (an HBU in American phraseology). We knew all too well that our white peers were not reading Fanon, and that even if they were, they would read Fanon in addition to the likes of Freud and Rogers and Beck, say, whereas for us it felt like we read Freud and Rogers and Beck in addition to Fanon. Such was the power of his challenge that it became the hammer by which the other, "more psychological" nails were measured.

Beyond the theoretical challenge, though, beyond the critique of a Freudian orthodoxy and a rarefied, wholly intrapsychic and individualized mainstream, Fanon also validated a psychology of the streets and the barricades, much of which was happening already and spontaneously. Many of us were already counseling activists, preparing them for arrest and incarceration, providing workshops on how to deal with interrogation, solitary confinement, conflict resolution, problem solving, organizational communication – and in many instances, we had to apply those very insights to our own predicaments as activists ourselves.

For others, perhaps a little more removed from Fanon the psychologist, we venture that Fanon was read predominantly through a Marxist-Leninist lens [not altogether unlike Adolfo Gilly's reading in the introduction to *A Dying Colonialism* (1965/1952)], even if it meant foregoing or overlooking the very critiques of Marxism that Fanon renders. The words with which to make a Marxist telling were certainly there – alienation and dis-alienation, for example, the insistence on the economic realities of the day and the material experience of the individual, and of course by choosing to announce the future of his final chapter with the heraldry of a passage from Marx's *Eighteenth Brumaire*. Yet, we also conveniently passed over his criticisms, for example those inhering to the heterodox views of the peasantry and the specific modifications a violent colonialism posed to any Marxist application. That the very activists who so passionately championed a Marxist-Leninist post-Apartheid abandoned that model upon assuming power perhaps had less to do with the seeming failure of the Russian adventure than Fanon's insight into the peril and seduction of postcolonial misadventures. One can wonder. Still others adapted Fanon to an inspirational Black Consciousness, Steve Biko being foremost in this appropriation, and call for "the liberation of the man of color from himself." And lest one forgets, for Biko this eminently involved a psychological process: Black Consciousness was fundamentally about a psychological liberation as much as it was a political and revolutionary program ["The most potent weapon in the hands of the oppressor is the mind of the oppressed" (Biko, in Woods, 1978, p. 92)].

Fanon is still read in South Africa, but there is a startlingly clear difference in the manner of reading from the pre-Apartheid years: Now, it seems the gateway text, in the aftermath of the Rhodes Must Fall movement[5], and after 25 years of formal Apartheid's demise, is the *Wretched/Damned of the Earth* (Fanon, 2004/1961). The decolonial and post-colonial language of this day seem to feature more prominently than the Marxist, new humanist, psychologically liberating language we learned at Fanon's lips in the 80s – "the search for postcoloniality may require more than *Black Skin, White Masks* offers" (Gordon, 2015, p. 17), and for many of these "born free's," those who never knew formal Apartheid, it feels like little or no progress has been made, the country's "new management" notwith-standing, and that "everything has to be started over from scratch, everything has to be rethought" (Fanon, 2004, p. 56). Hudis, too, notes Fanon's contemporary prominence in South Africa, among a "new generation (striving) to go beyond the nationalist-bourgeois dominance of the African National Congress … that has so clearly betrayed the hopes … for a fundamental transformation of social existence" (2015, p. 126). Without our offering explanation or understanding, necessarily, Fanon's closing words to the *Wretched/Damned of the Earth* somehow insists on also having this paragraph's last word; that "each generation must out of relative obscurity discover its mission, fulfill it or betray it" (Fanon, 2004).

Of the three editors here, all of us met Fanon in different clothes, and are often forced by acquaintance and academic conference, to slip in and out of different Fanonian regis-ters, ears, and grammar. Moreover, over time we have also come to "know" Fanon differ-ently, by our own experiences and the companionship we've enjoyed with his texts – as a salve to post-9/11 racist hate and profiling; as a white academic fascinated and troubled by coinages ("epidermalization," "corporeal malediction," "a zone of nonbeing") that were at once difficult to assimilate and yet undeniable in his South African post-Apartheid context; as a Black academic from South Africa, whose experience was precisely of the Marxist and praxis social interventionist sort described above, but whom, upon enrolling for a doctoral degree in the United States, in a specifically circumscribed psychoanalytic program, now also had to own up to the challenge of a psychoanalytic Fanon, so to speak. How is it that the phantasies of dirt and sex, of aggression and sex, so important in Fanon's analyses, come to play out against the Freudian universal and the specifics of the colonial setting? How is it that the "Negro is a phobogenic object, a stimulus to anxiety" by the imago and phantasm of cultural and historical mythmaking and racial praxis? It is worth reminding ourselves that Fanon never rejected the unconscious, only the orthodox psychoanalytic etiology thereof. For him, an unconscious rooted in the socius and history meant that the task of the analyst remains one that makes the unconscious conscious, but in a manner attuned to the depths of sociopolitical repression and associated "attempts at a hallucina-tory whitening," an unconscious struck on the anvil of race and the experiential socius as much as from racist myth, history, stereotype and habit – an epidermal unconscious, even, located in the skin. As with the unconscious, so too with the Oedipus, less universal now than understood in terms of a father that, for the Black man in the colonies, can never be. Even if the unconscious (and the inferiority complex) disguises its economic, material, and racist origins in everyday expression, it is precisely the work of the analyst to make those roots conscious in the twofold response to the socio economic and the psychological. Here, for the first time, at least in our training, was a psychoanalysis that took account of rac-ism, and of lives shaped by race and racism. For someone who reveled in the criticism of psychoanalysis, back in South Africa, for someone who would handily and gleefully retort to any Freudian to be, that "the rifle of the Senegalese soldier is not a penis but a genuine rifle, model Lebel 1916" (Fanon, 1994), it was quite the unsettling experience to now also wrestle with the imagined riposte, that "only a psychoanalytical interpretation of the black problem can lay bare the anomalies of affect that are responsible for the structure of the complex" (Fanon, 1994). In truth, though, and by the punning colloquialism of a snarky resolution, Fanon's was never yo' daddy's psychoanalysis.

As fate or the gods would have it, it was a mere few years later, upon relocation to the psychology department at Duquesne University, for sixty years a veritable Camelot for existential phenomenological psychology and psychology as a human science,[6] that another Fanon demanded attention. Studying Fanon there with no less an instructor than visiting professor Lewis Gordon, now brought into powerful relief the very question of lived experience, of what it is to *be* (a Black person) and how it is for the "Negro" to suffer "in his body differently than the White." To a department and tradition steeped in the phenomenologies and existentialisms of the likes of Husserl, Heidegger, Merleau-Ponty, or Gadamer – and to the methodological translations of such philosophical insights into often contested "schools" of phenomenological psychological research, such as the Utrecht school, the Van Manen camps, even the "Duquesne" schools – to all of that tradition came the very *j'accuse* that they ignored, overlooked, or otherwise violated the Black body in a racism of which, to appropriate Bernasconi's (2005) insightful use of Fanon's turn of phrase, "the European knows, and does not know." It was, of course, no coincidence that this challenge was carried by the appointment to this illustrious department of the first Black person to that faculty, and his invitation, as well, to as first a Black visiting professor. Such states of affairs are not new, and remain the lament of gay or lesbian faculty, women, or faculty of color who seemingly end up the only ones "qualified" to teach on such issues of difference and diversity in their departments. There might even be, where Fanon is concerned specifically, some commentary here on two rather tired and largely unexamined racist notions: First that his audience is a Black audience, that his work speaks to Black people, save then for some "progressive," "activist," or "well meaning" white folks and allies, at best, or white "voyeurs" and "cultural tourists" at worst. Second, that his work is derivative, at best influenced by, or otherwise some applied exercise of existing (white) theory. Lewis Gordon addresses this last point thus:

> How many biographies of Frederick Douglass, W. E. B. Du Bois, and Fanon do we need before it is recognized that they also produced *ideas*? It is as if to say that white thinkers provide *theory* and black thinkers provide *experience* for which all seek explanatory force from the former.
>
> *(Gordon, 2015, p. 5, italics in original)*

Yet, for all the different ways we've come to Fanon, for all the places Fanon traveled to, and even if he has changed for us over time, as we have, there is – we believe – a constant thread which binds us all. Whether Marxist, postcolonial, activist therapeutic, existential, phenomenological, psychoanalytic, cultural studies, postmodern, the manner and force of his writing left us changed at that level of witness to an other, and the other which is us. Reading Fanon was and is to be struck, to be profoundly unsettled and unmoored, to experience something from an elsewhere beyond words or reason, even as its gifts are the words and reason for that elsewhere. Here was and is an eminently rigorous and exemplary scholarship which nonetheless speaks in lyrical prose and transcendent poetry, able to reach an affective heart and an animating soul even as it does a thinking ego. That we believed we could reclaim, that we did reclaim, or that we are reclaiming what were and are denied us – an inner life, an individuality, a validation and a license both to our pain as to our worth and struggle, a charge to emerge from the genus and classification of "perverse anonymity" (Gordon, 2015) – is also because he spoke as he did, in a speech from a within and a beyond. Appropriating Toni Morrisson's eulogizing gratitude to James Baldwin, Fanon too gave us "a language to dwell in, a gift so perfect it seems my own invention" (Morrison, 1987).

We do not want to lose the force of that experience of Fanon's words, and of its effects on us – an all too easy betrayal in learned and scholarly texts. We venture that recall and reminiscence about "firsts," or "what were you doing," or "where were you when" is not entirely uncommon for events or encounters of great personal or cultural importance – occurrences that unsettled one, that shaped or moved one, or that stayed with one, and continue to haunt one, that follow or lead, depending on the angle of the sun, like a shadow before or behind us. Or like an unconscious, whether on or under the skin, whether within or between the other's (mis)recognition, or whether hiding in the plain sight of a children's story or the cultural sediment of a certain way we and they are believed to be. Perhaps, right about now, you, the reader, may be pausing for a moment to reflect on that meeting with Fanon, where you were, what you were doing, what it felt like, what the experience was like, and in which ways he has been a companion since. Almost like an examination of a lived experience, a proto-phenomenological exercise even.

THE BODY OF THIS BOOK: ITS MATTER AND HOW IT MATTERS

Having written some now about how this scholar and activist from Martinique, France, and Algeria, from South Africa and the streets of Chicago and Birmingham, Delhi and Santa Domingo, has come to speak to us, it is worth saying something about this book – about how it came to be and what we would like it to do, and to provide a capsule outline of its riches, which is of course also to say, of Fanon's gifts.

Firstly, all three the editors of this book are psychologists and derive professional and identitary investment, as well as struggle and frustration, from a location within that discipline. Additionally, all three editors also draw on some history of research and/or scholarship within a broadly phenomenological tradition. As such, they have noted a series of peculiar anomalies which have played a motivating role in developing this book. The first of these concerns a turn away from psychology, which seems surprising given the importance of Bulhan's (1985) instructive. There are exceptions, such as Erica Burman's (2018) *Fanon, Education, Action*, which makes inventive use of Fanon's work within critical and feminist psychology to think in radical – and inspiring – ways about pedagogy, education, and childhood. That being said, it remains true that Fanonian problematics and dilemmas have not always been thought in terms of psychological concepts or descriptions, and one will be challenged to find Fanon on most curricula within psychology departments and programs, certainly within the United States. One way to account for this is that the strong – and necessary – imperative to foreground the political as asserted by many Fanon scholars, operating mainly outside of psychology, along with the associated injunction to avoid at all costs falling prey to various forms of "psychological reductionism" became perhaps somewhat overly restrictive. This apparent critical suspension of the psychological in Fanon scholarship – "the psychological" here understood both as everyday vocabulary of experience and as a scholarly field – sometimes led to surprises. Encountering the sobering case studies at the end of *The Wretched of the Earth*, for example, as precisely *clinical* case studies, or being reminded of the fact that Fanon was as much psychiatrist as revolutionary, both could be considered wake-up calls for trajectories within Fanon scholarship which summarily replaced reference to the psychological with the cultural (or talk of national culture), the phenomenological with the dialectical, or the psychical with the revolutionary. And to be sure: Such a critical bypassing of the language of the psychological is motivated by sound political reasoning (and has important benefits) – as Fanon himself taught us in his dismantling of Octave Mannoni's (1950/1990) psychoanalysis of colonialism. And yet, to foreclose the psychological is also to sideline the acuity of so many of Fanon's critiques and analysis in *Black Skin, White Masks*. As David Marriott bluntly puts it in rejuvenating the notion of the "psychopolitical" as a guiding concept in how we approach Fanon's extraordinary conceptual innovations: "the language of neurosis … [is] never simply secondary to 'the language of political experience'" (2011, p. 39). That is to say: We should not leave the dimension of the psychological behind – "psychological" in the broadest sense, inclusive of the phenomenological *in* psychology, the unconscious and the psychopolitical – in how we take up Fanon today. If there is anything that Fanon is *not*, it is a one-dimensional theorist. The Fanonian challenge to the various academic disciplines and modes of scholarship that influenced him was always twofold. It involved, firstly, a rigorous and non-retreating critique of who and what was being excluded by such vocabularies of analysis, which of course entailed an omnipresent awareness of the racism perpetuated by such vocabularies. And it involved, secondly, an awareness that racism and what we might call a "colonial (un) consciousness" is never limited to one domain, but spreads across various (bodily, psychological, economic, cultural, political, epistemic) facets of experience in a saturating way. As such, breaking disciplinary boundaries, attempting to think the myriad intersection points and articulations between such domains remains forever a Fanonian critical imperative.

A second and perhaps even more conspicuous anomaly in Fanon scholarship concerns the virtual disappearance of the phenomenological. We can likewise posit a series of reasons for this historical omission, the first of which conceivably concerns the voluminous literature intent on exploring the connections between Fanon and psychoanalysis, and, perhaps more notoriously yet, between Fanon and Lacanian psychoanalysis. Without condemning or dismissing such literature – the domain of Fanonian scholarship should, or so we hope, be as inclusive of creative attempts to put Fanonian ideas to work as it is critical of how Fanon might be de-politicized, banalized – it seems clear that this psychoanalytic trend in Fanon studies occurred at the cost of a more developed exploration of psychological analysis and description, namely that of the phenomenological.

In addition, though, that phenomenology seemed, for a significant period, to have fallen out of the set of critical terms frequently referenced within Fanon studies could also be the historical consequence of shifts within the intellectual climate, the outcome of differing priorities in terms of what gained currency in scholarly and political debates of the time – most notably, a structuralist/post-structural interrogation of any direct ("naïve") appeal to the notion of experience. Some may also argue, contentious – or spurious, in our view - as the argument may be, that "Fanon is not a terribly sophisticated phenomenologist" (Macey, 1999, p. 10). Dermot Moran (2000) in his otherwise excellent *Introduction to Phenomenology*, not only has no dedicated section for Fanon, but the entire book has not a single reference to Fanon at all, omissions which can only lead one to assume some broader concordance with Macey's assessment, or an earlier stated notion of Fanon's phenomenology as derivative and secondary with nothing of "original" phenomenological note. Of course, while Macey also avers that "although Fanon is often described as a 'psychoanalyst,' he was not" (2012, p. 132), this did not stop Fanon's appropriation there, nor extensive scholarship about *his* "psychoanalysis." There may well be smoke to this "reason" for the neglect of phenomenological attention, but one can hardly claim fire.

Hence it was that a rigorous exploration of Fanon's distinctive uses and forms of phenomenology emerged as one of the foremost motivations for this edited collection. As we began the literature review that formed the first research task of this book, it quickly became apparent that there have been a number of excellent studies of Fanon's uses of phenomenology (many of which we have been fortunate enough to include in the pages that follow). The problem with this literature was not its content, but its distribution: Without dedicated searching and access to suitable academic databases and libraries, this literature remained so scattered and inaccessible that it has seemed, historically, as if it had almost completely fallen through the cracks of Fanon studies. What is problematic about this – and it helps to consult the indices of a cross-section of titles on Fanon for mention of "phenomenology" to make the point about its omission – is that the appeal to experience, and more directly yet, the appeal to the lived experience of the Black man, is an absolutely irreducible and crucial aspect of *Black Skin, White Masks*. At the risk of being dramatic: There would be no *Black Skin, White Masks* without this method of description and engagement. Fanon's uses of phenomenology – which, as several of the following chapters show, did not leave phenomenology unchanged – proved a condition of possibility for that book, and, extending our argument, for much of what was most compelling, visceral, and innovative within it. It is, in retrospect, unsurprising that Fanon is now being considered a founding figure, as Karera (2020) puts it, for a new era of a properly critical phenomenology (see Guenther 2020; Weiss, Murphy, & Salamon, 2020).

We've divided the book into five broad parts, covering a wide swathe of Fanonian scholarship, including with respect to: Phenomenology, psychology, embodiment, temporality, and the horizons of inquiry and action. Yet, whereas the contributions grouped within each section certainly speak to the section heading, none are entirely constrained by it.

Part I, "Situating Fanon's Phenomenology," opens with an original contribution by **Nigel C. Gibson**. Focusing on the decade of the 50s, Fanon's most active and sustained period as a clinician, Gibson closely examines Fanon's psychiatric writings of the day alongside the contexts of his work and life. It is abundantly clear from this chapter how profoundly close and even fundamental psychology and psychiatric practices were to Fanon, from his days as a student in Lyon, to his residency in the south of France, and his professional appointments thereafter in Algeria and Tunisia. Gibson also demonstrates both the development of Fanon's psychological insights and praxis, and clearly shows its close relation to his political development and involvements. An important contribution to Fanonian scholarship, this original contribution not only brings to an English-speaking world a body of Fanon's writings that is either unavailable in English, or has only very recently become so; it also privileges the psychological and psychiatric Fanon which is barely discussed and remains neglected. One even sees glimpses of Fanon in the mode of empirical qualitative researcher. The view of Fanon as an "incidental psychiatrist" (Keller, 2007) at best is thoroughly challenged, if not upended altogether, by this chapter.

Jean Khalfa's contribution opens with the enigmatic line that ends *Black Skin, White Masks*: "O my body, always make me a man who questions," signaling in so doing the close attention Khalfa will pay to "Fanon on flesh," to Fanon's description of the lived experience of the "body, this skin, this fire," the "Cogito" of a subject that cannot detach from his body. *Black Skin, White Masks* can be read as a long reflection on the body in historical time, suggests Khalfa, as well as a phenomenology of the colonized consciousness. Fanon was attempting, in Khalfa's view, to describe objectively what could only be perceived from the inside: The subjective experience of being objectified. Not only then is Fanon's work necessarily experiential, it is necessarily bodily, hence characterizations of the "exceptionally physical approach" of *Black Skin, White Masks* and the idea that the book is argued from the body. If we are to understand the trauma that racism is capable of inducing, we need to grasp the true risk it poses to the body, namely "the abolition of what is proper to the human ... the loss of *freedom* or *play* of *bodily being* within the world" (emphasis original). Describing Fanon's enrichment and challenge to previous (French) phenomenological notions of body and its relation to both world and the (ongoing) constitution of subjectivity, Khalfa ends his article by saying "there was no other way," the body is "an essential element in Fanon's conscious attempt at inventing a new theory of alienation and a new psychiatry, attentive to the historical and sociological context of the trauma."

Lou Turner's chapter, "Frantz Fanon's Phenomenology of the Black Mind," rounds out Part I. Highlighting the interconnected influences of Merleau-Ponty and Marx upon Fanon enables Turner to highlight a number of crucial themes in *Black Skin, White Masks*. Fanon's phenomenology of Black mind, for Turner, "begins with the sensuous certainty of language ... because language places our existence for others in question." While this has meant that Black existence within colonialism has been "fixed on the lowest rung of human evolution," it is nonetheless true that language remains – as Fanon realized – a potent instrument of protest. A second route of inquiry concerns questions of perception: "Insofar as our perceptions are realizations of the world, race and racial perceptions are realization of a racialized world; they are ... (e)race-ing the world." Issues of knowledge and truth are not far behind. What Fanon's phenomenology of mind discloses is "at once the negation of reflections of ... pre-existing 'truths' about race" and "the act (qua performance) of the (self) bringing forth of truth." A reoccurring theme is that of the "colonial situation," which, in Fanon's view, divides everything in the colonial world into the mutually exclusive categories of "civilized" and "primitive." It is via a phenomenology of this colonial situation that Fanon is able to disrupt the powers of racialization and begin the reflective and dialectical process of becoming whereby the oppressed and negated are able to take on the impulse of self-development.

Part II, "Fanon and the Psychological," brings Fanon even closer into a psychological orbit, with contributions from Desai, Maldonado-Torres, Bernasconi, and Hook. **Miraj U. Desai**'s chapter situates the role of psychological investigations in analyses of social problems such as colonialism and racism by means of a careful phenomenological reading of Frantz Fanon's writings. As Desai argues, an emerging scholarship on Fanon's use of psychology is beginning to elucidate how his style of analysis enables an interweaving of psychological insights with sociopolitical ones. Desai builds on such scholarship by explicating the essential moments of Fanon's approach, structured by a focus on experience, concrete examples, evidence, meaning, unprejudiced seeing from multiple perspectives, delineation of essential structure, and critical and liberating praxis. Desai then moves on to compare Fanon to other theorists operating at the level of the nexus of psychology and society in order to delineate an overall structure of psychopolitical investigations. Overall, the chapter attempts to sketch the ways in which psychology can be advanced as a science and praxis of human liberation.

Nelson Maldonado-Torres examines Fanon's "work in psychology," taking as inspiration the declaration, in *Black Skin, White Masks*, that he will "leave methods to the botanists and mathematicians." In the face of colonial methods and attitudes, Fanon searches for a decolonial attitude that seeks to "build the world of you." With the search for such an attitude at its core, Fanon's corpus makes the case for a decolonial turn in psychology that poses the primacy of attitude over method in knowledge production. In such a form, psychology becomes a decolonial transdisciplinary practice that is close to decolonized versions of other fields in the human sciences, such as philosophy, sociology, history, literature, and political theory, as well as to decolonial activism and praxis. As Maldonado-Torres puts it, citing Fanon: "the description and explanation of attitudes is structured so as to facilitate or provoke the emergence of a new, decolonial, form of attitude ... [the goal of which] is 'nothing less than to liberate the black man from himself.'" This notion of attitude is one that may reverberate not only within Fanonian and decolonial psychological circles, but within phenomenological ones as well, given their own histories with the term.

Robert Bernasconi's chapter, "Frantz Fanon and Psychopathology," provides a meticulous overview of Fanon's most important critiques of psychological understandings of Black experience and colonialism within *Black Skin, White Masks*. Psychological accounts, for Fanon, routinely misattribute problems caused by a racist environment to the patient's psychological constitution, failing thus to register the role of structural phenomena, the importance of economic realities, and the fact that genuine disalienation needs to occur in the most materialist sense. A restructuring of the world, and the conflicts therein, is, in the final analysis, required. General – and typically universalizing – psychological accounts are repeatedly shown by Fanon to be inapplicable to Black experience, particularly so within the conditions of anti-Blackness. The list of theories and theoreticians that Fanon accordingly calls into question is long and varied. Freud's idea that the origins of psychic trauma are repressed and unconscious, is, for example, refuted given that for Black men and women, the traumas of racism exist very much at the level of conscious awareness and concerns in/of the world. Mannoni's notorious psychoanalytic theorization according to which the Malagasy people themselves were responsible for their own colonization – because of their own supposed dependency complex – is likewise rejected. Rather than an absolute rejection of psychoanalysis – and Bernasconi upsets here some of the conclusions drawn in the secondary literature – Fanon intimates that psychoanalysis helps us understand how "White guilt cannot be separated from White supremacy and so is very much part of the problem that creates the Black world." So, while it is often assumed that *Black Skin, White Masks* is written almost exclusively about Blacks, Fanon is also deeply concerned with the deep-rooted myth concerning the Black man as he exists in the white unconscious. Finally, Bernasconi powerfully provokes us to consider where Fanon ends in *Black Skin, White Masks*, not in the tears of foreclosure at the end of Chapter 5, but in the "open dimension of every consciousness," and in action, especially towards the "transformation of the very structures of society."

Derek Hook's chapter is another original contribution to this text. Hook engages, creatively and rigorously, with the work of Black Consciousness psychologist Chabani Manganyi, alongside that of Fanon, arguing in so doing that Manganyi provides an important resource for developing Fanon's ideas on the disturbed dialectic between the body and the world that exists within the conditions of racism. "Racial ontologizing through the body" explores Manganyi's distinctive conceptualization of racializing (and, indeed, *racist*) forms of embodiment, utilizing facets of phenomenology and psychoanalysis conjointly to advance two modes of racial ontologizing through the body. Hook posits, firstly, the idea of an *imposed* embodiment which, reliant on the meaning of othered bodies, involves the transposition of a discursive frame of ideological symbolic values upon the realm of bodily experiences. This conceptualization, as exemplified in Manganyi's work, is supplemented by the idea of an *expressive* mode of embodiment which emphasizes somatic sensation and in which – as in Fanon's harrowing account of corporeal malediction – the body serves as a vessel of lived experience. In Hook's rendering, it becomes clear that racism infiltrates even into the very basic processes of bodily functioning, and their meanings, in its assault.

Proceeding to Part III, "Fanon's Uses of Phenomenology," contributions by Colman, Mahendran, Salamon, and Weate rigorously wrestle with, explore, and expand the very matter of this part title. **Athena V. Colman** examines the corporeal schema as part of the pre-thetic condition for the possibility of experience insofar as we experience through our bodies and their positioning(s) in space. Coupled with this notion of the corporeal schema is Merleau-Ponty's notion of the body image. In this chapter, Colman contextualizes the notion of the schema in its early psychological context, especially turning to the clear link between Fanon, Merleau-Ponty, and Jean Lhermitte. She addresses the significance of Fanon's idea of a historico-racial schema in relation to Merleau-Ponty's conception of the corporeal schema, showing how Fanon's thought in *Black Skin, White Masks* retrieves the lived experience of race, which allows us to expand our understanding of the phenomenological subject and thereby gives us greater insight into the nature of both the corporeal schema and the formation of body image. Toward this end, her chapter begins with a thorough discussion of what is meant by the corporeal schema and the body image in the work of Merleau-Ponty and some others (e.g. Lhermitte, Gallagher, and Meltzoff). She then turns to a discussion of Fanon's phenomenological account of the "lived experience of the black" in his *Black Skin, White Masks*. Although always tied to the corporeal schema, the body image should not be conflated with the former term. The body image, emerging from the corporeal schema, is our representation (including beliefs and images) of our own body. Reading Lhermitte and Merleau-Ponty, Frantz Fanon interrogates the notion of the corporeal schema and describes "the lived experience of the black" as an experience of being in the world as "an object among other objects." Whereas traditionally existential and phenomenological discourses mark the site of subjectivity precisely by distinguishing the subject's experience of being-in-the-world from the mere existence of "things," Fanon's description suggests that the lived experience of the Black is marked, in some way, by "thing-hood." The conception of spatiality this implies alludes more to the objective sense of being "in" space than the subjective sense through which we are embodied. Fanon's phenomenological account demonstrates that the lived experience of Blackness always already takes place within the horizon of being an *object* for an "other" and thus her lived experience – including her sense of spatiality and body image through which she experiences – is fundamentally determined in relation to the "Weltanschauung of a colonized people." Such a horizon, Fanon suggests, *precedes* the corporeal schema, and hence his need to "sketch," beneath the conception of the corporeal schema, a *historico-racial schema* to account for the oppression of the colonizer which shapes the corporeal schema and the body image.

Dilan Mahendran seeks to interrogate Frantz Fanon's phenomenological descriptions of the embodied experience of anti-Black racism and his critique of Merleau-Ponty's phenomenology of perception. Mahendran begins by arguing for an embodied understanding of racism rather than the dominant intellectualist account of race which posits an objective racial knowing, and which privileges race as a discursive formation – as the only definitive and legitimate account of race and racism. An outcome of this privileging of objective racial knowledge is to marginalize any subjective experience of race as always leaning towards an essentialist understanding. Since the linguistic turn in Continental and Anglo-American thought, the trend has been to disassociate power from the body, but this has only been made possible by an Enlightenment universal humanism that indemnified European man's humanity against all others. The linguistic turn thus jettisons the notion of the human, declaring it, in a move of staggering hubris, non-operative, even as it rests assured that the human status of its own leading practitioners (typically privileged, white scholars and critics) can be taken for granted. As such, this European universal subject's humanity is normatively guaranteed while those whose possibility of a subject position is not a given, those with Black and brown bodies, have to contend with their humanity dead on arrival. What is interesting is that for Frantz Fanon the body under racism poses a problem, while for Merleau-Ponty the body is a solution to the existential crisis of Western man. For Merleau-Ponty to address the crisis, Western man must get back to the things themselves, which is the already promised gift of the body in its primordial givenness. Fanon on the other hand sees, through the body, that a radically new conception of the human is needed even to begin to address this multidimensional crisis.

Writing from a gender theory standpoint, **Gayle Salamon** asks what bodily *being* consists of. She explores the social mediation of bodies, insisting that such mediations shape not only our *knowledge of* our bodies but our *feelings in* them as well. Phenomenology is a crucial ally here insisting, as it does, that hard and fast distinctions between body and the world, between inside and outside of the self, are difficult to discern at the level of experience. Phenomenology, indeed, allows us to think of embodiment as a dialectical relation, a relation, furthermore, characterized by constant movement between the inside of the self and the outside of the world. Merleau-Ponty's notion of "flesh," Salamon argues, helps us appreciate how this constant movement both engenders and dissolves the boundary lines between these two domains. Merleau-Ponty's phenomenology, furthermore, allows the prospect of a type of bodily retreat; the body is said to retain the power to withdraw from relations with the world, to transform bodily life into "anonymous life." Frantz Fanon also considers the question of embodied subjectivity, although crucially within the realm of anti-Black racism which consigns the Black subject to a "zone of indeterminacy in bodily being." It is not just the body in its visibility that is targeted by the racism projected at it, and that projects it in turn, a body marked by otherness that is forced into relentlessly surveyed objecthood, but the body in its innermost interiority, a region often posited as beyond the reach of the poisonous effects of an objectifying gaze. Not only does Fanon draw our attention to "the mimetic relation between the physical structures of colonialism and the psychic structures that they produce," he shows, furthermore, that access even to the body's most decidedly material and ostensibly universal aspects is shaped by its racialization.

Jeremy Weate's chapter, "Fanon, Merleau-Ponty, and the Difference of Phenomenology," takes up a recurring objection to phenomenology: The idea that phenomenology is often guilty of *repressing difference* by virtue of presuming a fundamental ground or unity in its descriptions of experience. Fanon's use of phenomenology proves illuminating in this regard inasmuch as it both exposes the core of phenomenology's problematic relation to difference and nonetheless shows how the theorization of lived experience can reveal "the key issues at work between agency, history and the world." Fanon's critique focuses on the equality that Merleau-Ponty's phenomenology assumes to exist across all able-bodied beings – an idea rendered naïve on the basis of Black experience. Illustrative recourse to the fiction of James Baldwin enables us, says Weate, to "display forcefully how difference denies the possibility of an already given community and commonality between human subjects." One appreciates in this respect how for Fanon ontology can itself be revealed as a strategy of legitimation for the repression of difference. Prior to the doing of ontology then, Fanon insists on the necessity of critical resistance to the dominating values, representations, and myths of a positively racializing and racist episteme. "Fanon's critique of phenomenology" for Weate "teaches us that the universal is the end of the struggle not that which precedes it." The hope then is that Fanon's critique might result in a productive phenomenology of difference which effectively repositions community as the deferred universal and not the given.

Part IV, "Temporality and Racism," offers important contributions by Al-Saji, Ngo, and Farred with respect to race, racism, postcoloniality, and temporality. **Alia Al-Saji** draws on Fanon's *Black Skin, White Masks* in order to explore temporal structures of racialized experience. Fanon proves a crucial ally in Al-Saji's attempt to ask how racism may be understood as a social pathology which, when internalized or "epidermalized," may result in aberrations of affect, embodiment, and agency that are temporally lived. Al-Saji analyses the racialized experience of coming "too late" to a world predetermined in advance, and the distorted relation to possibility – the limitation of playfulness and imaginative variability – that defines this sense of lateness. Racialization is not limited to the present, argues Al-Saji, but also colonizes and reconfigures the past, splitting in a duality of times: One open and civilizational, the other closed, anachronistic and racialized.

Helen Ngo examines how racialized and white bodies are differentially temporalized, drawing inspiration from Fanon's account of racialized "lateness," as elaborated by Alia Al-Saji. Extending their analyses of racialized bodies as predetermined by and tethered to the past, Ngo argues that such temporalization serves not only to anachronize the racialized body, but also to close off its projective possibilities for being or becoming otherwise. Drawing on Charles Mills' accounts of "white ignorance" and "white time," Ngo then examines how racialization relies on a forgetting or a disavowal and leaving behind of its own process. The result, she argues, is to render whiteness and white bodies as temporally present and even futural in their orientation, free from the vestiges of racism's history and free to adopt any number of stances on its continuing legacy. It is against this setting that Ngo argues exhortations to "get over it" – whenever charges of racism are leveled in the public domain by racialized subjects – are not only dangerous in their denial of racism, but also disingenuous in the way they purport to move beyond a racially divided world, when in fact this very gesture serves to reinscribe differential racialized temporalities. Further, looking to typical responses in the contestations over public commemorations of events and figures within "white time" (for example, calls to tear down the monuments of colonialism and slavery), Ngo examines how these responses cast the deep attachments and temporal "untetheredness" of whiteness in a different light.

Frantz Fanon and Heidegger are thinkers with such opposed political allegiances and histories that they are not often read together, despite the – perhaps unexpected – critical and philosophical benefits of doing so. **Grant Farred**'s chapter, "To Dwell for the Postcolonial," provides a case in point, offering an exploration of how Heidegger's notion of dwelling might inform the Fanonian project of beginning a genuinely *post*colonial nation. As quickly becomes apparent in Farred's exposition, the concept of dwelling provides an important phenomenological means of illuminating questions of postcolonial being and temporality alike. Indeed, this Heideggerian concept provides a way of framing Fanon's overarching agenda in *The Wretched of the Earth*, a text which can be understood precisely as "Fanon's struggle to build the postcolonial as a house for dwelling." Farred echoes Fanon's pronouncement in *The Wretched of the Earth*, "Perhaps everything needs to be started over again," and reads it in terms of the foregoing imperative, stressing that it is "the making of a dwelling that must be sought for, built, in the act of the 'starting over again'" that is required in the making of the postcolonial. Such a nation-building agenda, says Farred, overlaying Heidegger with Fanon, necessarily brings together the ideas of dwelling, building, and thinking. Thinking these terms conjointly brings with it crucial critical insights.

As Farred argues, "Thinking the postcolonial as a dwelling precedes, for Fanon, the act of building the nation." At the core of dwelling, moreover, is thinking. And building – to add the further Heideggerian qualification – is not so much an instrumentalist act, as in the making of the nation, "as it is the manifestation, the 'presencing,' of the thinking of dwelling."

Part V, "Phenomenology after Fanon," contains chapters by Gordon, Henry, and Ahmed, struggling as they do with the horizons and promise of Fanonism, particularly with respect to Africana phenomenology, the phenomenology of whiteness, and the important task of translating Fanon to local contexts. **Lewis R. Gordon**'s chapter explores how the political writings of Steve Biko, the charismatic leader of the Black Consciousness Movement in Apartheid South Africa, offer a profoundly *politically situated* understanding of consciousness. Gordon reminds us that phenomenology demands examining consciousness as a lived embodied reality, not a floating abstraction. He goes on, drawing vital parallels between the work of Biko and Fanon, noting how anti-Black racism structures Blacks *outside* of the dialectics of recognition and the ethical struggle of self and other. The result is, in Gordon's words, "a struggle *to enter* ethico-political relations, ironically to establish the self both as 'self' and 'other.'" Biko, crucially, shows how this struggle occurs within the historical context of white supremacy, that is, within a domain that *forbids the very possibility of the political* at least insofar as the latter brings with it the possibility of radically critiquing or transforming the existing social order. Biko's Black Consciousness brings these two realms (the ethical/intersubjective and the political) together in demonstrating how colonialism has left us with a situation that requires political intervention for ethical life to even become possible. Black Consciousness is, as such, identical with political life under such circumstances, "and those who are willing to take on the risk of politics … are, as their opposition mounts, blackened by such a process." Accordingly, Gordon asserts that Biko's genius included rendering politics *Black*. These insights are still of utmost political value today. How so? The phenomenology of Black Consciousness shows us that such a consciousness does not properly function merely as a negative term of a prior positivity of whiteness. This realization impacts dramatically upon popular liberal models of cosmopolitanism, which, upon reflection, maintain unacknowledged endorsements of white normativity. Given that white consciousness is rarely – if ever – relativized in reference to another positive term, it appears to transcend the status of the racial, asserting itself simply as consciousness itself. What this means then, as Gordon insists, is the cosmopolitanist fails to see that politics is at work in the illusion of transcending particularity. To insist upon this before a cosmopolitan viewpoint thus "constitutes an intrusion of the political in the dream world of ethical efficacy." It is to blacken the cosmopolitan world, "to begin its path into Black Consciousness."

Whiteness, argues **Sara Ahmed**, can be usefully approached through the lens of phenomenology, and could indeed be described as an unfinished history which orients bodies in specific directions, affecting how they "take up" space and what they "can do." Drawing on Fanon's analysis in *Black Skin, White Masks* to think of whiteness as involving a particular form of orientation, Ahmed goes on to consider how whiteness functions as a habit, which becomes a background to social action. Referring to experiences of inhabiting a white world as a non-white body, Ahmed explores how whiteness becomes worldly through the noticeability of the arrival of some bodies more than others. A phenomenology of whiteness helps us notice institutional habits; it brings what is behind to the surface in a certain way.

Paget Henry engages the work of Fanon alongside that of W.E.B. Dubois and Lewis Gordon so as to develop a remarkably concise intellectual historical account of Africana phenomenology. Henry describes phenomenology as "the discursive practice through which self-reflective descriptions of the constituting activities of consciousness are produced after the "natural attitude" of everyday life has been bracketed by some ego-displacing technique." He goes on to stipulate that an Africana phenomenology would thus be "the self-reflective descriptions of the constituting activities of the consciousness of Africana peoples, after the natural attitudes of Africana egos have been displaced by the de-centering techniques practices in these cultures." Henry shows how Africana phenomenology starts with a different foil, not scientism – as might be expected for a more traditional phenomenology – but racism. Henry also describes Fanon's response to the problem of double consciousness (first detailed by Dubois) and shows the relation of Fanon's penetrating insights to Fanon's skillful use of poetic and phenomenological reductions as well as to philosophical and psychoanalytic modes of investigation. For Henry, Fanon's achievements in *Black Skin, White Masks* remain unsurpassed: "There is no finer or more detailed account of the state of racial double consciousness."

Beyond the explicit aims and goals of the book – to bring the psychological in Fanon to greater prominence, and to address the scarce, and collate the disparately distributed work on the phenomenological in Fanon – the contributions here also highlight a greater truth, to wit that the field of Fanon scholarship has been subject to a number of reconfigurations. We could go so far as to say that this is the norm now within Fanon studies. The questions posed by Henry Louis Gates Jr. (1999), Stuart Hall (1996), and David Macey (2012) concerning the modalities, divisions, and often widely varying utilizations of Fanon's work, make this point strongly enough. The stories at the beginning of this introduction, of the many ways we came to face up to Fanon, do the same. Such diversity of reading and application is unsurprising inasmuch as there are many fields, both old and new – from cultural studies, sociology, political and postcolonial theory, to continental and Africana philosophy, the visual arts, and decolonial theory – that have attempted to channel the force of Fanon's various critiques. One such prospective reconfiguration of how one might read and approach Fanon is currently underway, and it is particularly deserving of our attention here.

Perhaps the single document that signals the prospective sea-change in critical Fanonism more than any other is David Marriott's (2018) *Whither Fanon?* a text which has not only interrogated many of the accepted approaches to Fanon, but that can reasonably claim to have genuinely revitalized the field. The salience of Marriott's work for our project here concerns the critique he launches upon "the Marxist-phenomenological tradition," which, importantly, is inclusive of Sartrean approaches that attempt to "map the *philosophical* importance of Fanonism in terms of a phenomenology of experience, giving rise (or birth) to a drama of freedom and alterity, recognition and authenticity" (Marriott, 2011, p. 35).

It may help here, by way of a broader intellectual contextualization, to briefly note the influence of two important Afro-Pessimist intellectuals on Marriott's arguments. We have in mind particularly the work of Jared Sexton (2011, 2015) and Frank Wilderson (2010, 2020), who equate Blackness – often via a reading of Fanon's notion of the zone of nonbeing – with the condition of social death. The claim here is that the historical institution of slavery has set the paradigm – epistemically, socially, politically – for how Blackness is to be understood and valued, that is, *as existing precisely outside of the category of the human*. Anti-Blackness is not, moreover, a temporary historical aberration for Afro-Pessimist theorists, a condition that might be overcome; it is the "constitutive outside," the fundamentally externalized condition of possibility for the category of the human as we know it.

One appreciates now the force of Marriott's (2011, 2018) critique of humanistic phe-nomenological and existentialist readings of Fanon whom, he says, persistently locates "blackness as a necessary contamination of traditional political thinking and ontology" (p. 36). The implication of this is that "racism interrupts the movement towards the human, and paradoxically makes ontology irrelevant for understanding black existence" (p. 36). As such, ethics and politics, in so far as they are grounded on humanism – particularly for Marriott of the Marxist-phenomenological tradition – "cannot simply be invoked … as a model for thinking black existence" (p. 36).[7]

This is not the place to attempt a viable response, or worse, a defensive reaction, to what is unquestionably a considered and seminal piece of critique. Marriott's position, suf-fice it to say, poses questions for the future of how "Fanon's phenomenology," and "Fanon's psychology," if those terms may be permitted, should be developed in the years to come. The contributions of critical phenomenology, of Africana existential philosophy, of phe-nomenology in its relation to colonialism, to Black Consciousness – indeed, in its relation to the conditions of anti-Blackness as outlined by Afro-Pessimism – all of these should preoc-cupy our attentions in articulating the future prospects of Fanonism. What we might call Fanon's archive of critique, referring thus to the various strategic mobilizations of Fanon's writings and revolutionary praxis, is far from exhausted.

It is our sincerest hope that this book does its part to advance those very future pros-pects; that the engagement with Fanon here, as with any engagement with Fanon, involves a demand for transformation. This would include potential transformations of all three domains referred to by the terms in the book title: Fanon(ism), phenomenology, and psy-chology. None of these, we hope, become seen in the same way after engaging the full scope of the authors' contributions and their challenges to, and interventions within, each. Posing this question of "what comes after the engagement" another way, we are forced to ask what, then, becomes of Fanonism, phenomenology, and psychology?

In reverse order, the psychology that has dominated the landscape of Western/Northern countries, and increasingly the world, is in need of radical revision. There needs to be a new way of doing and thinking through the psychological that is capable of attend-ing to the wider contexts of culture, society, politics, and imperialism, which current, main-stream psychology falls far short of. The problem of racism makes this abundantly clear. People who experience racism may painfully wonder why it is not among the first things any discipline or practice such as psychology deals with. Or, when it is dealt with, besides its nominal manner that often feels like an afterthought, or an obligatory imposition to cross the t's and say it has been done, its content, no less, is of the sterile and reductionistic positivist remove that does not resonate in the least with the everyday assaultive experience thereof. Fanon's phenomenology of racism and the racist world poses a wholesale challenge to such a psychology's understandings and concepts, the methods that have been used to arrive at understandings and concepts, as well as the practical disciplines that have been built up by these understandings, concepts, and methods. So if the call for transformation is directed at psychology's aims, methods, concepts, and practices, that is, its *structure*, then a radical repositioning is not only suggested but necessary. What is suggested, then, is not a psychology "of" this or that, but a radical revisioning of what comes before the "of." The question, in this day, seems less now about why such a radical revisioning is needed, than: Why not?

And why should the same questions and challenges not be applied to phenomenology, broadly construed? Towards what end and towards what world has much of phenomenol-ogy typically been directed? Is the vaunted world of phenomenological experience and description one within which all of us live and truly see ourselves? If we had let the things truly speak to us, then the constitution of the world as racist and as racially and economically stratified would have emerged clearly and centrally, with racial justice, liberation, and the actions these require being demanded by the things themselves. The pieces on Africana phenomenology teach us as much. The embodiment of Fanonian phenomenology questions as much.

And finally, with regard to Fanonism or Fanon studies, we are left with gratitude and mourning about what comes after. Our gratitude is towards a field that has left us with a rich and detailed engagement with what Fanon was, his life, ideas, writings, and actions. To borrow a phrase from Fanon, Fanonism has become its own foundation. But our mourning comes from the recognition that fidelity to an inheritance means that we resist the seduction of hermetic attempts to seal that inheritance in some or other notion of original "purity" or intent and that we continually re-invent, re-apply, and re-launch from an always present where we are, into a future without guarantees. Fanon never wanted Fanonism. He wanted us to look, together, within our own world to confront it with all the means at our disposal, whether experiential, psychological, poetic, political, actional, or otherwise. Thus, it may be that, for Fanonism, what comes after are not only investigations of Fanon but *Fanonian-inspired* investigations, interrogations, and actions on and in the world that faces YOU. To be sure, the final transformation that Fanon always points to is none of the three titular domains after all. It points to the world, always towards the world, which is failing us, derelict in its duty of providing a genuinely liveable, just, and loving space. And to the world, pointing back at us, questioning what *we* have done, individually and collectively, to realize our human, our humane, duty in this suffering world.

The "fierce urgency of now"[8] is the order of this day.

NOTES

1 The actual quote is from *Black Skin, White Masks* (1994/1952, p. 226), and reads "It is not because the Indo-Chinese has discovered a culture of his own that he is in revolt. It is because 'quite simply' it was, in more than one way, becoming impossible for him to breathe."

2 Bernasconi might be onto something when he says, of *Black Skin, White Masks*, that it "is difficult for Whites to read," and that Fanon's "phenomenological description of the lived experience of the Black in Chapter 5 presents an extraordinary challenge to his white readers ... not least because it obliges white readers, like myself, to consider what we prefer to ignore and what we too easily dismiss as beyond our understanding: the impact of racism, both personal and structural, on Blacks" (Bernasconi, 2005, p. 100).

3 In addition to the experiential and anecdotal, we've also examined this theme of Fanonian theoretical travel and movement academically, for example in Desai (2018) and Hook (2012, 2020).

4 One should also acknowledge Adams (1970) and McCulloch (1983) among those few early attempts at a psychological mapping and/or reading of Fanon's work.

5 A prominent statue of Cecil John Rhodes, one of the most iconic of colonialists, on the campus of the University of Cape Town, was the target of an initially small and localized campus protest. Very soon, though, the campaign for the statue's removal led to a wider movement to "decolonize" education in South Africa, and the pressure to remove colonial vestiges across the country. In fact, the reverberations of the Rhodes must fall movement crossed national borders, with students at Oxford, Edinburgh, Cambridge, Harvard, and the University of California, Berkeley, to name a few, mounting similar protests to remove statues and symbols of slavery and colonialism.

6 Until very recently, the graduate program in clinical psychology at Duquesne University was the only American Psychological Association (APA) accredited program in Human Science Psychology in the United States. Just a few years ago, Point Park University (also in Pittsburgh!) claimed the second such spot. There are precious few human science psychology programs in the United States that continue to provide some refuge to students interested in an existential, phenomenological, humanistic, or broadly human science psychology – in addition to Duquesne and Point Park, graduate psychology at the universities of West Georgia, Seattle, Dallas, Brigham-Young, Pacifica, and Boston College increasingly so, are the most prominent exceptions.

7 More specifically, in reference to Sartre, and as part of an extended critique of the phenomenological-existential orientation of Lewis Gordon, Marriott (2011) observes that "Fanon identifies in the subject a void-like nothingness-of-being which is ... linked to the problem of self-deception in Sartre" (p. 46). This link allows Fanon "to develop thoughts on how the black subject is always belated and dispersed ... *irrealized* and yet forever haunted by its non-appearance and who can only acquire a certain density of being by taking on the tragic neurotic role (of an imaginary whiteness) – which is also why phenomenology can never be grounded in the experience of this subject for its truth is literally void" (p. 46, emphasis original).

8 The allusion is to the memorable phrase of Martin Luther King Jr's, delivered at the March on Washington, on August 28, 1963.

REFERENCES

Adams, P. (1970). The social psychiatry of Frantz Fanon. *American Journal of Psychiatry, 127*(6), 809–814.

Bernasconi, R. (2005). The European knows and does not know: Fanon's response to Sartre. In M. Silverman (Ed.), *Frantz Fanon's* Black skin, White masks (pp. 100–111). Manchester, UK: Manchester University Press.

Bulhan, H. A. (1985). *Frantz Fanon and the psychology of oppression*. New York: Plenum Press.

Burman, E. (2018). *Fanon, education, action: Child as method*. London and New York: Routledge.

Caute, D. (1970). *Fanon*. London: Fontana/Collins.

Derrida, J. (1994). *Specters of Marx: The state of the debt, the work of mourning, and the new international* (P. Kamuf, Trans.). New York: Routledge.

Desai, M. (2018). *Travel and movement in clinical psychology: The world outside the clinic*. London: Palgrave Macmillan.

Dick, K., & Kofman, A. Z. (Writers). (2002). *Derrida*. A. Z. Kofman (Producer). United States: Zeitgeist Films.

Fanon, F. (1965). *A dying colonialism* (H. Chevalier, Trans.). New York: Grove Press. (Original work published 1959)

Fanon, F. (1994). *Black skin, White masks* (P. Markmann, Trans. New York: Grove Press. (Original work published 1952)

Fanon, F. (2004). *The wretched of the Earth* (R. Philcox, Trans.). New York: Grove Press. (Original work published 1961)

Fanon, J. (2014). *Frantz Fanon, my brother: Doctor, playwright, revolutionary* (D. Nethery, Trans.). Lanham, MD: Lexington Books.

Gates, H. L. (1999). Critical Fanonism. In N. C. Gibson (Ed.), *Rethinking Fanon: The continuing dialogue* (pp. 251–268). New York: Humanity.

Gendzier, I. L. (1973). *Frantz Fanon: A critical study*. New York: Vintage Books.

Gibson, N. (1999). Introduction. In N. Gibson (Ed.), *Rethinking Fanon* (pp. 9–46). New York: Humanity Books.

Gilly, A. (1965). Introduction. In F. Fanon (Ed.), *A dying colonialism* (H. Chevalier, Trans.). New York: Grove Press. (Original work published 1959)

Gordon, L. (2015). *What Fanon said: A philosophical introduction to his life and thought.* New York: Fordham University Press.

Guenther, L. (2020). Critical phenomenology. In G. Weiss, A. V. Murphy & G. Salaman (Eds.), *Fifty concepts for a critical phenomenology* (pp. 11–16). Evanston, IL: Northwestern University Press.

Hall, S. (1996). The after-life of Frantz Fanon: Why Fanon? Why now? Why Black skin White masks? In A. Read (Ed.), *The facts of blackness: Frantz Fanon and visual interpretation* (pp. 12–37). ICA: Bay.

Hook, D. (2012). *A critical psychology of the postcolonial: The mind of Apartheid.* New York: Taylor & Francis.

Hook, D. (2020). Fanon via Lacan, or: Decolonization by psychoanalytic means…? *Journal of the British Society for Phenomenology, 51*(4), 305–319.

Hudis, P. (2015). *Frantz Fanon: Philosopher of the barricades.* London: Pluto Press.

Karera, A. (2020). The racial epidermal schema. In G. Weiss, A. V. Murphy & G. Salaman (Eds.), *Fifty concepts for a critical phenomenology.* Evanston, IL: Northwestern University Press, pp. 289–294.

Keller, R. C. (2007). *Colonial madness: Psychiatry in French North Africa.* Chicago, IL: Chicago University Press.

Macey, D. (1999). Fanon, phenomenology, race. *Radical Philosophy, 95*, 8–14.

Macey, D. (2012). *Frantz Fanon: A biography.* New York: Verso Books.

Mannoni, O. (1990). *Prospero and Caliban: The psychology of colonization* (P. Powesland, Trans.). Ann Arbor, MI: University of Michigan Press. (Original work published 1950)

Marriott, D. (2011). Whither Fanon? *Textual Practice, 25*(1), 33–69.

Marriott, D. (2018). *Whither Fanon?* Stanford, CA: Stanford University Press.

McCulloch, J. (1983). *Black soul, White artifact: Fanon's clinical psychology and social theory.* Cambridge: Cambridge University Press.

Moran, D. (2000). *Introduction to phenomenology.* New York: Routledge.

Morrison, T. (1987, December 20). James Baldwin: His voice remembered; Life in his language. *The New York Times.*

Sexton, J. (2011). The social life of social death: On Afro-pessimism and Black optimism. *InTensions, 5*, 1–47.

Sexton, J. (2015). Unbearable blackness. *Cultural Critique, 90*(1), 159–178.

Silverman, M. (2005). Editor's introduction. In M. Silverman (Ed.), *Frantz Fanon's "Black skin, White masks": New interdisciplinary essays* (pp. 1–11). New York: Manchester University Press.

Wilderson, F. (2010). *Red, White and Black: Cinema and the structure of U.S. antagonisms.* Durham, NC: Duke University Press.

Wilderson, F. (2020). *Afro-Pessimism.* London and New York: Norton.

Woods, D. (1978). *Biko.* London: Paddington Press.

Weiss, G., Murphy, A. V., and Salaman, G. (Eds.). (2020). *Fifty concepts for a critical phenomenology.* Evanston, IL: Northwestern University Press.

PART I
Situating Fanon's Phenomenology

CHAPTER 1

DECOLONIZING MADNESS

The Psychiatric Writings of Frantz Fanon[1]

Nigel C. Gibson

This chapter centers on the clinical and psychiatric essays that consumed much of Frantz Fanon's intellectual and professional life during the decade of the 1950s. Doing so proves a challenging task on more than one account. Firstly, these texts are mainly viewed as peripheral to the three books and the collection of political writings that have been available to English readers for nearly fifty years.[2] It is, however, not only a question of perception, but also of access: As François Maspero put it, Fanon carried on a remarkably medical activity in his role as a psychiatrist in Algeria, "innovating at many levels" but "this material remains untouched … [and] too scattered" (2007, p. viii). Indeed, more than fifty years after Maspero's editorial comment, that material still remained to be assembled in France and translated into English.

A second challenge issues precisely from the attempt to translate these works, which is to say open up a space between two languages and cultures through which a unique voice can be ushered more or less successfully from one to the other. This is of course a difficult undertaking on the best of days, but complicated all the more so here by shared authorship, particularities of context, and the sometimes messiness of composition. Several of these texts are either unfinished articles, drafts for conference papers, or notes taken by a third person of a lecture given by Fanon – meaning that there are mistakes, typos, and incomplete sentences to contend with. Further, of the papers that were published, most of them were co-authored collaborations; we don't actually know who wrote them up. It is probably safe to assume from what we do know of Fanon's hectic schedule and predilection for dictation, though, that his interns or colleagues did some of the writing. Alice Cherki, who worked with Fanon in both Blida and Tunis, reminded me that the political writing of the time was done in great haste and with the specific task of fast and wide dissemination in mind, while the scientific writing was done in a similar vein, in preparation for a conference or publication deadline. Someone held the pen and the others spoke, or notes were collected to feed the article being written, but Fanon was almost always the instigator of the ideas being explored. He was, according to Cherki, involved in everything that went on and certainly the most formidable and exacting presence in the room.

Finally, attention to these writings involves plunging into the world of European and French psychiatry of the 1950s, almost three-quarters of a century ago, and particularly into the question of the relationship between neurology and psychiatry, which has developed considerably since. As such, some of these writings may appear at first quite dated. I maintain, however, that these psychiatric writings not only represent milestones and radical methodological innovation for its time, but importantly also concede the beginnings of Fanon's affirmation of the imbrication of social reality with the organization of mental disorders as he argues in his reading of Lacan's thesis in 1951 (Fanon, 2018, pp. 262–269). They already bear witness to Fanon's particular interest in thinking the alienated as whole persons in their own right, and, while not directly political as are Fanon's major works,

DOI: 10.4324/9781003037132-1

nevertheless what is found in his psychiatric writings are many of the important issues and challenges that we associate with Fanon, as well as critical and self-critical studies that serve to underline and illuminate the relationship between Fanon's work as a psychiatrist and his major works. Indeed, each one of these texts insists upon the apprehension and comprehension of alienation and the alienated through the entire social, cultural, and familial registers from which subjects of language and history are born and constructed.

It is worth remembering that Fanon did not arrive in Algeria in 1953 staunchly committed to a violent revolution against French colonialism. However critical he was of French society, Fanon at that time remained committed to what he called the French drama (2008, p. 179). It was the violent and oppressive reality of colonial Algeria and the issue of psychiatric healing in a colonial war that led him to embrace the liberation struggle that began on November 1, 1954. After he met with leaders of the Front de Libération Nationale (the National Liberation Front, or FLN), he continued to work at Blida-Joinville Psychiatric Hospital until his resignation in December 1956. And even after he started to work full-time for the FLN in Tunis, Fanon remained dedicated to psychiatry, insisting, as he put it while he was at Blida-Joinville Hospital, that psychiatry "has to be political" (Cherki, 2006, p. 72) and as he put it to his colleague Maurice Despinoy, "colonial psychiatry as a whole has to be disalienated" (see 2018, p. 417). In Tunis he continued to work in psychiatric hospitals and to publish in psychiatric journals, seeking to "clarify the relationship between psychiatric theory and colonial domination" (Keller, 2007a, p. 181). After all, while Fanon believed that organized political action was absolutely essential to individual and national liberation, he was under no illusion that it exhausted the problem of mental illness. In Fanon's view, there would continue to be a dialectical relationship between mental health and social change, which meant that a critical grounded psychiatry would continue to have a practical place after the conditions creating colonial alienation were ended. If the end of colonialism was necessary for mental health, and even if "only violence could remediate the psychical damage done by colonialism" (Zaretsky, 2005, p. 3), at the same time, the real psychiatric work of addressing trauma can truly begin with the end of colonial violence and on the basis of genuine self-determination. Hence, I take Fanon's work as a totality, and consider his psychiatric writings to be very much a part of his oeuvre. Moreover, whereas the specificity of Fanon's psychiatric essays frame a particular historic context and situation, a worthy motivation for scholarly examination in its own right, they *also* open up new avenues to reevaluate Fanon's thought in its totality, and in its relation to issues of the present.

FANON THE PSYCHIATRIST

It is no small stretch to assert a common assumption, in the Anglophone world especially, that Fanon was an "incidental psychiatrist" (Keller, 2007b, p. 825), at best. Detailed biographies of Fanon by David Macey (2000) and Alice Cherki (2006), alongside scholarly works such as those of Bird-Pollan (2014), Bulhan (1986), Hook (2011), Keller (2007a), Renault (2011), and Vergès (1991), have helped to re-establish a more even-handed approach to Fanon's psychiatric works as part of his oeuvre. In the 1980s, Homi Bhabha, perhaps more than anyone in the English-speaking world, helped reinsert the psychoanalytic into our understanding of Fanon by emphasizing his debt to Lacan. Readers could no longer ignore the significance of Fanon's engagement with psychoanalytic practice and psychoanalytic theory, even if Fanon was not a professionally trained psychoanalyst and never underwent analysis.[3] Additionally, Hussein Bulhan's *Fanon and the Psychology of Oppression* (1986) remains one of the most important engagements with Fanon's psychiatric work. Even so, Fanon's own writings on psychiatry have been up until now barely discussed. In the sections that follow, I address several of these neglected psychiatric writings through a mostly chronological and biographical scaffold.

Training at Lyon

Frantz Fanon left Martinique in 1944, at the age of 18, to join the Free French Army. By the time he had been deployed in North Africa and France, and after taking part in the Battle of Alsace in 1945, his initial enthusiasm for French civilization had turned bitter, and in a letter to his mother he wrote that he doubted "everything, even myself" and the decision "to fight for an obsolete ideal" (Joby Fanon, 2014, p. 34). After the war, he returned briefly to the Martinican capital of Fort de France to work on Aimé Césaire's election bid for mayor under the Communist ticket, and in 1946, he returned to France to pursue a medical degree at the University of Lyon.[4]

While at Lyon he continued studies in philosophy (especially phenomenology and existentialism), politics, and psychoanalysis, reading Marx, Sartre, Freud, and Lacan, and alongside his degree courses, he also enrolled in classes with Merleau-Ponty. Before completing his medical training, he switched to psychiatry and joined Lyon's psychiatry department, then headed by Professor Dechaume, a specialist in neurology who was fascinated by psychosurgery. The whole psychiatry department was "based on a very organicist approach to neuro-psychiatry" (Razanajao, Postel, and Allen, 1996, p. 500), with absolutely no interest in psychoanalytical inquiry or methods. The professional training of psychiatrists could simply be summed up as consisting of the conviction that under any circumstance the patient should be committed to the psychiatric institution. While under Dechaume's supervision, Fanon submitted a draft (in late 1950) of what would become parts of *Black Skin, White Masks* titled "Contribution to the study of Psychological Mechanisms likely to generate a healthy understanding between the different members of the French Community" as his doctoral thesis. It was rejected for political reasons. In response, he quickly wrote up a study on Friedreich's ataxia (a neurophysiological disorder) and delusions of possession that met Dechaume's approval: "Troubles mentaux et syndromes psychiatrique dans l'Hérédo-Dégéneration-Spino Cérébelleuse" (Mental Disorders and Psychiatric Syndromes in Hereditary Spinocerebellar Degeneration) (1951).

A section of Fanon's dissertation discusses the "limits of neurology and psychiatry" through three representatives, Kurt Goldstein (whose theory of neuropsychology was based on Gestalt theory), Henry Ey, and Jacques Lacan.[5] "Few men are as contentious as Lacan," Fanon writes in the dissertation, summing up Lacan's position, perhaps mistakenly, as "a defense of the rights of madness to exist in man" (see Fanon, 2018, p. 263). Asserting that "misrecognition is at the foundation of Lacan's thought," he argues, "Lacan goes beyond the concept of the image, making the projectional phenomena described by Levy-Bruhl as a corollary of primitive thought, the cornerstone of his system. He links the unhappy consciousness to a conception of magic" (see 2018, p. 269). Whereas Fanon does not develop this argument further, he does suggest that "[i]nternally Lacan seems to inhabit the meeting place of Hegel and Levy-Bruhl" (see 2018, p. 269). Lacan's discussion, in Fanon's view, "centers on the very limits of freedom, in other words, humanity's responsibility" (2018, p. 270).

While Lacan is discussed, Fanon does not engage Freud in the dissertation, and it should be noted that the only direct quote from Freud in *Black Skin, White Masks* (for which Fanon provides no citation) comes from the first and second lectures of Freud's (1990) *Five Lectures on Psycho-Analysis* (originally published in 1910).[6] If, for (the 1895) Freud, "there is determined Erlebnis at the origin of every neurosis" (Fanon, 2008, p. 123) – even if the "first trauma [is] … expelled from the consciousness and memory of the patient" (Freud, quoted in Fanon, 2008, p. 123) – then the event for the Black is "the traumatic contact with the white" (2008, p. 164), both as a continuing process and as the slow absorption of cultural stereotypes (alongside a "brutal awareness of social and economic realities" [2018, p. xiv]). While obviously critical of so-called scientific explanations of race based in phrenology and brain weight, Fanon was dismissive of the liberal colonial culturalist idea that neurosis and alienation were simply a result of prejudice, or the effect of European "modernization" and "civilization" on a colonized people (2008, 2007, pp. 31–44).[7]

"The North African Syndrome," an essay written at the same time as *Black Skin, White Masks*, and published in February 1952, before being included as the first chapter in Fanon's subsequent book *Toward the African Revolution* (1967), is a political-ethical critique of contemporary medical practices, which includes parodies of common attitudes about North Africans among medical professionals as lazy and criminal. Referring to a doctoral thesis from a Dr. Mugniery (who defended at Lyon in the same year as Fanon), Fanon quotes Mugniery's concern about the North African's considerable sexual needs, and the stereotypical conclusion that granting French citizenship to a "civilization still primitive … seems to have been precipitous" (p. 9). "The North African Syndrome" does not directly attack the then dominant ethnopsychiatric theories promoted by Professor Porot and the Algiers school of colonial psychology (about which we will say more shortly), but there is a direct connection between Fanon's criticism of the racist and orientalist attitudes toward North Africans in France, and the theories of the Arab mind promulgated by the Algiers school, notably the idea of racial/cultural hierarchy in terms of anatomic-physiology, i.e., the absence of cortical integration.

Fanon begins the essay with a belief that the human dilemma can be reduced to this existential question: "Have I not, because of what I have done or failed to do, contributed to the impoverishment of human reality … (H)ave I, in all circumstances, called forth the human inside me" (1967, p. 3). For Fanon, it is not enough to understand that the Algerian's "impulsivity" is a product of the colonial situation. Rather, he implores his readers to change the way they act, and take a stand against the alienated social reality that has created it. To change the world always requires openness to self-critique. Disalienation or demystification, as he puts it in *The Wretched of the Earth*, means "to demystify (de-alienate), and to harry the insult that exists in oneself" (1968, p. 304). "The North African Syndrome," Fanon argues, is based on a priori diagnosis founded on an idea: "The North African [is] … a foundation built by the European. In other words, the North African enters spontaneously, by his very presence, into a pre-existing framework" (1967, p. 4). The racist and dehumanizing pathology created and recreated by the medical establishment and reproduced in medical schools is rehearsed in every interaction between doctor and patient. Like the Black in *Black Skin, White Masks*, the North African is objectified: Spoken to as though lacking in intelligence and treated as a liar or shirker or, as Professor Antoine Porot (1932) opined, an impulsive criminal. While the French doctors continued to look for the diagnostic source of the symptom in a lesion, they refused to think in terms of the psychosomatic. Moreover, by thingifying the North African, they refused to consider the condition of these wretched people who are "without family, without love, without human relations, without the possibility of communion" and thus live "in a bodily struggle with death, a short death of death, a death in life" (1967, p. 10). The patient (the sufferer) is reified and "dissolve[d] on the basis of an idea"; instead of seeing a human being, the doctor reconstructs the North African as something empty of substance (p. 12). Once dehumanized, the patient's inability to express a specific symptom increases the doctor's disdain. Linguistic alienation simply reinforces the patient's sense of insecurity, along with the doctor's condescension and tendency to infantilize the patient. "The North African Syndrome" is an ethical statement that challenges the medical profession to act with genuine reciprocity and dignity toward the poor and suffering immigrants. Not acting in this way is a form of neo-hippocratism, he argues, and reveals the utter bankruptcy of the Hippocratic oath. The North African, Fanon concludes, would be happier at home. But, of course, in Algeria, Fanon would soon find that the North African was alienated; there too, he would continue to find himself repeating the plea that he had made in "The North African Syndrome," to treat the North African with dignity.

Residency at Alban-sur-Limagnole

Fanon escaped the intellectual desert that was the University of Lyon's psychiatry department to work and study with François Tosquelles as a resident at Saint-Alban-sur-Limagnole psychiatric hospital, in the highland region of Southern France. Fanon acknowledged Tosquelles as a mentor; he considered himself "a disciple" (Cherki, 2006, p. 20) in a totally committed and crucial relationship. The feeling was mutual. Years later, Tosquelles remarked that "Fanon had never really left us; he continued to be present in our memory in the same way he had filled the space around him. He questioned his interlocutors in body and voice" (quoted in Cherki, p. 20).

François Tosquelles[8] was one of the founders of Institutional Psychotherapy and Sociotherapy, a critical, humanistic psychotherapy based on a fundamental belief that the patient's self-liberation could be accomplished in a socialized setting. Its mission was the reintegration of the patient into the social community; as such the social needs of the patient took priority and the reification created by the psychiatric institution was criticized. For Tosquelles, the hospital itself was a sick organism set up to pacify patients and create docile receivers of care. Medical therapies were simply the products of this will to control and supervise. Thus the psychiatric hospital had to be radically restructured. Sociotherapy necessitated a different attitude toward mental illness and was opposed to the practice of ostracizing the mentally ill, and separating them from society. Tosquelles further believed that psychosis could not be magically accessed inside the four walls of a doctor's office, cut off from the social world; instead, just as the individual should not be pathologized, the institution itself needed to be de-pathologized and disalienated. Treating the patient, restructuring the hospital, and humanizing and socializing the mental institution were part of the same process that would create a new society inside the hospital. It would be accomplished by reforming social and spatial relations, treating patients as human and social beings, and thereby encouraging a sense of self instead of isolating them as controllable objects.[9]

When Fanon began his psychiatric residency at the Saint Alban Hospital, under the supervision of Tosquelles in 1951, Institutional Psychotherapy was still in its infancy, but it marked "the first time" that Fanon was "involved in a clinical situation that allowed patients to contribute to their own recovery" (Macey, 2000, p. 149). Fanon and Tosquelles presented some of their ongoing collaborative work in three short conference papers,[10] but perhaps more importantly, they *practiced* a belief that politics and medicine were not separate fields. Implicitly and often explicitly, sociotherapy was associated with a concern for social, indeed revolutionary, change.

Director of Psychological Services at Blida-Joinville Hospital, Algeria

Fanon took up his position as a director of psychological services at Blida-Joinville Hospital in Algeria in 1953, more than a year before the beginning of the Algerian revolution. Blida is located about 30 miles south-west of Algiers, at the base of the Atlas Mountains. The hospital, which was still a fairly new facility (opened in the 1920s), had become, by the 1950s, the largest psychiatric hospital in North Africa, with over 2,000 patients. The newly created position that Fanon stepped into was in part a response to the hospital's increasing size. With the other four section chiefs – Dequeker, Lacaton, Micucci, and Ramée – Fanon co-authored an article on the state of psychiatric care in Algeria. Written just a few months after arriving, "Current Aspects of Psychiatric Care in Algeria" (1955) is indicative of Fanon's organizing activity. Though the four section heads were far more conservative than Fanon, the article details a situation about which they all could agree, namely underfunding, understaffing, and massive overcrowding which was having an increasingly detrimental effect on care at the hospital. In addition, Fanon had already garnered support from his colleagues for his sociotherapy reforms. The patient's living conditions had improved, the article states, with new collaborations that had helped develop a patient newspaper, the Moorish café, film screenings, and trips to the seaside.

Under his care were 165 European women and 22 Muslim men. Though the Algiers School of Psychiatry was the dominant system of thought at Blida-Joinville Hospital, the directors were given quite a bit of autonomy, and Fanon immediately undertook reform. His goal was to humanize the institution and its therapeutic approaches by introducing a sociotherapy project along Tosquellean principles. If he didn't literally unchain the patients like a modern-day Pinel,[11] he did try to humanize relations and attitudes toward the patients, as well as develop cultural and social programs, even though, as he points out in his 1954 article, "Sociotherapy on a Muslim Men's Ward," large numbers of Muslim patients continued to be restrained.

The year after Fanon took the position at Blida-Joinville, the FLN signaled the beginning of the national liberation struggle. It began on November 1, 1954, with coordinated attacks on targets across the country. Initially dismissing the FLN as a bunch of criminals, in the language of the Algiers school, the French continued to refuse the FLN as a recognized political organization, and the authorities continued to deny that there was any kind of political struggle. The Algiers school provided the easy terminology of fanaticism and deviance to describe those responsible for the "savage" and "blood-thirsty barbaric acts" perpetrated on Europeans.[12] In this context, Fanon quickly learned that it was one thing to criticize racist medical practices in France, but quite another to take on the dominant paradigms in colonial Algeria, where medicine was directly related to colonial power (as he put it in later, "colonialism in its essence [is] … a fertile purveyor for psychiatric hospitals" [1968, p. 247]), and where any space for criticism was quickly shut down for "security" reasons.

But Fanon's political commitments were also changing. And it was in this changed political environment of Algeria in 1955 that he criticized Porot's Algiers school theory, linking it with John Carothers' idea of the African as a "lobotomized European," and in "Thoughts on Ethnopsychiatry," which appeared as an unsigned article in *Consciences Maghribines* (1955), Fanon notes that Carothers' report, "The African Mind," had just been officially sanctioned by the World Health Organization.[13]

The Algiers school deployed "an intellectual violence," argues the historian, Richard Keller, "a savagery concomitant with the brutality required to police Algeria's Manichean world" (Keller, 2007a, p. 159). After three years in Algeria, Fanon would agree, writing in his resignation letter that "the Arab – permanently alienated within his own country – lives in a state of absolute depersonalization" (1967, p. 53). And yet, it should not be forgotten that Fanon joined Blida-Joinville Psychiatric hospital to put into practice the challenge he set out in "The North African Syndrome," to get things done and be part of the "human work" of humanization so as to "call forth the human that is before you" (Fanon, 1967, p. 13).

Fanon became a political revolutionary at Blida-Joinville Hospital, even though he joined the institution with other work in mind. He immediately undertook a program of sociotherapy, the first to be conducted in North Africa. It was written up by Fanon and his intern Jacques Azoulay[14] and published in 1954 as "Sociotherapy on a Muslim Men's Ward." Fanon took the work of sociotherapy earnestly and sincerely and, as he admitted later, naïvely. For while sociotherapy assumed universality, specific contexts and experiences were the real testing grounds for the efficacy of treatment. At Blida-Joinville, the sociotherapy experiment was considered successful in the European women's ward (the hospital wards were strictly segregated), but it failed in the Muslim men's ward. Among the reasons for failure, Fanon and Azoulay argued, was their inability to speak Arabic. They had to rely on interpreters who, in the mind of the Arab patient, were associated with the police and the courts. The presence of the interpreter, Fanon and Azoulay conclude, "fundamentally vitiated the psychotherapeutic doctor-patient relationship" (1975, p. 11; see 2018, p. 367).

Additionally, alongside what might be considered normal problems of interpretation, such as a lack of detail, content, and nuance, Fanon noted a key point, namely that a specific aspect of technique in a psychodynamic situation is that the psychiatrist arrives at a diagnosis through language. "How could a structural analysis be possible if we bracketed off the geographic, historical, cultural, and social contexts?" (p. 1102; see Fanon, 2018, p. 362) "Aside from the need for an interpreter," they continue, "our attitude was absolutely not adapted to the Muslim men's ward. In fact, a revolutionary attitude was essential – for we needed to move from a position where the supremacy of western culture was self-evident to one of cultural relativism" (p. 1102; see Fanon, 2018, pp. 362–363). Underlining the importance of language to the psychodynamic process, Fanon quoted Merleau-Ponty – as he had done in *Black Skin* – that "to speak a language is to carry the weight of a culture" (2008, p. 16). Refusing to accept the Algiers school explanations for failure put forward by the staff, Fanon maintained that the problem wasn't with the Muslim men, but with the presuppositions of the experiment itself. As Fanon's co-author Jacques Azoulay put it:

> we proposed to implement a Western-based sociotherapy program that disregarded an entire frame of reference and neglected geographic, historical, cultural, and social particularities in a pavilion of mentally ill Muslim men. Are we not guilty of having thoughtlessly embraced a policy of assimilation?
>
> *(quoted by Cherki, 2006, p. 69)*

North Africa is French – and if you are not looking for it, you will not see why approaches should differ from one ward to the next. The psychiatrist unthinkingly adopts the politics of assimilation. Algerians do not need to be understood in their cultural originality. They are the ones who must make the effort to adapt and it is in their interest to resemble the kind of person being proposed.

(p. 1102; see Fanon, 2018, p. 362)

A "politics of assimilation," Fanon and Azoulay continued, "which does not propose a reciprocity of perspectives," but rather an insistence that one "culture must disappear for the benefit of the other ... This kind of assimilation does not suppose a reciprocity of perspectives: instead, one culture must disappear for the benefit of the other" (p. 1102; see Fanon, 2018, p. 362).

Thus, on reflection, Fanon and Azoulay "orchestrate[d] a major leap and undertook a transmutation of values ... to move from the natural to the cultural" (p. 1102; see Fanon, 2018, p. 363). Written before the outbreak of the Algerian liberation war, their initial Marxian spatial study, which Fanon would develop in *The Wretched of the Earth*, already recognized that the French occupation had brought about "The decline of the old nomadism ... as inescapable as the rise of its replacement: proletarianization." This seasonal migrant labor, meeting the demands of industries in France and the settler colonial farms of Algeria, was "leading to the dissolution of both sedentary and nomadic groups which also explain the formation of shantytowns [bidonvilles or Hay Kazdiri] on the outskirts of large cities" (p. 1105; see Fanon, 2018, p. 366). Before the outbreak of the revolution a few months later, Fanon and Azoulay were seeing that "Muslim society ... so often seen as fixed in its ways ... is fermenting at its base from the bottom up" (p. 1105; see Fanon, 2018, p. 367). Fanon shifted his perspective away from the colonial hospital and began to learn Arabic and spend time with his team visiting local Kabylian villages and undertaking basic research. In 1956, he co-authored a short, introductory paper with François Sanchez entitled "Maghrebi Muslim Attitudes to Madness" (1956). This, along with the draft paper "Introduction to Sexuality Disorders Among North Africans" written with Azoulay and Sanchez in 1955 (Azoulay, Sanchez, and Fanon, 1955), were not simply critiques of Porot's ethnopsychiatric generalizations about the North African, but part of a critical endeavor to begin from an entirely different standpoint, "from the inside" as Fanon and Sanchez would put it (1956, p. 24; see Fanon, 2018, p. 421). It is interesting to read both these papers alongside the studies collected in *A Dying Colonialism*. The paper "Introduction to Sexuality Disorders Among North Africans" is comprised of field notes written in 1955. Having come across many cases of sexual disorder in their psychotherapeutic practice, the authors embarked on an ethnographic study in Kabylia. The draft reports beliefs about sexual impotence – "all the more preoccupying as Muslim society is founded on male authority" (see Fanon, 2018, p. 385) – which are not dismissed as irrational or unscientific, but rather recorded. Rather than applying Western sociological methods, their report is based on an informant, a learned man with a "good reputation in the region," but "whose explanations left us rather confused" (see Fanon, 2018, p. 386). This "taleb," whose knowledge of the causes of sexual impotence was based on a medieval text on medicine and wisdom, is reproduced without further comment. Rather than a critique of Porot's ethnopsychiatry generalizations about the North African, the notes indicate Fanon's desire to begin a critical endeavor from inside the culture that their patients lived. As Fanon argued in "Maghrebi Muslim Attitudes to Madness," the Maghrebian view of therapy "possesses a value (on the human level) which cannot be limited solely to its 'effectiveness'" and should be studied for its own sake. Fanon was interested in North African conceptions of mental illness that were quite different from those held in capitalist Europe. For Fanon there is a logical inconsistency in the Western view that madness alienates (and separates the mad from society) and that the mentally ill are somehow responsible for their illness. In contrast, the Maghrebian views the mentally ill as "absolutely alienated" (see Fanon, 2018, p. 422), and thus not responsible for their actions. Because the mentally ill remain human, there is a respect and dignity in the Maghrebian attitude to mental suffering that is lost in the Western alienated view of madness. Rather than the embarrassment and distrust found in the West, the formerly ill can thus "resume their role in society without fear of arousing suspicion or ambivalence from the group" (see Fanon, 2018, p. 423).

Fanon continued the self-critique he began in "Sociotherapy on a Muslim Men's Ward" with a paper written in 1956 on "The Thematic Apperception Test (TAT) in Muslim Women" co-authored with his intern, Charles Géronomi (Fanon and Géronimi, 2021). The TAT, developed by American psychologist Henry Murray and lay psychoanalyst Christiana Morgan at Harvard University, is essentially a projective psychological test, where scoring and conclusions are based on the viewer's interpretation of ambiguous pictures on cards. Because the images on the cards were culture bound, the tests became an ordeal for North African Muslims; their "responses were disconnected and empty" and without narrative or drama the responses, Fanon and Géronimi conclude, "were without any psychoanalytic value" (Fanon and Géronimi, 1956, p. 366; see Fanon, 2018, p. 430). In other words, there was a complete disconnect between the card's "stimuli" and the patient's cultural context. While the idea of the test might be useful, it quickly became clear that the patients were "stumbling over a world [of images] that excluded them" (p. 368; see Fanon, 2018, p. 432) and that a "rich and varied narrative" could only be "animated by cultural dynamics consistent with the psycho-affective structures examined" (p. 368; Fanon, 2018, p. 432). Thus a critical and culturally sensitive psychiatry was sharply opposed to the Algiers school's so-called universalism and claims of primitivism that linked Muslims' inability to imagine to a genetic constitution. After all, given a blank card, the women were able to "unleash their imaginations" (p. 368; Fanon, 2018, p. 432). Fanon and Géronimi conclude that they are developing a test "intended for Maghrebi Muslims, based on the cultural research we conducted" where "imaginary life is not isolated from real life" which "nourishes, legitimates and groups the imaginary" (p. 367; Fanon, 2018, p. 432).[15]

Though the TAT was a "systematic failure," it illuminated the importance of historical, geographic, and cultural specificity to apperception. The patient's refusal and elemental resistance to cultural assimilation was far from hysterical and could not be read in Freudian terms. Rather, it indicated the importance of culturally lived experience to psychodynamic situations, and Fanon and his interns shifted their research orientation not simply toward a cultural relativism but toward what "the culture offered us" (Fanon and Azoulay, 1975, p. 1095). Reporting on the failure of some of the reforms at Blida Hospital, Fanon told Charles Geronomi that sociotherapy was not about applying a method, but owning a process that is implicitly political: "It is not simply a matter of imposing imported methods … I had to demonstrate a number of things in the process: namely that the values of Algerian culture are different from those of colonial culture; that these structuring values had to be embraced without any complexes by those to whom they pertained—the Algerian medical staff as well as Algerian patients." (quoted in Cherki, 2006, pp. 71–72). The project and results were all part of sociotherapy. "I needed to have the support of the Algerian medical staff in order to incite them to rebel against the prevailing method, to make them realize that their competence was equal to the European … Psychiatry has to be political" (quoted in Cherki, 2006, p. 72). Indeed, it was becoming clear that psychiatry was always political.

The psychiatric hospital creates institutionalized patients, which further alienates them from the community. Fanon sought to address this alienation by developing sociotherapy and a day hospitalization program. The idea of the day hospital was first developed while at Blida-Joinville Hospital and connected with his critique of sociotherapy confined to the hospital. It encouraged breaking down alienation and building up the social self, constituted by integrating the patient back into the community, and by bolstering the patient's sense of self through therapies in the "open" day hospital. It was at Charles Nicolle Hospital in Tunis that Fanon was able to put such a program into operation.

"The Conduct of Confessions in North Africa" (1955), another article written while at Blida-Joinville, was co-written with a fellow director, Lacaton, concerned with the idea of confession and notions of reciprocity and social reintegration. The article follows a similar critique of medical practices developed in the articles on the Thematic Apperception Test and on sociotherapy. Like other psychiatrists in Algeria's colonial hospitals, Fanon not only attended to patients at the hospital, but also was called on by the colonial justice system to evaluate the sanity of the accused. As well as the question of "confession," questions about language and culture in terms of non-recognition are also raised in the article. By definition, confessions require "reciprocal recognition" because for the court, the confession signals taking ownership of one's wrongdoing and guilt. This notion of guilt – and paying one's debt – is connected to the notion of reintegration into society. But when Algerians are interviewed by psychiatrists for the court, eighty percent of the confessions of guilt that had earlier been made were retracted. Something clearly was awry. If one dismisses the then hegemonic Algiers school notion of the North African as a pathological liar and criminal, not only does the idea of the role of the confession itself have to be investigated, but by extension so does the validity of the court itself. In other words, if the confession as well as the redaction of the confession is true, can the retraction of the confession be connected to an implicit refusal to recognize and to refuse reintegration? Logically, the truth of retraction can be understood as a rational response to the colonial society whose judicial system is utterly alien. Fanon and Lacaton suggest this is possible because the confession represents a truth that was built on pseudo-reciprocity. The pseudo-truth of the initial confession is a result of submission to colonial rule "not to be confused with acceptance," they say. Redaction in fact represents a real truth expressing the "total separation" (Fanon and Lacaton, 1955, p. 659; Fanon, 2018, p. 412) between the two social groups – the European and the North African. Thus, given "the refusal of the accused Muslim to authenticate the social contract" (p. 659; see Fanon, 2018, p. 412), the confession is an elemental resistance to European colonial rule.[16] Similarly, the idea of elemental resistance is found in the lecture notes taken by a student from Fanon's course on Social Psychopathology at the Institut des Hautes Études in Tunis, "The Meeting between Society and Psychiatry" (1959–60; see Ben Salem, 1984), where Fanon asks, "Is the colonized a lazy being?"[17] He responds,

> The idleness of the colonized is a means of protection, a measure of self-defense above all physiological. Work was conceived as forced labor in the colonies and, even if there is no whip, the colonial situation itself is a whip. It is normal that the colonized refuses to do anything since work leads nowhere for them.
>
> *(see Fanon, 2018, p. 530)*

The situation is Manichean. Already employed by the state to evaluate confession, psychiatrists actively participated with the colonial forces "in the most frightful most degrading practices" to force confession (Turner, 2011, p. 137).[18] This practice, what Fanon calls neo-hippocratism (the abandonment of a commitment to the care and the objectification of the patient) in "The North African Syndrome," expresses the utter lack of reciprocity, which results in the depersonalization of the patient. It is part of the logic of neo-hippocratism, what Lou Turner (2011, p. 137) calls "the degeneration of the ethics of the social and behavioral sciences and in particular the ethics of the psychological professions." Thus, Fanon argues for the need "to analyze, patiently and lucidly, each one of the reactions of the colonized," knowing that "every time we do not understand, we must tell ourselves that we are at the heart of the drama – that of the impossibility of finding a meeting ground in any colonial situation" (1965, p. 125). After all, while Fanon saw psychiatry in the colonies as part of the regime of violence, he did not view psychiatry as always already colonizing. Blida-Joinville Fanon was opening space for a different psychiatry, but in the context of the unfolding war in Algeria, it was becoming clear that mental and psychological decolonization, the recovery of the dignity of the human being crushed by colonial rule, had to be openly connected to the emerging political and social struggle.

Joining the FLN

Fanon made contact with the FLN in the spring of 1955, just a few months after the beginning of the Algerian revolution.[19] Pierre Chaulet, a few years younger than Fanon, was finishing his medical studies with a specialization in tuberculosis, and was part of the milieu of Europeans who supported the FLN by giving it practical assistance. It was through Chaulet that Fanon was asked to give psychiatric help to FLN fighters, and it was Chaulet who asked him to submit a critique of the Algiers school, which was published in the summer of 1955 in *Consciences Maghribines*.[20]

Fanon's critique came as Algiers school concepts were informing "counter-insurgency" army programs. The army's *Section Administrative Spécialisées* (Special Administrative Section), founded in 1955, fully employed Algiers school terminology about the Muslim's primitive mentality, and Algiers school graduates were working in its torture programs. By February 1955, just three months after the war had been declared, meetings organized by Chaulet were held between the FLN and Fanon, and soon Fanon was not only counseling FLN fighters, but also providing hiding places for local FLN leaders at Blida-Joinville Hospital.[21]

During the Battle of Algiers, the colonial regime issued orders to control the distribution of medicines and supplies to stifle the flow to FLN fighters. At Blida-Joinville, some staff surreptitiously distributed supplies, while others carried information or provided safe houses. Fanon was contacted to help counsel militants about how they might withstand the torture they were likely to face if caught. Later, Simone de Beauvoir recounted that Fanon "taught them to control their reactions when they were setting a bomb … and also what psychological and physical attitudes would enable them to resist torture best" (1992, p. 315). The FLN request was very practical and concrete, and he responded in kind.[22]

Fanon hewed out a critical space at the hospital, but the hospital was becoming increasingly caught up in the war. Indeed, both the torturer and tortured were being treated in the same space. As Fanon explains in one of his cases,[23] a policeman he had been treating privately had one day decided to walk around the grounds and became panic-stricken when he met one of Fanon's other patients whom he had questioned and tortured. Neither fared so well. Fanon administered sedatives to the policemen, who later, under Fanon's advisement, resigned and left the country, while the tortured patient was found in a toilet trying to commit suicide.

The police knew that some of the hospital staff was aiding the FLN. They had their informants. After the July 5, 1956 strike (called by the FLN to mark 126 years of French occupation), the situation at Blida-Joinville Hospital became untenable (see Fanon's resignation letter, Fanon, 1967, pp. 52–54). According to the police, the hospital had become known as a "den" of Fedahin. Clearly it was no longer safe; indeed, it had become a dangerous place to be.

One of Fanon's interns, Sanchez, who co-wrote "Maghrebi Muslim Attitudes to Madness," was arrested in January 1957, tortured, and then imprisoned. Another intern, Slimane Asselah, was arrested in March 1957 and disappeared. Pierre Chaulet was also arrested. When Lacaton, Fanon's closest colleague among the five directors at the hospital, who had already been arrested and tortured once, heard that he was going to be arrested again along with Fanon, he informed Fanon. A turning point had been reached. It became clear that their work inside the institution was impossible. The multiple projects that Fanon had begun, his work in sociotherapy and the beginnings of a critical ethnopsychiatry – Thematic Apperception Tests, the field work in Kabylia about attitudes to mental illness and sexuality – the staff reading groups and education programs all had to be left unfinished for now.

The program of institutional therapy expressed in part Fanon's belief in the mission of humanizing the hospital. When he confronted the failures of sociotherapy, he blamed their implementation, not the mission itself. Yet, it soon became clear that the idea of creating a neo-society in the hospital was itself based on a false premise. Rather than being rational and sane, the society itself was exactly like that in the colonial asylum, actively making its members mad and driving them to "desperate solutions." "If psychiatry is the medical technique that proposes to help man no longer be a stranger to his environment," Fanon wrote in the letter of resignation to the Resident Minister, "I can only but confirm that the Arab – permanently alienated within his own country – lives in a state of absolute depersonalization. What is the status of Algeria? A systematized dehumanization" (1967, p. 53). This was his final prognosis.

Leaving Algeria

Leaving Algeria for Paris at the end of December 1956 marked a real shift: It signaled the absolute end of any connection with the "French drama" and affirmed Fanon's self-identification as an Algerian and African revolutionary. Fanon would appeal to European leftists to aid the Algerian movement, but he would not expect anything from Europe. He would no longer publish in French medical journals. As summed up in the conclusion of *The Wretched of the Earth*, Europe had become a static, "motionless movement" that murders human beings in the name of humanity (1968, pp. 314–315).[24] A new humanism would come instead from those oppressed and objectified, those who Europe had considered backward and not fully human. Though Fanon would continue his work as a psychiatrist, it ceased to be his primary occupation. In Paris, Fanon stayed with Jean Ayme, one of Tosquelles' close colleagues, and an active Trotskyist with "a long history of anticolonial activism" (Cherki, 2006, p. 86). While at Ayme's apartment, Fanon made use of his library of revolutionary theorists, and one night, Ayme introduced Fanon to his comrade, Pierre Broué. The same age as Fanon, Broué had become a revolutionary socialist in 1944 and co-authored a definitive work on the Spanish revolution and its "betrayal" from the inside, a dialectic that Fanon would engage in *The Wretched*. All three talked through the night. The next day Fanon presented "Racism and Culture", which would go on to become the second chapter in *Toward the African Revolution* (1967), at the First Congress of Black Writers, and while the paper said little directly about Algeria, it was based in the Algerian struggle and absolutely radical in tone with its call for "total liberation" (1967, p. 43). By then Ayme had no doubt that Fanon would join a revolutionary movement; in truth, Fanon already had. Fanon was a revolutionary, who, as Ayme put it, had "been given the opportunity to take part in a revolution" (quoted in Cherki, 2006, p. 94). Meanwhile, through underground connections provided by Pierre Chaulet, Fanon had met the FLN leader in Algiers, Ramdane Abane. Abane would play an essential role in developing a platform for the revolution at the Soummam conference, which took place for twenty days right under French noses near Akbou in the Soummam Valley in August 1956. The platform created a national political body (the national council of the Algerian Revolution) and advocated for the primacy of politics over the military, and the internal over the external wings of the movement. It also, notably, gestured to secular and socialist strategies as well as to organizing agricultural workers, the landless, and urban poor, the "veritable pariahs" (Abane, 2011, p. 38) created by the colonial regime. Fanon and Abane met in December 1956, and it would not be an exaggeration to claim that the radical Abane (who would be later liquidated by an FLN faction), as well as the radical Soummam Platform, would continue to have a profound influence on Fanon's politics.[25]

Tunis and Full Time FLN

Fanon left Paris for Tunis in 1957 and began functioning full time for the FLN, working directly on its paper, *El Moudjahid*. At the same time, he also continued his work as a psychiatrist, first at The Razi Hospital in Manouba and later at Charles Nicolle Hospital. Treating both Tunisian patients and also a large number of Algerian refugees, many of whom were suffering from serious traumas inflicted by the colonial war, he attempted to introduce sociotherapy programs informed by his experiences and criticisms at Blida-Joinville. At first the programs were less than successful; Manouba had significant numbers of long-term patients, but the major program was resistance by the conservative nationalist director in charge of the hospital. An antisemite and racist, the director questioned Fanon's professional competence and claimed that because he didn't speak much Arabic "he couldn't understand Arabs" (see Cherki, 2006; Macey, 2000). He understood Fanon as a threat to his authority and tried to undermine him by fabricating a story that Fanon and his staff were involved in a Zionist plot (see Cherki, p. 114). This failed, but Fanon did not stay long at Manouba. He developed a new medical team at the neuropsychiatric ward of Charles Nicolle Hospital with Lucien Lévy, a communist who moved from Manouba with him, and Charles Géronimi, Fanon's former intern, who had left Blida-Joinville around the same time as Fanon and reached Tunis in 1958.

A Dying Colonialism, published two years after his move to Tunis in 1959, was addressed to liberals and leftists in France, and took aim at the sociologists and orientalists, as it reflected on the radical social and cultural changes occurring during the liberation struggle. The essays, especially "Algeria Unveiled"[26] and "This Is the Voice of Algeria," are original in the way that they explore the complexities of psychic life in colonial society. In "This Is the Voice of Algeria," Fanon not only speaks of the mutation that took place in people's attitudes toward the radio, but also saw a radical change in how the French language was perceived. For Fanon, the FLN's radio program, "This Is the Voice of Algeria," was not only an organizing and educational tool but also a new form of communication and participation. The linguistic hierarchy between French and Arabic, which could not previously be crossed, began to crumble, and French "acquire[d] new values," as the language of order began to lose its "accursed character." A real shift occurred in "psychopathology" as "sentences in French lost their automatic character of insult" (Fanon, 1965, pp. 89–90). For Fanon, this was a genuine development; it could be measured by the less aggressive use of French words by those who had hallucinated French voices.[27] A new divide had begun to develop between the French used by the movement and by Algerians, and the French used by the French in their continued effort to resist Arabization (see Lazali, 2011).

Fanon revisited his experiences at Blida-Joinville in the chapter "Medicine and Colonialism." There he argues that with medicine, "we come to one of the most tragic features of the colonial situation" (1965, p. 121). Again we see him confronting "The North African Syndrome" among the medical staff who consider that the problem central to psychiatric care is the patient. But here we also begin to understand another element of Fanon's originality. In his exploration of psychic life in a colonial society, we see that "For the colonized the visit [to the doctor] is always an ordeal ... The medicines, the advice, are but the sequels of the ordeal ... The technician's words are always understood in a pejorative way" (1965, p. 128). The colonized's Manicheanism is a product of real experiences, not an a priori abstraction. To say that the doctor was part of the same colonial system as the policeman is, in other words, not an illusion. Colonialism is systemic. Indeed, the truth of this statement includes not only the medical staff involved in tortures, but all those who were silent about torture and its administration as hospitals became "important as tools of pacification" (Keller, 2007a, p. 157). Its essence appeared as the medical technicians become torturers and the medicine became "weaponized" (Keller, 2007a, p. 151). Psychiatrists willingly administer shock treatments, the "truth serum," and all medical personnel become spokespeople for the colonial power (1965, p. 131). Every medical question is thus, according to Fanon, experienced as a "repetition of the torturer-tortured relationship" (1965, p. 137).

Yet, alongside the dehumanizing effects of torture and colonial violence, Fanon perceives the birth of a new collectivity and a "radical mutation" in social consciousness. In a seemingly spontaneous surge that is very much part of a historical moment, what had been seen as the colonized's indolence and laziness had become the subjective basis upon which the idea of freedom and the end of colonial mutilation could be thought about. In 1960, when he was appointed official representative of the Provisional Government of Algerian Republic (GPRA) in Ghana, he gave up his psychiatric position, vowing to take up practice again after the revolution.

Perhaps the most significant psychiatry writing from the Tunis period is his concluding chapter of *The Wretched of the Earth*, which also includes case notes from the Blida-Joinville hospital. Fanon warns his readers that the effect of the violence of pacification as a central theme for the study of psychiatric disorders among the "pacified" population (1968, p. 249) might seem "out of place in such a book" and "untimely." That time now has certainly come and with it we must be cognizant of Fanon's concept of time and healing. Fanon is hopeful that "time alone can bring some improvement" (Fanon, 1968, p. 263) to the psyche disrupted by colonial violence (social, psychic, and biological) while wary that some wounds may never heal. Reflecting on his work at Blida-Joinville Hospital he notes, "we have since 1954 in various scientific works drawn the attention of both French and international psychiatrists to the difficulties that arise when seeking to cure a colonized person" that is to say to fit into the "social environment of colonialism" (1968, p. 249; 2004, pp. 181–182). But the chapter "Colonial War and Mental Disorders" also appears as a different order because of its singular focus on the traumatic effects of colonial violence. Colonial wars, Fanon argues, constitute a "veritable apocalypse ... [and] a new phenomenon even in the pathology it produces" (2004, pp. 183–184).

Fanon's conscious decision to conclude *The Wretched of the Earth*, a work that begins with the chapter "On Violence," with this chapter on "Colonial War and Mental Disorders" is important. The apparent shift in perspective has also be put in the context of the anticolonial war.[28] The truth of colonialism is absolute violence that leads to a daily brutalization practiced so routinely that it becomes normal. The human legacy of France in Algeria, he argues, is "an entire generation of Algerians, steeped in wanton, generalized[,] gratuitous homicide with all the psycho-affective [psychosomatic] consequences that this entails" (1968, p. 205). As Homi Bhabha puts it in his Foreword to the 2004 translation of *The Wretched of the Earth*, "Fanonian violence," that is counter-violence, "is part of a struggle for psycho-affective survival and a search for human agency in the midst of the agony of oppression" (2004, p. xxxvi). One can hear in Fanon's earlier analysis of the psychiatric hospital the initial stages of his analysis of the colonial world as Manichean. Indeed, this is implicit in the quite technical and nonpolitical essay "The Phenomenon of Agitation" written with Slimane Asselah while at Blida-Joinville Hospital (Fanon and Asselah, 1957). Fanon and Asselah criticize Tosquelles' mechanistic typological distinction between agitation of the "excessive type" and agitation of the "percepto-reactive type." Rather than this dualistic typology, they insist that all forms of agitation are products of reciprocal relations triggered and sustained and aggravated by the sado-masochistic institution. What Fanon and Asselah call the lines of force, that mark out the geographical layout essential to colonial control in *The Wretched of the Earth* (see 1968, p. 38), is here seen in the medical institution through the exclusion and isolation of the patient. The staff's fear of out-of-control patients keeps reproducing the hospital's sadistic, repressive, and rigid regime. Sadism and imprisonment thus mark the lines of force in both the colonial and the hospital regimes, and the violence perpetrated in the asylum is intimately connected with colonial violence.

The brutal reality of colonialism and the tragic effects on the psyche are also made clear in the introduction to *A Dying Colonialism* where Fanon quotes a Swedish newspaperwoman's report about the brutalization of a seven-year-old boy. Marked by deep wounds made by the steel wire that bound him and whose eyes were forced open while French soldiers raped and killed his sisters and parents, Fanon asks, "Does anyone think that this child will forget both the murder of his family and his enormous vengeance?" (1965, p. 26) This is France's legacy, he argues, a theme that Fanon would repeat in "Colonial War and Mental Disorders": "Is this orphaned child growing up in an apocalyptic atmosphere the sole message that French democracy will leave?" (1965, p. 26) While Fanon was working with traumatized and brutalized children in Algeria and in Tunisia, he was painfully aware that the psychological trauma was a product of the colonial war and that the brutality of the war had already found its ideological justification in the Algiers School of Psychiatry.

Fanon's attitude remained constant, though the consequences of colonial psychiatry became more brutal. At the beginning of the decade, he had criticized Octave Mannoni's theory of colonial dependency in *Black Skin, White Masks*. What Mannoni had forgotten, Fanon argues, "is that the Malagasy no longer exists" (2008, p. 77). Traumatized by the shock of colonization, the Malagasy underwent "destructuralization": "The arrival of the white man in Madagascar inflicted an unmistakable wound. The consequences … are not only psychological, since, as everyone said, there are inner relationships between consciousness and social context" (2008, p. 77). Inverting Mannoni's causality, he argues that it is colonialism that causes a dependency complex rather than the other way round. Similarly, against Jean Sutter (Porot's mentee, formerly at Blida-Joinville and who became the chair of the clinic of neuropsychiatry in Algiers in 1958) and Antoine Porot, he continually makes the point that it is colonialism that produces "the degenerate Arab." In other words, Fanon does not attempt to counter the claims about the Algerian's violent impulsivity. Instead, he argues that criminality and violence are consequences of systematic exploitation and dehumanization. What becomes clear in Fanon's mind is that the revolutionary's work consists in channeling that violence and aggressivity away from self-destruction and immediate reactions toward its real source. Here the objective of the psychiatrist and the revolutionary converge.

In the introduction to *A Dying Colonialism*, Fanon characterizes the Algerian war as the most violent and "the most hallucinatory war that any people has ever waged to smash colonial aggression" (1965, p. 23). Again there is an analogy to Fanon's analysis of agitation where he views the "flight of ideas prepar[ing] the way for hallucination" which in turn, he says, "coincides with the annihilation of reality" (1965, p. 23). Just as confinement and isolation create the conditions for hallucinatory activity in the institution, the conditions for hallucinatory activity become more pronounced in a society that is becoming more and more totalitarian.

From "The North African Syndrome" onward, Fanon declares that colonialism creates a kind of living death for the colonized, and revolt becomes a biological necessity. In the conclusion to *Black Skin, White Masks*, he argues that the Vietnamese revolt "because it became impossible for them to breathe, in more than one sense of the word" (2008, p. 201). In *The Wretched of the Earth*, he describes the development of shantytowns as the colonized "biological decision to invade, at whatever cost and if necessary by the most cryptic methods, the enemy fortress." The shantytown inhabitants "endanger the 'security' of the town," and represent "irrevocable decay, the gangrene ever present at the heart of colonial domination" (1968, p. 129). And in "Algeria Unveiled," the first chapter of *A Dying Colonialism* (1965), he describes the colonized's very existence as a "combat breathing" within a totalitarian society where "the country as a whole, its history, its daily pulsation … are contested [and] disfigured … Under these conditions, the individual's breathing is an observed, an occupied breathing. It is a combat breathing" (1965, p. 50).

Life can only emerge from the death of colonialism. But Fanon does not think it is that simple. The inversion of colonial Manicheanism must undergo a dialectical change, or it is doomed to repetition. This is the dialectic of liberation espoused in *The Wretched of the Earth*, which is grounded by real movement. For example, if in the "Thematic Apperception Test" "imaginary consciousness is certainly unreal, but it is saturated by the real" (see Fanon, 2018, p. 431), in *The Wretched of the Earth* it is the liberation struggle that marks the end of "centuries of unreality." And yet perhaps it is only a shift in emphasis, for as Fanon continues, "the imagination and the imaginary are only possible to the extent that the real belong to us" (see Fanon, 2018, p. 431).[29] For Fanon, figuring out the radical humanist politics of "who am I" is what the anticolonial struggle has to address since colonialism "is systematic negation of the other person and a furious determination to deny the other person all attributes of humanity … [it] forces the people it dominates to ask themselves the question constantly" (Fanon, 1968, p. 249).

FANON THE THERAPIST

Fanon was eclectic in his use of therapeutic techniques. Certainly, he used therapies popular at the time (such as insulin therapy), which are now seen as crude if not dangerous. He was critical of electroconvulsive therapy and rejected lobotomies, which were used extensively on Algerian patients. But what is perhaps remarkable and undervalued, even dismissed, is Fanon's interest in psychoanalysis. Indeed, this almost seems counter-intuitive since Fanon connects mental illness primarily to the colonial war and thus mental health to the ending of that war. Additionally, the dreams of muscular activity – running, jumping, and so on – that he mentions in *The Wretched* result from the duress of colonialism's physical oppression (to "stay in place" [1968, p. 51]) are far from Freudian. And the elemental forms of resistance, including the sociotherapy work at Blida-Joinville Hospital and the Day Hospitalization program at Charles Nicolle Hospital in Tunis, are considered in a social and cultural frame rather than in an internal, psychic one. Fanon never retracted the critique of the Oedipus complex he made in *Black Skin, White Masks*, but by the end of the decade he was reconsidering psychoanalytic treatments and the importance of transference and counter-transference in the therapeutic sessions (see for example "Day Hospitalization in Psychiatry" – Fanon, 1959, and Fanon and Géronimi, 1959). At Blida-Joinville and in Tunis, Fanon continued to engage psychoanalytic concepts and practices and began to read Sandor Ferenczi and Melanie Klein among others as part of what Alice Cherki calls Fanon's return to Freud (2006, p. 121). Referring to a twenty-seven-year-old patient, who was in therapy with Fanon five times a week, Cherki writes that transference made Fanon "extremely uncomfortable," even though Fanon made "incredible progress" in the work. Perhaps as an existentialist, Fanon was reluctant to engage the classical notion of transference as the analysand's unconscious wishes and fantasy often expressed in dreams. In his last published article, "Day Hospitalization in Psychiatry: Its Value and Limitations" (Fanon, 1959), which includes individual psychotherapy sessions among its treatments,[30] Fanon seems to accept that the reconstruction of fantasy is essential to mutual analysis:[31] "Our psychoanalytic practice is one of appeasement in which we encourage the reconstruction of fantasies and generally adopt an active attitude in the Ferenczian sense" (see Fanon, 2018, p. 507). Clearly he had moved away from simply being made uncomfortable by manifestations of transference to wanting to take an active or interactive attitude. While we may debate Fanon's attitude to transference (which he seems at times to conflate with the money transaction between therapist and patient), one can speculate that Fanon found Ferenczi's work – the critique of medical hierarchy in the doctor/patient relationship and discussions of psychoanalytical technique – fruitful.

The Algerian-born psychoanalyst, Thierry Bokanowski (1996, p. 127), describes Ferenczi as we might Fanon, a man of independent temperament, "bold, creative, undogmatic, and determined to maintain his freedom and thought and action. After a decade of analytic practice, he came to the conclusion that clinical observation and experience (*Erlebnis*) were inseparable." In other words, just as Fanon had been a mentee of Tosquelles' inspired institutional therapy, which advocated opening up new therapeutic space by breaking down the barriers and ranks between patient and staff (including between doctors and nurses) in the institution, Fanon, one can safely assume, was drawn to Ferenczi's therapy, with its emphasis on empathy, kindness, and tenderness in an active, creative and flexible, cooperative, and respective practice.[32] Ferenczi insisted that a friendly and sympathetic objectivity was necessary in part as a response to the traumatic experience created by what he called elsewhere "the confusion of tongues."[33] Like Ferenczi, Fanon had a sensitivity to language and the use of language in therapy. "He also had a great insight," Cherki writes, "of using language to invoke the great tyrannical figures so that," – and here one can imagine the influence of Ferenczi – "through intervention of a third voice, these figures could be made to retreat or take on another aspect" (Cherki, 2006, p. 121).

As a clinical practitioner, perhaps Fanon appreciated Ferenczi's conclusion that the task was not to apply a clinical technique but to discover the necessary technique by "offering the analysands unconditional understanding and a right to find their own path to cure" (Bergmann, 1996, p. 154). Indeed, "in his final reflection," Ferenczi begins to reject "the concept of transference altogether," or perhaps to contextualize transference in a different way. He "reduces the analytic relationship to an everyday relationship, in which only therapeutic alliance remains intact" (Giampieri-Deutsch, 1996, p. 232). This notion of the everyday, of *Erlebnis* and overcoming the distinction between the analytical, the medicalized, and everyday relationships, can also be considered a goal of Fanon's praxis.

While in Tunis, Fanon was involved in the preparation of a film, *J'ai Hui Ans*,[34] which Nicholas Mirzoeff (2011) describes as "the product of a new therapeutic strategy of visualization that Fanon was experimenting with in his clinical work with Algerian refugees." The drawings by children from refugee camps along the Tunisian border, as well as interviews describing the military's repression and the children's traumas, were included as a therapeutic effort to present a child's voice. It also indicated the importance Fanon placed on child therapy and the idea that sociotherapy must continue after liberation in a new way. After all, insofar as the struggle for liberation is successful, it opens up new spaces for treatment, new sensibilities to trauma, and new avenues for mental health therapies to continue. While the old psychiatric hospitals "extended a protective mantle over the patient [which] … merely provoked lethargy – a state of waking sleep in which the patient would lead a vegetative life" (Fanon, 1959, p. 690; see Gibson and Beneduce, 2017, p. 205), in Fanon's view the attempt by sociotherapy to create "pseudo society" or the institutionalizing of any therapy within the hospital allows "no space for invention, or innovative dynamics … The institution remains the 'cadaveric cement' Mauss spoke of" (Fanon and Géronimi, 1959, p. 718; see Gibson and Beneduce, 2017, p. 208).

The development of the Psychiatric Day Hospital in Tunis, the first day hospital in North Africa, was one avenue, and in the case notes in "Colonial War and Mental Disorders" one can see that Fanon envisioned himself taking part in these developments after Algeria won independence. Breaking out of the traumatic cycle of violence is indeed one of the problematics that takes us back to the heart of the drama.[35]

FINALLY …

"Why did you do it?" Fanon, the psychiatrist, asks two adolescents who murdered a European playmate. "I'll tell you why," replies the fourteen-year-old, whose answer is less a confession than a statement of fact. "Have you heard of the Rivet business? … Two of my family were killed then … the French had sworn to kill us all … nobody was arrested" (1968, p. 272). Fanon had heard of the Rivet business, adding a note in the chapter on "Colonial War and Mental Disorders" that Rivet is a village near Algiers which was invaded in 1956 and where 40 men were dragged from their beds and murdered. Fanon was working at Blida-Joinville hospital when he spoke with these children during the year of the Battle of Algiers (which spread panic among the French). Writing of Rivet, David Galula, a French counter-insurgency officer, reported, "since it was hard to tell the difference between a fellaghas (bandit) from a peaceful Arab, they fired on whoever ran" (Galula, 2006, p. 50). The operation was considered a success. Afterward, "high-ranking military and civilian officers came from Algiers to congratulate the battalion." Photographers took pictures and "*Paris-Match*, a leading weekly magazine, printed on its cover a color picture of the battalion in operation" (Galula, 2006, p. 51).

"Well, there you are," the fourteen-year-old sums up. The tragedy is clear: There had been no choice. We are again at the heart of the drama. Fanon forewarns in "An Algerian Family" in *A Dying Colonialism* that "No revolution, can with finality, and without repercussion, make a clean sweep of well-nigh instinctive modes of behavior" (1965, p. 113). Again Fanon warns on the first page of "Colonial War and Mental Disorders," "for many years to come we shall be bandaging the countless and sometimes indelible wounds inflicted on our people by the colonialist onslaught." This warning also intimates the question, how a new society can be built on such bandaging, on the basis of people who have been traumatized by colonialism, destruction, and war?

Answering it is intimately connected with what Fanon calls the need for a second liberation struggle. Indeed, trauma bleeds into and is reproduced repeatedly in the postcolonial period. The colonial legacy is multifaceted – political-economic, social, cultural, and psychological – and just as the psychological traumas are often suppressed if not addressed, so too systems of policing and secret services, governance and courts, education and economy are often uncritically taken over, and alternative movements outside the state are viewed as threatening. It seems as if we are back to the beginning, cycling through a new neocolonial stage. What we also learn from Fanon's psychiatric writings and his commitment to the revitalizing nature and the constant praxis of radical humanism is that liberation is never a single event but continuous movement.

NOTES

1 This chapter is excerpted and edited from the introduction to an aborted translation of Fanon's psychiatric set to be published in 2014, "Decolonizing Madness." An English translation of these writings appeared in 2018 in *Frantz Fanon: Alienation and Freedom* edited by Jean Khalfa and Robert J. C. Young. Unless otherwise noted, the translations of Fanon's psychiatry articles used in this chapter are by Lisa Damon. An extended discussion of these writings can be found in Nigel C. Gibson and Roberto Beneduce, *Frantz Fanon, Psychiatry and Politics* (Rowman and Littlefield International, 2017 and University of Witwatersrand Press, 2017).

2 The English translation of *The Wretched of the Earth* by Constance Farrington was first published by Presence Africaine in 1963 (2004); *A Dying Colonialism*, translated by Haakon Chevalier, was published by Monthly Review Press in 1965 (1967); and *Black Skin, White Masks*, translated by Charles Lam Markman, by Grove Press in 1967. The posthumous collection, *Toward the African Revolution*, also translated by Haakon Chevalier, was published by Grove in 1967. All these books remain in print.

3 See Bhabha (1999/1986), Macey (2000). On the literary debates about Fanon as post-structuralist *avant la lettre*, see Gates (1999). On Fanon and Freud, see Bird-Pollan (2014).

4 According to his brother, Joby Fanon, Frantz was studying for three degrees: A Bachelors in Arts and a Bachelors in Sociology alongside the Doctorate in Medicine (2014).

5 On the Ey and Lacan dialogue, see Monique Charles' *Ey-Lacan: du dialogue au débat ou l'homme en question* (2004).

6 Fanon only quotes from the earlier section of the lectures, where Freud is speaking of the development of psychoanalysis prior to distancing himself from the seduction theory, in favor of the Oedipus complex as the nucleus neuroses. Bird-Pollan (2014) argues that Fanon was well aware that Freud moved away from his earlier theory but uses it to gain insight into

the "trauma" of the Black who makes contact with the white world – a "determined *Erlebnis*" (experience) at the origin of every neurosis. For Freud this is repressed in the unconscious; for Fanon, the Black plays out this drama in the open every day, and is a product of collective catharsis.

7 Fanon argues neither Freud, Adler, nor the "cosmic Jung," took the Black man into serious, if any, consideration in the course of their research. Of Jung he later adds that all the people Jung studied – "Pueblo Indians from Arizona or Blacks from Kenya in British East Africa ... have more or less traumatic contact with the white man" (2008, p. 164). In other words, rather than a permanent characteristic of people from Kenya or Pueblo Indians, the myths and archetypes of Jung's collective unconsciousness is "cultural, i.e., it is acquired" (2008, p. 165) – a product of the "traumatic contact with the white man."

8 Born in Catalonia in 1912, François Tosquelles passed his baccalaureate at the age of fifteen and enrolled in Barcelona University's medical school, where he met Sándor Eiminder with whom he was in analysis from 1931 to 1935. For Tosquelles, individual and social liberation, and psychiatry and politics were intimately connected. At the university he organized a seminar on Marx and Freud, and by the 1930s he was part of a group reading Lacan. During the Spanish Civil War he joined the anti-Stalinist workers' party, POUM, later becoming the head of the Republican Army's psychiatric services. Sentenced to death by Franco's regime, he escaped Spain for France in 1939, walking across the Pyrenees with little more than the two books in his suitcase (one being Lacan's thesis). Finally, at Saint Alban, after being interned in camps for "undesirables," Tosquelles created a refuge for suffering resistance fighters. For him, institutional therapy was a product of these experiences, and the struggle for liberation against Francoism and Nazism became inseparable from the struggle for liberation inside the mental asylum. He insisted that the institution had to be transformed into a caring community; rather than a professional administration of mental health that normalizes the institution and pathologizes the patients, the institution had to become a space where the inmates (staff and "guests") could work out therapies in a supportive, nurturing environment.

9 Fanon remained remarkably dedicated to these goals, and would carry many of them later to the Blida-Joinville Hospital. One can also see how this notion would be developed politically in *The Wretched*, where the administration of things – "development" from on high – is considered a deus ex machina and contrasted to the messy working out in day-to-day praxis (1968, p. 201).

10 Presenting at the *Congrès des médecins aliénistes et neurologistes*, Paris (July 20–26, 1953), these papers were titled *Sur quelques cas traités par la méthode de Bini, Indication de la thérapeutique de Bini dans le cadre des thérapeutiques institutionnelles*, and *Sur un essai de réadaptation chez une malade avec épilepsie morphéique et troubles de caractère graves*.

11 Active during the French revolution, Phillipe Pinel argued for a moral therapy, ordering not only the unchaining of the insane but careful observation of patients. He is considered one of the "fathers" of modern psychiatry. Fanon's biographers from the 1970s, Peter Geismar and Irene Gendzier, maintain, as does Hussein Bulhan, that Fanon's first act in Blida was an order to unchain patients. Macey questions this claim, arguing that those who worked with Fanon "deny that anyone was chained in Blida" (2000, p. 227). However, Joby Fanon, who toured the hospital with Fanon in 1954, was "horrified by what he saw." He states, "patients were strapped to their beds or attached to rings fixed to the wall" and adds that Frantz had taken him to a building that Frantz "had transformed by breaking the chains that tied the patients" (2014, p. 74).

12 Of course, this naming of political movements as a struggle between civilization and barbarity continues to this day.

13 The World Health Organization sponsored Carothers' *The African Mind* (1954), because he was, at the time, "the most internationally renowned ethnopsychiatrist with clinical experience" (Heaton, 2013, p. 44). In that volume, Carothers describes "The resemblance of the leucotomized European patient to the primitive African" (1953, p. 177). As for his clinical experience, McCulloch (1995) points out that when Carothers was appointed at Mathari Mental Hospital, he had no training in psychiatry, and the "empirical material" for

Carothers's description of the African mind as "lacking in spontaneity, foresight, tenacity, judgment and humility, inapt for sound abstraction and logic" (quoted in Heaton, 2012, p. 50) came from a collection of European observations of African workers (see Gibson, 2003). It should be noted that Carothers' thesis was dismissed almost immediately by Thomas Adeoye Lambo, who argued it was based on anecdotes and misleading information and could not be taken seriously (Lambo 1955). Porot and Carothers expressed similar attitudes to the emergent anticolonial struggles and had become influential colonial intellectuals. Just as Carothers was peddling the primitive and barbaric "mind of the Mau Mau" (1954) to give legitimacy to colonial violence against an anticolonial struggle in Kenya, Porot's Algiers school of "racial degeneration" was legitimating "psychological action" in Algeria, whose goal was "to reshape the Algerian mind by destroying its capacity for resistance" (Keller, 2007a, 159).

14 According to Macey (2005), Azoulay had not wanted to be a doctor but a philosopher. Feeling alienated at the faculty of medicine at the University of Algiers and disgusted by the racism and incompetence of his peers, he got a job at Blida a month after Fanon had arrived there, and immediately became involved in Fanon's sociotherapy project. Cherki (2006) points out that they had an intellectual affinity as well as overlapping experience of racism and antisemitism. Despite these affinities and their working relationship (as well as co-writing articles, Fanon also supervised his dissertation), Azoulay kept Algerian nationalism at arm's length. He never really knew of Fanon's practical commitment to Algerian liberation and left for France in 1956.

15 The project, Cherki notes, was abandoned in late 1956, to be returned to "after independence."

16 This realization is repeated in a footnote in *A Dying Colonialism*: "The colonized does not let on. He does not confess himself in the presence of the colonizer" (1965, p. 127n2)."

17 The idea of the African's innate laziness was echoed across the continent. Like Porot, Carothers' idea of the African's laziness was intimately connected to his idea of the African's mental development.

18 Recent revelations about medical/psychological staff's active participation in torture of detainees at Guantanamo Bay attest to this continuing practice. See http://ethicalpsychology.org

19 Joby Fanon argues that "Frantz's engagement with the Algerians ... began well before the date agreed on by his biographers" (2014, p. 75).

20 A short-lived journal published by a discussion group at the university of Algiers, called Association de la Jeneusse Algérienne pour l'Action Sociale.

21 The main intermediary between the FLN and Fanon was Mustapha Bencherchali, who drove through French roadblocks in his American convertible under the pretext of studying psychotherapy at Blida (see Macey, 2000, pp. 262–263).

22 An example of his axiom that middle class intellectuals need to be at the service of the revolution by donating the resources they have "snatched from the colonial universities" (see 1968, p. 150).

23 The case is named, "A European policeman in a depressed state meets while under hospital treatment one of his victims, an Algerian patriot who is suffering from stupor" (1968, p. 264).

24 In the 1959 article "Racist Fury in France" (1967b, pp. 163–166), Fanon advises Blacks to "jump ship" and leave Europe. The context for this statement was the colonial war coming to the metropole. For example, on October 17, 1961, the police attacked a demonstration in support of Algerian liberation in Paris, killing up to 200 people (many drowning after being thrown off the bridges into the Seine) and arresting up to 11,000. The police chief who ordered the attack, Maurice Papon, had overseen the torture of prisoners in Constantinople, and instructed his forces that "every Parisian officer that had been assassinated by the FLN" would be avenged by taking "the lives of ten FLN" (Feldman, 2014, p. 160). In practice the differentiation between the FLN and the Algerian population in Paris was null and void, and vicious persecution of the Algerian population in France had become accepted. It was in fact not until 1998 that any accounting of this event took place.

25 In 1955, Abane informed readers of the *French Observer* that the Algerian struggle was for "honor, justice and liberty." In the face of death, the struggle was "for the right to live as dignified free men" (Abane, 2011, p. 32). By 1956, Fanon had begun to make more and more contact with FLN militants and experienced face to face this new will to live with dignity or not live at all. The colonized, including some patients at the hospital, who had been overwhelmed by colonial reification, were changing in the new situation, shaking off the shackles of colonial subjugation and becoming "masters of their fates" (Abane, 2011, p. 30). For Fanon this was something completely new, and it affected him profoundly. It is likely that in the waning months of the Battle of Algiers, Abane, the professional revolutionary, convinced Fanon to leave and join him in Tunis.

26 The literal translation of Fanon's chapter title *"L'Algérie se dévoile"* is "Algeria unveils herself" or "Algeria unveiling herself" (it could also be "Algeria unveiling itself") quite different from the passive "Algeria Unveiled."

27 It should be noted that the "dialectical progression" that Fanon sees in the radical mutations are not guaranteed. French in contemporary postcolonial Algeria, like English in South Africa, carries with it most definite class significations.

28 Mass murder, rape, torture on an enormous scale, murder of civilians, execution, arbitrary detention, forced removal, the constant psychological terror, and small acts of daily violence: This was the reality of life in Indochina and Algeria in the wake of the liberation of France and the defeat of Nazi Germany. It is clearly manifested in the stark asymmetry of the Algerian anticolonial war, perhaps the most violent in history. On the French side, up to twenty-five thousand soldiers were killed (according to the French). On the Algerian side, over 20 percent of the population (one million people) was killed (according to the FLN) and two million people forcibly removed from their homes.

29 A point repeated in "This Is the Voice of Algeria," where Fanon argues that the real belongs to us through our actions – not the actions of a hysterical individual running down the street shouting "Long live independent Algeria" (1965, p. 78), but social action; even if it is a group sitting around a radio trying to decipher the broadcast jammed by the French, imagination would take on reality.

30 Making psychotherapy available to all was not only part of Tosquelles' institutional therapy, but also part of the psychoanalytical movement during World War One. Ferenczi became director of a clinic to treat shell-shock victims in 1916 and Reich, whose later "sex-pol" was basically therapy for working class people, began working in Freud's psychoanalytic outpatient clinic in Vienna in 1922. Often treating shell-shock, the clinic offered free or reduced fee psychoanalysis.

31 Mutual analysis is "the final development of the 'active' technique," according to Martin Stanton (1991, p. 198) "which involves exchanging places between analyst and patient where this seems fruitful."

32 It is worth noting that, like Tosquelles, Ferenczi had experience treating trauma during wartime as the director of a neurology clinic in Budapest in 1916 to treat shellshock victims, and writing about the psychoanalytic treatment of war neuroses.

33 The language of tenderness belongs to the child and/or childhood innocence, if you like, in contrast to the language of passion (and suffering) of the adult and genital sexuality. The point is that "premature imposition on a child of the adult language of passion shatters the child's innocence."

34 A film by René Vautier, Olga Baïdar-Poliakoff, and Yann Le Masson, released in 1961, is made from drawings and stories of children collected by Jacques Charby and Frantz Fanon.

35 In a discussion of the relation between psychology/psychiatry and politics, Miraj Desai (2014, p. 71) argues, "applied mental health is not merely applied psychology." A radical mental health is wary of new forms of psychologism: "Fanonian investigations call for an applied 'mental health' that is not merely applied psychology but ... also addresses the traumatizing social structures, racist narratives, and humiliating practices that suffocate human experience."

REFERENCES

Abane, B. (2011). Frantz Fanon and Abane Ramdane: Brief encounter in the Algerian Revolution. In N. C. Gibson (Ed.), *Living Fanon* (pp. 27–43). New York: Palgrave Macmillan.

Azoulay, J., Sanchez, F., & Fanon, F. (1955). Introduction aux troubles de la sexualité chez le Nord- Africain. [Introduction to sexuality disorders among North Africans]. In J. Khalfa and R. J. C. Young (Eds.) (2018), *Frantz Fanon: Alienation and freedom* (pp. 385–393). London: Bloomsbury.

Ben Salem, L. (1984). Rencontre de la société et de la psychiatrie, The meeting between society and psychiatry: Frantz Fanon's course on social psychopathology at the Institut des hautes études in Tunis. Notes taken by Lilia Ben Salem, Tunis, 1959–1960, Etudes et Recherches sur la psychologie en Algerie. Oran: CRIDSSH. In J. Khalfa and R. J. C. Young (Eds.) (2018), *Frantz Fanon: Alienation and freedom* (pp. 511–530). London: Bloomsbury.

Bergmann, M. S. (1996). The tragic encounter between Freud and Ferenczi and its impact on the history of psychoanalysis. In P. L. Rudnytsky, A. Bókay & P. Giampieri-Deutsch (Eds.), *Ferenczi's turn in psychoanalysis* (pp. 145–159). New York: NYU Press.

Bhabha, H. (1986). Remembering Fanon. Foreword to Frantz Fanon, *Black skin, White masks*. London: Pluto Press. Reprinted in Nigel C. Gibson (Ed.), *Rethinking Fanon*. Amherst, NY: Humanity, 1999.

Bird-Pollan, S. (2014). *Hegel, Freud and Fanon: The dialectic of emancipation*. Lanham, MD: Rowman & Littlefield Publishers.

Bokanowski, T. (1996). Sándor Ferenczi: Negative transference and transference depression. In P. L. Rudnytsky, A. Bókay & P. Giampieri-Deutsch (Eds.), *Ferenczi's turn in psychoanalysis* (pp. 120–144). New York: NYU Press.

Bulhan, H. (1986). *Fanon and the psychology of oppression*. New York: Plenum Press.

Carothers, J. C. (1953). *The African mind in health and disease: A study in ethnopsychiatry*. Geneva: World Health Organization.

Charles, M. (2004). *Ey-Lacan: du dialogue au débat ou l'homme en question*. Paris: L'Harmattan.

Cherki, A. (2006). *Frantz Fanon: A portrait*. Ithaca, NY: Cornell University Press.

DeBeauvoir, S. (1992). *The force of circumstance*. New York: Paragon.

Dequeker, J., Fanon, F., Lacaton, R., Micucci, M., & Ramée, F. (1955). Current aspects of psychiatric care in Algeria. *L'Information pychiatrique, 31*(1), 11–18.

Desai, M. (2014). Psychology, the psychological, and critical praxis: A phenomenologist reads Frantz Fanon. *Theory & Psychology, 24*(1), 58–75.

Fanon, F. (1951). Troubles mentaux et syndromes psychiatrique dans l'Hérédo-Dégéneration-Spino Cérébelleuse [Mental disorders and psychiatric syndromes in hereditary spinocerebellar degeneration]. Unpublished dissertation, University of Lyon, 29 November 1951.

Fanon, F. (1955). Considérations ethnopsychiatriques [Thoughts on ethnopsychiatry]. *Consciences Maghribines, 3*, 1–2.

Fanon, F. (1959). L'Hospitalisation de jour en psychiatrie: Première partie, Valeur et limites [Day hospitalization in psychiatry: Part one, its value and limitations]. *La Tunisie Médicale, 38*(10), 689–712.

Fanon, F. (1965). *A dying colonialism*. New York: Monthly Review.

Fanon, F. (1967). *Toward the African revolution*. New York: Grove Press.

Fanon, F. (1968). *The wretched of the earth*. Translated by Cinstance Farrington. New York: Grove Press.

Fanon, F. (2004). *The wretched of the earth*. Translated by Richard Philcox with a Foreword by Homi K. Bhabha. New York: Grove Press.

Fanon, F. (2008). *Black skin, White masks*. New York: Grove Press.

Fanon, J. (2014). *Frantz Fanon, my brother: Doctor, playwright, revolutionary*. Lanham, MD: Rowman and Littlefield.

Fanon, F. (2018). *Alienation and freedom* (Jean Khalfa and Robert Young, Eds.) (Steven Corcoran, Trans.). New York: Bloomsbury.

Fanon, F., & Asselah, S. (1957). Le Phénomène de l'agitation en milieu psychiatrique: considérations générales, signification psychopathologique. *Maroc médical*, 36 (380), pp. 21–24. [The phenomenon of agitation in the psychiatric milieu: General considerations, psychopathological meaning]. In J. Khalfa and R. J. C. Young (Eds.) (2018), *Frantz Fanon: Alienation and freedom* (pp. 437–447). London: Bloomsbury.

Fanon, F., & Azoulay, J. (1954, 1975). Contribution à l'étude de la social-thérapie dans un service d'aliénés musulmans: Difficultés méthodologiques, *L'information psychiatrique, 30*(9). Reprinted *L'information psychiatrique, 49*(10), 1975. Sociotherapy in a ward of Muslim men: Methodological difficulties. In J. Khalfa and R. J. C. Young (Eds.) (2018), *Frantz Fanon: Freedom and alienation* (pp. 353–371). London: Bloomsbury.

Fanon, F., Dequeker, J., Lacaton, R., Micucci, M., & Ramée, R. (1955). Aspects actuels de l'assistance mentale en Algérie. *L'information psychiatrique, 31*(1), 11–18. Current aspects of mental care in Algeria. In J. Khalfa and R. J. C. Young (Eds.) (2018). *Frantz Fanon: Freedom and alienation* (pp. 395–404). London: Bloomsbury.

Fanon, F., & Géronimi, C. (1956). Le TAT chez la femme musulmane: Sociologie de la perception et de l'imagination, *Actes du Congrès des médecins aliénistes et néurologues de France et des pays de langue française*, August 30 to September 4, 364–68, Bordeaux. The TAT among Muslim women: The sociology of perception and imagination. In J. Khalfa and R. J. C. Young (Eds.) (2018). *Frantz Fanon: Freedom and alienation* (pp. 427–432). London: Bloomsbury.

Fanon, F., & Géronimi, C. (1959). L'Hospitalisation de jour en psychiatrye: Deuxième partie, Considérations doctrinales, *La Tunisie Médicale, 38*(10), 712–732. Day hospitalization in psychiatry: Part two, doctrinal considerations. In J. Khalfa and R. J. C. Young (Eds.) (2018). *Frantz Fanon: Freedom and alienation* (pp. 473–494). London: Bloomsbury.

Fanon, F., & Lacaton, R. (1955). Conduites d'aveu en Afrique du Nord, presented at the *Congrès de Psychiatrie et Néurologie de langue française*, Nice, 657–659. Reprinted in *L'Information psychiatrique, 51*(10), 1975. The conduct of confessions in North Africa. In J. Khalfa and R. J. C. Young (Eds.) (2018), *Frantz Fanon: Freedom and alienation* (pp. 409–412). London: Bloomsbury.

Fanon, F., & Sanchez, F. (1956). Attitude du Musulman Maghrébin devant la Folie, *Revue pratique et sociologie de la vie sociale et d'hygiène mentale, 1*, 24–27. Maghrebi Muslim attitudes to madness. In J. Khalfa and R. J. C. Young (Eds.) (2018). *Frantz Fanon: Freedom and alienation* (pp. 421–426). London: Bloomsbury.

Feldman, H. (2014). *From a nation torn: Decolonizing art and representation in France, 1945–1962*. Durham, NC: Duke UP.

Freud, S. (1910; 1990). *Five lectures on psycho-analysis*. London: Norton.

Galula, D. (2006). *Pacification in Algeria, 1956–1958*. Santa Monica, CA: Rand Corporation.

Gates, H. L., Jr. (1999). Critical Fanonism. In N. C. Gibson (Ed.), *Rethinking Fanon* (pp. 251–268). Amherst, NY: Humanity Books.

Geismar, P. (1971). *Fanon*. New York: Dial.

Giampieri-Deutsch, P. (1996). The influence of Ferenczi's ideas on contemporary standard technique. In P. L. Rudnytsky, A. Bókay & P. Giampieri-Deutsch (Eds.), *Ferenczi's turn in psychoanalysis* (pp. 224–247). New York: NYU Press.

Gibson, N. C. (2003). *Fanon: The postcolonial imagination*. London: Wiley-Blackwell/Cambridge: Polity Press.

Gibson, N. C., & Beneduce, R. (2017). *Frantz Fanon, psychiatry and politics*. London: Rowman and Littlefield; Johannesburg: University of Witwatersrand Press.

Heaton, M. (2013). *Black skin, White coats: Nigerian psychiatrists, decolonization, and the globalization of psychiatry*. Columbus, OH: Ohio University Press.

Hook, D. (2011). *A critical psychology of the post-colonial: The mind of Apartheid*. New York: Routledge.

Keller, R. C. (2007a). *Colonial madness: Psychiatry in French North Africa*. Chicago, IL: Chicago University Press.

Keller, R. C. (2007b). Clinician and revolutionary: Frantz Fanon, biography, and the history of colonial medicine. *Bulletin of the History of Medicine, 81*(4), 823–841.

Lazali, K. (2011). The emergence of the subject in politics: Some reflections on the Algerian situation and on the work of Frantz Fanon. In Nigel C. Gibson (Ed.), *Living Fanon* (pp. 149–158). New York: Palgrave.

Macey, D. (2000). *Frantz Fanon: A life*. London: Granta.

Macey, D. (2005). Adieu foulard, Adieu madras. In M. Silverman (Ed.), *Frantz Fanon's black skin white masks* (pp. 12–31). Manchester: Manchester University Press.

McCulloch, J. (1995). *Colonial psychiatry and the African mind*. Cambridge, MA: Cambridge University Press.

Mirzoeff, N. (2011). *The right to look: A counterhistory of visuality*. Durham, NC: Duke University Press.

Porot, A., & Arrii, D. (1932). L'impulsivité criminelle de l'indigène nord-africain. Ses facteurs. *Annales médico-psychologique, 90*(2), 588–611.

Razanajao, C. L., Postel, J., & Allen, D. F. (1996). The life and psychiatric work of Frantz Fanon. *History of Psychiatry, 7*, 499–524.

Renault, M. (2011). *Frantz Fanon: de l'anticolonialisme à la critique postcoloniale*. Amsterdam: Editions Amsterdam.

Stanton, M. (1991). *Sandor Ferenczi: Reconstructing active intervention*. London: Aronson.

Turner, L. (2011). Fanon and the biopolitics of torture: Contextualizing psychological practices as tools of war. In N. C. Gibson (Ed.), *Living Fanon* (pp. 117–130). New York: Palgrave.

Vergès, F. (1999). *Monsters and revolutionaries: Colonial family romance and métissage*. Durham, NC: Duke University Press.

Zaretsky, E. (2005). *Secrets of the soul: A social and cultural history of psychoanalysis*. New York: Vintage.

CHAPTER 2

MY BODY, THIS SKIN, THIS FIRE

Jean Khalfa

Black Skin, White Masks ends on the enigmatic note of a prayer to the body: "My final prayer: O my body, always make me a man who questions!"[1] (Fanon, 1986, p. 206). Why should the interrogative stance be a prerogative of the body rather than the mind? Clearly *my* body must be more than simply *a* body within the world, a material object, if what is at stake in it is a stance vis-à-vis the world, a way of facing it, a questioning. Yet, there is for Fanon a risk, a danger that this body might not be what it should be, the body of a man (and the position of *toujours*, "always," gives the sense of an almost desperate urgency). The tone is thus that of a prayer, a paradoxical one, since it does not open onto a transcendence but rather signals an inner dialogue of the self with itself, a shaping of the self within the immanence of the body. Perhaps a meditation, one of these exercises or paths through which the self reforms or reshapes itself, but can only do so because it was all along precisely what it becomes, a consciousness or a being constantly shaping itself, albeit so far unknowingly. For who would make such a prayer if not one who interrogates radically, in particular one who questions even the familiar evidence of the body? A metaphysical meditation therefore, in a sense, but reversing the Cartesian movement, since what is asserted here is the inseparability of thought (as questioning), from body, since consciousness can only come to know itself through the body.

Remarkably, Fanon's prayer was chosen as an epitaph on the memorial plate in the family plot in Fort-de-France, but it was altered into: "My final prayer: make me always a man who questions." "O my body," has disappeared and the prayer now seems addressed to another, presumably transcendent, being. A prayer to the body in the context of a cemetery might have seemed too paradoxical. Perhaps there was a religious motivation, or in a land where, according to Fanon, Black skin always masked itself to itself, such reference to the body was perhaps not acceptable. Whatever the case, there is in this choice and transformation both the irreducibility of the figure of the questioner and a resistance to the issue of the body that should alert us.

Fanon himself was particularly aware that in his writing (and perhaps all writing that interested him), what was important was not so much the ideas expressed as what resisted expression. This is perhaps why the conclusion of *Black Skin, White Masks* is aphoristic. In his preface to the first edition (1952), commenting on the correspondence he had with Fanon regarding the manuscript, Francis Jeanson reports that Fanon stressed that some of his sentences aimed at the affectivity of the reader, at transmitting an experience, rather than an explanation or a system of concepts:

> Thus it can happen that in the middle of an argument Fanon will suddenly throw into the heart of an idea that charge of words, that dynamite which is revealed in them when they are no longer neutralised by their decorous enlistment in a coherent discourse. In these moments in which he explodes context, Fanon in one fell swoop disorganises our intellectual certainties and reproduces in us as if by magic the same explosion he experienced in slamming himself too brutally against the absurd, in telescoping himself against the limits of the human condition.[2]

DOI: 10.4324/9781003037132-2

There is indeed in this limitation of discursive writing and final recourse to the body and prayer something truly "ultimate," that is essential and final but not in a religious sense, as implied when the reference to the body is removed. In the long reflection on the body in history which is *Black Skin, White Masks*, Fanon sought the foundation of a new ethics, an ethics for a time when ethics could no longer seriously be grounded in transcendent and universal values, be they religious or secular:

> The starry sky that left Kant in awe has long revealed itself to us. And moral law has doubts about itself. As a man, I undertake to risk annihilation so that two or three truths can cast their essential light on the world.[3]

His own experience of racial discrimination, discovered in particular during the long journey that took him from Martinique to North Africa and across Europe during the Second World War as a volunteer in the Free French Forces, had soon dispelled for him the illusions of humanist universalism. This disillusionment would only be reinforced in the postwar period when, under the guise of secular, universalist republicanism, troops were sent to Algeria by a Socialist government, supported by the Communist Party.

EXPERIENCING

> "Dirty nigger!" or simply "Look, a Negro!" I came into this world anxious to elicit a meaning out of things, my soul desirous to be the origin of the world, and here I am an object among other objects.[4]

Black Skin, White Masks could be read as a phenomenology of the colonized consciousness. "Phenomenology" in a Hegelian sense first: It is the narration of the various stations and figures of consciousness through which mind, in history at large as well as in the history of an individual, first experiences and then endeavors to resolve the various forms of its own alienation. Accordingly, the exposé is inseparably subjective and objective, Fanon constantly shifting from the scientific "we" (the psychiatrist/philosopher) to the subjective "I" (the self as consciousness), to the objective "he" (the self as *nègre*). He was particularly aware of the inherent complexity of this voice, attempting to describe objectively what could only be perceived from the inside, the subjective experience of being objectified. This complexity meant that the book had to contain substantial material of a sociological or historical nature, and could not be submitted as a doctoral dissertation in psychiatry.[5] But there was no other way.

At the same time, the view which considers the body not only as a thing within the world but also as a "posture" or as a condition for a primordial interrogative relationship to the world, a condition for the constitution of the given as world ("to reveal a meaning in things"), this is a view which defines the intellectual world of Fanon's formative years, a world fundamentally influenced by Husserl's phenomenology. He encountered it first through Merleau-Ponty, whose lectures he attended in Lyon, and then through all those in the French phenomenological tradition who considered the incarnation or embodiment of thought here and now as structural to it, under the name of *existence* – Sartre in particular, who published Fanon in his journal, *Les Temps Modernes*, and later on famously prefaced *The Wretched of the Earth*.[6] For these philosophers, before the concepts of abstract thought can grasp it, the world is constructed in space as a synthesis of perspectives or projections from a situated point of view and in time or history as the synthesis of a multiplicity of possible projects. Here is a presentation Merleau-Ponty gave of this conception:

Our own body is not only *an object in the world* under the gaze of a separate mind, it shifts towards the position of the subject, it is *our viewpoint on the world*, the place where our mind becomes vested in a specific physical and historical situation … It is through the positioning of our body that we take possession of exterior space. At any given moment a "corporal" or "postural schema" gives us a practical and implicit global notion of the relationships between our body and things, and as it were its location in relation to them. An array of possible movements or *mobilising projects* extends from us on to our surroundings. Our body does not occupy space as things do: it inhabits space or haunts it.[7]

Merleau-Ponty's insistence on the body answers a classical difficulty in Husserl's phenomenology: An object, as such, and not just as a singular perceptual image, is the synthesis of an infinity of possible aspects or "profiles" given in perception. On the other hand, the world is understood as a synthesis of the infinity of all possible objects. Far from having a divine comprehension of the world as a whole, and in each of its details, we only perceive within horizons; there is always a beyond to all of our perceptions. Given that no world is perceptible without things and no thing is conceivable without at least the possibility of relationships with other things, each of these horizons – the internal horizon of the thing and the external horizon of the world – depends on the other. The problem is that such a structure of horizons seems to presuppose a focus, a center of organization and totalization, in other words an Idea, which in a sense would be nothing other than the thing or the world: Where would the tendency to link all these specific aspects come from, if not from a preconception of the object or of the world? Yet, these preconceptions or centers of organization can be neither the object nor the world since the object *is*, and is *only*, the collection of all "its" aspects and since none of these aspects or objects taken individually is an object or a world:

So it seems we are led into a contradiction: the belief in the thing and in the world can only signify the presumption of a completed synthesis – and yet this completion is rendered impossible by the very nature of the perspectives to be tied together, since each of them refers indefinitely to other perspectives through its horizons.[8]

In other words, is it possible to avoid postulating, under the guise of a will to stick strictly to the phenomenal alone, the very ontology that one had set out to ground in the phenomenal in the first place? Merleau-Ponty's solution is not Husserl's postulation of a transcendental consciousness, a hypothesis severely criticized by Sartre in his seminal essay of 1937, *The Transcendence of the Ego*, but rather the idea that it is the body itself, through the dialectic of its interaction with the world that gives sense to the given. *The Structure of Behaviour* (1942), for instance, shows through a study of the failure of behaviorism that even at the simplest levels of animal behavior the organism builds *structures* of behavior which allow it to *act* according to the stimuli of its environment rather than simply *reacting* to them. Thus when the conditioning labyrinth is flooded, the laboratory rat will swim towards the goal, food, which shows that through learning the animal has drawn a map of the relevant data of its environment, suitable for a variety of behaviors, and not just a precise and invariable sequence of muscular responses.

The main notion that such an explanation was based on and to which Merleau-Ponty would refer until his death, that of a *schéma corporel* ("body schema"), had been developed by the psychiatrist Jean Lhermitte in 1939.[9] This notion is so essential to Fanon that he too constantly came back to it, using it to describe scientifically the psychopathology of the "lived experience of the negro" ('l'expérience vécue du nègre') and later, as we shall see, in a political reflection on the transformations of Algerian women's relationships to their own bodies, brought about by the Algerian war.

"Look! A Negro!" It was a passing sting. I attempted a smile.

"Look! A Negro!" Absolutely. I was beginning to enjoy myself.

"Look! A Negro!" The circle was gradually getting smaller. I was really enjoying myself.

"*Maman*, look, a Negro! I'm scared!" Scared! Scared! Now they were beginning to be scared of me. I wanted to kill myself laughing, but laughter had become out of the question. I couldn't take it any longer, for I already knew there were legends, stories, history, and especially the *historicity* that Jaspers had taught me. As a result, the body schema, attacked in several places, collapsed, giving way to an epidermal racial schema. In the train, it was a question of being aware of my body, no longer in the third person but in triple. In the train, instead of one seat, they left me two or three.[10]

Here is the scandal, the true risk to the body: The sudden abolition of what was proper to the human, the pre-philosophical interrogative stance essential to "perceptual faith." This incarnated interrogation is an essential freedom or play in the individual's relationship to the world, even though this freedom and this play are constantly masked by the obvious, massive presence of the world that is also their work. Philosophy and art, in their reflexive practices, simply make this work explicit in their own interminable interrogation.[11] The system of racism leads to the real loss of this interrogative body, revealed by phenomenology, which is instantly turned into a thing.[12] Such a system is therefore based not just on the racist gaze, but also on the alteration of the consciousness it produces, on the interiorization of this gaze by its object, who necessarily responds to it either through self-hatred or in the affirmation of a difference: Servility or *négritude*. To the racist gaze, the opacity which is essential to the perception of the body of the Other as an Alter Ego (*Autrui*), as the irreducibly unpredictable source of possible worlds has simply vanished.[13] What is left is a surface:

Disoriented, incapable of confronting outside the Other, the white man, who had no scruples about imprisoning me, I transported myself that day far, very far, from my existence, and gave myself up as an object. What did this mean to me? Peeling, stripping my skin, causing a haemorrhage that left congealed black blood all over my body.[14]

The living, signifying body, source of all "orientation" or "perspective," of all direction constitutive of an exteriority, now perceived as that of a "Nègre," has been replaced by a Black skin.

Phenomenology clearly played a considerable role in the development of Fanon's thought, but one needs also to mention a second domain of reference, directly related this time to his training as a psychiatrist: The development of an experimental psychology revealing, on the one hand, the role of the body in the construction of the fundamental structures of objectivity in the child's development, and, on the other hand, confirming the existence and functions of such structures by studying psychopathologies of the relationship of the self to the body and of the body to the world. Piaget was probably an influence of the first sort: In *The Birth of Intelligence in the Child* (1936) and *The Child's Construction of the Real* (1937) he argues that during the phase which precedes the apparition of language, the first ontological categories (object, space, causality, and time) are produced via physical interactions with the world, along progressively more complex sensory-motor correlations ("schèmes sensori-moteurs"). Fanon was aware of these theories both directly and through philosophical readings – again Merleau-Ponty and Sartre. For instance, the idea that child play is an ontological apprenticeship is considered common knowledge by Sartre in *L'Être et le néant* (1943) which Fanon knew very well. Sartre uses it in his famous analysis of inauthenticity in the example of the waiter's "ballet":

Let us consider this waiter in the café. His movement is quick and forward, a little too precise, a little too rapid. He comes toward the patrons with a step a little too quick. He bends forward a little too eagerly; his voice, his eyes express an interest a little too solicitous for the order of the customer. Finally there he returns, trying to imitate in his walk the inflexible stiffness of some kind of automaton while carrying his tray with the recklessness of a tight-rope-walker by putting it in a perpetually unstable, perpetually broken equilibrium which he perpetually reestablishes by a light movement of the arm and hand. All his behavior seems to us a game. He applies himself to chaining his movements as if they were mechanisms, the one regulating the other; his gestures and even his voice seem to be mechanisms; he gives himself the quickness and pitiless rapidity of things. He is playing, he is amusing himself. But what is he playing? We need not watch long before we can explain it: he is playing at being a waiter in a café. There is nothing there to surprise us. The game is a kind of marking out and investigation. The child plays with his body in order to explore it, to take inventory of it; the waiter in the café plays with his condition in order to *realize* it.[15]

The difference is that at that stage the child plays without reference to an external norm, whereas the game the waiter plays "with" his body only makes sense in relationship with a third term, a norm, or a "condition" – the condition precisely which defines a waiter in general, or what is expected of him. Hence the contrived appearance of his behavior: "*a little too* precise, *a little too* quick … *a little too* solicitous …*"* (emphasis added). In his body, the relationship of the self with the self is mediated by a third term, the exterior norms of a job, and the waiter is performing for other human beings. But the empire of this norm is an illusion: He could always be something other than a waiter, and the ritualistic style of the performance immediately proves to all that he is something altogether different from any of his specific "incarnations" of the norm. Therefore, rather than being imprisoned by his own interpretation, through his variations, the style he imprints onto it, he is in fact immediately recognized as other than what he is or is occupied at being at any given time (a crucial point in Sartre's ontological phenomenology).

However, being Black is neither a game nor an "occupation"; it is a "condition" in a deeper sense. In the case of the "Nègre," that is, a consciousness seen and defined within the racist historical-social environment as a pure thing without any inner freedom, the third term, a specific norm or form of being, suddenly determines existence itself, not just the representation of the self. The "Nègre" cannot *directly* affirm his difference from all and any specific incarnations either in his work or in the fight for recognition with other individual alter-egos, as in the case of love. He always has to go through a third term to do that: The White. This is why, well before Fanon's psychiatric experience in Blida and his conclusion as to the impossibility of real psychotherapeutic work in Algeria, a psychology of the individual like that of Adler was for him no longer sufficient in the colonial environment:

> The Martinican compares himself not to the white man, seen as the father, the boss, God, but to his own counterpart under the patronage of the white man. [...]
> The Adlerian comparison comprises two terms; it is polarized by the ego.
> The Antillean comparison is topped by a third term: its governing fiction is not personal but social.[16]

The formation of the colonized self is therefore perverted from the very beginning. Hence Fanon's constant reference to, but also constant skepticism vis-à-vis psychoanalysis. The self of the colonized is essentially neurotic, but this is because it is inexorably constituted by history, not (or not just) by family. In her biography of Fanon, Alice Cherki stresses that this was also the view Lacan expressed in the fifties about patients from Africa: "Their unconscious was not that of childhood memories, they were only juxtaposed and their childhood was retroactively experienced through our [French] family categories. This unconscious had been sold to them together with the laws of colonisation."[17]

Fanon displayed a similar ambivalence towards Hegel's analysis of the process of recognition through the dialectical relationship of domination and servitude, popularized by Alexandre Kojève, whose pre-war lectures on Hegel were published to great acclaim in 1947.[18] Fanon accepted the model of the constitution of subjectivity through an antagonistic process of recognition: Consciousness only gains determination through a contest with another consciousness, thus gaining recognition as an alter-ego (*autrui*) and not simply as other (*autre*). But when race has become the foundation of domination, the slave is forever unable to transform and to change his or her relationship to the world through work, since he or she is made a prisoner of general physical determinations: A thing in the world and not a creator of this world, and thus unable to see in the master an alter-ego that will soon become superfluous, as in Hegel's dialectics. In colonial history, the "white" master has had no need to fight for recognition, and the "black" slave[19] has never been able to experience recognition in the transformation of the world through work, since this world excluded her or him *a priori* by its very "nature" (i.e. the naturalization of relationships of power). It is only when the colonized fights for his freedom (rather than being granted it) that he gains recognition and then, properly, *exists* as an autonomous consciousness. An assessment of the possible relationship of "le nègre et Hegel" must take into account geographical and "racial" dimensions of the conflict as well as historical ones. In that sense, if Marxism had a growing influence on Fanon's writing, he nevertheless considered, like Césaire in his *Letter to Maurice Thorez* of 1956, that the classical Marxist analysis of class struggle could not account for colonial alienation.[20]

Since his "body schema" is pathological from the outset in this society, the Black man may very well try to take refuge in a room, next to a fire, like Descartes in the *Discours de la méthode* or the *Méditations métaphysiques*. There he will discover neither his irreducible soul nor the certainty of his own rationality, but rather his body as a skin, the livery of a slave, and the risk of madness[21]: "I sit down next to the fire and discover my livery for the first time. It is indeed ugly."[22]

The slave is denied the radical experience of the Cogito: Skin has become the crystallization of history, an inheritance which suddenly bears down so heavily that the body, now flattened and fragmented into the anonymous taxonomies of a clinical gaze, is forced to crawl:

> I arrive slowly in the world; sudden emergences are no longer my habit. I crawl along. The white gaze, the only valid one, is already dissecting me. I am *fixed*. [...]
> I slip into corners, my long antenna encountering the various axioms on the surface of things: the Negro's clothes smell of Negro; the Negro has white teeth; the Negro has big feet; the Negro has a broad chest. I slip into corners; I keep silent; all I want is to be anonymous, to be forgotten.[23]

In the end, such Kafkaesque descriptions of a becoming-animal, not as a liberation process but as an entrapment, an alienation, echo the descriptions of the psychopathology of the image of the body which was a major theme of study in the psychiatry of the period, more than the psychoanalytical or Hegelian descriptions of alienation. It is through studying these pathologies that Lhermitte was led to his hypothesis of a *schéma corporel* "a function of integration of sensations and perceptions," patently disturbed in his patients: They perceived their bodies as objects or fragments of objects within the world, rather than as projects of action upon the world.[24]

Apart from the similarity of décor and the parodic description of a self withdrawing temporarily from historical turbulences into a phase of introspection, there is no direct reference to Descartes in this passage of *Peau noire, masques blancs*. But the comparison is revealing. When Descartes, in the third paragraph of the first of his *Méditations métaphysiques*, questions the nature and existence of his body, the fire he is seated next to, and the piece of paper he holds in his hands, he is far from experiencing the real danger of the reification or alienation of the subject that Fanon describes. In a similar skepticism vis-à-vis classical rationalism, Michel Foucault has argued that an authentic consideration of the possibility of madness had been eliminated from the outset – through the choice of the meditative, discursive form – from the process that ultimately leads to the *Cogito* and to the certainty of the real distinction of body and soul.[25] Fanon's analysis of the historical-social determination of existence through the body is close to Foucault's notion of discipline, and his practice as a psychiatrist and particularly his refusal of the institutionalization of madness anticipated the antipsychiatry of the 1960s. However, he consistently defined madness as an alienation of freedom, and wrote in his letter of resignation to the Ministre Résident: "La Folie est l'un des moyens qu'a l'homme de perdre sa liberté."[26]

QUESTIONING

We can now understand the meaning of Fanon's prayer, and also perhaps the link he saw and constantly wove, in all his books, between an analysis of the psychopathology of the colonized as object and the definition of the anticolonial struggle as constitutive of a subjectivity. For instance, "L'Algérie se dévoile," the first chapter of *Studies in a Dying Colonialism*,[27] is a study of the perception, within the colonial context, of the body of Algerian women and the impact this perception has upon their corporal schema. According to Fanon, within the pre-colonial culture, the veil is a traditional clothing feature (like the *fez*, the *djellabah*, etc.). Under the colonial gaze, the veil is reified as a feature of the culture which needs to be eradicated (the perception of cultures as monolithic wholes is a trait of colonialism, often reflected in the early developments of ethnology), and under the pretext of liberation it must be removed: "Every new Algerian woman unveiled announced to the occupier an Algerian society whose systems of defence were in the process of dislocation, open and breached."[28] This in turn produces a reaction and the veil suddenly becomes alive: "In the face of the violence of the occupier, the colonized found himself defining a principled position with respect to a formerly inert element of the native cultural configuration."[29] Associating the Sartre of *About the Jewish Question* with the Sartre of *Black Orpheus*, Fanon notes in this context that "It is the white man who creates the Negro. But it is the Negro who creates negritude."[30]

The final moment in this paradoxical dialectics between objectification and liberation is when colonized women taking part in the struggle removed their veil in order to infiltrate the colonizer's society. Their former corporal schema was destroyed, but it became possible for them to invent a new one and the structure of the traditional society was transformed, but this time from the inside:

> One must have heard the confessions of Algerian women or have analyzed the dream content of certain recently unveiled women to appreciate the importance of the veil for the woman's experience of her body. Without the veil she has an impression of her body being cut up into bits, put adrift; the limbs seem to lengthen indefinitely … A sense of incompleteness experienced with great intensity. The anxious feeling that something is unfinished. A frightful sensation of disintegrating. The absence of the veil distorts the Algerian woman's corporal schema. She quickly has to invent new dimensions for her body, new means of

muscular control. She has to create for herself an attitude of unveiled-woman-outside …
The Algerian woman who walks stark naked into the European city relearns her body, reestablishes it in a totally revolutionary fashion. This new dialectic of the body and of the
world is primary in the case of women.[31]

To this phenomenological description in the style of Sartre's *Being and Nothingness*, Fanon
added a footnote:

> Involved in the struggle, the husband or the father learns to look upon the relations between
> the sexes in a new light. The militant man discovers the militant woman, and jointly they
> create new dimensions for Algerian society.[32]

That said, Fanon had clearly anticipated the risk, in "neocolonial" societies, of an osmosis
between the old and the new order. He would probably have been dismayed to see postcolonial societies moving back against their own history and returning to the veil as a cultural or
religious symbol, adopting paradoxically the point of view he described as that of the former
colonizer. Several testimonies show that he became aware early on of the danger that the
national fight might be transformed into a traditionalist one, the revolutionary stance being
then replaced by a forced obedience to transcendent values and ossified styles of existence.

This constant attention to the structural relationship between colonialism and a power
exerted through the body also explains Fanon's impatient attitude towards the liberal left
in France which, at the beginning, mostly protested against the widespread use of torture
in Algeria (by 1960 independence would have become its aim). For Fanon, torture was not
an aberration:

> In reality, the attitude of the French troops in Algeria fits into a pattern of police domina-
> tion, of systematic racism, of dehumanization rationally pursued. Torture is inherent in the
> whole colonialist configuration.[33]

And, in a section of the same article entitled "Torture as a Fundamental Necessity of the
Colonial World," he added:

> Torture in Algeria is not an accident, or an error, or a fault. Colonialism cannot be under-
> stood without the possibility of torturing, of violating, or of massacring.
> Torture is a modality of the occupant-occupied relationship.[34]

In the conclusion to *Peau noire, masques blancs*, Fanon had already noted the conundrum of
the colonized, reified by the very nature of the colonial system, and then running the risk
of being reified again in the identity created by the struggle against this system:

> There should be no attempt to fixate man, since it is his destiny to be unleashed.
> The density of History determines none of my acts.
> I am my own foundation.
> And it is by going beyond the historical and instrumental given that I initiate my cycle of
> freedom.[35]

These Sartrean themes, expressed in the paradox of a "destin d'être lâché" while being perpetually at risk of reification, announce *The Wretched of the Earth*, a description of a hell on
earth in which temporality and the self are lost and all projects made impossible – except
that those souls who have faced hell through their skin, are now returning, as Sartre had
noted in *Black Orpheus*. Again, when Fanon analyzes the complicated links between national
culture and liberation struggle, his initial understanding of the body as the seat of an interrogative stance in relation to the world underpins his thought:

in a colonial situation any dynamism is fairly rapidly replaced by a reification of attitudes. [...] Every effort is made to make the colonized confess the inferiority of their culture, now reduced to a set of instinctive responses, to acknowledge the unreality of their nation and, in the last extreme, to admit the disorganized, half-finished nature of their own biological makeup. [...]

After one or two centuries of exploitation the national cultural landscape has radically shriveled. It has become an inventory of behavioral patterns, traditional customs, and miscellaneous customs. Little movement can be seen. There is no real creativity, no ebullience.[36]

When the revolution starts, in contrast, "The people's encounter with this new epic elicits a new breathing rhythm, arouses forgotten muscular tensions and develops the imagination."[37] His later work is largely dedicated to trying to prevent an ossification of this initial impetus in the new societies.

In the 1965 postface to the second French edition of *Black Skin, White Masks*, Francis Jeanson notes:

What struck me first about Fanon's thought, from the moment I had the opportunity of reading the manuscript of *Black Skin* and of meeting its author, was its exceptionally *physical* approach [sa démarche exceptionnellement *incarnée*], in which I cannot but see the surest guarantee of its universal scope and its revolutionary effectiveness. Fanon argued from the body [*à corps perdu*], from the heart, he confessed to being wounded in his very flesh, he spoke to us of having *howled, exploded,* almost gone mad.[38]

Human thought for Fanon, is *à corps perdu*, a useful metaphor: It throws itself headlong into action or creation. In a sense, all body, for Fanon, is a *corps perdu*, except when it is irremediably objectified by colonialism.[39]

David Macey devotes serious attention to the role of phenomenology in Fanon's thought, but largely in a negative way:

Just why Fanon chooses to analyse his *Erlebnis* [*expérience vécue*, lived experience] in Sartrean and Merleau-Pontyan terms is a surprisingly difficult question to answer ...

The question "why phenomenology" is hard to answer, mainly because we do not have any documentary evidence: there are no preparatory materials or drafts, no correspondence, and no helpfully revealing diaries or notebooks. We know relatively little of what Fanon had read, or of when he read it. We have only the evidence of the text itself. And the text suggests that Fanon turns to phenomenology after a process of elimination. Of the theoretical discourses available to him it is, apparently, the most suitable for his purposes.[40]

Phenomenology would have been appealing because of its concentration on experience and immediacy and because it is a philosophy in the first person: "no other philosophy would have allowed Fanon to say 'I' with quite such vehemence."[41] But the crucial question is why Fanon would have been interested in the first place in a thought that made immediate experience, (thought of as inseparable from the situation of a specific body in space and time) a condition of the institution of a subjectivity, thus turning philosophical rationalism on its head. Macey is also quite critical of Fanon's treatment of psychoanalysis, accusing him of interpreting the destructuring effect of the racist gaze through "the obscure notion" of corporal schema, rather than as the re-experiencing of a traumatic moment:

To speculate, which is all we can really do here: when Fanon is gazed at by that child, he is experiencing anew a traumatic moment in Martinican history and in the Martinican imaginary: he is being looked at by the *béké* [the white colon] and his eyes are burning.[42]

But it is clear that when he uses anecdotes in *Black Skin, White Masks*, Fanon does it in the manner of Sartre, to reveal what is meaningful in a specific lived experience: Here, the birth of a particular mode of being, induced by a racial gaze (and accompanied by a very clear racial comment). We have also seen that the notion of corporeal schema, when it is understood as an important articulation of the neurological and the psychological, is in fact an essential element in Fanon's conscious attempt at inventing a new psychiatry, attentive to the historical and sociological context of the trauma.[43]

MOVING

We have known, at least since the empiricists, that thought does not face reality as God faces the world. Rather, it develops as it moves within it. Fanonian freedom presupposes the structural incarnation of all thought and its essentially open temporality, in the endless construction of a world. This is why seeing the body of another human being, perceived as conscious, is not seeing a thing. It is, rather, the assignation of an intentionality and the immediate perception of another perspective, another world. There is, however, a historical-geographical situation which endangers this incarnated self: Colonialism, with its inherent racism. Very early on Fanon violently rejected *white masks* – the self-denegation joined to an acute consciousness of race – that was so widespread in his native Antilles. Born and raised in a place where no historical stance was possible, Fanon was to become an *écorché vif* (literally "skinned alive") when he was confronted with the reality of the racist gaze, his body flattened to a thing in the world, insignificant and yet perceived as vaguely menacing. In such a situation, in order to be perceived in its opacity, a free consciousness could only manifest itself through acts. Freedom had to be the result of a fight, a stance. It is thus no wonder that in the end he would so eagerly embrace a nation-building struggle and adopt a new ancestry.[44] It was for him, paradoxically, the first step towards a freedom from all identity.

NOTES

1 Frantz Fanon, *Black Skin, White Masks* (1952), Pluto Press, London, 1986, p. 206.

Mon ultime prière:
O mon corps, fais de moi toujours un homme qui interroge!
(Peau noire, masques blancs (1952), Le Seuil, Paris, 1971, p. 188,
Oeuvres, La Découverte, 2011, p. 251)

2 Fanon, *Peau noire*, ibid, p. 12 of the 1952 edition.
3 Frantz Fanon, *Black Skin*, op cit, p. 202. "Depuis longtemps le ciel étoilé qui laissait Kant pantelant nous a livré ses secrets. Et la loi morale doute d'elle-même. En tant qu'homme je m'engage à affronter le risque de l'anéantissement pour que deux ou trois vérités jettent sur le monde leur clarté essentielle." *Peau noire*, p. 184, *Oeuvres* p. 248. All biographies of Fanon, stress how racial discrimination within the Free French Forces during and after the war shocked him. On the situation of Black soldiers and prisoners during World War II, see Serge Bilé, *Noirs dans les Camps Nazis*, Monaco, Éditions du Rocher/Le Serpent à Plume, 2005, pp. 53–56. Bilé reports that tens of former Black Senegalese inmates in Nazi camps were executed on 1st December 1944 in a French military camp in Dakar where they had been repatriated, for having protested discriminations in pay and war indemnities compared to white soldiers. Such inequalities had provoked several revolts in camps in France, and the reports written by military authorities explicitly advocate the crushing of claims of

equality, which they accurately diagnosed as born from a loss of prestige of the White following the debacle: "Aux yeux du Noir qui n'est pas dénué de tout sens critique, le Blanc a perdu de son prestige."

4 *Black Skin*, p. 89. "'Sale nègre!' Ou simplement: 'Tiens un nègre!'"
"J'arrivais dans le monde, soucieux de faire lever un sens aux choses, mon âme pleine du désir d'être à l'origine du monde, et voici que je me découvrais objet au milieu d'autres objets." *Peau noire*, p. 5. *Oeuvres*, 153. "Faire lever un sens aux choses": this is the vocabulary of Merleau-Ponty. Not so much to give a meaning to things from the outside but to be one of these special beings – a consciousness – through which the world comes to have a meaning. A co-genesis of the world as world (not simply as a collection of objects) and mind (as freedom and not object within the world).

5 On this question, see my introduction to Fanon's psychiatric writings in Frantz Fanon, *Écrits sur l'Aliénation et la liberté, La Découverte*, Paris, 2018, pp. 163–202; Frantz Fanon, *The Psychiatric Writings from Alienation and Freedom*, Jean Khalfa and Robert J. C. Young, ed., Bloomsbury, London, 2020, pp. 1–38.

6 Fanon admired him so much, that during their memorable meeting in Rome in the summer of 1961 he said to Claude Lanzmann: "I would pay twenty thousand Francs per day to have the opportunity to talk to Sartre for two weeks, all day long." (*Je paierais vingt-mille francs par jour pour parler avec Sartre du matin au soir pendant quinze jours.*) Quoted in Simone de Beauvoir, *La Force des choses*, Gallimard, Paris, 1963, vol II, p. 421 in the Folio edition.

7 "le corps propre n'est plus seulement *un des objets du monde*, sous le regard d'un esprit séparé, il se déplace du côté du sujet, il est *notre point de vue sur le monde*, le lieu où notre esprit s'investit dans une certaine situation physique et historique … C'est à travers la situation de notre corps que nous saisissons l'espace extérieur. Un 'schéma corporel' ou 'postural' nous donne à chaque instant une notion globale pratique et implicite des rapports de notre corps et des choses, et comme son relèvement sur elles. Un faisceau de mouvements possibles ou de 'projets moteurs' rayonne de nous sur l'entourage. Notre corps n'est pas dans l'espace comme les choses: il l'habite ou le hante" (emphasis original).

"Un inédit de Merleau-Ponty" text published by Martial Guéroult in *Revue de Métaphysique et de Morale*, no. 4, October 1962, reprinted in Maurice Merleau-Ponty, *Parcours deux, 1951– 1961*, Jacques Prunair, ed. Verdier, Paris, 2000, p. 39. Cognitive sciences came back to the problem of the postural schema when it needed to be modelled in view of creating an artificial intelligence. See Daniel C. Dennett "Cognitive Wheels: The Frame Problem of AI" in Z. W. Pylyshyn, ed., *The Robot's Dilemma: The Frame Problem in Artificial Intelligence*, Ablex Publishing Corporation, Norwood, NJ, 1987.

8 "Ainsi, il semble que nous soyons conduits à une contradiction, la croyance à la chose et au monde ne peut signifier que la présomption d'une synthèse achevée – et cependant cet achèvement est rendu impossible par la nature même des perspectives à réaliser, puisque chacune d'elles renvoie indéfiniment par ses horizons à d'autres perspectives." Maurice Merleau-Ponty, *Phénoménologie de la perception*, in *Oeuvres*, Gallimard, Paris, 2010, *1030/ Phenomenology of Perception*, trans. Donald A. Landes, Routledge, London and New York, 2012, p. 345.

9 Jean Lhermitte, *L'Image de notre corps*, Éditions de la Nouvelle Critique, Paris, 1939.

10 Fanon, *Black Skin*, op cit, pp. 91–92, emphasis original.

"Tiens, un nègre!" C'était un stimulus extérieur qui me chiquenaudait en passant. J'esquissai un sourire.
"Tiens un nègre!" C'était vrai. Je m'amusai.
"Tiens un nègre!" Le cercle peu à peu se resserrait. Je m'amusai ouvertement.
"Maman, regarde le nègre, j'ai peur!" Peur! Peur! Voilà qu'on se mettait à me craindre. Je voulus m'amuser jusqu'à m'étouffer, mais cela m'était devenu impossible.
Je ne pouvais plus, car je savais déjà qu'existaient des légendes, des histoires, l'histoire, et surtout l'*historicité*, que m'avait enseignée Jaspers. Alors le schéma corporel, attaqué en

plusieurs points, s'écroula, cédant la place à un schéma épidermique racial. Dans le train, il ne s'agissait plus d'une connaissance de mon corps en troisième personne, mais en triple personne. Dans le train, au lieu d'une, on me laissait deux, trois places.

(Peau noire, p. 90, Oeuvres, p. 155, emphasis original)

11 For Merleau-Ponty, the world exists "on the interrogative mode" so that philosophy is much more the unfolding of this fundamental *interrogation* than the exposition of the knowledge of the totality of being. He constantly returned to Husserl's famous statement in *Méditations cartésiennes*: "It is [the] still-mute experience ... that we must bring to the pure expression of its own meaning." See for instance *Le Visible et l'invisible*, Gallimard, Paris, 1964, p. 171.

12 Racism, as analysed by Sartre, is a system based not only on the racist gaze but also on the interiorization of this gaze by its object who always adopts it when he/she encounters it, either in the form of self-hatred or in the form of the affirmation of a difference: Servility or négritude. Fanon often refers to "Orphée noir," Sartre's preface to Léopold Sédar Senghor, *Anthologie de la nouvelle poésie nègre et malgache de langue française*, PUF, Paris, 1948 and to his *Réflexions sur la question juive*, Gallimard, Paris, 1954.

13 In an essay on Michel Tournier's rewriting of *Robinson Crusoe* from the point of view of Friday, "Michel Tournier and the world without Other [*Autrui*]," Gilles Deleuze proposes to analyse "Autrui" as structure rather than object: But what is this structure? It is the structure of the possible. A frightened countenance is the expression of a frightening possible world, or of something frightening in the world – something I do not yet see. Let it be understood that the possible is not here an abstract category designating something which does not exist: The expressed possible world certainly exists, but it does not exist (actually) outside of that which expresses it. The terrified countenance bears no resemblance to the terrifying thing. It implicates it, it envelops it as something else, in a kind of torsion which situates what is expressed in the expressing ... The Other [*Autrui*] is the existence of the encompassed possible. Language is the reality of the possible as such. The self is the development and the explication of what is possible, the process of its realization in the actual. Proust says of the perceived Albertine that she encompasses or expresses the beach and the breaking of the waves: "If she had seen me, what could I have represented for her? At the heart of what universe was she perceiving me?" Love and jealousy will be the attempt to develop and to unfold this possible world named "Albertine." In short, the Other, as structure, is *the expression of a possible world*; it is the expressed, grasped as not yet existing outside of that which expresses it. Gilles Deleuze, *The Logic of Sense*, The Athlone Press, London, 1990, trans. Mark Lester, pp. 307–308.

14 Fanon, *Black Skin*, op cit, p. 92. "Ce jour-là, désorienté, incapable d'être dehors avec l'autre, le Blanc, qui impitoyable, m'emprisonnait, je me portai loin de mon être-là, très loin, me constituant objet. Qu'était-ce pour moi, sinon un décollement, un arrachement, une hémorragie qui caillait du sang noir sur tout mon corps?" *Peau noire*, op cit, p. 91; *Oeuvres* p. 155.

15 Jean Paul Sartre, *Being and Nothingness*, Methuen, London, 1969, trans. Hazel E. Barnes, p. 59, emphasis original.

16 Fanon, *Black Skin*, op cit, p. 190: "Le Martiniquais ne se compare pas au Blanc, considéré comme le père, le chef, Dieu, mais se compare à son semblable sous le patronage du Blanc ... La comparaison adlérienne comporte deux termes; elle est polarisée par le moi. La comparaison antillaise est coiffée par un troisième terme: la fiction dirigeante n'y est pas personnelle, mais sociale." *Peau noire*, op cit, pp. 174–175; *Oeuvres* p. 237.

17 Alice Cherki, *Frantz Fanon Portrait*, Éditions du Seuil, Paris, 2000, p. 38.

18 Alexandre Kojève, *Introduction à la lecture de Hegel*, Gallimard, Paris, 1947. See esp. pp. 12–34.

19 Or simply the "colored" slave, in this binary of uncolored/colored that turns the opposition of self and other into an ontology.

20 Fanon, *Black Skin*, op cit, pp. 191–197.

21 The parallel with Descartes is striking. See also "My Body, This Paper, This Fire," in Michel Foucault's *History of Madness*, Routledge, London, 2005. Fanon's analysis of the historical-social determination of existence through the body is close to Foucault's notion of discipline. His practice as a psychiatrist, in particular his refusal of the institutionalisation of

madness, was part of a movement soon to be known as "anti-psychiatry." But he saw madness as "one of the means man has to lose his freedom" (*l'un des moyens qu'a l'homme de perdre sa liberté*). See his letter of resignation from his post at the Hôpital de Blida-Joinville: "Lettre au ministre résident" (1956), reprinted in *Pour la révolution africaine* [1964] La Découverte Paris, 2001, p. 60. The historian of the Algerian War Mohamed Harbi wrote, in his postface to the 2002 French edition of *The Wretched of the Earth* (La Découverte, Paris), that the thought of Fanon on the revolutionary process must be considered together with his conception of madness as a form of subversion: "Fanon's inspiration also animates the conception he has of his own practice as a psychiatrist ... On the side of madness are to be found a truth and an authenticity which must be given free rein." But this truth and authenticity are those of an alienation and only indirectly part of a movement towards freedom. On Fanon's psychiatric work, see, among many other texts, C. L. Razanajao, J. Postel and D. F. Allen, "The Life and Psychiatric Work of Frantz Fanon," *History of Psychiatry*, vii, 1966, pp. 499–524; Hanafy A. Youssef and Salah A. Fadl, "Frantz Fanon and Political Psychiatry," ibid, pp. 525–532; Irène L. Gendzier, "Psychology and Colonialism: Some Observations," *Middle East Journal* no. 30 (4), 1976, pp. 501–507; Françoise Vergès, "Creole Skin, Black Mask: Fanon and Disavowal," *Critical Inquiry*, Spring 1997, pp. 578–595. Alice Cherki, *Frantz Fanon: Portrait*, op cit.

22   Fanon, *Black Skin*, op cit, p. 94: "Je m'assieds au coin du feu, et je découvre ma livrée. Je ne l'avais pas vue. Elle est effectivement laide." *Peau noire*, op cit, p. 92; *Oeuvres* p. 156.

23   Fanon, *Black Skin*, op cit, pp. 95–96, emphasis original. J'arrive lentement dans le monde, habitué à ne plus prétendre au surgissement. Je m'achemine par reptation. Déjà les regards blancs, les seuls vrais me dissèquent. Je suis *fixé* ...

Je me glisse dans les coins, rencontrant de mes longues antennes les axiomes épars à la surface des choses, – le linge du nègre sent le nègre – les dents du nègre sont blanches, les pieds du nègre sont grands – la large poitrine du nègre, – je me glisse dans les coins, je demeure silencieux, j'aspire à l'anonymat, à l'oubli.

(Peau noire, op cit, p. 93; Oeuvres p. 158)

24   On the psychiatry of the period see Stéphane Thibierge, *Pathologies de l'image du corps*, PUF, Paris, 1999. Thibierge shows how neurologists studying patients unable to recognise their own image, following cerebral lesions, described syndromes which in effect confirmed psychoanalytical understandings of the relationship of the self to the body:

What all these phenomena in fact invite us to consider is the way in which neurological lesions foreground the mention, in these patients' discourse, of something which blocks the recognition of their own image. Now, one need only go over their statements to realise that what is at issue here cannot only be defined negatively as a deficit. Rather their observations bear witness that, when the integrity of the body's image is threatened, appears, within the field of recognition ... something of the order of an autonomy and of an extraneousness [ie, the body as thing] of which the subject would be hard put to it to say how it relates to him or her, though the subject is burdened by it, since this "something," this autonomy and extraneousness, can act as a parasite on the body of the subject and on the image in which the subject recognises its body.

The order of reality evoked here is not far removed from what psychoanalysis has been able to isolate as the dimension of the *object* inasmuch as the latter is usually "clothed" in the image, in other words neutralised and suppressed by the particular form the image substitutes to it for the purposes of recognition.

(pp. 184–185)

Fanon often refers to Lacan's text on the mirror stage, which was of direct concern to a thinker interested in pathologies of the relationship to the body. Thibierge also comments on the reading Merleau-Ponty made of these neurological studies in his *Phénoménologie de la perception*, relating Descartes' dualism to Lhermitte's analysis of asomatognosia, ibid, p. 157,

n. 3. See also Catherine Morin, *Schéma corporel, image du corps, image spéculaire. Neurologie et psychanalyse*, Éditions Érès, Paris, 2013), Ch. 1 and 2.

25 See "My Body, This Paper, This Fire," appendix to Michel Foucault, *History of Madness*, pp. 550–574.

26 [Madness is one of the ways people have to lose their freedom.] *Lettre au ministre résident* (December 1956), in *EAL*, 367. In his postface to the 2002 edition of *Les Damnés de la terre* (Paris: La Découverte), the historian of the Algerian War, Mohammed Harbi, wrote: "l'inspiration de Fanon passe aussi dans la manière dont il comprend sa pratique de psy-chiatre [...] C'est du côté de la folie que se trouvent une vérité et une authenticité auxquelles il faut laisser son libre exercice" [Fanon's inspiration extends also to the way in which he understood his psychiatric practice [...] It is on the side of madness that a truth and authen-ticity are found, whose free exercise one is obliged to respect] (p. 311). It is important to note that this truth and authenticity are those of an alienation, and can only indirectly be part of the revolutionary process. On Fanon's psychiatric work, see *infra*, Ch. 7.

27 *Sociologie d'une révolution*, Maspero, Paris, 1959; *Studies in a Dying Colonialism*, translated from the French by Haakon Chevalier with a new introduction by A. M. Babu, Earthscan Publications, London, 1989.

28 Ibid, p. 42. "Chaque nouvelle femme algérienne dévoilée annonce à l'occupant une société algérienne aux systèmes de défense en voie de dislocation, ouverte et défoncée." Ibid, p. 25.

29 Ibid, p. 46. "Face à la violence de l'occupant, le colonisé est amené à définir une position de principe à l'égard d'un élément autrefois inerte de la configuration culturelle autochtone." Ibid, p. 29.

30 Ibid, p. 47. "C'est le blanc qui crée le nègre. Mais c'est le nègre qui crée la négritude," ibid, p. 30.

31 Ibid, modified translation, p. 59.

"Il faut avoir entendu les confessions d'Algériennes ou analyser le matériel onirique de certaines dévoilées récentes, pour apprécier l'importance du voile dans le corps vécu de la femme. Impression de corps déchiqueté, lancé à la dérive; les membres semblent s'allonger indéfiniment … Incomplétude ressentie avec une grande intensité. Un goût anx-ieux d'inachevé. Une sensation effroyable de se désintégrer. L'absence du voile altère le schéma corporel de l'Algérienne. Il lui faut inventer rapidement de nouvelles dimensions à son corps, de nouveaux moyens de contrôle musculaire. Il lui faut se créer une démarche de femme-dévoilée-dehors … L'Algérienne qui entre toute nue dans la ville européenne réapprend son corps, le réinstalle de façon totalement révolutionnaire. Cette nouvelle dia-lectique du corps et du monde est capitale dans le cas de la femme." *L'An V*, p. 43; *Oeuvres* p. 284. There are visual echoes of this passage in Gilo Pontecorvo's *Battle of Algiers*.

32 Ibid, p. 59, n. 14 "Engagé dans la lutte, le mari ou le père découvre de nouvelles perspectives sur les rapports entre sexes. Le militant découvre la militante et conjointement ils créent de nouvelles dimensions à la société algérienne." *Oeuvres*, pp. 294–295, n. 8.

33 *El Moudjahid*, no. 10, September 1957, reprinted in *Toward the African Revolution*, p. 64. "En réalité, l'attitude des troupes françaises en Algérie se situe dans une structure de domination policière, de racisme systématique, de déshumanisation poursuivie de façon rationnelle. La torture est inhérente à l'ensemble colonialiste." *Pour la révolution africaine, Oeuvres*, p. 745.

34 Ibid, p. 66. "La torture en Algérie n'est pas un accident, ou une erreur, ou une faute. Le colonialisme ne se comprend pas sans la possibilité de torturer, de violer ou de massacrer. La torture est une modalité des relations occupants-occupés." *Pour la révolution africaine, Oeuvres*, p. 747.

This position is similar to that of Césaire who wrote, in 1955, about the "Christian bour-geois," that "what he cannot forgive Hitler for is not *crime* in itself, *the crime against man*, it is not *the humiliation of man as such*, it is the crime against the white man, the humiliation of the white man, and the fact that he applied to Europe colonialist procedures which until then had been reserved exclusively for the Arabs of Algeria, the coolies of India, and the blacks of Africa." *Discourse on Colonialism*, trans. Joan Pinkham, Monthly Review Press, New York, 1972, p. 14.

35 *Black Skin*, op cit, p. 205.

Il ne faut pas essayer de fixer l'homme puisque son destin est d'être lâché.
La densité de l'Histoire ne détermine aucun de mes actes.
Je suis mon propre fondement.
Et c'est en dépassant la donnée historique, instrumentale, que j'introduis le cycle de ma liberté.

(Peau noire, p. 187; Oeuvres p. 250)

36 *The Wretched of the Earth*, trans. Richard Philcox, Grove Press, New York, pp. 170–172.

assez rapidement, dans la situation coloniale, le dynamisme est remplacé par une substantification des attitudes … Tous les efforts sont faits pour amener le colonisé à confesser l'infériorité de sa culture transformée en conduites instinctives, à reconnaître l'irréalité de sa nation et, à l'extrême, le caractère inorganisé et non fini de sa propre structure biologique …
    Au bout d'un ou deux siècles d'exploitation, se produit une véritable émaciation du panorama culturel national. La culture nationale devient un stock d'habitudes motrices, de traditions vestimentaires, d'institutions morcelées. On y décèle peu de mobilité. Il n'y a pas de créativité vraie, pas d'effervescence.

(Les Damnés de la terre, Maspero, Paris, 1961,
La Découverte, 2002, pp. 225–227; Oeuvres pp. 613–614)

37 Fanon, *The Wretched of the Earth*, op cit, p. 174. "Le contact du peuple avec la geste nouvelle suscite un nouveau rythme respiratoire, des tensions musculaires oubliées et développe l'imagination."' *Les Damnés*, p. 229; *Oeuvres*, p. 616.
38 Ibid, p. 221, emphasis added. This preface, one of the most perceptive readings of Fanon, contains many other passages on the colonized body. Remembering Fanon in an interview published by *Révolution Africaine*, December 1987, Josie Fanon also insisted on Fanon's own physicality: "He dictated [*Black Skin, White Masks*] to me … He walked back and forth like an orator improvising, which explains the rhythm of his style, the breath that animates all of his writings."
39 To understand the importance of the poetic dimension of all thought, for Fanon, one should have Césaire in mind. For instance the poem "Corps perdu," published in an eponymous volume in 1949, with Picasso. Césaire recognized this kinship. In the poem "par tous mots guerrier-silex," published in *Moi laminaire*, Gallimard, Paris, 1981, Fanon (whose name in French can mean a whalebone plate or blade) is compared to a flint stone. It ends with these lines:

> je t'énonce
> FANON
> Tu rayes le fer
> Tu rayes le barreau des prisons
> Tu rayes le regard des bourreaux
> Guerrier-silex
> Vomi
> Par la gueule du serpent de la mangrove

40 David Macey, "Fanon, Phenomenology, Race," *Radical Philosophy*, no. 95, May/June 1999, p. 11.
41 Ibid, p. 12.
42 Ibid, p. 13.

43 In his excellent biography of Fanon, Macey is more positive about the relationship between Fanon and Phenomenology. Giving more evidence of the extensive philosophical readings of Fanon, he concludes: "The classics of French phenomenology – Merleau-Ponty's *Phénoménologie de la perception* and Sartre's *L'Être et le néant* – are obviously not treatises on racism and anti-racism, but they provided tools that were much better suited to the analysis of 'the lived experience of the black man' than either Marxism or psychoanalysis" (p. 126). Alice Cherki's book gives a more nuanced reading of Fanon's relationship with psychoanalysis. On Fanon and phenomenology, see also Lou Turner, "Frantz Fanon's Phenomenology of the Black Mind. Sources, Critique, Dialectic," *Philosophy Today*, no. 45, (supplement), 2001, pp. 99–104.

44 See Édouard Glissant, *Le Discours antillais*, Gallimard, Paris, 1981, pp. 56–57, and Albert Memmi, "The Impossible Life of Frantz Fanon," *Massachusetts Review*, Winter 1973, pp. 9–39.

REFERENCES

Bilé, S. (2005). *Noirs dans les Camps Nazis*. Monaco: Éditions du Rocher/Le Serpent à Plume.

Césaire, A. (1972). *Discourse on colonialism* (Joan Pinkham, Trans.). New York: Monthly Review Press.

Cherki, A. (2000). *Frantz Fanon portrait*. Paris: Éditions du Seuil.

De Beauvoir, S. (1963). *La Force des choses* (Vol. II). Paris: Gallimard.

Deleuze, G. (1990). *The logic of sense* (Mark Lester, Trans.). London: The Athlone Press.

Dennett, D. C. (1987). Cognitive wheels: The frame problem of AI. In Z. W. Pylyshyn (Ed.), *The robot's dilemma: The frame problem in artificial intelligence* (pp. 41–64). Norwood, NJ: Ablex Publishing Corporation.

Fanon, F. (1989). *Studies in a dying colonialism* (Haakon Chevalier, Trans.). London: Earthscan Publications,

Fanon, F. (2007). *Toward the African revolution*. New York: Monthly Review.

Fanon, F. (2018). *Alienation and freedom* (Jean Khalfa and Robert Young, Eds.) (Steven Corcoran, Trans.). London: Bloomsbury.

Foucault, M. (2005). *History of madness*. London: Routledge.

Frantz F. (1986). *Black skin, White masks*. London: Pluto Press. Original work published in 1952 (French).

Gendzier, I. (1976). Psychology and colonialism: Some observations. *Middle East Journal, 30*(4), 501–507.

Glissant, É. (1981). *Le Discours antillais*, Paris: Gallimard.

Guéroult, M. (2000). Un inédit de Merleau-Ponty. In Maurice Merleau-Ponty, *Parcours deux, 1951–1961*, Jacques Prunair (Ed.). Reprinted from *Revue de Métaphysique et de Morale, 4*, 1962. Paris: Verdier.

Kojève, A. (1947). *Introduction à la lecture de Hegel*. Paris: Gallimard.

Lhermitte, J. (1939). *L'Image de notre corps*. Paris: Éditions de la Nouvelle Critique.

Macey, D. (1999). Fanon, phenomenology, race. *Radical Philosophy, 95*, May/June, 8–14.

Memmi, A. (1973). The impossible life of Frantz Fanon. *Massachusetts Review*, Winter, 9–39.

Merleau-Ponty, M. (2012). *Phenomenology of perception* (Donald A. Landes, Trans.). London: Routledge.

Morin, C. (2013). *Schéma corporel, image du corps, image spéculaire. Neurologie et psychanalyse*. Paris: Éditions Érès.

Razanajao, C. L., Postel, J., & Allen, D. F. (1996). The life and psychiatric work of Frantz Fanon. *History of Psychiatry, 7*, 499–524.

Sartre, J. P. (1948). Orphée noir. In Léopold Sédar Senghor (Ed.), *Anthologie de la nouvelle poésie nègre et malgache de langue française* (pp. ix–xliv). Paris: PUF.

Sartre, J. P. (1954). *Réflexions sur la question juive.* Paris: Gallimard.

Sartre, J. P. (1969). *Being and nothingness* (Hazel E. Barnes, Trans.). London: Methuen.

Thibierge, S. (1999). *Pathologies de l'image du corps.* Paris: PUF.

Vergès, F. (1997). Creole skin, Black mask: Fanon and disavowal. *Critical Inquiry,* Spring, 578–595.

Youssef, H. A., & Fadl, S. A. (1996). Frantz Fanon and political psychiatry. *History of Psychiatry,* 7, 525–532.

CHAPTER 3

FRANTZ FANON'S PHENOMENOLOGY OF BLACK MIND

Sources, Critique, Dialectic

Lou Turner

One may, no doubt, expect that given the title of this essay, my intention is to present something of an overview of the thought of Frantz Fanon. As the title would suggest, Fanon's 1952 *Black Skin, White Masks* is the specific object of such a description, a project that has had more than a few adventurers. After all, Fanon himself makes no secret of his intellectual debt to phenomenological existentialism. In fact, though, while my essay is something of an overview, one that focuses on Fanon's *Black Skin* (and I mean that not only as a quick reference to his book), my endeavor amounts to something more than collecting phenomenological bric-a-brac of so revolutionary a thinker and practitioner as Frantz Fanon, on this, the fortieth year of his death, which occurred not far from here, at Bethesda Naval Hospital, Maryland, under CIA guard. (It is also important to note, for purposes that will become apparent later, that last year [2000] marked the fortieth anniversary of the death, in Paris, of Richard Wright, a Black radical intellectual who had also come under the same kind of surveillance by U.S. watchdog agencies as Fanon. Wright and Fanon died a year apart at the beginning of what the United Nations designated as "the Africa Decade," under circumstances that remain murky to this day. The circumstances of their deaths, in countries from which each had exiled themselves, could not have been more revealing of the diasporic dialectic that made Black thought so revolutionary and international a dimension of the postwar world.)

In the end, I may or may not have succeeded in escaping the kind of arbitrariness that so often attends scholarly adventures into Fanonian dialectics. For it is also no secret – and Fanon is one of those rare twentieth-century intellectuals who makes us alive to this at a visceral level – that he had to have been passionately in search of a liberatory method to have so seamlessly gone from the kind of restless postwar veteran and French Caribbean intellectual who could never "return to his native land," to the radical clinical psychiatrist in revolutionary Algeria, to the self-identified African revolutionary theoretician whose thought would become synonymous with Third World liberation. One does not, in other words, go willy-nilly making phenomenological *bricolage* out of such compelling philosophical commitments without risking some critical blow-back. That polemic is for another time however. The expectation that my essay is an overview is, nonetheless, not misplaced. It is simply that by calling it "Frantz Fanon's Phenomenology of Black Mind," I mean nothing so essentialist or essentializing as negritude, toward which Fanon had at first an understandably ambivalent attitude that then evolved with his growing revolutionary commitments into a scathing critique. Nor have I in mind the kind of postmodernist eclecticizing of Fanon that anachronizes the revolutionary content of his thought. I have something else in mind.

DOI: 10.4324/9781003037132-3

SLOUGHING THE SKIN OF WESTERN MODERNITY

> Without adequate preparation, the Negro of the Western world lives in *one* life, *many* life-times ... The Negro, though born in the Western world is not quite of it; due to policies of racial exclusion, his is the story of *two* cultures: the dying culture in which he happens to be born, and the culture into which he is trying to enter – a culture which has, for him, not quite yet come into being; and it is up the shaky ladder of all the intervening stages between these two cultures that Negro life must climb. Such a story is, above all, a record of shifting, troubled feelings groping their way toward a future that frightens as much as it beckons.
>
> *(Wright, 1954, emphasis original)*

Merleau-Ponty's "flesh of the world" is an elemental fact that makes all apparent facts actual facts. Fanon's "black skin," too, is the flesh of the world, one that is caught up in other worlds of apparent and actual Blackness. Merleau-Ponty's "flesh of the world," in other words, is Fanon's "fact of blackness." I am privileging "fact of blackness" over the "lived experience of the black," recognizing that Fanon may have given the latter as the actual title of chapter 5 of *Black Skin, White Masks*, because "fact of blackness" comes closer to Fanon's phenomenological project. Both Merleau-Ponty's "flesh of the world" and Fanon's "fact of blackness" concentrate around them the meaning(s) of the world. That the inter-corporeality of the flesh/fact of the world is its phenomenological meaning means that my lived experience is not only in-itself but is for-others whose facticity is similarly involved in the "flesh of the world." We participate in the field of experience of others because we share, possess, and experience the same meaning ascribed to the "flesh of the world." We look back at those who look at us. Indeed, the perception of seeing becomes meaningful when it becomes a "look," i.e., an act of perception between two perceivers who reciprocally intend to construct a certain objective meaning or certainty of the world. For a racially constructed world, the meaning is Manichean. "Black skin," looked at, participates in that meaning or Being of the world that is elementally "flesh." Like touching a hand that touches the world and others in it for their sensuous meaning, which corresponds to the phenomenological reduction carried out in the concepts of labor found in the *pre-Phenomenology* philosophy of spirit of Hegel, and in Marx's *Economic-Philosophic Manuscripts of 1844*, looking sees the flesh that looks at the world for meaning. Looking not only gives facticity to what is seen, it lends meaning and intentionality to whomsoever looks back. It is that meaning, or if you will, Being, which we participate in that ignites and enlivens existence.

This "fact" marks the contingent boundaries of human realities. The other looking back at Richard Wright during his 1953 trip to Africa, for instance, was not his elite African counterpart, but his non-elite African "other" camped along the side of the road, haggling in the markets, practicing "fetish" in the bush. The encounter changed the lived experience of the world of Richard Wright that had been so overly determined by the southern white glare. As contingent as the flesh of these worlds may be there remains a historical determination that foresaw the fact of Wright's Blackness, a determination, as logical as it is historical, that was always already there, certain of the turn history would take to deliver him into the structures of different references and feelings.

Sartre's "Orphée Noir" provided something of an epistemological insight into negritude's "fact of blackness." Insofar as our perceptions are realizations of the world, race and racial perceptions are realizations of a racialized world; they are in some sense (e)race-ing the world. The flesh of this racialized world is the Black skin that is hidden, or otherwise made invisible, behind a gallery of white masks. No matter how much we understand these masks to be manifestations of the colored flesh of the world, the actual world remains hidden.

Spontaneously set off from the "flesh of the world," Fanon's body was always (al)ready for the "miracle of vision" (Kwant, 1966, p. 79). Historically, this "miracle" was preceded by its existential Good Friday in which the Black body was sacrificed in a social crucifixion (viz., lynching). Fanon meant a resurrection, a new humanism, a new intensity of beginning, to follow the long history of racial sacrifice. The fact that the flesh of the world "predestines [one] to see and to perceive" (p. 79) means that Black skin predestines one to see and perceive racially. The "fact of blackness" is the meaning of this form of perception. It, however, escapes the grasp of philosophy, for subject and object are so utterly differentiated by the fact of Blackness that it (the difference) gives rise to the most deceptive "objects" and objective appearances.

THE FANONIAN MILIEU OF PHILOSOPHY'S UNMASKING

Hence, the situation of philosophy, i.e., metaphysics, in the Fanonian milieu has the semblance of an ideological mask whose many appearances, like Herman Melville's Confidence-Man, mystifies, as well as manifests the "flesh of the world." Fanon's thought, or more precisely, the phenomenology of Black mind it discloses, may properly be called philosophy, in Merleau-Ponty's sense, because it is at once the negation of reflections of any so-called pre-existing "truths" about race, and is the act (qua performance) of the (self-)bringing forth of truth. The Marxian character of Merleau-Ponty's idea of philosophy also accords with Fanon's phenomenology of Black mind. Inasmuch as for both, "the only way to do away with [the *cogito*] is to fulfill it, that is, to show that it is eminently contained in interpersonal relations" (Merleau-Ponty, 1964, p. 133). As examples of this phenomenological experience of philosophy inhering, or originating, in the "flesh of the world," Merleau-Ponty tells us that just as "Hegel's logic is … 'the algebra of revolution,'" so "The 'fetishism of [commodities]' is the historical accomplishment of that alienation which Hegel enigmatically describes, and *Das Kapital* … is a concrete Phenomenology of Mind" (p. 133).

Now, as much as Fanon's *Black Skin, White Masks* discloses the intersection of multiple languages and discourses, its performativity or *praxis* is as much a spoken act aimed at making its readers/audiences conscious of what it means to be human through the transcendence of "our individual empirical understanding of the world" (Couture, 1998, p. 81). Though Fanon was interested in more than creating new rhetorical meanings of the world, wanting instead to actually change the world, it is no less true that he recognized that that was impossible without the force of ideas fitted to a language of disalienation and liberation. And yet, Fanon's performance was more than a spoken act, as rhetorically visceral as works like *Black Skin, White Masks* and *The Wretched of the Earth* are, but a written act, as well. Writing represented that kind of act for an intellectual like Fanon who had always been a politically marginal figure in whatever milieu he moved, principally because writing involved creating meaning and interpreting realities, especially rhetorically constructed realities, at the margins. The idea that ideas must hear themselves speak determines the way we must grasp them as inherent in our lived experience. For that reason alone, the myriad appearances (masks) or voices found in Fanon's *Black Skin, White Masks* make it a phenomenology of mind.

For Fanon such a phenomenology begins with the sensuous certainty of language, simply because language places our existence for others in question. "The black man has two dimensions" (Fanon, 1967, p. 17), one for other Black people, the other for white people. The latter has meant, among other things, that the social science methods of placing Black existence in question have been sources of Black alienation because historically they fixed the place of the Negro on the lowest rungs of human evolution. This has, today, been replaced by a new "culture of poverty" discourse that fixes Black folk within the political morphology of American society according to their alleged psychosocial pathologies and eugenic destinies. Language, too, not only means the assumption of a certain culture, it signifies the possession of the cultural world implied and expressed by a language. This possession (*qua* capacity or capital) opens up a social class divide between members of the same racial or ethnic group by virtue of the most proficient minority-group users of the dominant language gaining mastery over it. The overdetermination of language in the adaptive strategies of minority-group members leads to a mutation of cultural identity. This becomes evident in the compulsion to rid oneself of one's native dialect, for "Every dialect is a way of thinking" (p. 25). Finally, language becomes that province whence the first form of protest against domination issues, particularly in the form of literatures of protest. Here, language and revolution become intertwined when the oppressed begin to speak in the language of a philosophy of liberation (Marx). Owing to the conflict which arises, language comes to define the noble and the base consciousness, the "civilized" and the "savage" mind, the Manichean world of "colonizer" and "colonized."

Behind the empirical immediacy of language and the conflicting discourses to which race gives rise lies a colonial ontology, one which Fanon finds at once articulated and problematized in Octave Mannoni's controversial *Prospero and Caliban: The Psychology of Colonization*. This so-called colonial ontology is the thoroughly historicized, existential "colonial situation" formed by the "confrontation of 'civilized' and 'primitive' men" (Fanon, 1967, p. 85). The colonial *situation*, for which Mannoni "deserves our thanks for having introduced" (p. 84), owes more, however, to Fanon's reading of Merleau-Ponty than to Mannoni. In fact, Fanon feels that Mannoni "has not understood its real coordinates" (p. 84), despite having called the ontology of the "colonial situation" to our attention.

In spite of his well known critique of Mannoni, Fanon credits the French social-psychological anthropologist and colonial administrator with having not avoided African subjectivity in a field known for overdetermining "objectivity." Not only had Mannoni's purpose been to "prove the impossibility of explaining man outside the limits of his capacity for accepting or denying a given situation," but to demonstrate the "interrelations of objective historical conditions," unseparated from the "human attitudes toward these conditions" (Fanon, 1967, p. 84). Mannoni, however, betrays his own purpose when he allows "objectivity" to be overdetermined from the outside. Despite his debt to Merleau-Ponty, who theorized situation as the expression of "the ultimate unity of man with his surroundings" (Mallin, 1979, p. 7), Fanon's notion of situation bears an even closer affinity to the Marxian dialectic which comprehends the relations between human beings as mediated by the instrumentality of their historical material situation. In other words, Fanon, like Marx, is concerned with the conflict brought into question by the "historical objective conditions" and attitudes of the situation.

MARXIAN–FANONIAN HUMANISM

Marx's "historical materialism," though not usually understood in the humanist terms Fanon is working out, nonetheless, developed a concept of situation that signifies more than the so-called "set of facts" that constitute "external circumstances." Marxist positivism, usually called "orthodoxy," is the history of the eliding of this "new humanism." For very different reasons, Fanon's reading of Mannoni and Merleau-Ponty discloses the archeology of this humanism. For Fanon, the colonial situation not only constitutes a unique relationship of subject to object, but a thoroughly historicized ontology in which existence itself must be historically reinterpreted. The colonial situation makes everything Manichean; existence is either "civilized" or "primitive" (actually "savage"). Even the hybridities that the colonial situation gives birth to are only understood in Manichean terms.

What Hegel calls internal intuition ensures that the immediate sensuousness of this "flesh of the [colonial] world," i.e., the "fact" of Fanon's "black skin," doesn't remain at the level of perception, but is instead elevated, in the sense of its determination to appear, and reflected back in the look of the very subject whose bodily schema had been racialized. Internal intuition breaks down the ontology of the colonial or racialized situation into a process of becoming wherein the inherent defects of the Manichean world are also "endowed with the impulse of self-development" (Hegel, 1969, p. 829). This, in Fanon's terms, represents the agency of the Negro, or that which becomes the revolutionary process of decolonization in his later works. Internal intuition, in short, is the method and means by which Fanon's comprehension of the "colonial situation" entails both the logic of its existence, i.e., its phenomenology, and the dialectic of its overcoming.

The counter-factuality of Mannoni's internal intuition bears out Fanon's own, inasmuch as, in the face of the 1947 Madagascar revolt and French massacre, Mannoni did not so much feel the liberatory impulse to free man, nor recoil from the "civilizing mission" of the European butchery of men. He instead intuited the confusion of lost dependency and the violence bred by sudden abandonment. His internal intuition was of an African personality desperately and futilely seeking its destiny in a lost authenticity of the past, a Malagasy negritude, if you will. It is to this internal intuition of the European intellectual, and the Europeanized Black intellectual, that Fanon directs the passage from Marx's *Eighteenth Brumaire* that he uses as the epigraph to the last chapter of *Black Skin, White Masks*: "The social revolution ... cannot draw its poetry from the past, but only from the future. It cannot begin with itself before it has stripped itself of all its superstitions concerning the past" (Fanon, 1967, p. 223). Not unlike the social ontology formed at the inception of the colonial situation, "Earlier revolutions relied on memories out of world history in order to drug themselves against their own content" (p. 223).

Fanon's thought is a phenomenology of Black mind by which twentieth-century Third World revolutions "let the dead bury the dead" (Fanon, 1967, p. 223). Much more, then, is involved in his internal intuition of the "colonial situation" than grasping the revolutionary impulses by which colonialism is overthrown. His internal intuition is as much the comprehension of the "new humanism" by which the specters of Europe's memory of its conquering spirit in world history are finally buried, as it is comprehension of the burial of the African "cult of the dead."

This is what gives *Black Skin, White Masks* its performative character; it is dramaturgical (here reading Sekyi-Otu, 1996) only in this sense, that Fanon is "performing" this twin burial himself. He, however, is less dramaturgical and more theatrical, i.e., performative. His "narrative," if it is possible to call his thought a narrative, is a phenomenological performance, a poetics fundamentally aware of its own praxis of burying the dead, including Mannoni's "cult of the dead." I would be remiss were I not also to note that this obviously entails Fanon trucking with that other "cult of the dead" – negritude – in order to bury it.

Fanon is, according to Marx's term for the revolutionary occupation of the unemployed proletariat, a "gravedigger."

Richard Wright was himself engaged in this revolutionary internment. Fanon and Wright were nonetheless not involved in a Foucauldian archeology of dead discourses, but, instead, in the very alive and revolutionary pursuit of burying them. The interdisciplinary character of their thought is constitutive of that phenomenology of Black mind I have suggested. Psychoanalytical theories, existentialist philosophy, Marxian (and in Fanon's case, Hegelian) dialectics, social psychology, literary discourses such as surrealism and negritude, as well as anthropology, were all sources, critiques, and dialectics of Wright's and Fanon's phenomenological performances of the modern Black mind. Indeed, in Wright and Fanon one sees that the dialectic that differentiates the mind as "black" is its performativity, whether as reason or as revolution. And in their performances the two are inseparable.

REFERENCES

Couture, B. (1998). *Toward a phenomenological rhetoric: Writing, profession, and altruism.* Carbondale, IL: Southern Illinois University Press.

Fanon, F. (1967). *Black skin, White masks* (Charles Lam Markmann, Trans.). New York: Grove Press.

Hegel, G. W. F. (1969). *Science of logic* (A. V. Miller, Trans.). New York: Humanities Press.

Kwant, R. C. (1966). *From phenomenology to metaphysics: An inquiry into the last period of Merleau-Ponty's philosophical life.* Pittsburgh, PA: Duquesne University Press.

Mallin, S. (1979). *Merleau-Ponty's philosophy.* New Haven, CT: Yale University Press.

Merleau-Ponty, M. (1964). Hegel's existentialism. In Merleau-Ponty (Hubert C. Dreyfus and Patricia Allen Dreyfus, Trans.), *Sense and non-sense* (pp. 63–70). Evanston, IL: Northwestern University Press.

Merleau-Ponty, M. (1964). Marxism and philosophy. In Merleau-Ponty (Hubert C. Dreyfus and Patricia Allen Dreyfus, Trans.), *Sense and non-sense* (pp. 125–136). Evanston, IL: Northwestern University Press.

Sekyi-Outu, A. (1996). *Fanon's dialectic of experience.* Cambridge: Harvard University Press.

Wright, R. (1954). Introduction. In George Lamming (Ed.), *In the castle of my skin* (pp. v–viii). New York: McGraw Hill.

PART II
Fanon and
the Psychological

CHAPTER 4

PSYCHOLOGY, THE PSYCHOLOGICAL, AND CRITICAL PRAXIS

A Phenomenologist Reads Frantz Fanon

Miraj U. Desai

This chapter[1] situates the role of psychological investigations in analyses of social problems like colonialism and racism, via a phenomenological reading of the writings of Frantz Fanon. Emerging scholarship on Fanon's use of psychology is beginning to elucidate how his style of analysis enables an interweaving of psychological insights with sociopolitical ones (e.g., Hook, 2004, 2005, 2012). The present chapter builds on this research by explicating the essential moments of Fanon's investigations, specifically those found in *Black Skin, White Masks* (1952/1967). The chapter details the structure of these Fanonian investigations, which include a focus on experience, concrete examples, evidence, meaning, unprejudiced seeing from multiple perspectives, delineation of essential structure, and critical and liberating praxis.

Frantz Fanon, a Martinique-born psychiatrist, influenced such varied fields as philosophy, politics, history, communications, literary theory, and postcolonial and cultural studies (e.g., Gibson, 1999a, 2003; Gordon, Sharpley-Whiting, and White, 1996; Maldonado-Torres, 2008; Martinez, 2000). A key component of Fanon's writings was his ability to scrutinize oppressive social structures with incisive psychological analysis, in effect, bringing psychiatry and psychology to subject matter typically considered under the purview of other disciplinary frames (McCulloch, 1983). Consequently, his work has been usefully noted as a form of "psychopolitics" (Hook, 2005; Lebeau, 1998) or "psychophilosophy" (McCulloch, 1983). Along these lines, Bhabha (2004) argued that Fanon's great contribution to ethics and politics was his ability to relate topics like colonialism and nationalism to the "psycho-affective realm" of the body, the emotions, dreams, and the imagination (p. xix).

Until recently, and despite Fanon's training as a psychiatrist and consistent use of psychological concepts, the literature on Fanon and psychology has been limited (e.g., Adams, 1970; Bulhan, 1985; McCulloch, 1983). There is now an emerging line of scholarship that investigates his progressive clinical practice, his political psychology, his influence on the history of psychiatry, and his application to critical psychology, psychoanalysis, and multicultural counseling (e.g., Bulhan, 1999; Hook, 2004, 2005, 2012; Keller, 2007; Lebeau, 1998, 2005; Ponterotto, Utsey, and Pedersen, 2006; Utsey, Bolden, and Brown, 2001; Vergès, 1996). Hook, in particular, has advanced our understanding of Fanon's contributions to critical psychology by outlining the possibility of a psychologically informed politics and a politically informed psychology. Examples of Fanon's body of work in this respect include the ideas of sociodiagnosis, the internalization/epidermalization of inferiority, and cultural trauma under colonialism (see Hook, 2004, for an excellent exposition). Hook's (2012) work has provided a space for psychology to offer positive contributions to critical analyses of racism and colonialism while remaining politically astute – which this current chapter hopes to build on. Of importance here is the continued elaboration, utilizing

DOI: 10.4324/9781003037132-4

Fanon's work, of a "worldly" psychology, that is, a non-psychologistic psychology that does not remain naïve to the social, political, and historical dimensions of experience (Davidson and Cosgrove, 1991, 2002).

The literature on Fanon's use of psychology is growing, but more research is needed on the specifics of his multi-perspectival approach. Today, an increasing number of psychologists are interested in exploring, and responding to, complex and problematic social structures (see Bhatia, 2007; Davidson, 2003; Desai, Divan, Wertz, and Patel, 2012; Felder and Robbins, 2011; O'Hara, 1989, 2010; Ponterotto et al., 2006). Few in Fanon's own time, apart from contemporaries like Erich Fromm (1941, 1956; cf., McCulloch, 1983), made as critical a use of psychological insights as Fanon in examining the complex social, economic, and political dimensions of phenomena. An explication of the essential constituents of Fanonian investigations may thus help inform contemporary research and critical praxis related to the social problems of our day.

First, I attempt to detail the key constituents of Fanonian investigations by beginning with a concrete example of Fanon's analyses and discovering its invariant structure. I approach this task from a phenomenological perspective (e.g., Giorgi, 1970; Wertz, 2010; Wertz et al., 2011), taking Fanon's investigations as the phenomena of interest. By treating Fanon's investigations as phenomena, the current analysis brings to mind Husserl's (1977) lectures on phenomenological psychology, in which he describes how to render a creative process intelligible by examining the creative experience, including its essential acts, objects, motives, and goals. Specifically, he states that one can help illuminate the origin of a work of art by systematically describing the artistic experience from the artist's perspective, that is: "to project oneself into the living and striving of the artist, to bring it to an appropriate and fully living intuition and to make intelligible on the basis of his motives the system of goal-positings and realizing activities" (p. 7, section on Dilthey). Though not specifically examining an artistic creation, the first task of the present chapter adopts these same phenomenological principles. That is, in order to understand the structure of Fanon's investigations, I will study the experiences on which these investigations were based, including their acts, objects, meanings, goals, and motives. This phenomenological approach aims for fresh descriptions of, emerging from direct access to, the phenomena.

For the second task, the emergent structure of Fanonian investigations is compared to other writers, theorists, and movements operating at the nexus of psychology and society, thereby contributing to a sketch of a larger psychopolitical project. The chapter focuses on those traditions familiar to psychological audiences, such as psychoanalysis, critical psychology, humanistic psychology, and cultural psychology. In concluding, the chapter attempts to demonstrate ways in which Fanonian-style investigations contribute to a science and praxis of human liberation, capable of combining insights from psychological, political, economic, and even geographical domains.

BLACK SKIN, WHITE MASKS

To focus the current analysis, I analyze Fanon's (1952/1967) investigation of childhood trauma under colonialism in his early work *Black Skin, White Masks*. This investigation has been identified as one of Fanon's distinctly psychopolitical moments (Hook, 2004). Scholars have recently argued that the psychological sphere plays an important role in both the early and later Fanon (e.g., Hook, 2012), despite previous tendencies in the literature to significantly separate the two periods. However, given the current chapter's specific focus, the question of whether the current analysis applies to his later use of psychology is not explicitly addressed.

In *Black Skin, White Masks*, Fanon announced his study of race and colonialism as rooted in love and understanding with the intention of setting humans free. He explicitly stated it was a work of psychology with an emphasis on socioeconomic realities, and also a "clinical" work with cultivation of insight and life movement in mind. Fanon's approach is now detailed, proceeding first with the fruits of his labor then working back to describe its essential constitutive moments, that is, what makes it what it is. This kind of *descriptive* analysis of a researcher's approach has been previously done with respect to Freud (Wertz, 1993) and others in the history of psychology (See also Giorgi, 1970, 2009; Spiegelberg, 1972). The primary task of the present analysis is to read Fanon phenomenologically. In doing so, certain affinities of Fanon's mode of analysis to phenomenology become apparent, including a focus on experience, concrete examples, meaning, unprejudiced seeing from multiple perspectives, and attention to structure. In Fanonian investigations, however, all of these are employed in the service of critical and liberating praxis.

REFLECTIONS ON FANON'S APPROACH

Choice of Phenomenon

Fanon investigated childhood trauma and adult psychopathology under colonialism. In one particular section of *Black Skin, White Masks* (1952/1967; 1952/2008), he investigated the process by which Black persons come to feel threatened when venturing into colonial society beset by racial inequalities.[2] In Fanon's (1952/2008) words, it was to elucidate how "a normal [B]lack child, having grown up with a normal family, will become abnormal at the slightest contact with the white world" (p. 122). In the course of his investigation, he was able to delineate how this type of "neurosis," rather than being a mere individualistic phenomenon, traced its origins back to early exposures to racist values and sociopolitical inequities (Hook, 2004). This type of analysis of psychopathology and trauma extended a classical Freudian formulation insofar as the trauma experienced by Black children in the French colony of the Antilles, as will be shown, was constituted by colonizer–colonized encounters, geopolitical power structures, storybook media, and racist structures. He reflected on the experience of Black persons in the French colony of the Antilles, including his own experience and that of students and workers.

Process of Investigations

Fanon (1952/1967) proceeded with his investigations of psychopathology via a return to their origins in lived experience, or *"Erlebnisse"* (p. 144). Invoking psychoanalysis, this move allows Fanon to examine experiences and meanings that are outside of immediate awareness. Gibson (2003) highlighted Fanon's (1952/1967) "method of regression" (p. 123) as a move "backward" (Gibson, 2003, p. 213, n. 39). A type of looking back into the development of a phenomenon, similar to Freud's investigations of neurosis, the Fanonian difference was that he remained open to a full experiential analysis that considered sociopolitical influences, not merely familial ones. Fanon's simultaneous utilization and critique of psychoanalysis has been called a "demonstration by failure" (Gordon, 1996,

p. 76), a de-colonial reduction of psychoanalysis (Maldonado-Torres, 2008), a breaking of new ground for psychoanalysis in investigations of racism (Lebeau, 2005, p. 142, n. 5), and a movement between the psychological and the political (Hook, 2005). In the present analysis, Fanon's extension of psychoanalysis takes on another role: It is part of an approach that heuristically uses, but is not dependent on, the received theoretical constructions of psychology. Any preconceptions may merely point to new phenomena, which themselves must be originally investigated via a return to lived experience and the lived world. In these types of investigations, there is an insistence on the primacy of seeing and unprejudiced observation to which Freud was also committed in his philosophy of science (Wertz, 1993).

Fanon extended this approach to subject matter that Freud had not touched, namely racism and colonialism. However, a version of Freud's psychoanalytic analysis of overdetermination, or multiply layered meanings of experience, can remain operative in Fanonian investigations.[3] Fanon, mirroring Sartre's (1946/1965) analysis of antisemitism and overdetermination "from within," keenly noted that overdetermination in a racist world necessarily involves sociopolitical infections on one's embodied presence. As Fanon (1952/1967) stated: "I am overdetermined from without" (p. 116).

Focus on Experience and Concrete Examples

Fanon's (1952/1967) analysis of childhood trauma in the colonies will be delineated via a concrete example: His description of the insidious nature of racist childhood storybooks. This concrete evidence gave Fanon ample material by which to pursue his transdisciplinary reflections on colonial trauma. The specific descriptive section is selected for its psychological richness, links to the history of psychology, and anticipation of contemporary scholarship on cultural/historical trauma. It has also been identified as distinctly illustrative of Fanon's psychopolitics by his most prominent commentators in psychology (e.g., Hook, 2004). Further, Bhabha (1994), in his postcolonial theoretical and psychoanalytic engagements with Fanon, notably identified the passage as an instance of a "primal scene" of racism (p. 108; see also Hook, 2012). This selection from Fanon is analyzed in the present chapter for purposes of a descriptive phenomenological inquiry into the core structure of Fanonian investigations.

Fanon (1952/1967) wrote:

> In every society, in every collectivity, exists – must exist – a channel, an outlet through which the [energy] accumulated in the form of aggression can be released…each type of society, of course, requiring its own specific kind of catharsis. The Tarzan stories, the sagas of twelve-year-old explorers, the adventures of Mickey Mouse, and all those "comic books" [aim at releasing] collective aggression. The magazines are put together by white men for little white men. This is the heart of the problem. In the Antilles – and there is every reason to think that the situation is the same in the other colonies – these same magazines are devoured by the local children. In the magazines the Wolf, the Devil, the Evil Spirit, the Bad Man, the Savage are always symbolized by [Blacks] or Indians; since there is always identification with the victor [or good guys], the little [Black child,] quite as easily as the little white [child], becomes an explorer, an adventurer, a missionary "who faces the danger of being eaten by the wicked Negroes."
>
> *(pp. 145–146, translation modified in brackets, mostly via Fanon,*
> *1952/2008, pp. 124–125)*

The child of color in the colony identifies with the storybook hero, who is the white aggressor conquering "savages" of color. He does not identify with the latter group or as a Black man, who are instead perceived to be of distant, African origin, foreigners, and hunted enemies. Fanon noted that it was only afterward that the Antillean, upon traveling to Europe, recognized that these categories had all along been applied to himself. Here, Fanon described the process by which the person of color in the colony, who had originally identified with colonial aggressors in stark opposition to supposed "savages," lives through psychological conflict once realizing the full global reach of colonialism and its racist values. He is now and was always the hunted object of murder and humiliation. What was once a childhood dream of being a hero is now a childhood nightmare of being a hunted savage. As Fanon (1952/1967) stated, they are "made inferior" (p. 149). His embodied presence has been "epidermalized" (p. 11), that is, dehumanized and made to feel like an inferior object.

Analysis of Meaning

Fanon attempted reflections on the meaning of his and others' lived experience.[4] Fanon rigorously described various psychological phenomena and processes in his analyses of life under colonialism, with description serving a critical and liberating function. These processes included: Trauma, identification, the imagination, aggression, internalized oppression, stereotyping, prejudice, anxiety, death, overdetermination, psychological conflict and paradox, and family systems. In his descriptions, Fanon was influenced by Karl Jaspers and the phenomenological psychological tradition that placed emphasis on *meaning*, not on mere abstract facts or behaviors. Fanon (1952/1967) stated: "What matters for us is not to collect facts and behavior, but to find their meaning" (p. 168). This intention involved understanding the meaning of the world, self, others, objects, media, race/ethnicity, political and economic structures, and collective traditions, as they are given in lived experience and the lived world. His interest was an "intuitive," in-depth understanding of concrete examples.[5] Through such a method, Fanon discovered that their experiential meanings were all tied to the colonial structure.

Temporality, Change in Meaning, and Invariant Structure

The importance of the role of examining *changes* in meaning, and how these changes in meaning occasion conflict, is now discussed. What is evident is that Fanonian investigations, in order to reveal the full scope of colonial trauma, necessitate the explication of structure, meaning, and temporal shifts in each. Regarding temporality, Fanon (1952/1967) introduced the entire book as "rooted in the temporal" (p. 13) and referenced Jaspers' views on historicity (p. 112). This was an essential turn for Fanon because the colonial situation remained a quite unprecedented global and historical event in which exploitation permeated so much of everyday life and so many sociopolitical institutions in its wake (Maldonado-Torres, 2008). In the passage analyzed for this chapter, Fanon focused his witnessing on both individual and world history. Specifically, Fanon delineated the temporal shifts in meaning from the developmental context of early childhood in the colony (the Antilles) to adulthood in the colonial core (France), all in the context of a structural unity of part-to-part and part-to-whole correlations. Fanon delineated how a child in the colony entered into a world that communicated violent messages in the form of stories and illustrations concerning foreign, "wicked," Black "savages." As he traveled away from home, the meaning of the storybook characters changed, along with the identification process. He went from identifying with the adventurous hero (Self as hero – Other as savage) to identifying with the hunted savage (Self as hunted – Other as hunter). In terms of the logics of identification, he was made to hunt himself. The occasion for this conflict and shift in meaning was rooted in the temporal: From childhood innocence to adult awareness of transnational colonial relations, which themselves were historically situated.

Further, in order to move up in French colonial society – meanings and goals that implicate the horizon of the future – Fanon described how the Antillean must reject himself and his family:

> The Antillean has therefore to choose between his family and European society; in other words, the individual who *climbs up* into society – white and civilized – tends to reject his family – Black and savage – on the plane of imagination, in accord with the childhood *Erlebnisse* that we discussed earlier.
>
> *(Fanon, 1952/1967, p. 149)*

This situation brings to mind Alfred Schutz's penetrating phenomenological description of the stranger in which the stranger is denied a central core of humanity: History. He observed: "Seen from the point of view of the approached group, [the stranger] is a man without history" (Schutz, 1976, p. 97).[6] In Fanon's analysis, colonialism strips the Antillean of his childhood innocence, his family, and his culture. In a way, colonialism makes him a stranger, not only to the approached group, but to himself as well. His history then gets usurped by trauma – psychological, historical, and cultural.

Characterized by dehumanizing motives, the colonial world was now experienced as hunting him due to the color of his skin. This shift in meaning, which conflicts with the earlier one from his childhood, is revealed through anticipatory anxiety and in the person's embodied presence, as a "racial epidermalization." This type of "neurosis" is not exactly "unconscious" insofar as the neurosis is "on the surface": Sociopolitical reality is internalized, and inferiority is epidermalized (Hook, 2004, p. 121). Further, Fanon situated conflict in the context of the person's life goals and trajectory and also the goals of the colonial world; that is, he described the reasonable desire to move up in society as directly requiring the horrific condition of abandoning one's family and home culture.

Fanon showed that colonial trauma is essentially given through various experiential planes: Through the imagination, the body, colonial relationships, cultural materials, and geopolitical power dynamics. The explication of an invariant, general meaning of trauma across these manifestations gave Fanon's analysis its most powerful evidence regarding the destructive nature of colonialism. Fanon was evidently seeking a high level of generality that held across all imaginable instances of colonial trauma and racism *of this kind*, as evidenced by his varying the structure that he found in order to determine its essential core. What he found was that a comprehensive understanding of racist trauma under colonialism is unthinkable without attention to psychological *and* political processes. As Fanon (1952/1967) stated regarding racist childhood storybooks: "there is every reason to think that the situation is the same in the other colonies" (p. 146).

Multi-Perspectival Renderings via Meaning and Structure

Fanon's multi-perspectival mode of inquiry contained a genuine psychology while meaningfully integrating it with other human scientific modes of analysis. Fanon did not reduce reality to the psychological alone and ventured into the terrains that economics, geography, sociology, communications, and, particularly, politics typically thematize. That is, as he explicated psychological structures, he simultaneously related them to social and collective structures, given his comprehensive view of the lived world. In the above analysis, he situated the experience of trauma within complex *socioeconomic* spheres. He incorporated knowledge of cultural *geography* and geopolitical connections between the Antilles, Europe, and Africa, including the processes of displacement. He examined the *sociology* of children's magazines and storybooks, which was also an investigation within the field of *communications*. Above all, his understanding of the workings of racist, colonial power structures gave him an entrenched vantage point by which to approach the relationship between *politics* and psychology.

A NOTE ON FANONIAN INVESTIGATIONS AND THE MEANING OF PSYCHOLOGY

Though it is impossible to place Fanon as a theorist of only one particular field of study, it is possible to utilize Fanon's groundbreaking ideas to advance various human studies disciplines in their own right; the use of Fanon's thought for the purposes of disciplinary generativity is known as the "5th stage" of Fanon studies (Gordon et al., 1996, p. 6). The contribution of the present study, however, is not as much on the traditional discipline of psychology. The emphasis is on how the "psychological" can be meaningfully related to other human structures to address complex social phenomena like racism. Fanon, who was once called "the chronicler of colonialism" (McCulloch, 1983, p. 4), indeed relied heavily on psychological perspectives in his analyses of racism, as shown above and elsewhere (e.g., Bulhan, 1985; Gaines, 1996; Hook, 2004, 2005, 2012; Lebeau, 1998; McCulloch, 1983). However, Fanon never clarified his particular approach to psychological subject matter, which the above attempted.

This explication of approach may seem out of place given that Fanon (1952/1967) himself had eschewed such a task: "It is good form to introduce a work in psychology with a statement of its methodological point of view. I shall be derelict. I leave methods to the botanists and the mathematicians. There is a point at which methods devour themselves" (p. 12). However, I do not think it is mere coincidence that Fanon mentioned the methods he found in the mathematical and natural sciences of his day as being inadequate to the task of explicating the all-too-human phenomenon of colonialism. As was shown in the above analysis, Fanon indeed relied on principles consistent with approaches that free themselves of naturalistic biases and instead respond to the human demands of the subject matter through an exploration of experience, meaning, embodiment, temporality, and so forth. This non-naturalistic methodological turn places Fanon in consonance with the traditions springing from both Dilthey and Husserl who criticized naturalism vis-á-vis psychological life, and, as Wertz (2010) notes, placed focus on: "intentionality, embodiment, efficacy, values, temporality, sociality, holism, motivation, unity, and the potential for change, ... features [which] are also mutually implicit and inconceivable apart from each other" (p. 268). Radically and fundamentally social, human experience is inconceivable without relations to others, institutions, and moral orders, given that what is human is essentially constituted by community and history (Husserl, 1952/1989; Wertz, 2010). Though the achievement of a precise disciplinary meaning of psychology has yet to be achieved (Giorgi, 2009, p. 183), it may one day be able to offer much towards investigating trenchant social pathologies, given the principles suggested above. The allied Fanonian imperative for this kind of psychology necessitates the ability to link psychological structure – directly and meaningfully – to the world around it.

TOWARD A STRUCTURE OF PSYCHOPOLITICS: CONNECTIONS TO EXISTING MOVEMENTS IN PSYCHOLOGY

This section delineates how the above portrait relates to the existing literature on Fanon and psychology in addition to literatures from the critical psychological, phenomenological, psychoanalytic, and cultural psychology traditions. Implications for critical praxis are also discussed. In connecting Fanonian-style investigations to other work situated at the nexus of the psychological and the social – thereby identifying convergent and divergent themes – the remaining sections attempt to contribute to delineating an overall general structure of psychopolitics. Though politics is the main interrelating sphere, the intent of the sketch is to suggest ways of connecting the psychological to other human domains, be it the social, the cultural, the economic, or even the geographic. This general effort can be considered a type of phenomenological meta-analysis of extant theory and research.

The present sketch of Fanon's methods supports Hook's (2004, 2005, 2012) work on Fanon's psychopolitics, which involves critically applying psychological insights to politics and political insights to psychology. As Hook, following McCulloch (1983) and Lebeau (1998), argued, Fanon's greatest originality came from examining colonialism via the lens of psychopathology and personal identity via the lens of colonial violence. Hook (2005, 2012) articulated Fanon's "materialist psychology" that demonstrated how racist encounters and gazes strip away a person's embodied subjectivity and resources for personal and cultural identity. Drawing on Fanon, Hook (2012) encouraged returning critical psychology – which had ironically abandoned psychological forms of conceptualizing – to those very psychological and bodily workings of oppression, albeit via methods that are capable of accessing these in a non-psychologistic fashion. The methodological foundation articulated in the current chapter supports and extends this critical praxis by describing the meaning-oriented approach that was operative for Fanon in building his psychological/multi-perspectival lens in the first place, including as directed towards the problem of (dis) embodied subjectivity under colonialism.[7] The essential moments of this approach, as presented here, together suggest a critical avenue towards (non-psychologistic) psychological research on complex sociocultural phenomena, analogous to or even beyond the ones Fanon had examined himself. Conversely, such Fanonian investigations also call attention to the need for transdisciplinary *re*-analyses of traditional topics in psychology such as psychopathology, trauma, and child development. To be sure, as Gibson (1999b) notes, Fanonian thought both informs *and* limits psychology's role in addressing the scope of phenomena like colonial racism, given that psychology cannot account for the world as a whole. Adams (1970) similarly highlighted Fanon's strong critique of psychologism, in which social ills like poverty, antisemitism, racism, and colonialism were minimized to mere mental states. As was suggested above, Fanonian investigations necessarily connected psychological structures to political, socioeconomic, and geographical ones.

The emergent structure of Fanonian investigations also suggests a template for accessing other psychological theorists and researchers who have examined the nexus between the psychological and the sociopolitical. For instance, the psychoanalyst Erik

Erikson's (1950) investigation of the supposed "problems" of federally funded education of American Indian children bears close resemblance to Fanon's analysis from the Antilles. Erikson himself was aware of and praised Fanon's insights regarding the damages of colonialism (Friedman, 1999, p. 369; also for comparisons of Fanon's thought to Erikson's psychobiography of Mahatma Gandhi). Erikson's analyses showed that "educational problems" of American Indian children were not to be localized in the person but were mostly a consequence of indigenous conflicts with the colonialistic imposition of free-market values, bureaucratic structures, harsh internalized consciences, and routinized and hostile attitudes towards children's bodily functions. These forces threatened to destroy longstanding indigenous values and practices such as generosity, the giving away of property, and centrifugality, or outward- and other-oriented behavior. As in Fanon's analysis, the forced imposition of colonialist values had drastic effects on the psychological lives of the indigenous populations, suggesting a direct and meaningful link between individual and world history (see also, Gone, 2004). In each grassroots investigation, colonialism was found to permeate both political and psychological structures.

Other relations to psychoanalysis have already been discussed above and in much greater detail elsewhere (Gibson, 1999a, 2003; Gordon, 1996; Hook, 2012; Lebeau, 2005). For the purposes of the present chapter, two themes related to common practices of both Fanonian and psychoanalytic investigations are discussed: The analysis of meaning and the method of reflection. Freud and Fanon both shared a focus on uncovering meaning in their historical investigations of "psychopathology," Freud having noted psychoanalysis' discovery that "symptoms have a *sense* and are related to the patient's experiences" (p. 318, emphasis added; see Wertz, 1987, 1993, for a fuller discussion). For Fanon, the focus on meaning was necessary to reveal the structure of colonial trauma. This emphasis allowed access to the unique temporal structure of colonial trauma, which was not a process caused by some prior factual occurrence but was characterized by shifts in experienced meaning. This same focus on meaning and structure applies to Erikson's cultural-developmental analysis above (see also Wertz, 1986, on Erikson and the meanings of the body). The overall sensitivity to the change in the meaning of prior experiences is related to Freud's notion of *nachtraglichkeit*, revivified by Lacan and others, and generally translated as deferred action or afterwardsness (see Judy, 1996, pp. 68–69). In the experience of *nachtraglichkeit*, new experiences change the meaning of prior ones, possibly engendering a conflict between the new and old understandings (e.g., what was once considered a trustworthy relation is now and was always, on the basis of new information, a traumatic one). Freud and Breuer's (1895/2004) early case studies provide the most in-depth descriptions of this phenomenon, particularly in the case of Katharina. The non-causalistic phenomenon of *nachtraglichkeit* is rendered intelligible only if the investigator is sensitive to changes in meaning that can *restructure* the totality of experience: Past, present, and future.

Fanon also featured a method of reflecting on others' *and* his own experiences for service in psychopolitical and cultural-historical investigations of colonial neurosis. Hook (2005), for instance, illustrated Fanon's "materialist psychology" by describing a racially objectifying encounter in which a white child shrieks in fear at Fanon, due to the color of his skin. Here, Fanon reflects on his experience as an "an amputation, an excision, a hemorrhage that splattered my body with black blood" (Fanon, 1952/1967, p. 112), indicating that sociopolitical violence had been inflicted on his embodied subjectivity. In addition to serving the aims of inquiry, a type of critical self-reflection has also been identified by Biko and others as a key component in consolidating forms of political agency capable of challenging racist structures such as Apartheid (Hook, 2012, pp. 27–30). While perhaps less acknowledged as an explicit source of psychological knowledge in contemporary scholarship, reflection on others *and* self featured prominently, for instance, in Freud's psychoanalysis (Wertz, 1993) and later developments such as Kohut's self psychology – Kohut's (1979) notable "two analyses of Mr. Z" were likely based on himself (Geller, Norcross, and Orlinsky, 2005). Fanon's version of reflection is related to this tradition in psychology that uses one's own experience as a source of general knowledge, but, importantly, extends this enterprise into the realm of analyzing collective structures. Fanonian investigations rely on, and indeed may require, multiple sources of "data": Self, other, and cultural materials like children's storybooks. On the issue of personal materials and documents in particular, Allport (1942) wrote an extensive scientific justification for their use in psychology. These documents, Allport stated, can ably provide a "touchstone to reality" for the psychological investigator (p. 184; Giorgi, 2009; Wertz, 2001). Allport encouraged the use and development of personal documents as a legitimate method via "bold and radical experimentation" (1942, p. 190). Though writing in a different time and place, Fanon, in his own way, accomplished such bold and radical experimentation in his psychopolitical investigations. Wertz (2010), building on Husserl's eidetic analysis, detailed the phenomenological basis for utilizing the varieties of experiential data in generating valid – and scientifically justifiable – insights: One's own experience, communication with others via empathy, and cultural expressions and objects (of particular value in interdisciplinary research). Thus, Fanonian, humanistic, psychoanalytic, and phenomenological psychology all feature an "experimental" method, that is, bold and radical experimentation with multiple sources of insight. The continued links between Fanonian investigations and the phenomenological tradition are discussed next.

Fanon's approach began with a return to experience and the lived world. This emphasis on investigations from the grassroots puts him in consonance with the phenomenological movement (see Bernasconi, 2004; Gibson, 2003; Gordon, 1996; Maldonado-Torres, 2008; Martinez, 2000). Gordon (1996) articulated much of Fanon's underlying existential-phenomenological approach, including his emphasis on "evidence" akin to Edmund Husserl's usage,[8] appeals to context, and concrete descriptions of embodiment in a racist world (pp. 77–78). In fact, Fanon's fifth chapter title, although first translated to English as "The Fact of Blackness," was *"l'éxperience vécue du Noir"* in the original French, or "the lived experience of the Black" (Gibson, 2003; Gordon, 1996; Judy, 1996). Further, Maldonado-Torres (2008) identified Fanon's deeply loving attitude, critical philosophy, and commitment to the dehumanized as the basis for a novel kind of phenomenological reduction and attitude, which allows for a "de-colonial" ethics and politics. One horizon of assuming this de-colonial attitude is revealing the "inhuman pathologies of social structures" (Maldonado-Torres, 2008, p. 93).

Previous treatments of Fanon's analytic of lived experience outlined his relevance for philosophical concerns, whereas the present chapter thematizes his applications for human science and critical praxis. Consistent with and in support of the outlining of Fanon's phenomenological affinities, the present article delineated his approach to describing *what colonial trauma is* on the level of the psychological and how this rendering relates to what colonial trauma is in other spheres of existence (e.g., the political, the economic, the sociological, and the communicative). Fanon's grassroots psychological investigations, based on experiential evidence in cultural-historical context, provided a crucial foundation for his overall project of prosecuting social pathology. Often noted as a friend of Sartre's (1961/2004), who wrote the preface to Fanon's (1961/2004) *The Wretched of the Earth*, Fanon embodied the phenomenological spirit as distinctly indicated by: The focus on concrete examples and evidence, the use of Jaspers' fact-meaning distinction, the delineation of an essential core structure of trauma as given through numerous variations, the emphasis on intuitive and deep understandings, the critique of psychologism, and complex descriptions of the body, the imagination, and temporality (see Davidson, 2003; Davidson and Cosgrove, 1991; Giorgi, 2009; Husserl, 1900–1901/1970a, 1954/1970b, 1913/1982, 1952/1989; Wertz et al., 2011). In the phenomenological movement formalized by Husserl and extended to psychology, emphasis is placed on examining living or lived experience from the grassroots, from below, in a return to the "things themselves" in the "lifeworld" (Husserl, 1900–1901/1970a, 1954/1970b; Spiegelberg, 1972).

By bringing parallel rigor to the problems of colonialism and racism, Fanon ventured into previously untouched phenomenological territory.[9] What is suggested by Fanonian investigations may be the adoption of a phenomenological psychopolitical attitude towards the lifeworld that does not negate but places the psychological in relief.[10] The task here is to return to lived experience and the lived world in order to intuit the psychological and political structures of phenomena like oppression, in a manner akin to what Hook (2005) described as a shifting of "registers." Just as Maldonado-Torres (2008) found in Fanon the possibility of a new type of de-colonial philosophical phenomenological reduction, the present analysis finds the possibility of a psychopolitical phenomenological reduction for use in the human sciences.

Fanon's approach anticipated other contemporary research themes in psychology as well, including stereotype threat (Steele, 1997),[11] traumatic racial microaggressions in everyday experience (Sue et al., 2007), healthy cultural mistrust of societies with histories of slavery and oppression (Whaley, 2000, 2001), and the Westernization of mental illness (Watters, 2010). With each research domain, there is an implication that cultural-historical traumas are experienced on the individual level and that psychological structures directly relate to sociocultural ones. Part of Fanon's distinct approach, however, was to contribute understandings of what these traumas *mean* in the lives *and* worlds of the persons involved. Therefore, the extent to which various paradigms in psychology investigate experience, meaning, and social structure may determine whether they are able to access the complex lives, loves, and societal-level traumas in a manner like Fanon.

IMPLICATIONS FOR CRITICAL PRAXIS, OR CLINICAL PSYCHOPOLITICS

Fanon's approach to psychology carries implications for not only research, but also for critical practice, or praxis. As Fanon (1961/1963) stated, critical writing is done with the "intention of opening the future, as an invitation to action and a basis for hope" (p. 232). One of his major motivations was the possibility of healthy and harmonious racial relations (Fanon, 1952/1967, p. 80). Accordingly, Fanonian investigations contribute to the larger revolution in psychology in which, as Wertz (2011) suggests, methodological diversity is positioned to advance the urgent concerns of social justice and human liberation.

To begin this final discussion on praxis, I ask: What would a "clinical psychopolitics" look like? This question remains an open-ended one, but some suggestions will be offered here. Fanon provided evidence of the destruction inflicted by oppressive social structures, on both an individual and community level. Thus, "interventions" must operate at both levels. Fanon himself practiced a form of decolonized psychiatry characterized by "social" and "emancipatory" therapy in which community empowerment and the therapeutic relationship were emphasized; in addition, the culture of the institution respected and aligned with the culture of the person (Vergès, 1996). This type of psychiatry also respected the indigenous ways of addressing suffering (Bulhan, 1999; see also the indigenous psychology movement, Kim, Yang, and Hwang, 2006). However, at the same time Fanonian investigations call for an applied "mental health" that is not merely applied psychology but is one that also addresses the traumatizing social structures, racist narratives, and humiliating practices that suffocate human experience. This expanded concept of mental health dates back to scholar-practitioners like Erich Fromm (1956, 2006), who articulated the possibility of moving towards a loving society, that is, a mentally healthy one. Similarly, contemporary scholars have begun moving us towards psychologies of love, dignity, and liberation with a strong emphasis on culture and community (Davidson, 2011; Felder and Robbins, 2011; Lindner, 2010; Martín-Baró, 1994; O'Hara, 2010; Watkins and Schulman, 2008). Even the current evidence-based practice movement in psychology seeks to respect individuals' values, cultures, contexts, and experiences (APA Presidential Task Force on Evidence-Based Practice, 2006), but Fanonian investigations necessitate a radically expanded view of both evidence and practice, to say the least.

The liberation psychologist Ignacio Martín-Baró (1994), working in a Latin American context, warned against excessive individualizing that ignores pathological social realities. He instead argued for a praxis rooted partly in a non-psychologistic psychology that was at once personal, contextual, and historical. In the final analysis, Fanonian investigations too call for practices that do not colonize psyches or ignore social realities but instead deeply listen to, bear witness, collaborate, and eventually liberate people from the structures of oppression.

NOTES

1 This chapter reproduces the originally published article, with a few editorial changes.
2 I have updated the descriptions pertaining to the Black community from earlier translations of Fanon to reflect contemporary usage.
3 See Zakin (2002) for a concise description of Freud's concept of overdetermination.
4 See Gibson (2003), Gordon (1996), and Maldonado-Torres (2008), and of course the contributions of this edited collection, on Fanon as existential-phenomenological philosopher.
5 Jaspers' quote: "Comprehension in depth of a single instance will often enable us, phenomenologically, to apply this understanding in general to innumerable cases. Often what one has once grasped is soon met again. What is important in phenomenology is less the study of a large number of instances than the intuitive and deep understanding of a few individual cases" (Psychopathologie Générale, p. 49, as cited in Fanon, 1952/1967, pp. 168–169).
6 For reflections on Schutz's social psychology and science theory, see Embree (2003), and for interdisciplinary phenomenology more generally, see the work of the Interdisciplinary Coalition of North American Phenomenologists (http://www.icnap.org/).
7 Gordon (1996) articulated this racial-colonial process as the denial of human presence, a type of Sartrean bad faith.
8 See Drummond (2008) for a concise account of Husserl's notion of evidence.
9 Others have utilized Fanon's thought to elucidate a type of philosophical phenomenological reduction, but my concern here is delineating a type of "psychopolitical" phenomenological reduction. This psychopolitical reduction is akin to a kind of phenomenological attitude, described by Husserl and delineated for psychology/human science by Giorgi (2009) and others (e.g., Davidson, 2003; Wertz, 2010).
10 See Wertz (2010) on the utilization of various disciplinary "attitudes."
11 Steele (1997) referenced Fanon's (1952/1967) insights on the internalization of stereotypes as described in Black Skin, White Masks. Steele (1997) also framed his research with reference to the Sartrean (Sartre, 1946/1965) task of understanding human beings in situations.

REFERENCES

Adams, P. (1970). The social psychiatry of Frantz Fanon. *American Journal of Psychiatry, 127*(6), 809–814.

Allport, G. W. (1942). *The use of personal documents in psychological science.* (Bulletin 49). New York: Social Science Research Council.

American Psychological Association [APA] Presidential Task Force on Evidence-Based Practice. (2006). Evidence-based practice in psychology. *American Psychologist, 61*(4), 271–285.

Bernasconi, R. (2004). Identity and agency in Frantz Fanon [Sartre-Fanon symposium]. *Sartre Studies International, 10*(2), 106–109.

Bhabha, H. K. (1994). The Other question. In H. K. Bhabha (Ed.), *The location of culture* (pp. 94–120). London, UK: Routledge.

Bhabha, H. K. (2004). Foreword: Framing Fanon. In F. Fanon (Ed.), *The wretched of the Earth* (R. Philcox, Trans., pp. vii–xlii). New York: Grove. (Original work published 1961)

Bhatia, S. (2007). *American karma: Race, culture, and identity in the Indian diaspora.* New York: New York University Press.

Bulhan, H. A. (1985). *Frantz Fanon and the psychology of oppression.* New York: Plenum.

Bulhan, H. A. (1999). Revolutionary psychiatry of Fanon. In N. Gibson (Ed.), *Rethinking Fanon: The continuing dialog* (pp. 141–175). New York: Humanity Books.

Davidson, L. (2003). *Living outside mental illness: Qualitative studies of recovery in schizophrenia.* New York: NYU Press.

Davidson, L. (2011). Recovery from psychosis: What's love got to do with it? *Psychosis: Psychological, Social and Integrative Approaches, 3*(2), 105–114.

Davidson, L., & Cosgrove, L. A. (1991). Psychologism and phenomenological psychology revisited: I. The liberation from naturalism. *Journal of Phenomenological Psychology, 22*(2), 87–108.

Davidson, L., & Cosgrove, L. (2002). Psychologism and phenomenological psychology revisited: II. The return to positivity. *Journal of Phenomenological Psychology, 33*(2), 140–177.

Desai, M. U., Divan, G., Wertz, F. J., & Patel, V. (2012). The discovery of autism: Indian parents' experiences of caring for their child with an autism spectrum disorder. *Transcultural Psychiatry, 49*, 613–637.

Drummond, J. J. (2008). *Historical dictionary of Husserl's philosophy.* Lanham, MD: Scarecrow Press.

Embree, L. (2003). Reflective analysis in and of social psychology: A model for interdisciplinary phenomenology. In C-F. Cheung, I. Chvatik, I. Copoeru, L. Embree, J. Iribarne, & H. R. Sepp (Eds.), *Essays in celebration of the founding of the organization of phenomenological organizations.* Retrieved from http://www.lesterembree.net/ [Now available at: http://ipjp.org/images/e-books/OPO%20Essay%2010%20-%20%20Reflective%20Analysis%20in%20and%20of%20Social%20Psychology%20-%20By%20Lester%20Embree.pdf]

Erikson, E. H. (1950). *Childhood and society.* New York: Norton.

Fanon, F. (1963). *The wretched of the Earth* (C. Farrington, Trans.). New York: Grove. (Original work published 1961)

Fanon, F. (1967). *Black skin, White masks* (C. L. Markmann, Trans.). New York: Grove. (Original work published 1952)

Fanon, F. (2004). *The wretched of the Earth* (R. Philcox, Trans.). New York: Grove. (Original work published 1961)

Fanon, F. (2008). *Black skin, White masks* (R. Philcox, Trans.). New York: Grove. (Original work published 1952)

Felder, A. J., & Robbins, B. (2011). A cultural-existential approach to therapy: Merleau-Ponty's phenomenology of embodiment and its implications for practice. *Theory & Psychology, 21*, 355–376.

Freud, S., & Breuer, J. (2004). *Studies in hysteria* (N. Luckhurst, Trans.). New York: Penguin Books. (Original work published 1895)

Friedman, L. J. (1999). *Identity's architect: A biography of Erik H. Erikson.* Cambridge, MA: Harvard University Press.

Fromm, E. (1941). *Escape from freedom.* New York: Henry Holt and Company.

Fromm, E. (1956). *The art of loving.* New York: Harper & Row.

Fromm, E. (2006). *Beyond the chains of illusion: My encounter with Freud and Marx.* New York: Continuum.

Gaines, Jr., S. O. (1996). Perspectives of Du Bois and Fanon on the psychology of oppression. In L. R. Gordon, T. D. Sharpley-Whiting, & R. T. White (Eds.), *Fanon: A critical reader* (pp. 24–34). Cambridge, MA: Blackwell.

Geller, J. D., Norcross, J. C., & Orlinsky, D. E. (2005). The question of personal therapy: Introduction and prospectus. In J. D. Geller, J. C. Norcross, & D. E. Orlinsky (Eds.), *The psychotherapist's own psychotherapy: Patient and clinician perspectives* (pp. 3–11). New York: Oxford University Press.

Gibson, N. (Ed.). (1999a). *Rethinking Fanon: The continuing dialog.* New York: Humanity Books.

Gibson, N. (1999b). Introduction. In N. Gibson (Ed.), *Rethinking Fanon: The continuing dialog* (pp. 9–46). New York: Humanity Books.

Gibson, N. (2003). *Fanon: The postcolonial imagination.* Cambridge, UK: Polity.

Giorgi, A. (1970). *Psychology as a human science: A phenomenological approach.* New York: Harper & Row.

Giorgi, A. (2009). *The descriptive phenomenological method in psychology: A modified Husserlian approach.* Pittsburgh, PA: Duquesne University Press.

Gone, J. (2004). Mental health services for Native Americans in the 21st century United States. *Professional Psychology: Research and Practice, 35*(1), 10–18.

Gordon, L. R. (1996). The black and the body politic: Fanon's existential phenomenological critique of psychoanalysis. In L. R. Gordon, T. D. Sharpley-Whiting, & R. T. White (Eds.), *Fanon: A critical reader* (pp. 74–84). Cambridge, MA: Blackwell.

Gordon, L. R., Sharpley-Whiting, T. D., & White, R. T. (1996). Introduction: Five stages of Fanon studies. In L. R. Gordon, T. D. Sharpley-Whiting, & R. T. White (Eds.), *Fanon: A critical reader* (pp. 1–8). Cambridge, MA: Blackwell.

Hook, D. (2004). Fanon and the psychoanalysis of racism. *LSE Research Online.* Retrieved from http://eprints.lse.ac.uk/2567/

Hook, D. (2005). A critical psychology of the postcolonial. *Theory & Psychology, 15,* 475–503.

Hook, D. (2012). *A critical psychology of the postcolonial.* London, UK: Routledge.

Husserl, E. (1970a). *Logical investigations* (L. Findlay, Trans). London, UK: Routledge and Kegan Paul. (Original work published 1900–1901)

Husserl, E. (1970b). *The crisis of European sciences and transcendental phenomenology* (D. Carr, Trans.). Evanston, IL: Northwestern University Press. (Original work published 1954)

Husserl, E. (1977). *Phenomenological psychology* (J. Scanlon, Trans.). The Hague, Netherlands: Martinus Nijhoff.

Husserl, E. (1982). *Ideas pertaining to a pure phenomenology and to a phenomenological philosophy: First book. General introduction to a pure phenomenology* (F. Kersten, Trans.). The Hague: Martinus Nijhoff. (Original work published 1913)

Husserl, E. (1989). *Ideas pertaining to a pure phenomenology and to a phenomenological philosophy: Second book. Studies in the phenomenology of constitution* (R. Rojcewicz & A. Schuwer, Trans.). Dordrecht: Kluwer Academic Publishers. (Original work published 1952)

Judy, R. A. T. (1996). Fanon's body of black experience. In L. R. Gordon, T. D. Sharpley-Whiting, & R. T. White (Eds.), *Fanon: A critical reader* (pp. 53–73). Cambridge, MA: Blackwell.

Keller, R. C. (2007). Clinician and revolutionary: Frantz Fanon, biography, and the history of colonial medicine. *Bulletin of the History of Medicine, 81,* 823–841.

Kim, U., Yang, K.-S., & Hwang, K.-Ks. (2006). Contributions to indigenous and cultural psychology: Understanding people in context. In U. Kim, K.-S. Yang, & K.-K. Hwang (Eds.), *Indigenous and cultural psychology: Understanding people in context* (pp. 3–25). New York: Springer.

Kohut, H. (1979). The two analyses of Mr. Z. *International Journal of Psychoanalysis, 60,* 3–27.

Lebeau, V. (1998). Psychopolitics: Frantz Fanon's *Black Skin, White Masks.* In J. Campbell, & L. Harbord (Eds.), *Psycho-politics and cultural desires* (pp. 113–123). London, UK: UCL Press.

Lebeau, V. (2005). Children of violence. In M. Silverman (Ed.), *Frantz Fanon's Black skin, White masks* (pp. 128–145). Manchester, UK: Manchester University Press.

Lindner, E. (2010). *Gender, humiliation, and global security: Dignifying relationships from love, sex, and parenthood to world affairs.* Santa Barbara, CA: Praeger/ABC-CLIO.

Maldonado-Torres, N. (2008). *Against war: Views from the underside of modernity.* Durham, NC: Duke University Press.

Martín-Baró, I. (1994). *Writings for a liberation psychology.* Cambridge, MA: Harvard University Press.

Martinez, J. A. (2000). *Phenomenology of Chicana experience and identity: Communication and transformation in praxis.* Lanham, MD: Rowman & Littlefield.

McCulloch, J. (1983). *Black soul, white artifact: Fanon's clinical psychology and social theory.* Cambridge, UK: Cambridge University Press.

O'Hara, M. (1989). Person-centered approach as *conscientização*: The works of Carl Rogers and Paulo Freire. *Journal of Humanistic Psychology, 29*(1), 11–35.

O'Hara, M. (2010). Another inconvenient truth and the developmental role for psychology in a threatened world. *The Humanistic Psychologist, 38*(2), 101–119.

Ponterotto, J. G., Utsey, S. O., & Pedersen, P. B. (2006). *Preventing prejudice: A guide for counselors, educators, and parents* (2nd ed.). Thousand Oaks, CA: Sage.

Sartre, J.-P. (1965). *Anti-Semite and Jew.* New York: Schocken Books. (Original work published 1946)

Sartre, J.-P. (2004). Preface. In F. Fanon (Ed.), *The wretched of the Earth* (R. Philcox, Trans., pp. xliii–lxii). New York: Grove. (Original work published 1961)

Schutz, A. (1976). The stranger: An essay in social psychology. In A. Schutz & A. Brodersen (Ed.), *Collected papers: Vol. 2. Studies in social theory* (pp. 91–105). The Hague: Martinus Nijhoff.

Spiegelberg, H. (1972). *Phenomenology in psychology and psychiatry.* Evanston, IL: Northwestern University Press.

Steele, C. M. (1997). A threat in the air: How stereotypes shape intellectual identity and performance. *American Psychologist, 52*(6), 613–629.

Sue, D., Capodilupo, C. M., Torino, G. C., Bucceri, J. M., Holder, A. B., Nadal, K. L., & Esquilin, M. (2007). Racial microaggressions in everyday life: Implications for clinical practice. *American Psychologist, 62*(4), 271–286.

Utsey, S. O., Bolden, M. A., & Brown, A. L. (2001). Visions of revolution from the spirit of Frantz Fanon: A psychology of liberation for counseling African Americans confronting societal racism and oppression. In J. G. Ponterotto, J. M. Casas, L. A. Suzuki, & C. M. Alexander (Eds.), *Handbook of multicultural counseling* (2nd ed., pp. 311–336). Thousand Oaks, CA: Sage.

Vergès, F. (1996). To cure and to free: The Fanonian project of "decolonized psychiatry.". In L. R. Gordon, T. D. Sharpley-Whiting, & R. T. White (Eds.), *Fanon: A critical reader* (pp. 85–99). Cambridge, MA: Blackwell.

Watkins, M., & Schulman, H. (2008). *Toward psychologies of liberation.* New York: Palgrave McMillan.

Watters, E. (2010). *Crazy like us: The globalization of the American psyche.* New York: Free Press.

Wertz, F. J. (1986). Common methodological fundaments of the analytic procedures in phenomenological and psychoanalytic research. *Psychoanalysis and Contemporary Thought, 9*, 563–603.

Wertz, F. J. (1987). Meaning and research methodology: Psychoanalysis as a human science. *Methods, 1*(2), 91–135.

Wertz, F. J. (1993). The phenomenology of Sigmund Freud. *Journal of Phenomenological Psychology, 24*, 101–129.

Wertz, F. J. (2001). Humanistic psychology and the qualitative research tradition. In K. J. Schneider, J. F. T. Bugental, & J. F. Pierson (Eds.), *The handbook of humanistic psychology: Leading edges in theory, research, and practice* (pp. 231–246). Thousand Oaks, CA: Sage.

Wertz, F. J. (2010). The method of eidetic analysis for psychology. In T. F. Cloonan, & C. Thiboutot (Eds.), *The redirection of psychology: Essays in honor of Amedeo P. Giorgi* (pp. 261–278). Montréal, QC: Le Cercle Interdisciplinaire de Recherches Phénoménologiques (CIRP), l'Université du Québec.

Wertz, F. J. (2011). The qualitative revolution and psychology: Science, politics, and ethics. *The Humanistic Psychologist, 39*, 77–104.

Wertz, F. J., Charmaz, K., McMullen, L. M., Josselson, R., Anderson, R., & McSpadden, E. (2011). *Five ways of doing qualitative analysis: Phenomenological psychology, grounded theory, discourse analysis, narrative research, and intuitive inquiry.* New York: The Guilford Press.

Whaley, A. L. (2000). Cultural mistrust of White mental health clinicians among African Americans with severe mental illness. *American Journal of Orthopsychiatry, 71*(2), 252–256.

Whaley, A. L. (2001). Cultural mistrust: An important psychological construct for diagnosis and treatment of African Americans. *Professional Psychology: Research and Practice, 32*(6), 555–562.

Zakin, E. (2002). Overdetermination. In E. Erwin (Ed.), *The Freud encyclopedia: Theory, therapy, and culture* (pp. 406–407). New York: Routledge.

CHAPTER 5

FRANTZ FANON AND THE DECOLONIAL TURN IN PSYCHOLOGY

From Modern/Colonial Methods to the Decolonial Attitude

Nelson Maldonado-Torres

The idea of method as a guarantor of truth and knowledge in the sciences emerged from a certain confidence about the capacities of the cognitive subject and the status of the object, method being that which allows the subject to produce and secure true knowledge about the object – that is, objective knowledge. Psychology and the entire edifice of the social sciences were built on these foundations. With psychology, a peculiar terrain of reflection became gradually solidified: That where the human mind is not only the subject but also the object of scientific investigation.

The transformation of the subject into an object of scientific inquiry via specific methods led to multiple breakthroughs in the understanding of human beings, yet it had various risks that became realities. To start, Western methodic knowledge acquired normative status and led to the rejection or subordination of other forms of knowing. This is an important dimension of what some have referred to as epistemicide and epistemic colonization (Gordon, 2006; Lander, 2000; Santos, 2016). Then there was the extension of objectification from the area of knowledge to that of being, leading to what could be characterized as ontological colonization, which is part of the coloniality of being (Maldonado-Torres, 2007).

Epistemic and ontological colonization did not happen in isolation, nor were they merely contingent results of the search for objectivity through methodic science. More than mere risks, these forms of colonization were preconditions of the rise of modern psychology and the social sciences. They were not happening in isolation either: Undergirding them there was a more encompassing coloniality of being, power, and knowledge in the modern West (Lander, 2000; Mignolo and Escobar, 2010; Quijano, 2000; Walsh, 2005; Wynter, 2003).

This coloniality of being, power, and knowledge was grounded on the notions that humanity was unevenly divided among groups that appeared to be human and, furthermore, that the gap between these groups was Manichean in character (Fanon, 2004). This is arguably the foundation of the differentiation between the idea of human being as *humanitas* as opposed to human being as *anthropos*, the first one referring to human beings as subjects, and the other one to a sub-set of beings, for the most part in colonized territories, that may in some cases be formally classified as humans but are seen for the most part as lesser kind of beings, or as I would call them, entities that generate anxiety, fear, desire, and rage (Nishitani, 2006). This coloniality of being, power, and knowledge emerged and unfolded globally in the process of European expansion since at least the long sixteenth century (Quijano and Wallerstein, 1992).

DOI: 10.4324/9781003037132-5

The European Enlightenment involved a rationalization and secularization of the basic ideas and institutions that emerged in the process of the unfolding of modernity/coloniality, leading to new social formations and new sciences. Given the understanding of Man in the European Enlightenment and the decades that followed, the success of the science of the mind and of the social sciences in general depended on their ability, not only to bridge the distance between the subject and the object via the methodical production of knowledge, but also to further clarify and cement the notion of fundamental differences (differences of being and nature) between some humans who could properly occupy the position of subjects and others whose ontological status seemed closer to nature and were therefore destined to be, at best, objects of investigation. Method and science therefore played a role in securing the boundaries between populations that seemed to embody different levels of humanity. In this, modern science went hand in hand with modern colonialism. The effect of this coloniality of the modern human sciences was particularly felt in areas like psychology, whose goals were not only cognitive but also clinical: Coloniality shaping both the research and clinical practice of the science.

The Enlightened confident march of reason, linked to the production of what seemed like eternal Western empires in the nineteenth century, provided a solid ground for the coloniality of psychology and the human sciences, but it did not take long for the context to change quite radically. The combined effect of two World Wars, the holocaust, and the loss of colonies dramatically challenged some of the fundamental presuppositions of these sciences. These events led both to major critiques of modern rationality and the sciences in Europe, as well as to a massive decolonial turn outside Europe (Maldonado-Torres, 2006, 2011a, 2011b). Front and center in this decolonial turn was the psychiatrist, theorist, and political revolutionary Frantz Fanon, and his critique as well as creative recreation of psychology, philosophy, ethnography, and social study.

I will here explore some basic considerations of the Fanonian decolonial turn in psychology with reference to his critical engagement with the idea of method and the study of attitudes. For Fanon, attitudes are both a key object of study in the effort to understand the human being and to offer a prognosis of psychological maladies and a significant dimension in the production of knowledge and in the attention to epistemological problems that plague the modern cognitive and scientific subject. Fanon proposes, or so I will aim to show here with specific references to psychology, the primacy of attitude over method as part of his attempt to decolonize psychology, psychiatry, and the human sciences (on the roles of attitude in knowledge production, see also Maldonado-Torres, 2015). As I have put it elsewhere, Fanon's work approaches attitude as no less than "the dimension of the subject by virtue of which the subject can seek to challenge [established] knowledge, power, and being" (Maldonado-Torres, 2016, p. 23). A fundamental component of consciousness – as opposed to pure biology – attitude is key in the decolonial turn and the decoloniality of not only psychology but also knowledge, being, and power more generally.

A NOTE ON ATTITUDE

Before analyzing Fanon's approach to attitudes in relation to method, it is important to clarify that, for him, attitude is far from being simply a matter of subjective intention or purpose as opposed to structural conditions and power struggles. This would be a subjective, maybe psychological, reductionism of attitude. Fanon engages in a non-reductionistic psychology that, as we will see, is highly inter- and trans-disciplinary. Taking a different direction from psychological reductionism, Fanon approaches attitudes considering what he refers to as sociogeny, which accounts for the genesis of modes of subjectivity, meaning, and power relations with attention to the interplay between subjectivity and sociality (see Fanon, 2008, p. xv). For Fanon, social structures both reflect and reinforce collective attitudes, both of which play a role in the formation of subjectivity.

Subjectivity is, therefore, partly formed at the nexus of social structures and collective attitudes, which is why cultural and structural analysis are part of Fanon's psychology. He suggests as much not only in his definition of sociogeny but also in his description of the "collective unconscious" as not "inherited cerebral matter" but as "the repository of prejudices, myths, collective attitudes of a particular group" (Fanon, 2008, p. 165). However, cultural and structural analyses are not enough to explore the fundamental role of attitudes in the formation of subjectivity, of collectives, and of structures. For this, Fanon takes a philosophical approach that considers the role of attitudes in the formation of subjectivity as subjects relate to basic aspects of human experience: embodiment, intersubjective contact (via language and love), time, and space (Maldonado-Torres, 2016). Time, space, embodied subjectivity, and intersubjectivity play a key role in the formation of what is often defined as Being. From this perspective, attitude is, therefore, not only connected to knowledge production, as the exploration of the relation between attitude and method in the sciences has it, but also to the very production of being, which is why Fanon engages in a critique of ontology and dedicates a section of a chapter to a critical review of Hegel's account of the relation between the master and the slave (see Fanon, 2008, p. 191). Fanon's approach to attitude is, therefore, as I already pointed out, far from a form of psychological reductionism. It reflects a view of the subject as dynamic inter-relationality and therefore as always-already part of a larger field of social and cultural arrangements.

In addition to knowledge and being, attitudes are connected to action. Fanon considers this approach crucial in the goal of identifying ways in which subjects can become healthy, by which Fanon means, actional. As Fanon (2008, p. 197) puts it, "To induce man to be actional, by maintaining in his circularity the respect of the fundamental values that make the world human, that is the task of utmost urgency for he who, after careful reflection, prepares to act." Fanon endeavors to identify the kind of attitude that can lead subjects to become agents in a process that involves the rehumanization of the world: Individuality, the family, and society. For this, he examines the ways in which subjects position themselves with respect to the basic aspects of human reality that I have already mentioned (body, Other, language, etc.) and the horizons of possibility (in time and space) that open in certain ways or close depending on such attitudes. Attitude is that which prepares subjects to act or not to act, as well as to act or react in particular ways, including in the task of producing knowledge.

Fanon (2008), then, seeks to identify the basic components of an attitude that can lead human beings to become agents, both in thinking and practice, in a context that persists in understanding and organizing humanity in terms of the production of boundaries that segregate human beings and that deprive subjects and groups of a proper experience of spatiality, temporality, and intersubjective relations. This decolonial attitude is as much about decolonizing the sciences (conceptions of subject, object, and method) as about decolonizing society and the world (the world understood as both existing structures and the horizon of possibilities) through forms of individual and collective agency that lead to health in subjects and communities. Fanon's attention to attitudes, then, far from representing an evasion of responsibility and action by a focus on feelings and intentions, is an indispensable part of re-evolutionary work, by which I mean the re-introduction of human temporality

into the life of embodied subjects and society within an also re-humanized space that is
conducive to intersubjective interactions beyond coloniality and all kind of dehumanizing
lines of differentiation as those that are produced in epistemological and ontological colonization. This explains his focus on attitude and his critique of method.

ATTITUDE AND METHOD IN FANON'S
BLACK SKIN, WHITE MASKS

> It is good form to introduce a work in psychology with a statement of its methodological
> point of view. I shall be derelict. I leave methods to the botanists and the mathematicians.
> There is a point at which methods devour themselves.
> I should like to start from there. I shall try to discover the various attitudes that the Negro
> adopts in contact with white civilization.
>
> *(Fanon, 1968, p. 12; see a different translation of the passage in*
> *Fanon, 2008, p. xvi)*

Given the extent to which the social sciences have tended to differentiate themselves from
the humanities and claimed their right to the label of science by virtue of their methods,
one could hypothesize that Fanon's break with the usual practice of introducing a work
in psychology with a statement on its methods played a role in *Black Skin, White Masks* not
being accepted as his doctoral dissertation. After all, his main advisor, Jean Dechaume,
"was interested solely in psychosurgery, and he viewed things through a neuropsychiatric
lens that attributed all psychiatric conditions to organic origins" (Cherki, 2006, p. 17).
Fanon took a completely different approach, his early manuscript of *Black Skin, White Masks*
causing "quite a scandal" (Cherki, 2006, p. 18). This was the reaction to the manuscript
in the early stages, before Fanon developed his position further considering that he "could
not ignore certain elements, [that] however psychological they may be ... generate consequences in the realm of other sciences" (Fanon, 2008, p. 32). The final version of *Black Skin,
White Masks* was therefore even more critical of psychological reductionism than the copy
that led to its rejection as a thesis.

If one considers works such as Galton's (1869/1892) *Hereditary Genius*, which pioneered
quantitative methods in psychology to engage in investigations that would "conclude" that
"the range of mental power between – I will not say the highest Caucasian and the lowest
savage – but between the greatest and least of English intellects, is enormous" (Galton,
1869/1892, p. 26) and which would therefore justify racial inferiority, there should have
been no surprise that Fanon was skeptical of methods. But Fanon's view on methods can
also be explained with reference to other approaches that were not at least explicitly racial,
but still referred to the natural sciences and mathematics as exemplars of a norm.

Just five years after Galton's *Hereditary Genius* was published, Franz Brentano (2015), in
his Foreword to the 1874 edition of his influential *Psychology from an Empirical Point of View*,
stated that

> Our most urgent need in psychology is not the variety and universality of the tenets, but
> rather the unity of the doctrine. Within this framework we must strive to attain what first
> mathematics and then physics, chemistry, and physiology have already attained, i.e. a core
> of generally accepted truths capable of attracting to it contributions from all other fields of
> scientific endeavor. We must seek to establish a single unified science of psychology in place
> of the many psychologies we now have.
>
> *(p. xix)*

In this spirit, at the start of his reflections on "Psychological Method with Special Reference to Its Experiential Basis," Brentano calls attention to the relation between psychology and mathematics. He writes that

> Scientists have begun to pay very special attention to the method of psychology. In fact you could say that no other general theoretical sciences are as noteworthy and instructive in this regard as psychology, on the one hand, and mathematics, on the other.
>
> *(Brentano, 2015, p. 28)*

In line with his mention of mathematics in the Foreword, Brentano adds that "mathematics reveals in clear and understandable ways the fundamental nature of all true scientific investigation" (Brentano, 2015, p. 28). Yet, he also reserves a very special place for psychology:

> Psychology alone, on the other hand, demonstrates all the richness to which scientific method lends itself, by seeking to adapt itself to successively more and more complex phenomena. The two together shed light on the methods of investigation which are employed by the intermediary sciences.
>
> *(Brentano, 2015, p. 28)*

Brentano, taking mathematics as the model for science and method, posits psychology at the opposite end within the same conception of scientific inquiry. In doing this, Brentano (2015) was counting that the "scientific method" could "adapt itself" continuously as it faced "successively more and more complex phenomena." But what if the complexity of "phenomena" turned to be such that it defied this primacy of method? Ironically, it was Brentano's own contribution to the understanding of "phenomena" that led to what perhaps became the greatest challenge to his presupposition about the nature and scope of mathematics and scientific methodology (what Fanon referred to as "the botanists and the mathematicians," 2008, p. xvi). The challenge came from phenomenology and from phenomenological hermeneutics.

Phenomenology built from Brentano's idea of the intentionality of consciousness (the idea that consciousness is always the consciousness of something) and, through the writings of Edmund Husserl and then more radically Jean-Paul Sartre, it became more a description and critical analysis of the "attitudes" that consciousness takes in the face of objects, leading to the constitution of the meaning of "phenomena," than an attempt to make of psychology a unified science. Husserl saw his phenomenology as an effort to establish a form of philosophy as a "rigorous science" (Husserl, 1981), yet his analysis of attitudes led him to consider the natural sciences less as paradigms of rationality, and more as peculiar extensions of a "natural attitude" that limited the exploration and proper consideration of consciousness and phenomena (Husserl, 1970). With Sartre, whose work informed Fanon's, even the idea of "rigorous science" took the back seat, and philosophical anthropology became the primary concern (see, for example, Sartre, 1966).

Sartre's (1966) philosophical anthropology focused on the description and analysis of attitudes, starting with a general and overarching attitude of self-deception to which he referred to as bad faith. For Sartre (1966),

> It is best to choose and to examine one determined attitude which is essential to human reality and which is such that consciousness instead of directing its negation outward turns it toward itself. This attitude, it seems to me, is *bad faith (mauvaise foi)*.
>
> *(p. 48)*

In bad faith, consciousness deceives itself about itself and engages in projects that seek to maintain such deception. Sartre's *Being and Nothingness*, where he elaborates this perspective, reads less as a confident, if not triumphant, celebration of the scientific search for truth and of the Western idea of method, and more as an attempt to identify deception and lies.

Fanon's work is closer to Sartre, with its goal of identifying forms of self-deception, than to Brentano's emphasis on further solidifying methods and securing scientific truths. Both Sartre's and Fanon's work reflect a situation where faith in scientific truth and methods was arguably getting in the way of critique. But for Fanon it is clear that modern colonialism and its multiple modalities of knowledge, being, and power (i.e., coloniality) presents as strong or even more of a challenge to critical reflection as scientificism. This is something that Fanon took neither from Descartes nor from Sartre, but from his Martiniquean teacher Aimé Césaire. The initial epigraph in *Black Skin*, taken from Césaire's (2000) *Discourse on Colonialism*, suggests as much. Césaire's *Discourse on Colonialism* can be interpreted as a critical response to Descartes's own *Discourse on Method* (Maldonado-Torres, 2006), also focusing on deception and self-deception, but with particular attention to genocidal lies that ontologize and naturalize colonialism and similar views of human difference. The result is that rather than taking authenticity, absolute truth, or even "rigorous science" as goals, Fanon focuses on liberation and decolonization as indispensable areas for any discourse about the former. In that sense, decolonization takes the form of first philosophy.

Fanon's rejection of absolute truths might be linked, as I have noted already, to the suspension of methods, as methods are often conceived as the guarantor of repetition of results, prediction, and truths. Yet, Fanon nonetheless states that: "The attitudes I propose describing are true. I have found them any number of times" (Fanon, 2008, p. 16). This passage conveys the idea that there might be truths that become evident through descriptions, different from the presumably "absolute truths" that are asserted through methods. This is a theme that became central in hermeneutic phenomenology, such as it appears in Hans Georg Gadamer's *Truth and Method*.

In *Truth and Method*, Gadamer (2004) argues that

> The hermeneutic phenomenon is basically not a problem of method at all. It is not concerned with a method of understanding by means of which texts are subjected to scientific investigation like all other objects of experience. It is not concerned primarily with amassing verified knowledge, such as would satisfy the methodological ideal of science – yet it too is concerned with knowledge and with truth. In understanding tradition not only are texts understood, but insights are acquired and truths known. But what kind of knowledge and what kind of truth?
>
> *(p. xx)*

Gadamer (2004) refers to a hermeneutics of texts, while Fanon engages in a hermeneutics of lived experience (although also of texts as part of this larger endeavor). Both Gadamer and Fanon struggled with the tension between truths that emerge through "description" and the knowledge obtained and preserved through methods, leading them to different types of hermeneutics and to an appreciation of language and literature. The link between literature and phenomenological description is already established (see, for example, Gosetti, 2001), and Fanon himself uses cultural and cinematic texts in his effort to describe the attitudes of Black subjects. That Fanon (2008) saw the value in language and literature is evinced in his own literary production as well as in his examination of language in the first chapter of *Black Skin, White Masks* where he states,

> We attach a fundamental importance to the phenomenon of language and consequently consider the study of language essential for providing us with one element in understanding

the black man's dimension of being-for-others, it being understood that to speak is to exist absolutely for the other.

(p. 1)

Furthermore, Fanon states in *Black Skin, White Masks* that "The structure of the present work is grounded in temporality" (Fanon, 2008, p. xvi), and while time is usually associated with history, it is also equally central in the understanding of narrative (Ricoeur, 1984).

Where Fanon departs from Gadamer is not so much in the appreciation of the value of texts and in the skepticism toward methods that emerges out of the appreciation of phenomenological description and hermeneutical understanding, but in the view of "tradition." For, when Gadamer asks "what kind of knowledge and what kind of truth" are proper to the insights acquired in "understanding tradition" (Gadamer, 2004, p. xx), Fanon would have added the question: "what tradition?" Consider that given the predominance of anti-Blackness in the European tradition that informed Fanon's work and the European sciences, Fanon would not have even started a book describing the attitudes of Black subjects or exploring the "lived experience of the black" (Fanon, 2008, p. 89) in any scientific investigation. If he had, his scientific pursuit would have been limited to observing Black subjects as pathologies. Additionally, because of the links of the modern conception of Blackness with colonialism and slavery, Black subjects have a different relation with tradition than what Gadamer's (2004) hermeneutics would seem to pose if directly applied to Black subjects: Black people are often as banned from any true relation of kinship as they are from belonging to a tradition (Hartman, 1997; Spillers, 1987). Instead of finding a home in tradition, they have to get used to being banned from any legitimate tradition and are put in the position of trying to reconstruct some version of tradition, never certain of the success of the enterprise and always sure that the result will never amount to a legitimate construct.

Fanon's research does not aspire to produce "absolute truths" to be sustained by scientific methods just as he cannot rely on a hermeneutics of experience with reference to tradition to convey the things that he thinks need to be said (Fanon, 2008, p. xi). Instead, he focuses on the failures of Black subjects in becoming what they are, that is, human beings. Or rather, in *Black Skin, White Masks* he provides a narrative ("grounded [like literary narrative often is] in temporality") (Fanon, 2008, p. xvi) that will take the reader through a voyage that goes from the description of self-denial among Black subjects in the first three chapters to the rise and fall of the Black intellectual's dominant attitudes in the fifth chapter up to the birth of a new, decolonial, attitude at the end of the fifth chapter and through the rest of the book. This study in the form of a narrative offers descriptions (typical of the humanities) as well as providing explanations (typical of the social sciences), but the main goal is clinical.[1] As Fanon puts it, "This book is a clinical study. Those who recognize themselves in it will, I believe, have made a step in the right direction" (Fanon, 2008, p. xvi).

Fanon's description of attitudes (in chapters 1 to 5) and his explanations (in chapters 6 and 7) are meant to serve as a window as well as a mirror to the reader: A window to the lived experience of Black subjects and to the uncovering of dehumanizing behavior in whites, and a mirror that can reflect attitudes that the readers take in the world. The goal is to "get my brother, black or white, to shake off the dust from that lamentable livery built up over centuries of incomprehension" (Fanon, 2008, p. xvi). The result of "shaking off" this "dust" that often goes as tradition but that Fanon describes as "centuries of incomprehension" is less the attainment of a particular truth or a method, and more a radical change in attitude. That is, the narrative focused on the description and explanation of attitudes is structured so as to facilitate or provoke the emergence of a new, decolonial, form of attitude. The goal of this attitude is "nothing less than to liberate the black man from himself" (Fanon, 2008, p. xii).

FROM THE MODERN/COLONIAL TO THE DECOLONIAL ATTITUDE

In face of the entire arrangement of modernity/coloniality, Fanon's cure of the colonized, but also of psychology, psychiatry, and the human sciences involves, not the application of specific methods, nor the understanding of tradition, but the cultivation of a decolonial attitude, which is profoundly epistemological as well as ethical, political, and aesthetic. This is an attitude of comprehension or understanding that involves the proper description and explanation of attitudes. The opposite of this form of comprehension is deception and self-deception, which connects with the analysis of bad faith and with Césaire's assessment of Western civilization and the modern human sciences (see Césaire, 2000; Gordon, 1995; Sartre, 1966). Fanon makes a call and engages in the decolonization of both the subject and the object of psychology, and he spells out implications for psychology as a scientific enterprise and a clinical practice. This is why philosophy and psychology become very close in Fanon's work, and why he continued to do theoretical work alongside his medical practice.

The questioning attitude of the psychologist who seeks to "understand" rather than to punish is part of a more general decolonial attitude of questioning that Fanon proposes, through the critical engagement with psychology and psychiatry, for the entire range of the human sciences. In "The North African Syndrome" he states that

> It must be possible ... to describe an initial, a basic dimension of all human problems. More precisely, it would seem that all the problems which man faces on the subject of man can be reduced to this one question:
> "Have I not, because of what I have done or failed to do, contributed to an impoverishment of human reality?"
> The question could also be formulated in this way:
> "Have I at all times demanded and brought out the man that is in me?"
> *(Fanon, 1988, p. 3)*

Fanon here radically counters the logic of the modern/colonial attitude and its constant questioning of the full humanity of the colonized. In face of colonization and dehumanization, Fanon rather suggests that the cognitive subjects/scientists/therapists direct the question about the presence and lack of humanity to themselves. That is, the attitude of comprehension or understanding requires that the subjects of knowledge question themselves, not about the humanity of others, but about the extent to which they are expressing their own humanity. One's humanity, in turn, is expressed when one re-claims the subjects and peoples that one encounters in the world and who live in precarious conditions.

Reclamation of sub-others is a decolonial attitude of "love and understanding" that is crucial in the task of epistemic and ontological decolonization. It is an epistemic (as well as ethical, social, and political) attitude that must not be subordinated to the desire for recognition, or to method. Fanon makes these points in the final lines of the essay, now directly questioning the interlocutor and giving us a better sense of what he had in mind with the idea of "building the world of YOU" at the conclusion of *Black Skin, White Masks*.

> If YOU do not reclaim the man who is before you, how can I assume that you reclaim the man that is in you?

If YOU do not want the man who is before you, how can I believe the man that is perhaps in you?

If YOU do not demand the man, if YOU do not sacrifice the man that is in you so that the man who is on this earth shall be more than a body, more than a Mohammed, by what conjurer's trick will I have to acquire the certainty that you, too, are worthy of my love?

(Fanon, 1988, p. 16)

"The North African Syndrome" helps to explain the meaning and significance of the reference to the world of YOU in *Black Skin, White Masks*. The world of YOU is one where subjects treat others as YOUs, instead of as "the black" or "Mohammed," and where they struggle to make this world a reality. It is in the gift of the self beyond recognition where Fanon finds the core of the decolonial attitude and the true meaning of human subjectivity, intersubjectivity, and community, the maintenance of which is crucial for the proper production of knowledge beyond the confines of any tradition or the strictures of any given method. This is also where the decolonial search for knowledge, decolonial ethics and politics, and decolonial creative activity find a common nexus.

It is not a coincidence that "The North African Syndrome" and *Black Skin, White Masks* engage in non-reductionistic psychology/philosophy/sociogeny and that they were published in the original French in the same year (1952). The pairing of these texts helps make clear that *Black Skin, White Masks* is as much about the understanding of the devastating effects of anti-Black racism and colonialism in the development of identity and personality, social formations, culture, and knowledge, as about the fragile and difficult emergence of a decolonial attitude of love and understanding that involves the reclamation of sub-others in the effort to counter epistemic and ontological colonization, along with the coloniality of knowledge, being, and power. Without this attitude, both tradition and methods, to the extent that they are relevant, along with the sciences and approaches based on them, become vehicles of coloniality. The decolonial attitude, along with the actions that it promotes, appears then as a sort of cure to epistemic and ontological colonization in the modern/colonial world. A decolonial psychology, linked with other fields as well as with social and artistic movements, can greatly contribute to the understanding and further propagation of this cure.

NOTE

1 Consider Lewis Gordon's reading of *Black Skin, White Masks* in relation to the mythopoethics of hell in Dante Alighieri's *Inferno* (Gordon, 2015, p. 23).

REFERENCES

Brentano, F. (2015). *Psychology from an empirical standpoint*. London, UK: Routledge.
Césaire, A. (2000). *Discourse on colonialism*. New York: Monthly Review Press.
Cherki, A. (2006). *Frantz Fanon: A portrait*. Ithaca, NY: Cornell University Press.
Fanon, F. (1968). *Black skin, White masks*. New York: Grove Press.
Fanon, F. (1988). *Toward the African revolution: Political essays*. New York: Grove Press.
Fanon, F. (2004). *The wretched of the Earth*. New York: Grove Press.
Fanon, F. (2008). *Black skin, White masks*. New York: Grove Press.

Gadamer, H. G. (2004). *Truth and method*. London, UK: Continuum.

Galton, F. (1892). *Hereditary genius: An inquiry into its laws and consequences*. London, UK: Macmillan. (Original work published 1869)

Gordon, L. R. (1995). *Bad faith and antiblack racism*. Atlantic Highlands, NJ: Humanities Press.

Gordon, L. R. (2006). African-American philosophy, race, and the geography of reason. In L. Gordon & J. A. Gordon (Eds.), *Not only the master's tools: Theoretical explorations in African American Studies* (pp. 3–50). Boulder, CO: Paradigm Press.

Gordon, L. R. (2015). *What Fanon said: A philosophical introduction to his life and thought*. New York: Fordham University Press.

Gosetti, J. A. (2001). Phenomenological literature: From the natural attitude to 'recognition'. *Philosophy Today, 45*, 18–27.

Hartman, S. V. (1997). *Scenes of subjection: Terror, slavery, and self-making in nineteenth-century America*. New York: Oxford University Press.

Husserl, E. (1970). *The crisis of European sciences and transcendental phenomenology*. Evanston, IL: Northwestern University Press.

Husserl, E. (1981). Philosophy as rigorous science. In P. McCormick & F. A. Elliston (Eds.), *Husserl: Shorter works* (pp. 166–197). Notre Dame, IN: University of Notre Dame Press.

Lander, E. (Ed.). (2000). *La colonialidad del saber: Eurocentrismo y ciencias sociales. Perspectivas latinoamericanas*. Buenos Aires: El Consejo Latinoamericano de Ciencias Sociales.

Maldonado-Torres, N. (2006). Césaire's gift and the decolonial turn. *Radical Philosophy Review, 9*, 111–137.

Maldonado-Torres, N. (2007). On the coloniality of being: Contributions to the development of a concept. *Cultural Studies, 21*, 240–270.

Maldonado-Torres, N. (2011a). El pensamiento filosófico del "giro descolonizador" [The philosophical thought of the 'decolonizing turn']. In D. Enrique, M. Eduardo, & B. Carmen (Eds.), *El pensamiento filosófico latinoamericano, del Caribe y "Latino" (1300–2000)* [Latin American, Caribbean, and Latino philosophical thought (1300-2000)] (pp. 683–697). Mexico City: Siglo Veintiuno Editores.

Maldonado-Torres, N. (2011b). Thinking through the decolonial turn: Post-continental interventions in theory, philosophy, and critique: An introduction. *Transmodernity: Journal of Peripheral Cultural Production of the Luso-Hispanic World, 1*(2), 1–15.

Maldonado-Torres, N. (2015). Transdisciplinariedad y decolonialidad. *Quaderna*. Retrieved from http:// quaderna.org/?p=418

Maldonado-Torres, N. (2016). Outline of ten theses on coloniality and decoloniality. Foundation Frantz Fanon. Retrieved from http://frantzfanonfoundation-fondationfrantzfanon.com/article2360.html

Mignolo, W., & Escobar, A. (Eds.). (2010). *Globalization and the decolonial option*. London, UK: Routledge.

Nishitani, O. (2006). Anthropos and humanitas: Two Western concepts of "human being." In N. N. Sakai & J. Solomon (Eds.), *Translation, biopolitics, colonial difference* (pp. 259–274). Aberdeen: Hong Kong University Press.

Quijano, A. (2000). Coloniality of power, eurocentrism, and Latin America. *Nepantla: Views from South, 1*, 533–580.

Quijano, A., & Wallerstein, I. (1992). Americanity as a concept, or the Americas in the modern world-system. *International Social Science Journal, 44*, 549–557.

Ricoeur, P. (1984). *Time and narrative*. Chicago, IL: The University of Chicago Press.

Santos, B. de S. (2016). *Epistemologies of the South: Justice against epistemicide*. New York: Routledge.

Sartre, J.-P. (1966). *Being and nothingness: A phenomenological essay on ontology*. New York: Washington Square Press.

Spillers, H. (1987). Mama's baby, papa's maybe: An American grammar book. *Diacritics, 17,* 264–281.

Walsh, C. (Ed.). (2005). *Pensamiento crítico y matriz (de)colonial: Reflexiones latinoamericanas [Critical thinking and (de)colonial matrix: Latin American reflections]*. Quito, Ecuador: Editorial Universidad Andina Simón Bolivar.

Wynter, S. (2003). Unsettling the coloniality of being/power/truth/freedom: Towards the human, after man, its overrepresentation – An argument. *The New Centennial Review, 33,* 257–337.

CHAPTER 6

FRANTZ FANON AND PSYCHOPATHOLOGY

The Progressive Infrastructure of
Black Skin, White Masks

Robert Bernasconi

Frantz Fanon's writings, like his life, were a call to action, a call that still resonates today, but the arguments that he used to promote action –or *praxis* as he preferred to call it in key moments of *The Wretched of the Earth*[1] –are not always understood in all their complexity. I largely confine myself here to clarifying the overall argument of his first book, *Black Skin, White Masks*. I will focus on the book's sixth chapter, "The Negro and Psychopathology," as I believe it is the key chapter. The book's original title, before Francis Jeanson proposed a change, was *Essay on the Disalienation of the Black Man*.[2] In keeping with the original title, Fanon described *Black Skin, White Masks* as "a mirror with a progressive infrastructure where the black man can find the path to disalienation."[3] That is to say, the reader –and for reasons I will explain, particularly the Black man as reader –is invited to follow a progressive path. This gives the book its *dialectical* structure (to employ a term Fanon himself made use of on several occasions), but one must always be aware of the point within the overall argument in which any one of Fanon's dramatic and eminently quotable lines is to be found. As I proceed, I will give some examples of claims that Fanon makes that some of his commentators have treated as if they were his final view, when in fact they are modified or even reversed by him later in the book.

Fanon published *Black Skin, White Masks* when he was only 27 years old. In the previous year he had submitted his dissertation at the University of Lyon medical school under the title "Mental Alterations, Character Modifications, Psychic Disorders and Intellectual Deficit in Spinocerebellar Heredodegeneration."[4] The dissertation helps our reading of *Black Skin, White Masks* insofar as it shows his preoccupation with unpicking the links between hereditary neurological disturbance and the psychiatric symptoms to which it gives rise under specific social and cultural conditions. Much of *Black Skin, White Masks* is a continuation of this polemic. It takes the form of an attack on the way many psychological accounts emphasize biology and heredity at the expense of the social dimension of existence.[5]

I am not going to address the vexed question of the role of women, and especially Black women, in Fanon's account because it is a subject of its own and by no means an easy one to negotiate. The strategy of concealing the problem by assuming that whenever he says *le Noir* he means both men and women will not work in every case, and I will avoid doing so here. When Fanon used the term *le Noir*, I will usually translate it as "the Black man" even though it is only in some cases that one can be sure that he meant specifically to exclude women from the descriptions that follow, and so in other cases the translation is over determined. But there is another translation issue that is at least equally offensive to our ears, if not more so. He frequently used the term *le Nègre*, which I will translate as "the Negro," because on certain occasions the distinction between *le Noir* and *le Nègre* is important. Fanon frequently, although not always, uses *le Nègre* with all its negative connotations, not as a

DOI: 10.4324/9781003037132-6

synonym, but to highlight how Blacks are seen by whites in a racist context. On this, as on many points, neither the Markmann translation, nor the Philcox translation, are remotely adequate. [6]

Fanon's starting point was that one must never lose sight of the role of society, not just culturally but also economically.[7] Contrary to the exaggerated focus on the individual that he associated with Sigmund Freud, Fanon's own position was that "the alienation of the black man is not an individual question." He believed that genuine disalienation would occur only when "*in the most materialist sense*" things had resumed their rightful place.[8] In other words, one cannot address the psychological problems facing Blacks by relying only on psychology to the neglect of the other sciences.[9] He explained at the end of chapter 3: "We shall see that another solution is possible. It implies restructuring the world."[10]

This solution was predicated on the conviction that psychological problems were not hereditary, but were caused by the environment. For that reason, significant portions of the book were devoted to combating the way in which, in much of the psychological literature, problems that were caused by the environment and its culture were being misattributed both explicitly and implicitly to the patient's constitution. That was the theme of chapter 2 of *Black Skin, White Masks* where he posed the question of "whether the *basic personality* is a constant or a variable."[11] At the same time Fanon sought to show the inapplicability of standard theories to Blacks. One would never guess from the secondary literature that the primary purpose of his discussion of Mayotte Capecia's novels, a discussion that has caused heated debate, was largely directed at showing that the withdrawal of the ego, which Anna Freud described as "a normal stage" in the development of the ego, is impossible for Blacks because they seek white approval.[12] Turning to Abdoulaye Sadji's novel *Nini*, which in its first incomplete version was published in installments in *Présence Africaine*, Fanon highlighted how its heroine, Dedee, gained white approval through marriage.[13] (Fanon called this particular form of abnormal behavior which supported Dedee "affective erethism," with the implication again that this was "a cultural phenomenon" and not something constitutive.[14])

Similarly, when in the third chapter Fanon gave a reading of *Un homme pareil aux autres* (*A Man Like the Others*), Rene Maran's semi-autobiographical novel, it was primarily the occasion for him to demonstrate that, even if a problem with a patient persists after a change of environment, it does not prove the environment was not the main cause.[15] Maran's hero, Jean Veneuse, wonders whether he has not been betrayed by everyone around him, both by the whites who deny him recognition as one of their own and by the Blacks who repudiate him.[16] But by reading the novel through the lens supplied by Germaine Guex's *The Abandonment Neurosis*, Fanon showed that Veneuse's sense of betrayal is nothing other than a classic symptom of the negative-aggressive type.[17] On this basis Fanon sought to demonstrate that the changes Veneuse prescribed for himself were intended only to corroborate his externalizing neurosis.[18] Fanon described Veneuse as someone who is "accidentally black" but who is a neurotic who needs to be released from his infantile fantasies.[19] In other words, the novels of Capecia, Sadji, and Maran were not Fanon's real subjects; their books were merely the backdrop of an engagement with the psychological literature in service of the larger issue of improving understanding between Blacks, as well as between Blacks and whites.

The most egregious error in the psychological literature that Fanon wanted to expose in the book's early chapters was represented by Octave Mannoni's *Prospero and Caliban*, explored in chapter 4. Mannoni, drawing on the theories of Alfred Adler, placed responsibility for the colonization of the Malagasy not so much on the colonizers as on the dependency complex that he attributed to the Malagasy themselves.[20] Fanon returned to this critique in chapter 7, where he suggested that an Adlerian would conclude from a reading of Mannoni that the Malagasy should accept their place in society and not strive for anything else.[21] Fanon believed that the error arose from an insistence on locating psychological problems in the individual, whereas "in some circumstances the *socius* is more important than the individual."[22] In support of this conclusion Fanon cited Pierre Naville's critique of Sigmund Freud, according to which the real conditions in which the individual's sexuality is expressed are explained by the economic and social conditions of the class struggle.[23] Hence Fanon's judgment in the context of his reading of Mannoni that "Freud's discoveries are of no use to us whatsoever."[24] This is one of the basic themes of the book. Fanon made a similar critique when, in the context of his reading of Lacan's account of the mirror stage, he announced that he had already demonstrated that for the Black man, as compared with the white man, one must take into account historical and economic realities.[25] Echoing what he had written at the end of chapter 3, the main conclusion of chapter 4 was that the source of the conflict lay not in the dependency complex but in the social structure –the solution therefore was to change it.[26]

Chapter 5, "The Lived Experience of the Black," is the most accessible and best-known chapter in Fanon's book. It was originally published as a stand-alone essay,[27] but when read in isolation it is misleading for three reasons. First, it exaggerates Fanon's distance from Sartre as I have explained elsewhere.[28] Secondly, it ends with the words "I began to weep," thereby giving a false impression of where Fanon ended up;[29] this is especially clear if one compares it with the calls for action as well as the more hopeful tone adopted at the end of the book where he asked the reader to feel the open dimension of every consciousness.[30] Above all, thirdly, the fifth chapter highlights the lived experience of the individual at the expense of the individual's social and economic context and so, when read in isolation, runs counter to the main thrust of *Black Skin, White Masks*.

The fifth chapter is not my main topic here, but for the sake of my theme of the progressive structure of the book it is important to make one observation. In "Black Orpheus," a preface written for Léopold Sédar Senghor's *Anthologie de la nouvelle poésie nègre et malgache de langue française*, Sartre, taking his cue from some of the Marxist poets anthologized there, applied the dialectic, conceived in a somewhat elementary and vulgar form to make the point that Blacks were called upon to sacrifice their negritude in favor of "the realization of the human in a raceless society."[31] Every reader of *Black Skin, White Masks* seems to remember that this led Fanon to say that "Jean-Paul Sartre has destroyed black enthusiasm";[32] but, in part because of the poor translations, few English-speaking readers realize that Fanon himself had already in the preface warned against enthusiasm.[33] These same commentators also tend not even to comment on the fact that what Sartre had destroyed was described by Fanon himself as an illusion, an "unthinking position."[34] Certainly there is a criticism of Sartre here, but it largely derives from the fact that Sartre was white and so could forget that "the negro suffers in his body differently than the White."[35] In other words, in Fanon's view, Sartre was in no place to make the comment.[36] Most commentators assume that Fanon was saying Sartre should not have applied the dialectic so as to look beyond the present to a time when negritude had given way to a society without race. They ignore Fanon's statement in chapter 6, where he says very clearly in the context of a reading of Aimé Césaire "we can understand why Sartre sees in the black poets' Marxist stand the logical end to negritude."[37] The point is that Fanon's dramatic rejection of "Black Orpheus" is only one stage on the reader's journey, one that he explicitly re-evaluated later.

Another aspect of the book's progressive structure is revealed when one compares the provisional claim at the end of the second chapter that both Freud and Adler would "help us understand the notion of the world of the man of color,"[38] to the beginning of chapter 6 when he questioned the extent to which the psychoanalytic findings of Freud and Adler could be applied "in an attempt to explain the vision of the world of the man of color."[39] In chapter 6 he highlighted the incongruity between the psychoanalytic schema and the reality of the Black man,[40] just as in chapter 7 when he eventually turned to Adler and explained his opposition to any application of Adler's theory to the Black man again because of its concentration on the individual to the neglect of society: "If there is a flaw, it lies not in the 'soul' of the individual, but in his environment."[41] What Fanon did not appear to deny was that Freud and Adler could help us understand whites, and this meant that they could contribute to what it was that Blacks had to deal with in negotiating the white world. Indeed, the majority of the chapter is devoted more to whites than to Blacks.

The broader perspective that Fanon argued for in *Black Skin, White Masks* was not simply a theoretical concern but was at the heart of the approach he developed in his own psychiatric practice as an intern at Saint-Alban under the direction of François Tosquelles, the founder of "social psychotherapy" (later known as "institutional psychotherapy"). Subsequently, Fanon adopted it in his own right at the psychiatric hospital in Blida in Algeria. There is some uncertainty about when Fanon actually completed *Black Skin, White Masks* and thus some uncertainty about whether the manuscript was already complete by the time Fanon came under Tosquelles' direction. Certainly there was a synergy between the two men. Félix Guattari, who also collaborated with Tosquelles, wrote a description of "institutional psychotherapy" in terms of its determination, first, never to isolate the study of mental illness from its social and institutional context, and secondly, to analyze institutions always in terms of the real, symbolic, and imaginary effects of society on individuals.[42] This is Fanon's approach in a nutshell, and nobody before him seems to have thought to apply it to the investigation of the effects of racism as rigorously as he did.

The sixth chapter of *Black Skin, White Masks* already shows Fanon moving in the direction of social psychotherapy. The chapter begins with the immediate contrast between the environment of the Antillean and the very different environment that psychoanalysis takes for granted. Against Jacques Lacan's claim that "the psychic object and circumstance" is the family,[43] Fanon responded that the model of the family among Europeans is very different from that in the Antilles. In other words, universal structures had been presupposed where what was called for is "a concrete understanding."[44] He extended this observation to include the fact that there is a proportionality between the white family and the social milieu that is lacking for the Black family as a result of the racist context.[45] The trauma that Black children suffer when confronted with images of themselves in magazines and nursery rhymes means that "a normal black child, having grown up with a normal family, will become abnormal at the slightest contact with the white world."[46] Fanon turned to the French translation of Sigmund Freud's 1909 *Five Lectures on Psycho-analysis* to show that he believed that the origins of psychic traumas are repressed in the unconscious.[47] In response, Fanon argued that this was simply not the case for the Black man for whom everything takes place at the level of existence: "he exists his drama."[48] This difference – Fanon calls it at this point a "dialectical substitution" – is even more apparent if the Black man leaves the Antilles for Europe, as Fanon did, thereby indicating how the discussion in chapter 5 fits into chapter 6 as a kind of evidence, but now presented in the form of a testimony that initially did not fully understand itself, for the reasons given above.

The inapplicability of Freudianism to a discussion of the man of color, like the inapplicability of Adlerism later, should not be read as a total dismissal of psychoanalysis. It is necessary to remember Fanon's statement from the Introduction: "only a psychoanalytic interpretation of the black problem can reveal the affective disorders responsible for this network of complexes."[49] But what did he have in mind? This remark was made in the context of his announcement that the book was aiming at the lysis of the morbid universe, a reference to Angelo Hesnard's book *L'univers morbide de la faute* (*The Morbid Universe of Transgression*).[50] When he returned to that book in chapter 6 it was to make the point that both Jews and Blacks are scapegoats for a society that is suffering from collective guilt.[51] Psychoanalysis helps us understand how white guilt cannot be separated from white supremacy and so is very much part of the problem that creates the Black world. This shows how this book, so often read as if it were written almost exclusively about Blacks, hinges on the account of whites given in this chapter, which is concerned with "the deeprooted myth" concerning the Black man as he exists in the white unconscious.[52] This myth impacts both Blacks and whites and contributes to the alienation of both of them.

In chapter 6, Fanon also explored two prevalent myths about the Black man that contributed to how he was seen and thus also to how he came to see himself under oppressive conditions. According to the first, the Black man is genital, and here Fanon again referred to Freudianism, even though the word *imago*, which he used to describe the mechanism at work here, is more properly associated with Jung and Lacan.[53] According to the second myth, the Black man is evil, and this led Fanon to initiate a critique of Jung's account of the collective unconscious in this context. Initially he called the collective unconscious indispensable to an account of a racist society,[54] but subsequently he introduced serious qualifications on the grounds that Jung confused instincts, which are invariable, with habits, which are acquired.[55] Once that distinction is made, it becomes clear that what Fanon calls the figure of the bad negro is not an archetype in Jung's sense.[56] In an effort to dispel that confusion, Fanon replaced the role of collective unconscious in Jung with a mechanism to which he gave the name "cultural imposition."[57]

In addition to identifying these two myths, Fanon highlighted in chapter 6 two "errors of analysis."[58] What is important about these two errors is that they represent positions that are readily attributed to Fanon himself if one takes some of his remarks out of the context of the dialectical presentation of the argument in which they are embedded. The first error he identified was that of insisting that there is "only one type of negro."[59] The refutation of this error turns out to be more complex than it might seem at first. In chapter 5, in the context of a discussion of Sartre's "Black Orpheus," he had written: "The negro experience is ambiguous, for there is not *one* negro – there are *many* negroes."[60] In keeping with this criticism, in the following chapter, he quoted, seemingly approvingly, Gabriel d'Arbousier's critical remarks on Sartre's "Black Orpheus." The long quotation from d'Arbousier begins:

> This anthology that puts Antilleans, Guyanese, Senegalese, and Malagasies on the same footing creates a regrettable confusion. It thus poses the cultural problem of overseas territories by detaching the cultural issue from the historical and social reality of each country as well as the national characteristics and different conditions imposed on each of them by imperialist exploitation and oppression.[61]

Fanon commented: "The objection is valid. It concerns us too. At the start, we wanted to confine ourselves to the Antilles."[62] This is a reference to his comment in the Introduction that "our observations and conclusions are valid only for the French Antilles."[63] But Fanon had in his own account deliberately failed to abide by this restriction that he had placed on himself at the beginning of the book.

Although Fanon conceded that d'Arbousier's objection could be used against him just as it could be used against Sartre, that was not his last word. He began chapter 6 by focusing on the Antilles, but after conceding the validity of d'Arbousier's point, he tried to explain to d'Arbousier that "dialectics, whatever the cost, got the upper hand and we have been forced to *see* that the Antillean is above all a Black (Noir)."[64] Fanon acknowledged that "the universal situation of the Negro is ambiguous," which is not exactly the same as what he said earlier when he acknowledged the ambiguity of negro experience. In any event, the ambiguity was resolved in "concrete existence": "In order to counter the alleged obstacles above, we shall resort to the obvious fact that *wherever he goes a negro remains a negro.*"[65] As the concluding chapter showed, Fanon was not insensitive to the different forms of alienation suffered by a physician from Guadeloupe and an African construction worker,[66] but he recognized that in concrete existence both of them were subject to the same inferiorizing gaze of whites. Indeed, not only were both treated as Negroes by whites, but they had a culture imposed on them that made them see themselves as Negroes, that is to say, see themselves as whites see them, thereby compromising the diversity of Black experience. In spite of his admission that d'Arbousier's objection was valid, Fanon refused to concede the point because he recognized that in spite of local variations, these two myths concerning the Negro are sufficiently widespread as a result of colonialism that they operated across all societies characterized by anti-Black racism. In short, the restriction of the analysis to the Antilles was overcome in the course of the book.

I quoted Fanon as saying that "the universal situation of the negro is ambiguous, but this is resolved in his concrete existence." He followed that comment with the sentence: "This in a way puts him alongside the Jew."[67] This takes us to what for him was the second error of analysis, which is said to be that of "equating anti-Semitism with negrophobia."[68] Throughout *Black Skin, White Masks*, Fanon drew parallels between these two forms of racism, mainly by way of Sartre's *Anti-Semite and Jew*. However, in chapter 5 he made the point that, as opposed to the Jew, as described by Sartre, the Black man is over determined from the outside.[69] In chapter 6 it was Joachim Marcus who exhibited the error, as illustrated by a long quotation in a footnote where it is said of antisemitism that the attitude finds the content.[70] But Fanon's point was that, whatever the formal similarities, one must take into account the concrete differences that can be traced back to the myths: "No anti-Semite, for example, would ever think of castrating a Jew. The Jew is killed or sterilized. The negro, however, is castrated."[71] To that extent, there is not racism as such: there are racisms.

Fanon's question about whether psychoanalysis can take account of the man of color gave way to two questions that are related to each other: "can the White man behave in a sane manner toward the Black man and can the Black man behave in a sane manner toward the White man?"[72] He was least hopeful about whites. To make the point, the chapter ends with an extended discussion of a white woman who had a fear of imaginary Negroes. Fanon had observed the woman in 1951 during his time at the Saint-Ylie hospital in Dole.[73] Fanon's conclusion was that, even if one were to attribute part of her problem to her "constitution," her "alienation" was aggravated by predetermined circumstances, and until those circumstances had been addressed any improvement in her illness was going to be limited.[74] The conclusion is clear: white people also need a change in the structures of the world if they are ever to become sane, or, as he also put it, if they are ever to achieve their ambition to become human.[75] Fanon did not exclude disalienation for either group: "Disalienation will be for those Negroes and Whites who have refused to let themselves be locked in the substantialized 'Tower of the Past.'"[76] He understood that the cause of the problems lay in the past, and so a knowledge of history was requisite for assessing the situation. But he highlighted an additional option for those Negroes who refused to treat their actuality as definitive.

More precisely, Fanon offered clear indications of what would constitute a solution for Blacks. Indeed, he used the word "solution" twice at the end of chapter 6 in conjunction with a discussion of Aimé Césaire.[77] The solution turns on the earlier diagnosis that the Black man suffers from a collapsed ego that renders him re-actional, in the sense that his actions are dependent on the "Other" as the source of valorization.[78] For Fanon the answer lay in action: "to induce man to be actional."[79] He had already said it in chapter 4: The Black man must choose action with regard to the true conflictual source, which is the social structure of society.[80] By the time the reader reaches chapter 6, Fanon was able to explain himself more clearly. The Black man must, once he has discovered the white man in himself, kill him.[81] This is the heart of *Black Skin, White Masks*, and it does not necessitate literal violence, although it does appear to entail risking one's life in the fight for freedom.[82] Chapter 5 may end in tears, but, as chapter 6 shows, the path to disalienation is ultimately by way of action directed toward a transformation of the very structures of society. This would be different depending on the situation, the context. The question of what kinds of action that necessitates, in the various contexts in which he found himself, exercised him in his subsequent works until his death in 1961 at the age of only 36.

NOTES

1 Fanon, *Oeuvres*, 543; *Wretched*, 97–98.
2 Cherki, 24, 277 n41.
3 Fanon, *Oeuvres*, 211; *Black Skin*, trans. Philcox, 161.
4 Fanon, *Ecrits sur l'aliénation*, 168–232; *Alienation and Freedom*, 203–275.
5 Khalfa, *Poetics*, 209–235.
6 Fanon, *Black Skin*, trans. Philcox; *Black Skin*, trans. Markmann. There is, in addition, a problem posed by the fact that Fanon sometimes capitalizes *le Noir* and *le Nègre* and sometimes not. In quoting Fanon I have followed his usage, but when speaking in my own voice I have followed current usage by always capitalizing *Black* and *Negro*.
7 Fanon, *Oeuvres*, 66; *Black Skin*, trans. Philcox, xv.
8 Fanon, *Oeuvres*, 66; *Black Skin*, trans. Philcox, xv. Emphasis mine.
9 Fanon, *Oeuvres*, 96; *Black Skin*, trans. Philcox, 31.
10 Fanon, *Oeuvres*, 125; *Black Skin*, trans. Philcox, 63.
11 Fanon, *Oeuvres*, 97; *Black Skin*, trans. Philcox, 31. Italicized phrase in English in the original.
12 Anna Freud, *Das Ich*, 120; *The Ego*, 102–103. Fanon, *Oeuvres*, 99; *Black Skin*, trans. Philcox, 34.
13 Sadji, "Nini," 498.
14 Fanon, *Oeuvres*, 105, 187; *Black Skin*, trans. Philcox, 41, 130–131.
15 Fanon, *Oeuvres*, 124; *Black Skin*, trans. Philcox, 62.
16 Maran, *Un homme*, 36. Cited Fanon, *Oeuvres*, 119; *Black Skin*, 55.
17 Guex, *La névrose*, 28; *Abandonment*, 18. Cited Fanon, *Oeuvres*, 119; *Black Skin*, 55.
18 Fanon, *Oeuvres*, 124; *Black Skin*, trans. Philcox, 62.
19 Fanon, *Oeuvres*, 123; *Black Skin*, trans. Philcox, 61.
20 Mannoni, *Psychologie*, 71n; *Prospero*, 70n.
21 Fanon, *Oeuvres*, 237; *Black Skin*, trans. Philcox, 190–191.
22 Fanon, *Oeuvres*, 146; *Black Skin*, trans. Philcox, 86.
23 Naville, *Psychologie*, 151.
24 Fanon, *Oeuvres*, 145; *Black Skin*, trans.Philcox, 84.

25 Lacan, "Le complexe," 5. Cited Fanon, *Oeuvres*, 194n; *Black Skin*, trans. Philcox, 139n.
26 Fanon, *Oeuvres*, 142; *Black Skin*, trans. Philcox, 80.
27 Fanon, "L'experience."
28 Bernasconi, "On Needing."
29 Fanon, *Oeuvres*, 176; *Black Skin*, trans. Philcox, 119.
30 Fanon, *Oeuvres*, 251; *Black Skin*, trans. Philcox, 206.
31 Sartre, "Orphée Noir," xli; "Black Orpheus," 137. Quoted Fanon, *Oeuvres*, 171; *Black Skin*, trans. Philcox, 112.
32 Fanon, *Oeuvres*, 172; *Black Skin*, trans. Philcox, 113. Translation modified.
33 Fanon, *Oeuvres*, 64; *Black Skin*, trans. Philcox, xviii. Translation modified.
34 Fanon, *Oeuvres*, 175, 173; *Black Skin*, trans. Philcox, 116, 114. Translation modified.
35 Fanon, *Oeuvres*, 175; *Black Skin*, trans. Philcox, 117. Translation modified.
36 Bernasconi, "The European," 107.
37 Fanon, *Oeuvres*, 221; *Black Skin*, trans. Philcox, 174; Bernasconi, "The Assumption."
38 Fanon, *Oeuvres*, 107; *Black Skin*, trans. Philcox, 43. Translation corrected.
39 Fanon, *Oeuvres*, 179; *Black Skin*, trans. Philcox, 120. Translation corrected.
40 Fanon, *Oeuvres*, 186; *Black Skin*, trans. Philcox, 129.
41 Fanon, *Oeuvres*, 235; *Black Skin*, trans. Philcox, 188.
42 Guattari, "L'etudiant," 104.
43 Lacan, "Le complexe," 5. Cited Fanon, *Oeuvres*, 179; *Black Skin*, trans. Philcox, 120.
44 Fanon, *Oeuvres*, 75; *Black Skin*, trans. Philcox, 6. Translation corrected.
45 Fanon, *Oeuvres*, 180; *Black Skin*, trans. Philcox, 121.
46 Fanon, *Oeuvres*, 181; *Black Skin*, trans. Philcox, 122.
47 Sigmund Freud, *Psychologie collective*, 140; *Two Short Accounts*, 52.
48 Fanon, *Oeuvres*, 186; *Black Skin*, trans. Philcox, 129. Translation modified.
49 Fanon, *Oeuvres*, 65; *Black Skin*, trans. Philcox, xiv.
50 Hesnard, *L'univers morbide*.
51 Fanon, *Oeuvres*, 218 (see also 210); *Black Skin*, trans. Philcox, 170 (see also 160).
52 Fanon, *Oeuvres*, 185, 222; *Black Skin*, trans. Philcox, 128, 175.
53 Fanon, *Oeuvres*, 199; *Black Skin*, trans. Philcox, 146.
54 Fanon, *Oeuvres*, 136, 181; *Black Skin*, trans. Philcox, 72, 123.
55 Fanon, *Oeuvres*, 214; *Black Skin*, trans. Philcox, 165.
56 Fanon, *Oeuvres*, 214; *Black Skin*, trans. Philcox, 164.
57 Fanon, *Oeuvres*, 216–219; *Black Skin*, trans. Philcox, 167–171.
58 Fanon, *Oeuvres*, 210; *Black Skin*, trans. Philcox, 160–161.
59 Fanon, *Oeuvres*, 210; *Black Skin*, trans. Philcox, 160. Translation modified.
60 Fanon, *Oeuvres*, 173; *Black Skin*, trans. Philcox, 115. Translation corrected.
61 D'Arbousier, "Une dangereuse," 38–39.
62 Fanon, *Oeuvres*, 202; *Black Skin*, trans. Philcox, 150.
63 Fanon, *Oeuvres*, 70; *Black Skin*, trans. Philcox, xviii.
64 Fanon, *Oeuvres*, 202; *Black Skin*, trans. Philcox, 150. Translation modified.
65 Fanon, *Oeuvres*, 202; *Black Skin*, trans. Philcox, 150. Translation corrected, emphasis original.
66 Fanon, *Oeuvres*, 245; *Black Skin*, trans. Philcox, 198.
67 Fanon, *Oeuvres*, 202; *Black Skin*, trans. Philcox, 150.
68 Fanon, *Oeuvres*, 210; *Black Skin*, trans. Philcox, 160.
69 Sartre, *Reflexions*, 102; *Anti-Semite*, 95. Fanon, *Oeuvres*, 158; *Black Skin*, trans. Philcox, 95.
70 Marcus, "Structures familiales," 282. Cited Fanon, *Oeuvres*, 191–192; *Black Skin*, trans. Philcox, 136.
71 Fanon, *Oeuvres*, 194; *Black Skin*, trans. Philcox, 140. Translation corrected.
72 Fanon, *Oeuvres*, 199; *Black Skin*, trans. Philcox, 146.
73 Macey, *Frantz Fanon*, 133–134.
74 Fanon, *Oeuvres*, 229; *Black Skin*, trans. Philcox, 184. Translation corrected.
75 Fanon, *Oeuvres*, 65; *Black Skin*, trans. Philcox, xviii.
76 Fanon, *Oeuvres*, 247; *Black Skin*, trans. Philcox, 201. Translation modified.

77 Fanon, *Oeuvres*, 219, 221; *Black Skin*, trans. Philcox, 171, 174.
78 Fanon, *Oeuvres*, 189, 235; *Black Skin*, trans. Philcox, 132, 187.
79 Fanon, *Oeuvres*, 243; *Black Skin*, trans. Philcox, 197.
80 Fanon, *Oeuvres*, 142; *Black Skin*, trans. Philcox, 80.
81 Fanon, *Oeuvres*, 222; *Black Skin*, trans. Philcox, 175.
82 Fanon, *Oeuvres*, 240; *Black Skin*, trans. Philcox, 194.

REFERENCES

Bernasconi, R. (2002). The assumption of Negritude: Aimé Césaire, Frantz Fanon, and the vicious circle of racial politics. *Parallax, 8*(2), 69–83.

Bernasconi, R. (2005). "The European knows and does not know": Fanon's response to Sartre. In M. Silverman (Ed.), *Frantz Fanon's "Black skin"* (pp. 100–111). Manchester: Manchester University Press.

Bernasconi, R. (2007). On needing not to know and forgetting what one never knew: The epistemology of ignorance in Fanon's critique of Sartre. In N. Tuana & S. Sullivan (Eds.), *Race and the epistemologies of ignorance* (pp. 231–239). Albany, NY: SUNY Press.

Capecia, M. (1948). *Je suis Martinique*. Paris: Corrêa.

Capecia, M. (1950). *La négresse blanche*. Paris: Corrêa.

Cherki, A. (2006). *Frantz Fanon. A portrait* (N. Benabid, Trans.). Ithaca, NY: Cornell University Press.

D'Arbousier, G. (1949). Une dangereuse mystification: la théorie de la nègritude. *La Nouvelle Critique, 1*(7), 34–47.

Fanon, F. (1951). L'experience vecue du Noir. *Esprit, 179*, May, 657–679.

Fanon, F. (1967). *Black skin, White masks* (Charles Lam Markmann, Trans.). New York: Grove Weidenfeld Press.

Fanon, F. (2005). *The wretched of the Earth* (Richard Philcox, Trans.). New York: Grove Press.

Fanon, F. (2008). *Black skin, White masks* (Richard Philcox, Trans.). New York: Grove Press.

Fanon, F. (2011). *Oeuvres*. Paris: La Decouverte.

Fanon, F. (2015). *Écrits sur l'alienation et la liberté*. Paris: La Decouverte.

Fanon, F. (2018). *Alienation and freedom* (Steven Corcoran, Trans.). London: Bloomsbury.

Freud, A. (1936). *Das Ich und die Abwehrmechanismus*. Vienna: Internationaler Psychoanalytischer Verlag.

Freud, A. (1973). *The ego and the mechanisms of defense*. New York: International Universities Press.

Freud, S. (1950). *Psychologie collective et analyse du moi: Suivi de "Cinq Leçons sur la psychanalyse."* Paris: Payot.

Freud, S. (1962). Five lectures on psycho-analysis. In *Two short accounts of Psychoanalysis* (James Strachey, Trans.) (pp. 31–87). Harmondsworth: Penguin.

Guattari, F. (1969). L'etudiant, les fous, et les Katangais. *Partisans, 46*, February–March, 104–111.

Guex, G. (1950). *La névrose d'abandon*. Paris: Presses Universitaires de France.

Guex, G. (2015). *The abandonment neurosis* (Peter D. Douglas, Trans.). London: Karnac.

Hesnard, A. (1949). *L'univers morbide de la faute*. Paris: Presses Universitaires de France.

Khalfa, J. (2017). *Poetics of the Antilles*. Bern: Peter Lang.

Lacan, J. (1938). Le complexe, facteur concret de la psychologie familiale. *Encyclopedie française, 8*(40), 5–16.

Macey, D. (2001). *Frantz Fanon: A biography*. New York: Picador.

Mannoni, O. (1950). *Psychologie de la colonization*. Paris: Seuil.

Mannoni, O. (1956). *Prospero and Caliban* (Pamela Powesland, Trans.). New York: Frederick A. Praeger.

Maran, R. (1947). *Un homme pareil aux autres.* Paris: Albin Michel.

Marcus, J. (1949). Structures familiales et comportements politiques. *Revue française de psychanalyse, 2* (April–June), 277–313.

Naville, P. (1948). *Psychologie, Marxisme, Matérialisme. Deuxième édition revue et augmentée.* Paris: Marcel Riviere et Cie.

Sadji, A. (1947–1948). Nini. *Présence Africaine, 3*, 89–110, 276–298, 458–504, 647–666.

Sartre, J.-P. (1946). *Réflexions sur la question juive.* Paris: Paul Morihein.

Sartre, J.-P. (1948). Orphée Noir. In L. S. Senghor (Ed.), *Anthologie de la nouvelle poésie nègre et malgache de langue française* (pp. ix–xliv). Paris: Presses Universitaires de France.

Sartre, J.-P. (1976). *Anti-Semite and Jew* (George J. Beker, Trans.). New York: Schocken.

Sartre, J.-P. (2001). Black Orpheus (John MacCombie, Trans.). In R. Bernasconi (Ed.), *Race* (pp. 115–142). Malden, MA: Blackwell.

CHAPTER 7

RACIAL ONTOLOGIZING THROUGH THE BODY

Derek Hook

TROUBLING EMBODIMENTS

It is impossible not to notice the prevalence of the bodily in Frantz Fanon's (1952/1986) *Black Skin, White Masks*, especially the bodily suffering of the Black body as it is contrasted against insignias of whiteness. Few, indeed, have evoked the painful and disjunctive dimensions of racializing embodiment for Black persons in racist contexts as powerfully as Fanon did. His rendering of the violated dialectic of the body and the world in *Black Skin, White Masks* highlights that "In the white world the man of color encounters difficulties in the development of his bodily schema" (1952/1986, p. 112). Accordingly, the Black man or woman's "[c]onsciousness of the body is a solely negating activity" (1952/1986, p. 112). Fanon thus memorably asserts – to repeat the oft-cited refrain – that "the black man suffers in his body quite differently from the white man" (p. 117).

While Fanon's work on the disturbed dialectic between the body and the world is often revisited, there is a valuable supplementary historical analysis of race and embodiment that remains, unfortunately, neglected. I have in mind the work of the South African psychologist and Black Consciousness intellectual Chabani Manganyi. Manganyi's early essays (1973, 1977, 1981), influenced as much by Fanon's (1952/1986) anti-colonial and psychological concerns as by the imperatives of Black Consciousness and the struggle against the white supremacist system of Apartheid, stress the factor of embodiment as an indispensable mode of analysis.

In this chapter, I offer a detailed engagement with Manganyi's conceptualization of embodiment in racist contexts. This is followed by a discussion of what I take to be a complementary mode of analysis, that offered by Fanon in *Black Skin, White Masks*. My overarching objective is to explore two analytical perspectives on what Steve Pile (2000) refers to as "racial ontologizing through the body" (p. 29). The first of these – which Manganyi's work illuminates – is what I call an *imposed* mode of embodiment. The second – Fanon's work here being still the most pertinent instantiation – I consider an *expressive* mode of embodiment. I have a further agenda in bringing the work of Manganyi and Fanon into a dialogue. Both of these theorists help us think differently about how facets of psychoanalysis and phenomenology might intersect in exploring the experiences and processes of embodiment under the conditions of anti-Black racism. This meta-theoretical consideration is not merely of academic significance. It may well be, as I will indeed argue, that we need both analytical frameworks if we are to adequately grasp the complexity of the phenomenon at hand.

THE BODILY AND ITS SYMBOLIC MEDIATION

In an era where psychoanalytic and phenomenological conceptualizations are typically understood as being mutually exclusive, if not in fact mutually *antagonistic*, it comes as a

DOI: 10.4324/9781003037132-7

surprise to find an example of how they have historically been interwoven within a particular strand of Black Consciousness critique. This is the case in Chabani Manganyi's (1981) psycho-existential theorization of embodiment in the Apartheid context. In Manganyi's estimation, the body presents as a psychological and existential problem. It is worthwhile to play out the steps of Manganyi's argument in his single most important essay on racializing embodiment, namely, "The Body-for-others" (1981). Doing so enables us to both replicate the structure of this discussion, and to develop links to other conceptualizations of racism and its disjunctive modes of embodiment.

The problem that the body poses to both the ego and culture more generally is multifaceted in nature. The body is not just problematic in view of the ego's rejection of its crass physicality (bodily wastes, instinctual urges, the animality underlying the human condition, etc.) and its evident mortality (the fact that it ages, fails, eventually dies). Nor is it problematic only because it becomes a vehicle of alienating depersonalization (as is the case in respect of women's bodies, which, so memorably for Simone de Beauvoir [1949/2011], are in their comportment, dress, and lived experience, constantly subjected to a patriarchal framework of norms). The body represents also a cultural problem and perhaps particularly so for societies premised on a sense of their own cultural superiority. In Wilhelm Reich's (1970) *The Mass Psychology of Fascism* we find the following:

> "Away from the animal; away from sexuality" are the guiding principles of the formation of all human ideology ... whether disguised in the Christian form of man's "spiritual and ethical nature," or the liberal form of "higher human values" ... all this adds up to an overemphasis of the intellect, of ... logic and reason as opposed to instinct ... the superior man as opposed to the inferior man.
>
> *(Reich, 1970, p. 339)*

For Manganyi then embodiment presents us with *the existential dilemma of the disharmonious body-to-ego relationship as it is transformed into a pragmatic socio-cultural problem.* That is to say, for Manganyi the unpalatable physicality of the *bodily* often gives rise to a series of discriminatory social and ideological formations. More straightforwardly: What is disagreeable about the bodily dimension of human existence is typically managed by projecting those features onto (cultural/racial) others. *They* have, or better yet, they *are* bodies; we, the superior group, transcend the merely bodily and attain the status of properly cultural beings. As Manganyi puts it: The problem of bodily disavowal becomes "in race supremacist cultures, a medium for the development of racist systems and fantasies" (1981, p. 105).

Perhaps we are moving too quickly. The point is perhaps yet to be made strongly enough: Why the disavowal of the bodily? Why allocate this crass corporeality to some other abjected social figure rather than simply assume and own it? Is corporeality really as troubling to individual subjects and societies as Manganyi claims it is? This is perhaps an instance where the psychoanalytic vocabulary of the excremental seems fully justified. It is precisely this lower range of values, of waste matter, indeed, of shit and all its extended socio-symbolic equivalences and associations, that drives home the problem Manganyi confronts us with. His arguments in this respect strike up an unexpected kinship with Milan Kundera's (1984) *The Unbearable Lightness of Being*, which poses the philosophical quandary of the incompatibility of God and shit: If "man" was created in God's image, then does it not follow that God must defecate? How then might God and shit be thought together; can the idea of shitting be consolidated with our sense of God as divine, Holy, pure? It is for this reason that Kundera argues that "Shit is a more onerous theological problem than is evil" (p. 246).

A brief historical allusion might be in order here, both to preface Manganyi's argument, and to connect more overtly the themes of the excremental and racism. In his description of township life during Apartheid, Jacob Dlamini (2009) cites J. E. W. Mathewson's (1957) account of the sewage costs particular to the establishment of a new Black township:

> In the case of the Daveyton sewage disposal works, which will serve a township consisting entirely of Bantu residents, a factor which warranted special consideration was the nature of the Bantu diet, which being principally carbohydrate in character ... is deficient in protein and this necessitates a very much higher consumption of food than that of Europeans who live on a more concentrated diet. In consequence the amount of faecal matter to be treated per capita is greater than that of a mixed township and the capacities of the sludge digestor and sludge drying beds will therefore be greater than that normally provided for a European township.
>
> *(Mathewson, cited in Dlamini, 2009, p. 132)*

Dlamini concludes that for Mathewson – and for what we might term the "faecal imaginary" of Apartheid – "blacks are literally full of shit" (p. 132). It is precisely such longstanding historical racist associations that hinge on the relation to matter, to the bodily, that motivates Manganyi's early work. Indeed, it is in light of such examples, that Manganyi seems justified in adopting a rather dramatic turn of phrase:

> At the core of human existence is a devastating contradiction – the contradiction between the fate of creatureliness and the infinitude of the symbolic.
>
> *(p. 123)*

It is worth noting that Manganyi's theme of body-ego disjunction can be conceptualized somewhat differently, as a disjunction at a different level of analysis (precisely that between "creatureliness and ... the symbolic" [p. 123]). In other words, what a psychoanalytic approach might view as a disjuncture realized between ego and body, a critical phenomenological perspective might conceptualize as a disturbance between body and world occasioned by deleterious quasi-transcendental social structures (Guenther, 2020). As we progress, it will be important to keep such different levels of analysis jointly in mind, highlighting more the prospect of intersections between theoretical conceptualizations than points of evident incompatibility. One of the ideas I will develop as we continue is that a degree of conceptual ambidexterity will be crucial in grappling with the topic of racializing and racist embodiment.

Importantly, Manganyi's account does not rely on the assumption that it is chiefly the *sexuality* of the body that makes corporeality troubling, as in much of psychoanalysis. It is the body's inevitable fate of decay and death, the body as itself waste-matter, as inescapable proof of finitude, that make it, and all the ideological values that become associated with it, so in need of symbolic mediation and/or denial. For Manganyi, the threat of deathliness far outweighs the force of sexuality: "the reality which is feared most and defended against is death ... the denial of death is first and foremost a denial of the body" (1981, p. 121). At this point Manganyi takes a decisive step outside the parameters of Freudian psychoanalysis.

The above contradiction of mortality and infinitude presents as both a psychical and an ideological crisis. This is the double crisis of allocating a variety of bodily values and experiences a place, both in a given psychical economy, and within an existing discursive network of meanings. It results, as Manganyi puts it, in two psychological responses, repression and symbolization, of which he focuses predominantly on the latter. The displacements of ideological symbolization make it possible for individuals to have and maintain the polarization evident in the body-ego relation. They are able to drive a wedge between a set of imaginary ego-properties and those less habitable aspects of bodily-ness, those facets of corporeal experience that are typically delegated to others. For Manganyi the role of ideology in this respect might be understood as the "symbolic transformation mediating fundamental human needs for normative sanity" (p. 118). Or, to reiterate the description of Manganyi's argument offered above: The potentially traumatic aspects of having – of *being* – a body are managed, particularly in white supremacist culture, by those properties being projected unto others, who thereby assume the weight of objectification, of being reduced to what often seems a merely bodily existence.

Although the symbolic realm – the domain of culture, language, laws, prohibition – provides some relief from this pressing existential anxiety of the body, this strategy is ultimately inadequate. The conflicts and tensions between the factor of bodily experience, the ideological symbolic domain, and the imaginary force of racist fantasy proves considerably more complex than this. The body itself becomes a means for the articulation and projection of ideological values. It is not just the case that corporeal dilemmas are played out within the symbolic; symbolic dilemmas are also played out at the level of everyday bodily experience:

> [T]he human body is a perfect medium for the symbolic elaboration of social meanings, including the irrational substratum of superordinate/subordinate relationships. When this bodily symbolism is considered within the wider symbolic matrix which equates the body with creatureliness, finitude, excrement, sin … [then] the social and individual [psychic] dimensions of the body become manifest.
>
> *(p. 112)*

For Manganyi then the body is not merely a socially constructed object. The phenomenological ideas that he draws on in developing his analysis clearly inform this facet of his argument. The fraught nature of embodiment cannot as such be captured solely through the lens of socio-historical and discursive contextualization. His implications are clear and instructive. Not every social object is constructed in the same way; not every object poses the same challenge to given processes of symbolic mediation across varying socio-historical locations. More to the point: Not every object makes as potent an underlying factor in the making of racist ideology as does the body.

Bigoted social logics are one mode of response to this impasse, to the threat with which the bodily plagues the ego. In more direct terms, the facts of the body's corporeality, its death-bound-destiny, its most unpalatable features, and its prospective status as object, all of these facets of bodily experience are delegated, in white supremacist cultures, to Blacks. As a result we should be unsurprised to find that Blacks are more easily associated with death than are whites in racist cultures, indeed, that Blackness and death are strongly aligned signifiers, and that we find a disproportionate number of images of Black bodies in states of suffering and death (Hook, 2013) than we do of whites in such cultures.

It is from this "irresolvability," from this traumatic potential of the body-ego relation, that a variety of racist symbolic articulations and fantasies spring. We encounter here, in this reference to what is disjunctive, non-reconcilable, or incommensurable unto itself, an instantiation of the Lacanian psychoanalytic notion of the "real." This idea of a "non-relation" which can never be fully harmonized, which remains minimally traumatic, of a constitutive deadlock or impossibility underlying both psychical and bodily experience, helps, I think, to highlight a key facet of Manganyi's argument.

The delegation of a type of excess physicality to Black subjects is thus understood as an attempt, within the historical and political life of white supremacist cultures, at resolving just this "real" dimension – this impasse or "non-resolveability" – of the body-ego relation. Racism, in Manganyi's terms, insists on a polarization in the individual's interpretation of their body-to-ego experience such that it comes to be expressive "of an elaborate symbolic matrix" (1981, p. 118). Racist fantasies and narratives may thus be said to exploit the conflictual potentials of the body-ego disjunction, so as to entrench a type of radical realism to notions of racial difference. That is to say, race takes on a type of ontological status in racist contexts inasmuch as it is constantly affirmed and reiterated by the difference between those who *are* bodies as opposed to those who transcend a mere bodily existence.

To avoid a potential misreading: Foregrounding the "real" of the body-ego relation should not be taken as a license for a kind of lazy universalism. Highlighting, as Manganyi does, the psycho-existential dimension does not allow us to bypass considerations of socio-historical specificity. We might put it this way: Although the "real" of the body-ego relation represents a recurring psycho-existential dilemma in different historical eras, it does not remain unaffected by the historical flux of social constructions and racial fantasies.

DIFFERENTIAL ORDERS OF EMBODIMENT

Returning to Manganyi's idea of the "elaborate symbolic matrix" generated by the denial of the body: One of the most persistent and categorical of the available symbolic equations in Western culture, Manganyi insists, is that which traces an equivalence between whiteness and mind, and between Blackness and the bodily. These sociological schemata are essentially elaborations of a single dichotomy "between body and inner symbolic core (mind) which reflects and is supported by the symbolic variations of up and down (above and below), good and evil" (p. 112). We have thus two chains of ideas: The upward trajectory of whiteness-mind-goodness-life and the downward trajectory of Blackness-body-evil-death. These two ideological chains of symbolic values have a literal dimension. What has hitherto been a predominantly psychoanalytic analysis (on the "real" of the body-ego relation) now takes on a more phenomenological quality. Manganyi insists that the subject's bodily-experiential domain – the lived physicality of "up" and "down" – re-codes and reaffirms this racist division of values. "Being above somebody and being below somebody" he comments, "are fundamental and deep-seated orienting constructions of the racist consciousness" (p. 110).

These polarized chains of symbolic value not only replay the rudimentary dynamics of racism (its logics of superiority and inferiority), they also represent routes of *identification*: The upper pole (whiteness) provides a means of narcissistic self-valorization, affording its subjects the position of symbolic idealization; the lower pole (Blackness) represents that which is devalued, deserving of denial and repression. What thus needs to be built into these sociological schemata (or chains of signifiers) are two general subject-categories – the prospect, that is to say, of negative self-evaluation – if one is the subject of racist objectification – and of aggrandizing, positive self-over-evaluation – if one is its beneficiary. The former instance is something that Manganyi and Fanon, amongst others, have long since insisted upon: The problem of the unconscious dimension of the negative evaluation resulting from the incorporation of such stereotypes. Referring directly to Manganyi: "In racist societies the white body is denied through a frivolous kind of idealism … [whereas] the black body … is something unacceptable in its entirety" (p. 115). The implication of

Manganyi's argument is that being a "stakeholder of whiteness" enables some degree of sublimation in respect of one's own abject corporeality. This, by extrapolation, is less the case in respect of Blackness in racist contexts, where there are less symbolic supports for the sublimation of corporeality. A more recent theoretical contribution to these issues is worth highlighting here. I have in mind Frank Wilderson's (2020) reflections on the historical specificity of anti-Black racism. This is a form of racism which entails an ongoing physical and psychical type of violence which amounts to "a necessary violence ... a health tonic for everyone who is not black" (2020, p. 40). Such a condition is likened by Wilderson to a state of deathliness in which one comes to realize as a Black person that "the world tells you you are needed, needed as the destination for its aggressivity and renewal" (2020, p. 41).

Back though to Manganyi: We should not be surprised, he avers, that the existential challenge of body-ego integration is more complicated in the case of those who are the targets of racist objectification. It is certainly true, says Manganyi, for Black children who are exposed to "the experience of negative stereotypes of the black body espoused by racist cultures" (p. 115). Here Manganyi offers a point of historical contextualization. While this experience of bodily objectification is to be anticipated during eras of white supremacy, the influence of Black Consciousness will, he hopes, increasingly mitigate against such effects in the future.

The two opposed chains of symbolic value discussed above construct and affirm racial difference at a variety of modalities of human experience. This is not just a case of the contrast of the physicality of the lower (genital) body with the higher, cerebral qualities of mind. Whether we compare the spatial orientations of the upwards transcendence of spirit with the downward earthly destiny of flesh, or the realm of disciplined moral order versus that of base, unprincipled, instinctual action, each such comparison affirms two mutually exclusive racial categories. Racial difference, we might venture, is given a radical (phenomenological and psychical) reality, is constantly substantiated by reifying Blackness and whiteness as two distinct modes of being. This is a prime example of *racial ontologizing through the body*. Race here is not simply a reality of meaning or signification, but an experiential reality of embodied, affective, and pre-reflective depths. Racialization, for Manganyi, thus occurs in a saturating and experiential – which is not to say an exclusively *conscious* – manner, within the phenomenological dimension of how we make sense of our social and bodily "being-in-the-world." Racism thus exploits the "real" of bodily existence, so as to accentuate and extend social constructions of racial difference, making of them both a physical and metaphysical reality of difference:

> The negative values associated with blackness (blackness as dirt, impurity, smell) become vehicles in race supremacist cultures for the racist's attempts to adapt to his estrangement from the reality of the human body. The projection of these undesirable attributes of the human body to the victim of racism as a convenient scapegoat, is part and parcel of the process of denial and self-deception which characterizes the cultural heroics of Western culture and civilization.
>
> *(1981, p. 113)*

Manganyi thus clearly endorses Fanon's (1952/1986) depiction of the Manichean dynamics of colonial racism whereby a "metaphysics" of whiteness, as embodied by the higher values of culture, intellect, civilization, and spirituality, is opposed to the irreducible corporeality of Blackness, which by contrast, gravitates around values of nature, sexuality, criminality, and deathliness. Achille Mbembe invokes many of the terms highlighted by Manganyi's account of two opposed chains of symbolic value (object/spirit, animal/

human, death/transcendence) when he disconcertingly mimes what we might call the ontology of colonialism:

> [T]he colonized individual ... [was] the very prototype of the animal ... [this] individual ... was subordinate to power and the state and could not be like "myself." As an animal he is strictly alien to me. His way of viewing the world, that is, his mode of being, is not mine. No power of transcending himself can be perceived in him. Encapsulated in himself, he is a bundle of drives, not abilities ... To that extent, in the colony the body of the colonized individual is considered, in its profanity, one object among others. Indeed, being no more than a "body-thing," it is neither the substrate nor the affirmation of any mind or spirit.
>
> *(Mbembe, 2001, pp. 26–27)*

Lewis Gordon's (1995) influential schema of racialized absence and presence – itself derived from a reading of Fanon's *Black Skin, White Masks* – provides another means of understanding the Manichean dynamics of white/Black embodiment:

> [T]o look at a black body is to look at mere being-among-beings ... [But] the white body, being human (Presence), doesn't live as a mere-being-among-beings. It lives with the potential to be a being that stands out from mere beings.
>
> *(Gordon, 1995, p. 101)*

As Wilderson (2008) notes in his commentary on Gordon's work, Black presence is itself a form of absence, a type of voiding; Blackness amounts to the destruction of presence, the negation of what this presence may promise.

REGISTERS OF DISJUNCTURE

For Manganyi, the fact that the most creaturely and traumatic qualities of the bodily self might be located externally (which is to say, projected onto the racial other) proves crucial if we are to understand the historical obduracy of racism. We have here a shifting up of registers in which a psycho-existential dilemma (that of the individual subject's own abject corporeality) is transposed upon a higher symbolic, sociological, and socio-cultural level of experience (in which certain others are considered problematic and abject because they are reduced to the merely bodily). With this facet of his analysis – the fact of the upward transmission of non-resolvable conflict to a different (societal, socio-political) domain – Manganyi (1981) gives us a distinct perspective on the apparent intransigence of racism. Although this account must be viewed as contributing only one possible originating factor amongst a host of others within the complex genealogy of racism, it does highlight one reason why racism seems so difficult to eradicate. This attention to the historical tenacity of racism leads us to a methodological consideration, to how facets of psychoanalysis and phenomenology might be utilized alongside one another.

I noted above that it would be necessary to keep different levels of analysis jointly in mind, that we would need to exercise a type of conceptual ambidexterity in grappling with the theme of embodiment in racist contexts. This notwithstanding, it seems worthwhile anticipating a possible phenomenological critique of the analysis developed so far. Such a critique might go like this: Why, in your discussion of embodiment, do you so prioritize dissonance, conflict, disjunction, when the everyday experience of embodied physicality is, for the most part, relatively harmonious? The foregrounding of incommensurability, of disjuncture, could thus be said to be less than justified.

One response here would be simply to suggest that a study of the incommensurability between kinds of embodiment remains squarely within the remit of phenomenology. The experience of such dissonance of embodiment is highlighted, as we shall see, in a disturbing yet exemplary fashion by Fanon. The prospect of such an incommensurability also exists, if in more de-politicized terms, within phenomenology itself, as in the elementary distinction "between the body as subject and the body as object" which, as Zahavi (2018) proclaims "is a phenomenological distinction" (p. 83).

Perhaps the point here is simply that racism, as a traumatic factor, exacerbates a variety of interconnected "reals" (or registers of disjuncture) as they occur at symbolic, subjective, and bodily levels of experience. If this is the case, then we may well need more than one theoretical approach to plot the reverberating impacts of racism on such different yet connected levels of analysis. Whether we place the relation of incommensurability between ego and body as existing between different modes of embodiment (as in, for example, between the imaginary body and the symbolic body, were one to adopt a Lacanian approach[1]), or indeed, as Fanon does, as a type of traumatic disconnection in the dialect between body and world (a more phenomenological approach), we can focus on the prospective rift in question as something that will be exacerbated and exaggerated by racism.

In justifying the recurring reference to incommensurability and disjuncture in the foregoing analysis, we might make extended reference to Axelle Karera's (2020) account of why Fanon should be considered a founding figure for a properly *critical* form of phenomenology. Fanon (1952/1986), Karera reminds us, explicitly replaces Merleau-Ponty's notion of the corporeal schema with that of the racial epidermal schema. In fact, Fanon's description of a traumatizing objectifying gaze

> already invokes the failure of Merleau-Ponty's concept. If the corporeal schema gives us at every moment a global, practical, and implicit notion of the relation between our body and things that informs us of our agential presence in the world, Fanon exposes us to a contrasting rupture between body and world or, perhaps more precisely, between a corporeality and the involuntary dissolution of the coherent corporeal schema … Rather than offering us, as Merleau-Ponty does, a corporeal schema that epitomizes the felicitous relational exchange between body and world, a second historical-racial schema is imposed on the … body of the racially captive … For Merleau-Ponty, the body is free insofar as it acts and can transform the historically given, but as Fanon demonstrates, the black body's historical efficacy is amputated.
>
> *(Karera, 2020, pp. 289–291)*

Helen Ngo (2017) makes a very similar argument. While Merleau-Ponty (1945/2012) explicitly refutes Descartes' mind-body dualism in *The Phenomenology of Perception*, and goes on to secure the centrality of embodied experience for philosophical and phenomenological critique, such an understanding of the phenomenal body "seems to sit jarringly with … many descriptions of racialized embodiment" (Ngo, 2017, p. 62). The problem here, to be a little more precise, is that Merleau-Ponty's model of embodied existence stresses that the body is the very condition of phenomenological experience. The phenomenal body as such, to cite Ngo's commentary on Merleau-Ponty,

> cannot move away from itself, it cannot be severed from itself in such a way to be taken away, or *put in front of* itself … the phenomenal body … is marked with a fluidity and ease, since the body is co-extensive and co-present with itself, never wholly absent nor fully visible before itself.
>
> *(2017, p. 62, emphasis original)*

And yet it is precisely the opposite of this condition that occurs in moments of racist objectification where, as Ngo (2017) notes, the body of the racialized subject is, in a very marked sense, taken away, put in front of the (subject's) self, made hyper-visible. "The racialized body ... seems to cross over from subject to object" (Ngo, 2017, p. 64).

Perhaps unexpectedly then, a psychoanalytic attention to various instances of disjuncture (or, in Karera's terms, *rupture*) proves an ally to a critical phenomenological description of the multiple ways in which racism proves injurious. An interesting point of intersection between psychoanalytically and phenomenologically oriented accounts of racist embodiment now comes to light. The Lacanian "real," which, as I have argued, is one way of thinking Manganyi's attention to the conflictual ego-body relation, resonates powerfully with a critical phenomenological attention to how racism disrupts the dialectic of the body and the world.

RACISM'S *CORPS MORCELÉ*

At the outset of this chapter I suggested that Manganyi's work can be profitably read alongside Fanon's analysis of racializing/racist embodiment. As we have seen, Manganyi explores how the often troubling or disjunctive bodily/corporeal facets of human experience become components of racist ideology. More than this, he helps us better understand how such ideological symbolic values get damagingly replicated within the discursive and subjective experiences of communities and individuals.

What remains somewhat under-emphasized in Manganyi's (1981) approach – at least in his discussion of "The Body-for-others" – is the experiential aspect of embodied subjectivity, an attention to how *bodily phenomena themselves speak*. We might put this as a question: Manganyi's account emphasizes the necessary roles of symbolization and repression in the body-ego relation, but does he capture enough of the visceral somatic experiences of the ego-body disjuncture he so adeptly theorizes? It is imperative that we consider the disjunctive features of the "imposed" modes of embodiment that Manganyi has so helpfully sensitized us to. Yet we must likewise prioritize the somatic field, emphasizing that the body is a vessel of expressivity, and that bodily sensation is itself a kind of data. It perhaps helps to turn here to Calvin Schrag's (1980) thoughts – inspired by Merleau-Ponty – on how best one might analytically approach the bodily dimension of human subjectivity:

> Clearly there is a socio-historical horizon to lived experience, but there is also a psychico-natural horizon. Man can neither be lifted out of history nor out of nature ... The lived-body is neither historical nor natural in the categorical sense. It is the base of operations and the centre of concernful projects which envelop at the same time a sense of lived through history and a concrete experience of nature.
>
> *(1980, pp. 57–58)*

If we were to offer an – admittedly, *improvisational* – attempt, inspired by Schrag's (1980) comments, at identifying two lines of analysis in the above accounts of racist/racializing embodiment, we might arrive at something like the following. On the one hand, we have something akin to an "imposed embodiment" which is reliant on the meaning of other (and *othered*) bodies, a concern with the transposition of a discursive frame of ideological symbolic values upon the realm of bodily experiences (correlating perhaps to Schrag's [1980] socio-historical horizon of lived experience). Manganyi's (1981) work might be seen as exemplifying this approach. On the other hand, we might aim also to engage with the factor of bodily experience itself, with what we might call the "expressive embodiment" of the lived body as vessel of experience (roughly corresponding to Schrag's psycho-natural horizon). Fanon's account of "corporeal malediction," the result of his being fixed and figuratively broken apart by the white gaze, is the most historically powerful example of such an approach.

The corporeality of Fanon's language in *Black Skin, White Masks* invokes the psychical effects of what we might call racism's *corps morcelé* (body in pieces), effects which involve the fragmentation and objectifying "re-composition" of the bodily schemas of racism's objectified others. The notion of "corporeal malediction," the disjunction, to recall, of a particular corporeal schema (of inhabiting a Black body) in a given historico-racial schema (of the racist white world), is thus offered by Fanon as a means of conceptualizing the brutal psychological effects of racism:

> [C]ompletely dislocated … I took myself far off from my own presence … and made myself an object … What else could it be for me but an amputation, an excision, a hemorrhage that splattered my whole body with black blood.
>
> *(1952/1986, p. 112)*

A recurring motif of traumatized corporeality grounds the text's phenomenological concerns with racism. The hatred of this racist world is evinced in the experience of a mutilated, radically objectified body, just as the metaphysics of racism are, correspondingly, read into the natural features of a hostile, white world:

> My body was given back to me, sprawled out, distorted, recolored, clad in mourning in that white winter day. All around me … a white song … [A] whiteness that burns me.
>
> *(Fanon, 1952/1986, pp. 113–114)*

The result of such disruptions is that – as we have seen – the balance of the body's relation to the world, to other bodies, to its own positive identity, and to an array of cultural and historical values is constantly imperiled. No stable dialectical interchange can be maintained, be it with respect to Fanon's basic phenomenological bodily stability in the world, or in view of his relation to his own history, culture, or lifeworld. Hence the idea, so prevalent in Black Consciousness thought, of the "disfigurement" of the colonized's culture and history (as in Biko, 1978), a phrase that, as we have by now seen, should not be read as merely metaphorical.

We could argue then that no meaningful analysis of racism – or of any egregious form of social asymmetry – can be adequate without due attention being paid to the somatic field, to the experiential realm of corporeality and bodily sensations. Hence the importance of the emergent tradition of explicitly politically engaged critical modes of phenomenology (Guenther, 2020; Karera, 2020; Weiss, Murphy, and Salaman, 2020).

And yet, the foregoing analysis seems not to go far enough. To highlight a disturbed *dialectic* still implies that the component elements of that dialectic (the world, one's body, the realm of culture, etc.) might remain somehow beyond the scope of racism. The implication seems, in short, that there may be some refuge, some respite from racism in at least one of the underlying component elements of the dialectic. A closer examination of Fanon's text suggests something different. Indeed, Fanon shows us a disconcerting mismatch of physical and psychological properties: A violent disjunction at multiple registers of experience.

In *Black Skin, White Masks*, we have not only the overdetermination of the soul by the body (the effects, in other words, of epidermalization, of race and racism getting "under the skin"), and not only the metaphysical permeation of the material domain by racist subjectivity ("a whiteness that burns"). We have both of these occurring simultaneously and in conjunction: A state of objectified souls and materialized racist animosities. It is not just then that the dialectic between the body and the world is disturbed; each of these two foregoing ontological categories (body and world) are internally fractured, ruptured, made non-reconcilable, traumatic, within the conditions of colonial/anti-Black racism. So, while we should certainly heed Ngo's (2017) warning "to be careful ... to avoid the pathologizing of racialized bodies," we should likewise note her emphasis on "the depth and ubiquity" of racism as affecting "a kind of existential instability" (p. 70), an existential instability which, I would add, constantly ruptures bodies, worlds, cultures from within.

With this in mind, it helps to revisit Fanon's scene of corporeal malediction and to consider again both the nature of the corporeal and racial epidermal schemas and their relationship to one another. The racial epidermal schema which imposes itself upon Fanon "is woven out of thousands of stories, anecdotes, images and so on" says Pile (2010, p. 29) paraphrasing Fanon's memorable words from *Black Skin, White Masks*. And yet this schema is comprised "of more than racist imagery and discourse" because, crucially, "[i]t is also bodily" (Pile, 2010, p. 29). So while Fanon implicitly sets up a "real dialectic" between a corporeal schema (his body) and a racial epidermal schema (the world), the relationship between these two schemas cannot be reduced simply to one of replacement. The distinction between the corporeal schema and the racial epidermal schema is thus for Pile, muddier, more complex, than it at first appears. How so? Well,

> both schemas are bodily, and both racialized; further, both appear to be experiential and also psychological; and, both are social ... Neither exacts a space of the body that is simply internal or external: these [schemas] ... constantly switch, bleed, blur ... there is a tension, a dialectic, between them ... the dialectical play between the corporeal and the epidermal schemas is simultaneously worldly, psychological and experiential.
>
> *(Pile, 2010, p. 29)*

We are not thus dealing with a strictly sequential replacement of the corporeal by the racial epidermal schema. There is, by contrast, something of a reverberation effect in play, a type of cycling dissonance between the two schemas. This dialectic does not lead to a resolution; it is as such better qualified as a "negative" dialectic in which the schemas clash and remain constantly unreconciled (Pile, 2010) (another instance, so it would seem, of the Lacanian "real"). Moreover, both corporeal and epidermal schemas are, as Pile insists, simultaneously social *and* bodily. They defy such conventional categorizations, blurring analytical boundaries, the experiential features of each schema bleeding into, interrupting, undermining those of the other.

ANALYTICAL INCOMPATIBILITIES

This returns us to the meta-theoretical concern noted in the chapter's introduction (regarding the combined uses of facets of psychoanalysis and phenomenology). As is by now evident, neither of the two approaches to racializing/racist embodiment discussed above – those, schematically, of imposed embodiment (as exemplified by Manganyi) and expressive embodiment (as invoked by Fanon) – can be neatly categorized as belonging exclusively to either psychoanalysis or phenomenology. While the ego-body disjunction that Manganyi discusses is arguably psychoanalytic in origin, the ideological values it entrenches are played out at the level of everyday phenomenological bodily experience. As

I stressed above, race, for Manganyi, is not merely a function of meaning and signification, but is inscribed within the phenomenological dimension of how we make sense of our social and bodily "being-in-the-world."

Similarly, while there is much of value, from a phenomenological standpoint, in conceptualizations of expressive modes of embodiment – which, to be sure, invaluably reiterate the role of somatic experience and bodily sensation in any analysis of racism – they too are helpfully supplemented by more psychoanalytically inflected accounts of racializing/racist/embodiment. As I have tried to show, a handful of phenomenological tools – the idea of a harmonious dialectic (or felicitous relational exchange) between body and the world, Merleau-Ponty's assertion, that the phenomenal body cannot be severed from itself – are helpfully critiqued and extended by means of a psychoanalytic attention to disjuncture, rupture, and conflict. Indeed, one unexpected finding of the above analysis is that the Lacanian notion of the "real" resonates powerfully with a critical phenomenological attention to the wide-ranging and often insidious existential effects of racism. The overlaying of phenomenologically and psychoanalytically inspired types of analysis proves helpful also in expanding upon Fanon's account of the relationship between corporeal and epidermal bodily schemas.

FANON'S LANGUAGE OF THE BODY

Where does this leave us then, methodologically, when it comes to future analyses of racializing/racist embodiment? To avoid a possible misunderstanding: I am not suggesting that psychoanalysis and phenomenology are, ultimately, compatible. The relationship between these two traditions, despite certain shared themes and conceptual intersections, can perhaps best be characterized – repurposing here phrases used above – as, one of non-reconcilability, disjuncture, "irresolvability," even, possibly, as that of a negative dialectic. That being said, and counter-intuitive as such a claim might sound, apparent incompatibilities between conceptual frameworks may be a strength rather than a fatal weakness when it comes to phenomena as complex and insidious as racializing/racist embodiment.

What more is there to be said about the theme of racial ontologizing through the body, particularly in reference to future – and potentially de-racializing – modes of embodiment? Fanon links these two themes – the body and the future – in the conclusion of *Black Skin, White Masks*. Scholars have offered a variety of speculations on the closing sentence of that book ("O my body, make of me always a man who questions!" (1952/1986, p. 232), in which Fanon confers upon his body a critical and interrogative form of agency (Gordon, 2015; Khalfa, 2008; Marriott, 2018). Of such Fanon scholars, it is perhaps Achille Mbembe (2019), who provides the most memorable commentary. Mbembe's remarks take the form of a poetic reformulation, one which combines Fanon's ideas on racializing/racist embodiment with his own thinking on the body of colonial existence. They are worth citing here at length as a way of concluding the theoretical work undertaken above:

> It is practically impossible to read Frantz Fanon and come out unscathed. It is difficult to read him without being interpellated by his voice, by his writing, his rhythm, his language, his sonorities …
>
> In the era of the Earth [the Earth as common to all, as indicative of a prospective universality], we will effectively require a language that constantly bores, perforates, and digs … Each of the fragments of this terrestrial language will be rooted in the paradoxes of the body, the flesh, the skin, and nerves. To escape the threat of fixation, confinement, and

strangulation, as well as the threat of dissociation and mutilation, language and writing will have to … rise up and loosen the vice that threatens the subjugated person with suffocation as it does his body of muscles, lungs, heart … [T]hat dishonored body … [is] made of several bodies … on the one hand, the body of hatred, of appalling burden, the false body of abjection crushed by indignity, and, on the other … the originary body, which, upon being stolen by others, is then disfigured and abominated … [Hence] the matter is literally one of resuscitating it, in an act of veritable genesis.

Rendered to life and thereby different to the fallen body of colonized existence, this new body will be invited to become a member of a new community. Unfolding according to its own plan, it will henceforth walk along together with other bodies and, doing so, will re-create the world. This is why, with Fanon, we address it in this final prayer: *O my body, always make me a man who questions!*

(Mbembe, 2019, p. 189, emphasis original)

NOTE

1 Without going on a lengthy digression, let me note that the Lacanian differentiation highlighted above (that of the imaginary as opposed to the symbolic body) cannot easily be reducible to the oft critiqued Cartesian dualistic mind-body differentiation. The imaginary body is always, by definition, the *subjective* image of the body (the experiential and the corporeal cannot be separated), just as the symbolic body is both the lived body and the lived body as it is "imprinted," or over-written, with symbol values. As such, these Lacanian concepts – or at least my use of them – need not be seen as necessarily antithetical to phenomenological conceptualization. This being said, I concede that certain of the psychoanalytic conceptualizations utilized within this chapter could indeed be said to cling to a Cartesian ego/body dualism. Suffice to say that such differentiations might be better conceptualized in the terms above (i.e. of imaginary as opposed to symbolic modes of embodiment). One last comment: Technically, in Lacanian theory, we would need to add a third category to the above two modes of embodiment, namely that of the bodily "real," that is the unmediated physicality of the body that remains beyond the remit of both imaginary and symbolic mediation.

REFERENCES

Beauvoir, S. (1949/2011). *The second sex*. New York: Vintage.
Biko, S. (1978). *I write what I like*. London: Bowerdean.
Dlamini, J. (2009). *Native nostalgia*. Auckland Park: Jacana.
Fanon, F. (1952/1986). *Black skin, White masks*. New York, NY: Grove Press.
Gordon, L. (1995). *Bad faith and antiblack racism*. Atlantic Highlands, NJ: Humanities Press.
Gordon, L. (2015). *What Fanon said*. New York: Fordham University Press.
Guenther, L. (2020). Critical phenomenology. In G. Weiss, A. V. Murphy & G. Salaman (Eds.), *Fifty concepts for a critical phenomenology* (pp. 11–16). Evanston, IL: Northwestern University Press.
Hook, D. (2013). The racist bodily imaginary: The image of the body-in-pieces in (post) apartheid culture. *Subjectivity, 6*, 254–271.
Karera, A. (2020). The racial epidermal schema. In G. Weiss, A. V. Murphy, & G. Salaman (Eds.), *Fifty concepts for a critical phenomenology* (pp. 289–294). Evanston, IL: Northwestern University Press.
Khalfa, J. (2008). My body, this skin, this fire: Fanon on flesh. *Wasafiri, 20*(44), 42–50.
Kundera, M. (1984). *The unbearable lightness of being*. London: Faber.

Manganyi, N. C. (1973). *Being-black-in-the-world.* Johannesburg: Ravan Press.

Manganyi, N. C. (1977). *Mahangu's reverie and other essays.* Johannesburg: Ravan Press.

Manganyi, N. C. (1981). *Looking through the keyhole: Dissenting essays on the black experience.* Johannesburg: Ravan Press.

Marriott, D. (2018). *Whither Fanon? Studies in the blackness of being.* Stanford, CA: Stanford University Press.

Mathewson, J. E. W. (1957). *The establishment of a Bantu township.* Pretoria: Van Schaik.

Mbembe, A. (2001). *On the postcolony.* Berkeley, CA: University of California Press.

Mbembe, A. (2019). *Necropolitics.* Durham, NC: Duke University Press.

Merleau-Ponty, M. (1945/2012). *Phenomenology of perception.* New York, NY: Routledge.

Ngo, H. (2017). *The habits of racism.* Lanham, MD: Lexington.

Pile, S. (2010). Skin, race and space: The clash of bodily schemas in Frantz Fanon's *Black skin, White masks* and Nella Larsen's *Passing. Cultural Geographies, 18*(1), 25–41.

Reich, W. (1970). *The mass psychology of fascism.* New York: Farrar.

Schrag, C. O. (1980). *Radical reflection and the origin of the human sciences.* West Lafayette, IN: Purdue University Press.

Weiss, G., Murphy, A. V., & Salaman, G. (Eds.). (2020). *Fifty concepts for a critical phenomenology.* Evanston, IL: Northwestern University Press.

Wilderson, F. B. (2008). Biko and the problematic of presence. In A. Mngxitama, A. Alexander, & N. C. Gibson (Eds.), *Contesting the legacies of Steve Biko* (pp. 95–114). London: Palgrave.

Wilderson, F. (2020). *Afropessimism.* New York: W.W. Norton.

Zahavi, D. (2018). *Phenomenology: The basics.* London: Routledge.

PART III
Fanon's Uses of Phenomenology

CHAPTER 8

CORPOREAL SCHEMAS AND BODY IMAGES

Fanon, Merleau-Ponty, and the Lived Experience of Race[1]

Athena V. Colman

In the *Phenomenology of Perception*, Maurice Merleau-Ponty (1962) writes:

> my body appears to me as an attitude directed towards a certain existing or possible task. And indeed its spatiality is not, like that of external objects or like that of "spatial sensations," a *spatiality of position*, but a *spatiality of situation*.
>
> *(p. 100, emphasis original)*

These words are emblematic of Merleau-Ponty's corpus, which retrieves perception from its secondary reduction to restore it to its primacy. Indeed, his work constituted a sustained effort to reconfigure and undermine idealist or positivistic assumptions, which cleave experience off from its own reflection only to "rediscover" it as an "original" separation. The Cartesian division of reality into two essential substances, *res cogitans* and *res extensa*, not only rigidified the division of mind and body, but also secured the mind's dominion over the body. Through vigilance to the phenomenological method of bracketing one's preconceptions about the nature of experience(s) (or, performing the *epoché*), the development and tradition of the phenomenological method attempted to describe experience on its own terms, including an attempt to reflect on the experience of its own reflection. The endeavor of phenomenological reflection thus meant turning away from the assumptions of the mundane understanding of the world – including the very assumption of that mundanity – toward an attentiveness to description more adequate to the relational pulls of which experience consists.

Taking up early phenomenological methods, which began in the work of Husserl, Merleau-Ponty attempted to develop an even more refined analysis of the "essences" of experience by including within the purview of phenomenology a more robust theorization of embodiment.[2] This, of course, is already a problematic claim, for it would be hard for us to imagine what experience without embodiment could mean. Indeed, accounts of experience that assert a separation between mind and body, or reduce experience to biochemical, physiological, or functional processes altogether, are not only contrary to our lived experience, but are also theoretically impoverished as these views cannot account for the subsequent *connection* between the mind and the body, nor the intentional richness of phenomenal experiences as they are actually lived, i.e., such accounts are inadequate to the phenomena they attempt to explain. They disregard, or fail to account for, the most significant aspects of our experience: The socio-historical world in which we oppress, delight, kill, and love one another.

Merleau-Ponty's phenomenological refocusing on experience as it is lived allows him to locate the subject in its inextricability with the body, others, and the world: "This subject, which takes a point of view, is my body as the field of perception and action" (1964a, p. 16). What it means to have a body, or to be a body, is to be spatially and temporally *situated*. We are not in our bodies as "pilots in ships" but we *are our bodies*.[3] In other words, aspects of "myself" are not tacked onto some substratum called the subject: My subjectivity is the

DOI: 10.4324/9781003037132-8

dynamic interaction between all aspects of my experience. Hence, Merleau-Ponty's oft-quoted expression: "To be a body, is to be tied to a certain world ... our body is not primarily *in* space: it is of it" (1962, p. 148, emphasis original).

In elaborating this phenomenology of the body, Merleau-Ponty explicates a pre-reflexive "implicatory structure" in the unity of spatio-temporal experience, the *corporeal schema* [*schéma corporel*] (sometimes translated as *body schema* or *bodily schema*) through which the "unity of the body" is made possible (p. 149). This unity is given in spatiality and the subject's own bodily perception. Coupled with the corporeal schema is the term *body image*, which is either taken to be entirely synonymous with the term *corporeal schema* or a secondary structuring of embodiment in its own right. To clarify, the corporeal schema can be understood as having to do with a pre-representational mode of experience through which we continually, but without conscious effort, dynamically orient and restructure our body in the world according to our projects; whereas, the body image encompasses the more representational aspects of our embodiment, or what we can call boundary inscriptions of the figuration of our body (consciously or not). Frequently there is no distinction drawn between what is indicated by the terms, *corporeal schema* and *body image*, and even where the distinction is drawn, it is not done so consistently. This is not surprising when one examines the use of these terms in the psychological texts of the early twentieth century which significantly inform Merleau-Ponty's own thought. For example, in the introduction to his *L'image de Notre Corps* [*The Image of our Body*] (1939), Lhermitte writes:

> In reality, postural schema (H. Head), bodily schema (P. Schilder), self-image (Van Bogaert), somatopsyche (Wernicke-Foerster), body image of the self (Lhermitte), *constitute various names for the same thing*: the body image [*l'image de notre corps*].
>
> *(p. 12, translation and emphasis mine)*[4]

Whether or not Merleau-Ponty recognizes a clear distinction between corporeal schema and body image has been a matter of some debate. For example in her work *Body Images: Embodiment as Intercorporeality*, Gail Weiss (1999) suggests that Merleau-Ponty uses the two terms interchangeably, whereas Shaun Gallagher and Andrew Meltzoff (1996) contend that "[a]lthough Merleau-Ponty does not make an explicit conceptual distinction between body image and body [corporeal] schema, he is much more careful and consistent than the psychological literature is on this point" (p. 217).[5] This debate is complicated depending on how one discerns this difference, if at all, and by the subsequent differences in what constitutes the body image as such. That is to say, the complexity is redoubled since accounts of what constitutes the body image vary – as do theories of its relation to the corporeal schema (Gallagher, 1986).

If Merleau-Ponty does draw a distinction between the corporeal schema and the body image, both aspects of embodiment would be found at the level of the pre-reflexive and would contribute different things in initiating, structuring, and renewing social bonds and self-relation. In what follows, I do not want to simply offer an argument for the distinction between the corporeal schema and the body image; rather, I consider the very emergence of the question of this distinction in Merleau-Ponty, or in general for that matter, as an indication of an issue in phenomenological accounts of embodiment that require further investigation.

I claim that this perhaps nascent distinction in the early psychological texts, which Merleau-Ponty's thought inherits, is *implicitly* taken up by Frantz Fanon (1967[1952]) in his critique of the corporeal schema as elaborated in his seminal work *Black Skin, White Masks*. While Fanon does not explicitly draw a distinction between the *corporeal schema* and *body image*, his critique of the corporeal schema nonetheless discerns what is at stake in the question of this distinction. I suggest Fanon's analysis of "the lived experience of the black" [*L'expérience vécue du noir*] provides a significant resource for thinking through the notions of corporeal schema and body image (and the subsequent relation between them), in ways that enrich and transform phenomenological and psychological thought on embodiment and the structures of subjectivity.

The corporeal schema is central to Merleau-Ponty's phenomenological rethinking of spatiality, meaning, and the body. The term appears consistently throughout his corpus after *The Structure of Behavior*, from the *Phenomenology of Perception* to the posthumously published *The Visible and the Invisible*. Merleau-Ponty's account of the corporeal schema is developed in close dialogue with prior psychological descriptions and interpretations of the idea. As Lhermitte is quick to point out, it was Pierre Bonnier (1905) who first proposed the term *schema* [*schéma*], as well as *topographical representation* and *posture* in his article, *L'Aschématie* (p. 605). Notably, the term *schema* was developed in an effort to clarify *disorders* of the subject's own bodily perception (Lhermitte, 1939, p. 12). Lhermitte's work is of particular interest since it is a key source for both Merleau-Ponty and Fanon on the topic.[6] It is worth lingering with Lhermitte in a lengthy quotation:

> What we find at the origin of our activity, at the source of all our sensations and our perceptions, is ... the notion of space. And it is appropriate to give the denomination of *"sense of space"* [*sens de l'espace*] to all parts of sensibility, both peripheral and central, which help to define our objective orientation and our subjective orientation: this last term, which especially interests us, responds to the perception of our position in relation to the world, and of our posture [*attitude*] and the variations in our positions; that is to say, of our own movements and displacements ...
>
> Bonnier ... taught that morbid processes could affect and damage this schema in different ways, this "topographical figuration, this posture [*attitude*]" of our corporeality; that there was a need to describe special disorders which arose when "certain parts of ourselves cease to be represented in our notion of the body. When they take up too much space, there is *hyperschematicism*, too little, *hyposchematicism*, and a place which is not their own: *paraschematicism*." Finally, when the schema is shown to be completely disorganized, as is the case during vertigo, this disturbance can be characterized by the term *aschematism*.
>
> *(pp. 12–13, emphasis original)*[7]

As is evident in this passage, an emphasis on sensibility and spatiality mark the corporeal schema as the link between our objective and subjective orientations, including "our postures [*attitudes*] and our *situation in space*" (Lhermitte, 1939, p. 11, emphasis added). Indeed, as Lhermitte avers, prior to his introduction of the term *schema*, Bonnier had already wedded sensation, perception, and spatiality to the body and world under the expression *sense of space* [*sens de l'espace*] (p. 12). And yet, while it is clear these early thinkers inform Merleau-Ponty's own account of the corporeal schema, it was his retrieval of a primordial intentionality through his phenomenology of the perceiving body that enabled him to rethink the corporeal schema, radically reconfiguring *sense of space* from a "situation *in* space" (Lhermitte, p. 11) to a *"spatiality of situation"* (Merleau-Ponty, 1962, p. 100).

Beneath Husserl's appropriation of the Cartesian *I think*, which is structured by constituting consciousness, Merleau-Ponty discerns an "operative" intentionality – an *I can* of the perceiving subject (p. 137), which *founds* any acts of judgment or intentionality of consciousness (Merleau-Ponty, 1962, p. 243). Operative intentionality is pre-reflexive and is "a pre-personal cleaving to the general form of the world, as an anonymous and general existence [that] plays beneath my personal life" (p. 84). In the simplest of terms, the *I can* of operative intentionality is one way of saying that there must already be a perceiving subject that has the possibility of perceiving, i.e., a point of view on the world – in the world and of the world – as a condition for any intentional acts of consciousness. The idea that a more primordial intentionality founds an intentionality of consciousness is not meant to imply either a hierarchy or a temporal priority between the two modes of intentionality. Rather, we can think of operative intentionality as a more primordial moment of reciprocity in the inextricably woven fibers of the real (1962). This pre-reflexive or operative intentionality discloses Merleau-Ponty's revision of the corporeal schema in the modality of a "primitive spatiality ... [which] merges with the body's very being" (p. 148) and "secretly nourishes" life (p. 84).[8]

For Merleau-Ponty, the corporeal schema is not a mere topographical figuration of the body in space that ensures a one-to-one correspondence between the movement of my body and meaning. He criticizes this view as assuming a *partes extra partes* concept of spatiality, a view that reduces embodiment to a "spatiality of *position*," as if space were a large container and, correspondingly, my body an object or a thing in that container (1962, p. 100). In contrast, "we grasp external space through our bodily situation. A 'corporeal or postural schema' gives us at every moment a global, practical, and implicit notion of the relation between our body and things, of our hold on them" (Merleau-Ponty, 1964a, p. 5). Thus, Merleau-Ponty cautions us to "avoid saying our body is *in* space, or *in* time. It *inhabits* space and time" (1962, p. 139). The so-called objective measurement of space, i.e., in miles or coordinates, and of time, i.e., in hours or years, is only coherent because there is already a primordial spatio-temporality to carve up. In a similar vein, this recasting the corporeal schema clarifies Merleau-Ponty's subsequent distinction between movement and motility. Whereas movement implies a spatiality of position, motility denotes the possibilities of movement, and so Merleau-Ponty claims *motility is already meaning* (1962, p. 142). It is in this sense that we mean lived experience is not the experience of being *in* a body but rather of embodiment.

To be clear, the corporeal schema is not a mere coordination of the various aspects of the body (i.e., the senses, motor capacity, etc.) but an ever emergent "envelopment" (p. 148) in which my body is the unity of my senses transposed across sensory registers, commingled, and "pregnant one with the other" (p. 235). This unity is evident in embodied time. I do not experience time in discreet units of equally distributed temporal moments; times of boredom or illness seem indefinitely long and carry a different temporal weight and intensity than do times of excitement, which seem to speed by too quickly. In this same way, I do not collect, or recollect, my past as a series of equidistant, equally intense *times* receding into the past. The death of a loved one is not limited to the date of its occurrence but can bleed into months or years. Even after many years, the experience of that loss can become acutely and intensely present once again without a need to dial back through the distance of years. For instance, it *may* happen that when a favorite shared song comes on the radio, my past loved one becomes instantly present to me. My past lines my present as the invisible threading of my future now and yet-to-be. Thus, our corporeality is already an *attitude*, a *spatiality of situation*, and a dynamic worlded investiture. For this reason, Merleau-Ponty rejects any account of the corporeal schema which reduces it to a schema of "the actual bodily state" and instead describes it as a "scheme [sic] of *all possible activities*" (1973, p. 68, emphasis added).

If, in addition to the corporeal schema, there is a *body image* that constitutes a *distinct* moment of structuring embodiment, this is, as already noted, a matter of dispute. With regard to Merleau-Ponty, this distinction is unthematized and muddied by his occasional synonymous use of the terms.[9] Nonetheless, I claim that a nascent account of this distinction is available in Merleau-Ponty's articulation of child development as is particularly evident in his lecture on "The child's relations with others" (1960; 1964a; 1964c). In such an account, the body image can be seen in relation to the corporeal schema in the intersubjective structuring of embodied subjectivity.

In his reading of Wallon and Lacan, Merleau-Ponty claims that perception "presupposes a minimal bodily equilibrium [or] the operation of a postural [corporeal] schema" (1964a, p. 122). He locates the child's ability to experience perception between the third and sixth month of their development. It is only *after* six months that the child develops consciousness of their "own body and … specular image" (p. 125). The English translator of this piece, William Cobb, helpfully clarifies that there should be no conflation between the terms *specular image* [*L'image spéculaire*] and *mirror-image* [*L'image du miroir*]. Cobb notes that Merleau-Ponty is careful to reserve the term *specular image* to refer to the developmental aspect of the child's becoming whereas he reserves the term *mirror-image* for the visual event of the child being captured by their own image (p. 125). "By means of the image in the mirror he becomes capable of being a spectator of himself. Through the acquisition of the specular image the child notices that he is visible, for himself and for others" (p. 136).[10]

I suggest the *specular image* is included in, or even a nascent version of, a notion of the *body image* implicit in Merleau-Ponty's thought. On this view, the body image is dynamically engaged with the corporeal schema in a continually reshaped pre-reflexivity of our bodily self, the constituting and reconstituting of subjectivity. There is an emergence of the body image through our relation to others as ongoing restructuring of pre-representational aspects of subjectivity. The body image cannot be reduced to a mode of representation or the beliefs and attitudes one holds about oneself even as these can be included in the body image. "But there is initially a state of pre-communication … wherein the other's intentions somehow play *across* my body while my intentions play across his" (p. 119). To clarify, the corporeal schema is the implicatory structure of the unity of the body in its spatiality, which dynamically re-situates ever-emergent body image (imaging) in and as an ongoing and variously charged transcription of our relations with others, and which always includes the world, others, and the otherness of ourselves. Thus, the "entire placement [*mise en place*] of the corporeal schema is at the same time a placing of the perception of others" (p. 123).

> There is thus a system (my visual body, my introceptive body, the other) which establishes itself in the child … imperfectly, with gaps. It is founded on *the indistinction of the several elements that enter into it*, rather than on an ordered relation and a two-way correspondence of its different elements.
>
> *(p. 135, emphasis added)*

This passage recalls Merleau-Ponty's notion of spatiality and the body. A *spatiality of situation* requires a rejection of any *point to point* correspondence in the child's development (or the subject's identificatory practices) with the specular image. Merleau-Ponty affirms the developmental priority of the child's ability to distinguish the difference between the other's body and the other's specular image *as prior to and constitutive of* making this distinction for the self. Crucially, it is "the other's specular image [which] helps him arrive at an understanding of his own" (p. 127). The virtue of reading the specular image in this way – as an aspect, a kernel, or a lining of the body image, is that it enables us to index the identificatory scaffolding of otherness through which subjectivity distills and deflects itself. Merleau-Ponty underscores the centrality of this process: "The acquisition of a specular image, therefore, bears not only on our *relations of understanding* but also our *relations of being,* with the world and with others" (p. 137, emphasis original).

And yet, despite the foregoing attempt to delineate a distinction between the corporeal schema and body image in Merleau-Ponty's thought, his own claim of an *"indistinction … of several elements"* in the "system" of constituting subjectivity (p. 135) may be more clarifying, if enervating, of the attempt at hand. To wit, Merleau-Ponty's comprehensive and nuanced rehearsal of developmental psychology and the constitution of subjectivity in "The child's relations with others," is peculiarly prefaced by an account of *psychological rigidity* – the exemplar of which is the holding of "racist opinions" (p. 107) and "prejudice" with regard to "Negros, Jews, or any other minority" (p. 106). Merleau-Ponty asserts *rigid subjects,* from rigid racism to "abstract or rigid liberalism," refuse to see "striking differences of *situation*," whereas the "truly liberal" [*vraiment des libéraux*] notices these differences as disclosed in the action of cultural and "historical situation[s]," but somehow, and presumably *despite* these differences, is able to treat "each man (*in so far as his situation permits him to be a man*) like any other" (p. 106, emphasis added).[11]

In this extended and considered account of the subject's development, it would seem that what *situation* "permits" a man to be "a man," or, what it means for *a man not to be a man,* would be central. However, it is notable that Merleau-Ponty relegates racism and prejudice apart from history and politics in his claim that racist *opinions* are a function of a *"psychological mechanism" of a rigid subject* (again, the development of which, rigid or otherwise, he has yet to elucidate), as they are based on "myth." He continues, it is not the *content* of the opinions that characterize this rigidity, but rather the *"manner* in which one adopts this thesis [of racism or prejudice] and tries to justify it" (p. 107).[12]

It is of critical interest to our discussion to point out that Merleau-Ponty only addresses race and prejudice from the perspective of the subject who is *psychological rigid* and *fails to consider the experience of the subject toward whom this rigidity is directed.* This omission is telling, and, I suggest, illustrative of the importance of drawing a distinction between the corporeal schema and body image. In this way, it is only in attempting to be present to the accounts of lived experience, from the perspective(s) of *those toward whom the rigidity of racism and prejudice is directed,* that the full argument for the importance of the distinction can be indicated. Fanon shows us that the phenomenological and psychological traditions can be most forcefully read in relation to the sites of thinking that cover over this tension, even as they may resource aspects of its articulation.

Fanon's description of "the lived experience of the black" [*L'expérience vécue du noir*] discerns a missed register of experience, another structuring of spatiality and subjectivity. Fanon describes the lived experience of the Black as an experience of being in the world as "an object among other objects … sealed into … crushing objecthood" (Fanon, 1967, p. 45; p. 109). Yet, traditional existential and phenomenological discourses (such as Merleau-Ponty's as it is articulated above) mark the site of subjectivity precisely by distinguishing the subject's experience of *being-in-the-world* from the mere existence of *things.*[13] Fanon's description suggests that the lived experience of the Black is marked by *thing-hood,* i.e., object-hood. The inversion of being-in-the-world into a *crushing objecthood,* which "seals in" the Black, colonized subject (which is itself discovered phenomenologically, i.e., within the very lived experience being described), cannot be adequately accounted for by the notion of the standard account of the corporeal schema. The sense of spatiality operative in Fanon's description of the colonized subject denotes an objective sense of being *in* space, i.e., a spatiality of *position,* and not the sense *of* space, which indexes the phenomenal sense of (embodied) subjectivity. Fanon's account of the colonized subject takes place within the horizon of being an *object* for an *other*, and thus the lived experience of the racialized subject, including her sense of spatiality and body image, is fundamentally determined in relation to the "*Weltanschauung* of a colonized people" (1967, p. 109).

In contrast to the universality of the corporeal schema, Fanon discovers a multiplicity of schemas that shape those subjects and moments excluded by the corporeal schema. The point here is that Fanon's rereading of phenomenology and psychology opens up the question of structuring schemas, which structure our *subjectivity*, and our connection to others. In the situation of colonization, constitutive elements of the Black subject's experience are given, through oppression, as the very denial of subjectivity, through which they are nonetheless constituted. In other words, the subjectivity of a colonized person is constituted through the denial of that subjectivity. "Below the corporeal schema, I had sketched a historico-racial schema. The elements that I used had been provided for me not by 'residual sensations and perceptions primarily of a tactile ... and visual character,' but by the other, the white man" (Fanon, p. 111).

When Fanon finds the historico-racial schema *beneath* the corporeal schema, it crumbles, its place taken by a "racial epidermal schema" (p. 112). This disintegration of the corporeal schema is brought about by the articulation of a representation *at first alienated from and then taken into* the lived experience of Black subjectivity. Fanon illustrates this in his account of a child on the train, pointing him out *at him* "Look, a Negro!" The child's representations, stories, and anecdotes are "woven" together (p. 111). "The eternal victim of an essence, of an appearance for which he is not responsible" (p. 35). "The Negro has to wear the livery that the white man has sewed for him. Look at the children's picture magazines" (p. 34). The corporeal schema crumbles for the Black subject in the phenomenal field of the white man, as the Black man, reduced to appearance and epidermalization, symbolizes the biological (p. 167) and thus, "impedes the closing of the postural [or corporeal] schema of the white man – at the point, naturally, at which the black man makes his entry into the phenomenal world of the white man" (p. 160). Black skin created via the colonizing, white gaze, becomes a "burden of ... corporeal malediction" (p. 111). "Hence a Negro is forever in combat with his own image" (p. 194).[14]

Fanon suggests that the oppression of the colonizer shapes the body image *and* the corporeal schema (or other schemas) of the colonized subject. Moreover, the lived experience of the colonized calls into question the very legitimacy of the claim of priority the corporeal schema expresses. If the unifying function of the implicatory structuring of experience is itself dependent upon a primary "disparity" underlying the constitution of subjectivity (which is, in turn, always covered over in its global assumption), then the primacy of the corporeal schema, and the very way in which we think the nature of bodily perception, is put into question.

This is Fanon's extension of the insight: Perhaps the body image was not discerned by Merleau-Ponty precisely because it did not register at the level of an appearance which would make it possible for Merleau-Ponty to apprehend. Merleau-Ponty's corporeal schema's "global" grasp of being, again, which is not *in* space like an object, but *of* space as a subject, illuminates the nature of certain forms of privilege which are pre-reflective, and part of the very structuring of subjectivity in the formation of the most profound inscriptions of embodiment. Thinking in terms of Fanon's logic, Merleau-Ponty might not have grasped a distinction between the corporeal schema and the body image because his privilege allowed him to experience the dimensions of his subjectivity as a "global" possibility of motility. In this sense, *his privilege meant that his corporeal schema was his body image.*

Consider the function of privilege in the example of "whiteness." As a term, "whiteness" betrays itself as awkward and untrustworthy because it never really seems to be able to hook onto its referent. A white subject may opt to put on the "livery" of interrogating race one moment, and then absentmindedly forget their earnest project the next. Fanon reminds us that racialized subjects cannot simply take off the *livery* of their skin.[15] When it comes to the body images of white subjects, whiteness does not stick, not, in any case, *as whiteness.* And yet, while this account of the privilege of whiteness may be typical, it remains inadequate and does not reach to the ground-up perceptual stylizing of race. This account of whiteness implies a passivity and a lack of perspective, horizon, or sense beyond the white perspective. Merleau-Ponty's articulation of the visible and invisible is helpful here. It is not as if there are not invisible aspects to being visible. Whatever is invisible to white people about being white is not invisible to others! Racialized subjects understand that what is visible about them is also often understood in terms of an invisibility.

The *whiteness* of the white continually recedes, giving way to a *self* generating movement of subjectivity. In contrast to the corporeal schema as an "open circuit" of connection (Merleau-Ponty, 1964b, p. 168), Fanon describes being *abraded* "into non-being" (p. 109). Indeed, if *motility is meaning* (Merleau-Ponty, 1962, p. 14), then Fanon uncovers structuring schemas where movement is a highly mediated space of positionality in which the subject can be diminished, denied, or locked back in on itself. In this context, *movement* (again, not motility), may be volatile, torn up, stuttering, hypervigilant, etc., at the same time as fragmented or bound across schemas, i.e., physically, psychically, historically, etc.

According to Fanon, the racialized subject has "difficulties in the development of his bodily [corporeal] schema [*schéma corporel*]" (p. 110). In Fanon's description of his lived experience, there is a withdrawing or fragmenting *implicatory* structuring unity of spatiality and the body (p. 109). Fanon describes his body in its reduction to an object or appearance for the white, colonizing gaze. In a similar way, Fanon's description of *traveling* on a train is marked by a lack of unity or equilibrium in spatiality. He tracks expansions of space, e.g., being allotted an extra two or three chairs, and sudden fragmenting or contraction, e.g., "I am *fixed*," (p. 116) or feeling his body as an "amputation" from his own bodily presence, or being "dislocated" (p. 112). Fanon discovers schemas of disconnection and fragmentation: "My body was given back to me sprawled out, distorted" (p. 113).

Here, I suggest it is illuminating to read Lhermitte's (1939) emphasis on Bonnier's "*L'Aschématie*" (1905) with Fanon's phenomenological descriptions. Recall Bonnier's rehearsal of different spatial-schema disorders: "too much space ... *hyperschematicism*, too little, *hyposchematicism*, and a place which is not their own: *paraschematicism*. Finally, when the schema is shown to be completely disorganized ... *aschematism*" (Bonnier, 1905, p. 605; Lhermitte, 1939, p. 13). Fanon tracks the dilation and restriction of his bodily spatiality in the everyday experience of the Black subject: Too much space, not enough space, being beside space (an object for colonizing subjects), having no space, a dissolution of space, etc. Unlike Bonnier's psychological account, in which having one disorder of the schema would necessarily exclude the other disorders, Fanon's phenomenological description discloses these disorders in their in/compossibility in the everyday lived experience of the Black. His description demonstrates his critique – the only interpretation of the Black *corporeal schema* is that it is *spatially pathological.*

On the one hand, Fanon's description of his lived experience problematizes the corporeal schema in its universality, revealing it as a particular structuring of subjectivity, i.e., white, colonizing subjects. He demonstrates the inadequacy of the corporeal schema to account for his lived experience, "as an object in the midst of other objects" (p. 109). On the other hand, and at the same time, Fanon thinks through this very same description of lived experience – leaving the assumptions of the corporeal schema intact (without resolving its tension with the first moment).

In this second moment, Fanon writes, he was always required to navigate multiple, unstable spaces that do not appear for the white subject. It was not enough to "construct a physiological self, to balance space, to localize sensations … [he] was called on for more" (p. 111). His body had to bear a triplicate burden: He was responsible for his body, race, and ancestors, *and* keeping vestibular, tactile, kinesthetic balance, etc. Lewis R. Gordon speaks to this point brilliantly: "The logic of anonymity is, however, perverted in an antiblack world. If a black is overdetermined, then to see that black is to see every black" (1997, p. 75). In this second moment, Fanon leaves the logic of the claim intact and shows his lived reality outstrips the adequacy of the corporeal schema.

At the very least, Fanon suggests, the corporeal schema thought in isolation from the historical context which shapes embodiment is problematic of its perspective. The corporeal schema is not the unifying, global structuring of pre-reflexive life we all share. Fanon is demarcating a register of Black, colonized experience, which is not commensurate with or reducible to the corporeal schema. Indeed, Fanon writes, the "reality" of the Black subject reveals a "disparity between the corresponding schemas" (p. 150). In other words, the irreconcilability of the "agile," "fragmented," "exploded," and "immobile," of racialized, colonized subjectivity, cannot be absorbed by a better survey of the corporeal schema (p. 116).

To suggest such a view reasserts global assumptions and grants that an overarching shared perspective is more valuable than the attentiveness of sharing perspectives in their historical situatedness and through an awareness of the differential structuring schemas. On this reading of Fanon, the historico-racial schema and the racial epidermal schema are *not fuller accounts* or *more inclusive* versions of the corporeal schema; they are a different register of structuring experience, subjectivity, and spatiality.

Fanon's only explicit reference to Merleau-Ponty in *Black Skins, White Masks*, is a passage quoted *verbatim* from *The Structure of Behavior*, from the final section on the "Relations of the Soul and Body" (1942, p. 220), and *not Phenomenology of Perception*, as is mistakenly cited in Fanon's original text and reproduced without correction in the English translation (Fanon, 1952, p. 225). He prefaces his quote from Merleau-Ponty's *Structure of Behavior*, with this statement: "There are times when the black man is locked into his body" (Fanon, 1967, p. 225). The sentences from Merleau-Ponty, that follow, in fact reveal Fanon's own aiming at an account between the connection of our corporeality and the ensuing representations which effect and shape such a schema. Merleau-Ponty states "the relations of the soul and body – obscure as long as the body is treated in abstraction as a fragment of matter – are clarified only when one sees in the body the bearer of a dialectic" (1963, p. 204).

Fanon responds to this historical sensibility in Merleau-Ponty's words by taking the historical more seriously and hence "sketching" a "historico-racial schema," showing us how one of the most fundamental claims about embodiment and world-situatedness fails that very situatedness. Fanon's own engagement with Merleau-Ponty's notion of the corporeal schema returns that situatedness to phenomenological thought and offers an opening up of the possibilities of discovering registers of the body image. Fanon writes, "In the white world the man of color encounters difficulties in the development of his bodily schema. Consciousness of the body is solely a negating activity" (Fanon, 1967, p. 110).

In describing the lived experience of the Black, Fanon uncovers the way in which traditional phenomenological accounts – and not necessarily the phenomenological methodology itself – fails to attend to the particular historical-racial situation of marginalized, colonized, and Black subjects, which, Fanon assumes, is part of Merleau-Ponty's ambition. Fanon addresses this failure in terms of Merleau-Ponty's account of the "corporeal schema." Beyond the "global" and "unifying function," the corporeal schema that assumes a possibility of movement and psychic motility, Fanon finds another register of schemas, including a "historico-racial schema" and a "racial epidermal schema." In attending to the tensions which emerge in Fanon's reading of the corporeal schema in Merleau-Ponty – and in relation to Fanon's own articulation of the historico-racial schema in response – we can read Merleau-Ponty and Fanon together in order to refine an account of the corporeal schema and body image. Such a reading provides resources for developing ways of thinking the pre-reflexive as historical. Such resources are required if we are to begin to adequately grasp the racialized texture of embodied experience.

NOTES

1 This paper was first drafted in Robert Bernasconi's graduate course on Fanon (though he is not to be blamed for its shortcomings). Written in 2000, the work has benefited from the many kind folks at Gordon R. Lewis' roundtable – including Professor Lewis' gracious comments to this unknown student. It was from Gordon's phenomenology roundtable photocopy and website that a variously named Athena Colman/Coleman found some longevity. I have immense gratitude to those who generously engaged with this unpublished text. Finally, I owe a debt of gratitude to the editors of this volume who solicited this piece into its final form. Their patience and care for this piece has been a great act of collegiality. I am happy this work finds its home amongst the very thinkers who have deeply inspired the beginnings they fostered.

2 It is his inclusion and focus on the body that allowed Merleau-Ponty to reach a different conclusion from Husserl regarding the phenomenological method. Taking account of the body enabled Merleau-Ponty to assert that there is no completion to the phenomenological reduction (1962, p. xiv).

3 To be fair – the legacy of Cartesian dualism notwithstanding – the implicit critique of mind-body dualism leveraged here is in fact Descartes' critique of Aristotle on the soul's relation to the body. Merleau-Ponty takes this image to be helpful in his own account of the body. He writes, "Descartes once said profoundly, the soul is not merely in the body like a pilot in his ship; it is wholly intermingled with the body" (Merleau-Ponty, 1964a, p. 5). For the distinction between Descartes and *Cartesianism* see Cottingham (1998).

4 Lhermitte writes "we are in possession, in the penumbra of our consciousness, of an image of our bodily self, of our body of flesh [*chair*], unceasingly in the background of our memories, our representations, and our sensations of even the simplest sense of our body ... [for] how could we act on the world if we did not have a schema of our bearings [*attitudes*] and our situation in space, if we had not already presented, in our mind, the idea of our body? There can, therefore, be no doubt that our activity is based on a psycho-physiological foundation that is none other than the image of our bodily self [*l'image de notre moi corporel*]" (1939, p. 11). All translations of Lhermitte are my own.

5 This problem is not helped by Colin Smith's English translation of *Phenomenology of Perception*, which translates the term *schéma corporel* as body image, with the exception of one instance where Smith translates *schéma corporel* as corporeal schema (Merleau-Ponty, 1962, p. 142).

6 Indeed, from reading *Black Skin, White Masks* it is unclear if Fanon was even aware of Merleau-Ponty's work on the corporeal schema. His only explicit reference to Merleau-Ponty is from

The Structure of Behavior (1942, p. 220; 1963, p. 204). In *The Structure of Behavior*, Merleau-Ponty had not yet elaborated his notion of the corporeal schema despite his brief reference to Paul Schilder's (1923) *Das Körperschema* in the context of his critique of reflex theory (Merleau-Ponty, 1963 [1942], p. 30). Whether or not Fanon was, in fact, aware of Merleau-Ponty's particular elaboration of the corporeal schema is not consequential to the current discussion. Fanon's interrogation of this central phenomenological idea brings into relief an essential clarification of the ambiguities which have plagued these accounts (e.g., the question of the corporeal schema and body image). Fanon's thought shows us that these theoretical tensions run along the same fault-line of the failure to attend to the actuality of embodied subjectivity in its situated, historical and lived experience.

7 The purpose of such lengthy quotation is two-fold. First, Lhermitte's rehearsal of Bonnier contextualizes Merleau-Ponty's thought on the corporeal schema in terms of spatiality and the body, i.e., the meaning (direction) or *sense* of space which is the body. Second, I take the summary of the general categories of the so-called disorders of the schema to be more relevant to Fanon's discussion of the racialized subject's bodily expansion and contraction under the white or colonized gaze than Merleau-Ponty's more specific examples of anosognosia and phantom limb syndrome.

8 Correspondingly, Merleau-Ponty will also note this same "fabric of brute meaning" in terms of "primordial historicity" (1964a, p. 161).

9 For example, in speaking of phantom limb syndrome, Merleau-Ponty writes "the illusion is founded on a corporeal scheme or body image" (1973, p. 68, emphasis original).

10 In a working note from May 2, 1959, Merleau-Ponty will go so far as to say that the corporeal schema is the *"hinge* of the for itself and the for the other – To have a body is to be looked at (it is not only that), it is to be *visible*" (1968, p. 189, emphasis original).

11 *"[L]es hommes en tant qu'ils ont la possibilité d'être tous des hommes"* (Merleau-Ponty, 1964b, p. 15). Merleau-Ponty is close to generalizing *situation* at the expense of the very specificity it putatively commits to apprehending. Situation emptied out in this way risks surreptitiously staging phenomenological ambiguity in terms of psychological ambivalence, eliding historical, lived experience.

12 In the later approved version of the course notes, Merleau-Ponty is much more ambiguous in his claims. He also removes any mention of the "true liberal" (1964c).

13 Following Heidegger and Sartre, Merleau-Ponty uses the term *being-in-the-world* throughout his writings.

14 The notion of body image in Fanon is not limited to a discussion of Merleau-Ponty. In his discussion of the mirror stage, Fanon problematizes Lacan's understanding of the body image in noting it does not hold for the black subject, "[t]he Other is perceived on the level of the body image, absolutely as the not-self ... For the black man, as we have shown, historical and economic realities come into the picture" (1967, p. 161ft).

15 Borrowing Fanon's use of the term "livery."

REFERENCES

Bonnier, P. (1905). L'Aschématie [Aschematie]. *Revista de Neurología 13*, 605–609.

Cottingham, J. (1998). *Descartes*. Oxford: Oxford University Press.

Fanon, F. (1952). *Peau noire, masques blancs*. Paris: Éditions du Seuil.

Fanon, F. (1967). *Black skins, White masks*. New York: Grove Press.

Gallagher, S. (1986). Body image and body schema: A conceptual clarification. *The Journal of Mind and Behavior, 7*(4), 541–554.

Gallagher, S., & Meltzoff, A. N. (1996). The earliest sense of self and others: Merleau-Ponty and recent developmental studies. *Philosophical Psychology, 9*(2), 211–233.

Gordon, L. R. (1997). Existential dynamics of theorizing black invisibility. In L. R. Gordon (Ed.), *Existence in Black: An anthology of Black existential philosophy* (pp. 69–79). New York: Routledge.

Lhermitte, J. (1939). *L'image de Notre Corps*. Paris: Éditions de la nouvelle revue critique.

Merleau-Ponty, M. (1942). *La structure du comportement* [*The structure of behavior*]. Paris: Presses Universitaires de France.

Merleau-Ponty, M. (1960). *Les relations avec autri chez l'enfant* [*The child's relations with others*]. Paris: Centre de Documentation Universitaire. (Course notes 1950–1951).

Merleau-Ponty, M. (1963). *The structure of behavior* (A. Fisher, Trans.). Boston, MA: Beacon Press. (Original work published 1942)

Merleau-Ponty, M. (1962). *Phenomenology of perception* (C. Smith, Trans.). New York: Routledge. (Original work published 1945)

Merleau-Ponty, M. (1964a). *The primacy of perception*. Evanston, IL: Northwestern University Press.

Merleau-Ponty, M. (1964b). *Signs* (R. McCleary, Trans.). Evanston, IL: Northwestern University Press. (Original work published 1960)

Merleau-Ponty, M. (1964c). 'Les relations avec autri chez l'enfant' [The child's relations with others]. *Bulletin de Psychologie, 18*(236), 295–336. (Course notes 1950-1951).

Merleau-Ponty, M. (1968). *The visible and the invisible* (A. Lingis, Trans.). Evanston, IL: Northwestern University Press. (Original work published 1964)

Merleau-Ponty, M. (1973). *Consciousness and the acquisition of language* (H. J. Silverman, Trans.). Evanston, IL: Northwestern University Press. (Original work published 1964)

Schilder, P. (1923). *Das Körperschema: Ein Beitrag aure Lehre vom Bewusstsein des Eigenen Körpers* [*The corporeal schema: A contribution to the study of the consciousness of one's own body*]. Berlin: Springer-Verlag.

Weiss, G. (1999). *Body images: Embodiment as intercorporeality*. New York: Routledge.

CHAPTER 9

THE FACTICITY OF BLACKNESS

A Non-Conceptual Approach to the Study of Race and Racism in Fanon's and Merleau-Ponty's Phenomenology

Dilan Mahendran

REPRESENTATION AND PRESENTATIONS OF BLACKNESS

This chapter is an attempt to flesh out the significance of an embodied perception of race in lived experience. Today skin is no longer privileged as the threshold of either identity or particularity. I argue that there is a need for a *non-conceptual* understanding of race, racialization, and racism. To set the stage for this argument, I start with three powerful quotes. Gilroy (2002, p. 47) writes that "The idea of epidermalization points toward one intermediate stage in a critical theory of body scales in the making of 'race,'" while Fanon (1967, p. 116) notes "I am overdetermined from without. I am the slave not of the idea that others have of me but of my own appearance." These two quotes powerfully highlight the marked difference in scholarship in theorizing race today, while the third, from Maurice Merleau-Ponty (2002, p. 66), points to where science would indeed need to go in order to describe the relation between theory and practice. Merleau-Ponty writes that

> The first philosophical act would appear to be to return to the world of actual experience which is prior to the objective world, since it is in it that we shall be able to grasp the theoretical basis no less than the limits of that objective world, restore to things their concrete physiognomy, to organisms their individual ways of dealing with the world, and to subjectivity its inherence in history.

The eminent scholar, Lewis R. Gordon (2005), announces this as the space of experience and situation.[1]

Gilroy (2002) makes an explicit critique of Fanon's understanding of the process of racialization and declares it no longer relevant. Gilroy understands Fanon's concept of epidermalization[2] of race as being synonymous with skin color – as a referent to the idea or concept of race. In this way, one's skin color designates[3] or refers to a concept or idea, and it is that concept which holds the meaning for that skin color. For Gilroy, Fanon's privileging of skin color is not relevant today because what many contemporary critical race theorists have done is to primarily locate postmodern notions of racialization in the space of what is representable generally and in genomic[4] representations in particular. However, Fanon is actually not concerned with (re)presentations of race, as concept or cogitation, but its immanence in lived experience from the position of one who shows up as Black in an anti-Black world. Rather than (re)presentations, Fanon sheds light on the *presentation* of race, meaning how racial intelligibility is manifest to us immediately in perception. To dismiss the quotidian way racial minorities in the West experience the violence of race and racism as no longer critical in contemporary theory is incredibly disconcerting and shows the investment that scholars have in the detachment of their research from the real world and their continual disparagement of experience as a foundational and valid form of

DOI: 10.4324/9781003037132-9

knowledge. In a double move, this peculiar Western rationality has condemned both "lived experience" as well as those that are understood as only experiential beings (not mindful), that is, people of color, to be non-existent in history.

In *Black Skin, White Masks* Fanon (1967) compares the existential crisis of being Jewish with that of being Black. For a Jewish person whose appearance is immediately like that of his white Aryan oppressor, he can conceal for at least a moment his Jewishness because his Jewishness is but a collection of objective facts about him (that he is from Warsaw, from the ghetto, that his name is Goldstein, etc.). The Jew appears to white others as another white person, in other words, a human. Fanon concludes that for a Black person there is no such possibility in an anti-Black world because a Black person is immediately caught out by white eyes in the visual field of human perception as either hyper-visible or invisible, as Ralph Ellison (1993) articulates in *Invisible Man*.[5] Therefore it's not the *idea* of race but the immediate pre-reflective and pre-linguistic appearance of what we call Blackness or more generally "racedness." Contrarily, (re)presentations of race must be cognizable and therefore within the positive sciences there is a tendency toward rational and explanatory models of race theory. What Fanon argues is that ideas of race as abstracted representations of lived experience miss the gravity of the phenomena of showing up as a "nègre" and the formation of the self-consciousness of a person who appears to others in this way. I would argue that the relevance of a phenomenology of race is as much a contemporary issue as it was in post war France. Gilroy's (2002) honest mistake is that he confuses the lived experience of race for its (re)presentation. It is the representation of Blackness and its commoditization in popular culture that Gilroy sees as shifting in the history of "raciology," and not the lived experience of showing up Black which has been durable in the long history of racism in the West.

Gilroy is probably not alone here, and one can argue that the bulk of race theory leans toward the privileging of mind in prioritizing idea, concept, and cognition rather than including bodily experience of being perceived as such and such a race. How we live the process of racialization and "showing up" in such and such a racial way is difficult to describe. As Linda Martín Alcoff (2001) argues, the process of being raced appears to us as self-evident; it occurs via a sort of common sense which does not resort to categories and classifications or call upon (re)presentations. This does not simply mean that racial intelligibility is sublimated to the unconscious and therefore rendered unrecoverable. Merleau-Ponty writes: "I can experience more things than I represent to myself … there are feelings in me which I do not name, and also spurious states of well-being to which I am not fully given over" (2002, pp. 345–346). We can say that the fund of perceptual experience is pregnant with meaning, but meanings that are not always readily articulable in cognition and through language. To pass over the most mundane experiences such as the intelligibility of human bodies seems to implicate that their depths go far deeper than merely that which is thought. It implies, furthermore, that there are sedimented layers of experience which impinge on our ability to see others as who they really are, as human. If race and racism were simply ideas and ideologies,[6] it should stand that we could rationally rethink our way out of it but, as I argue, racial perception is implicated at a more fundamental level of who we are and how we experience the world.

Philosophers Linda Martín Alcoff (2001), Athena Coleman (2005), Lewis R. Gordon (2005), and Jeremy Weate (2001) are but a few scholars who take up Fanon's phenomenology and his re-articulation and challenge to Merleau-Ponty's descriptions of corporeal existence. In this chapter I attempt to extend Merleau-Ponty's (2002) theory of perception and his subsequent development of a radical primordial ontology to the study of racial difference and racism. What makes Merleau-Ponty's existential phenomenology interesting is that we can take a close look at the experience of race and racism – along with much of what we understand as "race difference" – as it is *lived* by the body. Much of the theorization of race theory privileges abstract epistemological concepts of racialization that explain structural and discursive formations of racial ideology and representation. This area of race scholarship, objective racial knowledge, can be seen as an *epistemological* approach to the study of race. The result of this is that race is reducible to a concept that is cognizable by the mind on an abstract *de-worlded* level. However, emphasis on the abstract objective constructions of race that appear at the structural level neglect the problem that race is lived and experienced through the body, both individually and generally. It can be said that aside from the objective knowing of the positive sciences there is also a *bodily* knowing that founds the possibility of any knowing at all – certainly the objective and abstracted knowing of the positive sciences. Merleau-Ponty would say that we are existent in the world and moreover that we are already thrown into a shared world. For Merleau-Ponty these abstractions of race would be a sort of intellectualism that cannot account for the phenomena of racism as experienced in our average everydayness.

THE PITFALLS OF INTELLECTUALISM

Fanon describes a point in his intellectual career where he maintained an objective view of racism, one he subsequently found to be inadequate. In *Black Skin, White Masks* he notes,

> I have talked about the black problem with friends, or, more rarely with American Negroes … But I was satisfied with an intellectual understanding of these differences. It was not really dramatic … And then the occasion arose when I had to meet the white man's eyes. An unfamiliar weight burdened me. The real world challenged my claims.
>
> *(1967, p. 110)*

What Fanon reveals here is that even though he had an objective and critical view of racism, once he experienced racial discrimination in the *flesh*, he realized that intellectualist accounts of racism had in no way prepared him for the subjective experience. Fanon doesn't necessarily jettison an objective account of racism, but asserts that an objective general account needs the subjective[7] individual account in order to attain a comprehensive interpretation of racism(s). The linguistic turn in Anglo-American Eurocentric scholarship has conflated experience with identity essentialism. Appeals to personal, ethnic, racial, gender, and class identity have come to be seen as a bounded and often rigid set of discursive categories with exclusive characteristics. These discursive boundaries, when policed, include some but exclude others, therefore reproducing the same levels of epistemic violence that the groups' members were trying to avoid in the first place. However not all meaning is discursively produced, so to say that experience and personal identity is always already a discursive formation is problematic. This narrow view of experience as "condemned to language" inhibits the possibility for a comprehensive interpretation of existence and experience. Merleau-Ponty's phenomenology is critically important on this account because taken seriously, the body as the locus of meaning – as lived body amongst other beings in the world – offers a radical perspective on experience.

I would argue that dismissing sustained attention to the body and experience has come to pervade post-colonial studies, which, ironically, maintains the project of elucidating the violent experience of colonial, neo-colonial, and imperial racism. In the following passage from *Culture and Imperialism*, Edward Said (1993) invokes Gramsci to describe the problems of essentialism and essences in regards to ethnic identity:

> If one believes with Gramsci that an intellectual vocation is socially possible as well as desirable, then it is an inadmissible contradiction at the same time to build analyses of historical experience around exclusions, exclusions that stipulate, for instance, that only women can understand feminine experience, only Jews can understand Jewish suffering, only formerly colonial subjects can understand colonial experience.
>
> *(p. 31)*

Said goes on to write:

> if at the outset we acknowledge the massively knotted and complex histories of special but nevertheless overlapping and interconnected experiences – of women, of Westerners, of Blacks, of national states and cultures – there is no particular intellectual reason for granting each and all of them an ideal and essentially separate status.
>
> *(1993, pp. 31–32).*

Said is correct in pointing out the pitfalls of overinvested and essentialized identities, but for Said, essentialism seems to be an inevitable outcome of privileging a specific experience, whether being Jewish, a woman, Black, etc....

What is striking is that Said invokes Gramsci's important notion of an intellectual, which he (Gramsci, 1999) expands from the "traditional" intellectual to include the "organic" intellectual, produced "organically" from the ranks of the oppressed classes to articulate its experiences and challenge an oppressive hegemonic order. A close reading of Gramsci's (1999) section on intellectuals in *The Prison Notebooks* reveals that in order to obliterate the bourgeoisie's monopoly on intellectual life, Gramsci needed first to expunge the dominant Cartesian mind/body split. In the Marxian dialectical sense, mind would refer to the bourgeois intellectual while body refers to the proletarian factory wage worker. Gramsci does this by bringing the body and mind back together where the body and bodily skill were also part and parcel to mind and thinking. Once this dualism is shattered, it becomes possible to see that the craftsman and worker have as much to bear on intellectual life as the professional philosopher. Said (1993) does not bring Gramsci's expanded notion of intellectual to bear on experience and resigns himself to the Cartesian one.

Said's schema of an "intellectual" is one made in his own image where only a theoretical understanding of bodily experience is sufficient to understanding what it means to be racialized, colonized, or oppressed. This I would argue is a one-dimensional view of identity and experience as only discursively produced rather than co-dependent on identity as *lived*. In short, Said only proffers an intellectualist approach to the interrogation of identity and one that nominalizes experience, approaching it as forever "condemned to language" and therefore as subordinate to it.

BLACK TO THE THINGS THEMSELVES

Merleau-Ponty never applied his theory of perception and primordial ontology to an interpretation of the colonial situation; his project was to establish a universal ontology irrespective of society, culture, and institutions. From his *Phenomenology of Perception* to his last working notes, Merleau-Ponty consistently placed the perceiving body[8] as the centerpiece to his new ontology. It would be this primordial ontology that would then explain epistemology, culture, society, etc.

Merleau-Ponty starts his phenomenological project with the *perceiving* body; human perception is therefore a prerequisite for his ontology. For Merleau-Ponty's philosophical project, furthermore, it becomes important to foreground the primalness of perception as something universal to all of humankind. Anthropology is ripe with empirical data that can be drawn upon as reference to man and the "state of nature." What I mean here is that anthropology has, historically, offered up the concept of "the primitive," a concept necessary to embark on the approach of perception as first philosophy put forth in *Phenomenology of Perception*. True perceptual experience in which man could perceive things and space as they were in and of themselves was something that modern European man had, in a sense, lost. In this way Merleau-Ponty is in the shared company of French Enlightenment thinkers Jean-Jacques Rousseau and Etienne Condillac, both of whom made thorough critiques of Cartesian dualism, Rousseau (2009) in his *Essay on the Origin of Human Languages* and Condillac (2001) in his *Essay on the Origin of Human Knowledge*. This influence extends to the anthropology of Claude Levi-Strauss (1966), who, like Merleau-Ponty himself, was Rousseauian in his deployment of the anthropological category of the "primitive" as a means to critique European man and rationalism.

The inability to see, feel, hear, taste, and smell the things as they appeared to the perceiving body was in effect the foundational part of the crisis of European man. This crisis was only made visible by looking and comparing oneself to non-European man, essentially primitive man. Merleau-Ponty writes: "a primitive man in the desert is always able to take his bearings immediately without having to cast his mind back, and add up distances covered and deviations made since setting off" (2002, p. 115). No doubt this is a fantastical image of the savage. He goes on to say, "Primitive peoples, in so far as they live in a world of myth, do not overstep existential space, and this is why for them dreams count just as much as perceptions" (2002, p. 332). Much like Rousseau's "savage," the primitive here functions as means to show how the world should appear as it is to the pre-personal corporeal schema or to a schema unfettered by the "crypto-mechanisms" of the modern perceiving European subject. The problem of the modern intellectual European man is that he cannot see the thing as it appears to his body because he has allowed reason to colonize his very perception of himself, others, and world. Merleau-Ponty writes: "We must therefore stop wondering how and why red signifies effort or violence, green restfulness and peace; we must *rediscover* how to live these colours as our body does, that is, as peace or violence in concrete form" (2002, p. 245, emphasis original). The power to see things as they really are is the already contained promise of our perceiving body; we need only to "rediscover" it. Merleau-Ponty makes the rediscovery of bodily perception the primary project of the *Phenomenology of Perception*.

MERLEAU-PONTY'S NORMATIVE BODY

In the following pages I want to describe Fanon's appropriation and critique of Merleau-Ponty's description of bodily perception as articulated in *Black Skin, White Masks*. In this text, devoted almost exclusively to "being,"[9] or more correctly *non-being*, in the colonial situation, Fanon appropriates and challenges Western phenomenological and psychoanalytical traditions – the Hegelian ontological position of Jean-Paul Sartre (1992) and the Freudian view of the unconscious of Jacques Lacan respectively. Merleau-Ponty's theory of perception likewise figures prominently in *Black Skin, White Masks*. Though Fanon is critical of these Western conceptualizations, I argue that his phenomenology is not entirely incommensurable with that of Merleau-Ponty.

There are two fundamental philosophical themes Fanon and Merleau-Ponty agree on: The phenomenology of appearances, and the condition of human freedom. Freedom is for both philosophers derivative of the phenomena of the perceptual world being disclosed. The fundamental critique that Fanon indirectly levels against Merleau-Ponty concerns the latter's argument that there is a normative pre-personal corporeal schema that all humans share, a corporeal schema that exists as a biological given that cannot be fundamentally altered by society, culture, and language. Fanon argues that if we take this normative corporeal schema and subject it to a history of anti-Black racism and anti-Black existence, Merleau-Ponty's universal corporeal schema loses some of its universal givens. In short, Fanon implicitly charges that Merleau-Ponty's theory of the normative corporeal schema[10] is based upon European man, a white man.

Merleau-Ponty does show that the universal corporeal schema can be subtended by other cultural schemas, such as a sexual schema. Yet for Merleau-Ponty, these second-order schemas only influence or impinge on the corporeal schema and never have the capacity to overtake the primordiality of perception. Fanon argues that in an anti-Black world a Black person has in addition other schemas, a "historico-racial schema" and a "racial epidermal schema." The historico-racial schema is the sedimented personal experiences of anti-Black racism that a Black person endures. These are not memories imprinted on the brain but sedimented experiences that pre-delineate the exterior horizons of what is possible and what to anticipate in an anti-Black world. The historico-racial schema is a set of dispositions about how to accept the world and live in it. The racial-epidermal schema is the interior horizon of self and others within the immediate perceptual experience of the world. The racial epidermal schema impacts a Black person's tacit sense of self and is immediately in play in the phenomena of appearing or showing up as Black in an anti-Black world.

For Fanon the historico-racial schema and the racial epidermal schema tacitly inform a Black person's sense of self. The question is to what extent, if any, and in what relation, do the historico-racial schema and the racial-epidermal schema colonize the biological perceptual system, the system that according to Merleau-Ponty establishes the possibility for any level of consciousness (pre-reflective, reflective, intersubjective consciousness etc.)?

Firstly, it is necessary to look at the phenomenological description of bodily perception that Merleau-Ponty articulates in *Phenomenology of Perception*. Merleau-Ponty writes:

> [the perceiving body's] spatiality is not, like that of external objects or like that of "spatial sensations," a *spatiality of position*, but a *spatiality of situation* ... If I stand holding my pipe in my closed hand, the position of my hand is not determined discursively by the angle which it makes with my forearm, and my forearm with my upper arm, and my upper arm with my trunk, and my trunk with the ground. I *know* [my emphasis] indubitably where my pipe is, and thereby I know where my hand and my body are.
>
> *(2002, pp. 114–115)*

What Merleau-Ponty (2002) argues against is a cognitivist or intellectualist perspective on how the lived body forms its own space and has a tacit sense of self. The intellectualist perspective on perception holds that our bodies are like any other object that we re-present, that in our minds we calculate the dimensions, distance, and movement our bodies have, and then act. For the intellectualist the act of smoking a pipe is purely a mental activity where mind determines through calculation what the body can and should do in an atomistic fashion. This is a Kantian metaphysical conception of the human and the body, where a conscious, knowing subject represents the world, including one's body, through mentalist activities as representable objects splayed out before the knowing subject. However,

Merleau-Ponty's (2002) challenge is that the lived human body in its everydayness does not exist as subject[11] or object but rather as what he calls the "third term" or the perceiving body. In this view the body perceives the world and objects holistically in unity rather than as discrete and atomic sensations that are compiled together by the mind and then represented to the knowing subject.

Merleau-Ponty's (2002) bodily "knowing" is tacit knowing or what he calls the *tacit cogito*, a pre-reflective consciousness of the body in its own spatial field. This entails a certain sense of itself in the world, but not one that implies a subject formation or an "I." For Merleau-Ponty, the perceiving body is not simply another object in the world of objects, even in the pre-personal biological sense of perception. Merleau-Ponty's notion of this pre-reflective consciousness of one's own body in space is an important aspect of how Fanon experiences his own body but with additional schemas: The historico-racial schema and racial-epidermal schema. Merleau-Ponty presents the corporeal schema as a universal given of human being. For him, human perception is foundational for human existence and being-in-the-world; it is the primordial point where human being becomes possible at all.

FANON'S BODY AS ALWAYS FOR OTHERS

Next let us look at the problem of the Black body for Fanon. Fanon introduces us to these issues by way of his own experience in France as a Black Caribbean immigrant in a white world. It is worth here quoting Fanon in full to reveal his position on a post-colonial situation:

> In the white world the man of color encounters difficulties in development of his bodily schema. Consciousness of the body is solely a negating activity. It is a third-person consciousness. The body is surrounded by an atmosphere of certain uncertainty. I know that if I want to smoke, I shall have to reach out my right arm and take the pack of cigarettes lying at the other end of the table. The matches, however, are in the drawer on the left, and I shall have to lean back slightly. And all these movements are made not out of habit but out of implicit knowledge. A slow composition of myself as a body in the middle of a spatial and temporal world – such seems to be the schema. It does not impose itself on me; it is, rather, a definitive structuring of the self and the world – definitive because it creates a real dialectic between my body and the world ... Below the corporeal schema I had sketched a historico-racial schema. The elements that I used had been provided for me not by "residual sensations and perceptions primarily of a tactile, vestibular, kinesthetic, and visual character," but by the other, the white man, who had woven me out of a thousand details, anecdotes, stories.
>
> *(1967, pp. 110–111)*

Taking a cue from Merleau-Ponty's (2002) *Phenomenology of Perception* and Sartre's (1992) *Being and Nothingness*, Fanon describes phenomenologically the establishment of his body in space and time and the body's use of the tacit knowledge of abstract movement. Fanon concurs with Merleau-Ponty that the givenness of the body and knowledge of itself "seems to be the [body] schema" (1967, p. 111). This givenness of the body is for itself, not given by the other. At the same time however, the historico-racial schema is imposed by white others; therefore, consciousness of himself is subtended in such a way that the pre-personal biological schema has no autonomous bearing on Fanon's consciousness of himself. Fanon is forced to only see himself through the white others' eyes, through their stories about Negroes and savages. Directly challenging Merleau-Ponty's theory of the general existence of the lived body, Fanon places a historico-racial schema below that of the corporeal schema. The historico-racial schema is not discursively produced. It is made up of the sedimented experiences of racism that subtend one's corporeal schema. It is what Fanon refers to as the affective field (Merleau-Ponty's phenomenal field), "the definitive structuring of self and of the world" (1967, p. 111) that is not as such imposed but given by the body and being-in-the-world. The body is the locus of the *tacit cogito*, the primordial pre-reflective consciousness of self and world.

Merleau-Ponty would certainly agree with the possibility of the existence of the historico-racial schema. However, the assertion that it could nullify the pre-personal corporeal schema would, in all likelihood, be rejected by him. Fanon proves instructive here. Fanon was conscious of himself but *through the eyes of whites as a body always for others*. It could be argued that Merleau-Ponty's pre-personal corporeal schema was in fact subtended by this historico-racial schema in a similar way that Merleau-Ponty (2002) himself argued that the *sexual schema* subtended the pre-personal corporeal schema. Yet Fanon argues adamantly that the corporeal schema for the Black man is obliterated to such an extent that it is never able to establish itself as it can for whites. However, in the situation Fanon describes above, he can still stand and act and his body continues to be the primary locus of this action. Fanon continues:

> Then assailed at various points, the corporeal schema crumbled, its place taken by a racial epidermal schema. In the train it was no longer a question of being aware of my body in the third person but in triple person. In the train I was given not one but two, three places. I had already stopped being amused. It was not that I was finding febrile coordinates in the world. I existed triply: I occupied space. I moved toward the other … and the evanescent other, hostile but not opaque, transparent, not there, disappeared. Nausea.
>
> *(1967, p. 112)*

How can Fanon assert that what he calls the corporeal schema, a description that is commensurable with that described by Merleau-Ponty, be trumped by the historico-racial schema and then later a racial-epidermal schema? One could argue that what Fanon is describing are two separate phenomenal descriptions of consciousness. The first being the pre-reflective tacit knowledge of one's own body in the world. The second being the "third person" consciousness of self that is imposed by the white other's gaze. So rather than a corporeal schema, what Fanon may be describing is his own subjective body image, a reflection of himself through white others' eyes. Perhaps Fanon is conflating two types of consciousness, one that is a universal biological given, originating at the level of the perceiving body, and the other a reflective consciousness of himself that is discursively produced by a racist culture. We might, however, ask: Is the latter so-called reflective third-person consciousness of the self really a reflective consciousness of the self, or is it directly linked to the pre-reflective consciousness of body schema?

The racist phenomena Fanon describes have their apparent origin in the visual field of perception, when the white other directs his/her gaze upon Fanon. Making a hard and fast distinction based upon state and content of consciousness seems, as such, problematic. If the second phenomena, generated by the white gaze, is a pure reflective consciousness, then this would require an isolated subject, one who is removed from the world. This however is not the case with the phenomena that Fanon describes, existential phenomena pertaining to active being-in-the-world and being with others. The phenomena that Fanon experiences cannot be reduced to an intellectualist conceptual articulation of racist stories and anecdotes. They are better understood as the interpretation of these stories as projected onto his epidermis by the white gaze.

Fanon possesses a viable corporeal schema, inasmuch as he – like every other human entity – possesses tacit knowledge of his body. Yet at some fundamental level this other layer of significance (that of the historico-racial and racial-epidermal schemas) does not allow for the possibility of complete human recognition. This is what negates the possibility of intersubjectivity or being with others in a direction towards reciprocity. Fanon shows up for whites in postwar France not as a human being, and not as an object, but as something quite outside of the subject/object relation. It is the one-way street of the white's gaze that articulates the uncanny ontological status of Fanon.

Fanon is not a subject like the European man, nor is he an Other, or an object. He is a thirdly thing that is there as a living body but not there as human.[12] He exhibits the behavior not of a thing but of a human that is caught out there living in the world, while at the same time not being afforded the self-consciousness of the normative subject. So, for Fanon inter-subjective consciousness of the self with others is not simply posterior to pre-reflective consciousness of the corporeal schema. For him, biology is not always anterior to sociality. We can see now how the earlier hypotheses – referring here to Fanon's description of two types of consciousness, a pre-reflective consciousness and perception of others and others of him – is incorrect. Rather, anonymous biological existence and personal human existence are interwoven, one effecting the other, simultaneously, and in both directions.

Merleau-Ponty (2002) is for the most part clear about the distinction of the biological facticity of the body as comprehensively determinant of the pre-personal corporeal schema. This corporeal schema is, for him, universal to humans and is anterior to personal and cultural human existence. Indeed, for Merleau-Ponty the pre-personal corporeal schema is fundamental. The crisis of modern being for Merleau-Ponty is that *personal* human existence is thought to overrun the primordial perceiving body. If getting back to the things themselves is the phenomenological spirit for Merleau-Ponty then it becomes necessary to get back to primal perception. Merleau-Ponty does see our biological existence in synchronization with our human or social existence as a general way of existing. He allows for exceptions or aberrations of this order where the synchronization of the pre-personal to personal is not always seemingly given:

> so it can be said that my organism, as a pre-personal cleaving to the general form of the world, as an anonymous and general existence, plays, beneath my personal life, the part of an *inborn complex*. It is not some kind of inert thing; it too has something of the momentum of existence. It may even happen when I am in danger that my human situation abolishes my biological one, that my body lends itself without reserve to action. But these moments can be no more than moments, and for most of the time personal existence represses the organism without being able either to go beyond it or to renounce itself; without, in other words, being able either to reduce the organism to its existential self, or itself to the organism.
>
> *(2002, p. 97, emphasis original)*

Here it seems that in moments of danger the human situation can overrun the biological anonymous existence of the body. Merleau-Ponty stresses that these moments of danger can only be fleeting moments. His description of the phenomenon of mortal danger, of life and death in times of war, is one of the few places in *Phenomenology of Perception* where Merleau-Ponty concedes to an abolition of the pre-personal corporeal schema. This has an important impact on his foundational thesis on perception. For realists who take seriously the thesis of lived bodily perception that Merleau-Ponty expounds, the possibility of human existence taking on a type of dominance over the prospect of its synchronicity with biological existence will be seen as an aberration.

Is the phenomenon of racism that Fanon describes an exceptional moment in his everyday life? Perhaps, rather than focusing on the moment as anomalous, we should look to the essence of that moment as apparent also in other situations. In average everydayness – which is of course different from exceptional moments of mortal danger – Saint-Exupéry says that "meaning is not at stake" (cited in Merleau-Ponty, 2002, p. 97). So, it is not death itself but the possibility of death that evokes meaning; the essence of the moment is the *contingency* of life and meaning itself as presented to the self. Is then meaning at stake for Fanon? In that terrible moment of racism Fanon writes "Look at the nigger! ... Mama, a Negro! ... Hell, he's getting mad. Take no notice, sir, he does not know that you are as civilized as we" (1967, p. 113). Fanon then describes his experience of himself and being with white others:

> The white world, the only honorable one, barred me from all participation. A man was expected to behave like a man. I was expected to behave like a black man – or at least like a nigger ... I resolved, since it was impossible for me to get away from an *inborn complex*, to assert myself as a BLACK MAN. Since the other hesitated to recognize me, there remained only one solution: to make myself known.
>
> *(1967, pp. 114–115, emphasis original)*

Does the violence of the phenomena that Fanon describes constitute a challenge to existential meaning for him? It is clear that the enduring effects of white racism that Fanon describes call into question consistently the meaning of being human, of human existence. The experience of racism by the racialized seems inevitably to always put one's existence at stake. We might ask then: Are these racist experiences simply anomalous moments, or is it the case that the general existence of the racialized one constantly calls into question the meaning of being human?

NOTES

1 As Gordon writes: "Between Reason and History, Theory and Practice, there is experience which in this case is the realization of a situation that stimulates an existential struggle against sedimented, dehumanized constructions" (2005, p. 16).

2 In *Black Skin, White Masks* Fanon (1967) utilizes what can be understood as pathological metaphors to describe the colonial condition. Fanon deploys "epidermalization" to characterize the phenomena – both perceptual and psychical – of anti-Black racism, emphasizing the primacy of vision that, in a sense, metastases as a cancer on the body of Blacks who must live with that skin, never being able to escape it. Epidermalization is the processual intertwining of the "historico-racial schema" and "racial epidermal schema." The "historico-racial schema" designates the sedimented and knotted fabric of self experiences of anti-Black racism alongside its interpellating discourses, something akin to the prereflective conscious memory of lived experiences of racist violence. The "racial epidermal schema" is the immediately manifest intelligibility of Blackness or showing up as such.

3 See Charles Taylor's (1980) influential essay "Theories of Meaning" where he describes two areas of theorizing meaning in the philosophy of language: (1) designative and (2) expressive.

4 The significance of bio-technological articulations of race is not to be dismissed, yet genetic concepts of race help little in situations of DWB (driving while Black) or looking "Arab" in a U.S. airport.

5 Ellison writes: "When they approach me they see only my surroundings, themselves, or figments of their imagination – indeed, everything and anything except me" (1993, p. 3).

6 Representational racial politics in a sense assumes such a reality. The implication of such a view is that once civic, state, and corporate institutions are peopled with "representative"

minorities at all levels, race will cease to be an issue. However, if one takes a non-representational or non-conceptual approach to understanding the reality of racism, it is conceivable that an anti-Black world is more than possible, even when these institutions are replete with minorities at all levels of institutional authority. In other words, simply having Blacks in positions of authority does not mean that anti-Black racism will go away. One could conceive of a white supremacist nation being run by an executive branch that was predominantly filled with racial minorities. This possibility points to the pervasiveness and embeddedness of racism not only in how we see the world, but in how we inhabit and dwell within it.

7 Alcoff (2001) writes about this difference between objective and subjective accounts of race and racism and calls for a combined approach in order to gain a richer understanding about how racial intelligibility functions in society and for the individual consciousness. My understanding of Fanon and Merleau-Ponty is quite similar to that of Alcoff except in respect of the question of what subjectivity is for human perception. Beginning with Merleau-Ponty, I move in a different direction from Alcoff's notion of "body image" and "body schema." The two are not interchangeable. "Body image" refers to one's conscious reflection on how they see their own bodies. For example, the "body image" is that which is a self-conscious representation like an anorexic's view that they are always too fat and never thin enough. Our "body schema," on the other hand, is tacit yet unreflective knowledge about our body, its movements, its generation of space; it is body as being-in-the-world. The "body schema" is not the result of habit or mere repetitive movement in the world but of implicit knowledge of our own space and movement toward objects and humans. It is anterior and foundational to cognition. I consequently fundamentally differ with Alcoff on two key aspects of Merleau-Ponty: In respect of the conflation of "body image" with "body schema," firstly, and in terms of the conflation of "perceptual practices or habits" with tacit bodily knowledge and bodily skill secondly.

8 According to Merleau-Ponty, human perception, along with the consideration of the body as locus of meaning, results in a state of subjectivity without anthropocentrism. This means that the subject, or what Sartre (1992) would call the *for-itself* (*poursoi*), is not our normative and general way of being-in-the-world. Our general mode of existence is neither subject nor object but that of *bodily experience*. Some have translated this as "body subject" but this is incorrect because designating the body as some sort of subject drags perception into a privatization of experience, to a mere psychologism.

9 The subject of ontology, or the doing of ontology (the science of being), proves problematic for Fanon because as he correctly argues, the Black has no ontological resistance to the self/ Other dialectic of whites and therefore has no possibility of appearing as human in an anti-Black world. However, Fanon is clearly doing ontology and describing a postcolonial ontology. Therefore it is not ontology as a science itself that he rejects but *the ontological assumptions of the West* in general, and of Sartre and Merleau-Ponty in particular. Even more fundamentally, Fanon critiques implicitly Heidegger's fundamental ontology of *Dasein* because if we understand generally the entity of *Dasein* as "being-there," then for the Black, according to Fanon, it's "*nicht-sein*," "not being" or "not-there." Fanon articulates this precisely when he writes "I moved toward the other ... and the evanescent other, hostile but not opaque, transparent, not there, disappeared. Nausea" (1967, p. 112).

10 Iris Marion Young (1980) and Don Ihde (2001) make similar critiques of Merleau-Ponty's normative corporeal schema.

11 The issue of the subject is fundamental for Merleau-Ponty. Some have incorrectly called the perceiving body or "third term" the "body-subject." This is misleading because it implies a "subject." Merleau-Ponty never actually uses such a description as "body subject."

12 Here we do well to recall that the consciousness of the body for the Black man is "a third-person consciousness" (Fanon, 1967, p. 110) that the imposition of the historico-racial schema upon the racial-epidermal schema results in Fanon's experience of being split "into a triple person ... I existed triply: I occupied space. I moved toward the other ... and the evanescent other, hostile but not opaque, transparent, not there, disappeared" (Fanon, 1967, p. 112).

REFERENCES

Alcoff, L. M. (2001). Toward a phenomenology of racial embodiment. In R. Bernasconi (Ed.), *Race* (pp. 267–283). Oxford: Blackwell.

Coleman, A. (2005). Corporeal schemas and body images: Fanon, Merleau-Ponty and the lived experience of race. Unpublished paper.

Condillac, E. (2001). *Essay on the origin of human knowledge.* Cambridge: Cambridge University Press.

Ellison, R. (1993). *Invisible man.* New York: 20th Century Library.

Fanon, F. (1967). *Black skin, White masks.* New York: Grove Press.

Gilroy, P. (2002). *Against race: Imagining political culture beyond the color line.* Cambridge, MA: Belknap Press.

Gordon, L. R. (2005). Through the zone of nonbeing: A reading of Black skin, White masks in celebration of Fanon's eightieth birthday. *The CLR James Journal, 11*(1), 1–43.

Gramsci, A. (1999). *Selections from the prison notebooks.* New York: International Publishers.

Ihde, D. (2001). *Bodies in technology.* Minneapolis, MN: University of Minnesota Press.

Lévi-Strauss, C. (1966). *The savage mind.* Chicago, IL: University of Chicago Press.

Merleau-Ponty, M. (2002). *Phenomenology of perception.* New York: Routledge.

Rousseau, J. J. (2009). *Essay on the origin of languages and writings related to music.* Hanover: Dartmouth College Press.

Said, E. (1993). *Culture and imperialism.* New York: Vintage.

Sartre, J. P. (1992). *Being and nothingness.* New York: Washington Square Press.

Taylor, C. (1980). Theories of meaning. *Man and World, 13,* 281–302.

Weate, J. (2001). Fanon, Merleau-Ponty and the difference of phenomenology. In R. Bernasconi (Ed.), *Race* (pp. 169–183). Oxford: Blackwell.

Young, M. I. (1980). Throwing like a girl: A phenomenology of feminine body comportment, motility and spatiality. *Human Studies, 3,* 137–156.

CHAPTER 10

"THE PLACE WHERE LIFE HIDES AWAY"

Merleau-Ponty, Fanon, and the Location of Bodily Being

Gayle Salamon

In much critical writing about the body, the notion persists that the body is something of which we have unmediated knowledge, that the body is a material thing that we possess or *are* unproblematically, effortlessly, utterly. Philosophy in general, and phenomenology in particular, is forever asking us to interrogate truth claims: *How do we know what we know?* Interestingly, truth claims that emanate from the body, or the body itself as a truth claim, often escape our epistemological scrutiny. However, like most kinds of knowledge, our epistemological certainty about our own bodies is not given, but is delivered by processes and interactions – mostly mundane and largely unremarkable – that connect us to the world through which we move. This chapter will examine some of the ways in which our knowledge of the body is mediated in an attempt to show that this social mediation shapes not only our *knowledge of* our bodies but our *feelings in* them as well. These are structurations that take place at the border between the body and the world and exemplify the ways in which the outermost edge of the body is malleable and permeable. In the first section of this paper, I will discuss Maurice Merleau-Ponty's descriptions of proprioception and its creation of the outermost edge of the body. In the second section, I look at the idea of "flesh" that Merleau- Ponty outlines in *The Visible and the Invisible,* and examine the function of perception as the means by which relations between myself and the world are organized. Through perception, I apprehend the other, located just beyond the sensate border of my body; I also find the limit of my own body through perception. In the third section, I turn to bodily inwardness – in Merleau-Ponty's words, "anonymous life" – in *Phenomenology of Perception* and Frantz Fanon's *Black Skin, White Masks.* There, I ask if it is possible to consider the inner experience of embodiment without postulating a deep core of bodily being that exists unaffected by structures of race and gender. I aim to challenge the common assumption that the outside envelope of the body may be subject to the shaping press of the world that is its context, but that there exists beneath this outer surface an inner core of the embodied self that is immune to these pressures. An account of gender and race that understands "surface" interventions to be secondary or auxiliary modifications that are overlaid on the ungendered, unraced materiality of the body cannot explain the pervasiveness of the structures of either race or gender. This parsing of inside and outside necessarily posits another body beneath the surface of the visible and the bodily scene of difference, an "underneath" that is untroubled by dramas and dilemmas of racial or sexual difference, and thus restores an embodied subject whose ostensible "universality" critical studies of race and gender have taught us to view with skepticism. Even those aspects of the body that would seem to escape or evade structures of gender and race, that is, the body as it exists beyond the scope of the visible, are in fact still marked by them. Gender and race *are* often read from the surface of the body (though in quite different ways); however, gender and race cannot be said to be *located* there, but must also be understood to structure and shape the ways in which all subjects relate to their own bodies and, in turn, to the world. Here, I will argue that gender

DOI: 10.4324/9781003037132-10

and race can determine our very ability to retreat into the body, to experience the body *as* a core or a haven into which the self might retreat.

Put another way: We are by now comfortable enough with the notion that "gender" and "race" are socially constructed categories. I am suggesting that we do not yet have a thorough enough account of how the body's inner life is constructed by these categories and want to suggest that the accounts of bodily being offered by Merleau-Ponty and Fanon give us a way of understanding the retreat into the body as a difficult but necessary achievement that paradoxically both is born of social relations and opens the way for a body and a subject to exist in the world.

PROPRIOCEPTION AND EXTERNALITY

A phenomenological view of subjectivity understands the self to be formed proprioceptively, through our daily, and mostly mundane, encounters with the world around us. Proprioception is a constant movement between the inside of the self and the outside of the world, where that movement sometimes creates a boundary between inside and out and sometimes blurs the distinction between them altogether. Proprioception, particularly the model of proprioception used by Merleau-Ponty, is vital to an explication of bodily being in two ways: First, it shows that the relation between the materiality of the body and our *knowledge* of the body is more complex than it might first appear. Second, understanding the body proprioceptively underscores the extent to which the body is an amalgam: Not only matter and not wholly ideality, but found somewhere in the relation between the two. This last is crucial in its disjunction of bodily material from bodily truth, and allows us to chart the ambivalent presences of the body and to account for the ways in which ambivalent presences manifest themselves in the embodied experiences of transgendered and transsexual subjects.

Proprioception is that process through which we apprehend and make sense of our own bodies; it is what enables the psyche to construct a unified and coherent body from the body's disparate parts. Proprioception creates a body from the fragmented, disjointed chaos of the body in bits and pieces.[1] It is that *felt sense* that I have of my body, both as it relates to itself and to the world in which my body is always inescapably situated. At the level of the senses, proprioception is both a concatenation of the input that I receive from my sensory organs and something that exceeds my senses. It might seem a curious choice of focus, when inquiring after the materiality of the body, to concentrate on a "felt sense" that is decidedly nonmaterial. Yet, as Merleau-Ponty's *Phenomenology of Perception* argues, the body does not belong entirely to the realm of the material; it can only be located in the juncture between the psychic and the physiological. It is this hinge between the material and the phantasmatic, the physiological and the psychic, the present and the absent, that is the subject of *Phenomenology of Perception* and the site at which the embodied subject emerges.

Merleau-Ponty illustrates this juncture by describing bodily supplements and bodily absences, illustrating the former by describing the blind man's cane and the latter in his discussion of phantom limbs. The cane is, to be sure, an external object, unlikely to be mistaken for an organic part of the body. The cane's function as a tool would also seem to place it in the class of things that are used *by* the body but are not part *of* the body. And even the most cursory of examinations would seem to confirm the commonsense certainty that a cane is not a body part, since it is not attached to the body. And yet, the blind man is not only able to experience the cane proprioceptively, in the same way that we might interact with any object that we pick up, but his sense of proprioception itself relies upon it. "Its point has become an area of sensitivity" (Merleau-Ponty, 1962, p. 145); it has ceased to become an object and become a part of his body. It is what Merleau-Ponty will call a "bodily auxiliary" (p. 152), an extension of the bodily synthesis. Many different objects in the world can be taken up and utilized in an instrumental way, but the cane belongs to a special class of objects in that it is not just something that the blind man can feel but *the means by which* he can feel. It has become an organ of perception.

This is a becoming effected by a double movement, rather than a simple graft. The cane becomes something other than, something more than, an object in the world; so, too, does the blind man's body become something that exceeds its corporeal contours. "To get used to a hat, a car, or a stick is to be transplanted into them, or conversely, to incorporate them in to the bulk of our own body" (Merleau-Ponty, 1962, p. 143). This transformation is not a mere addition, not a matter of my cementing an object onto my corporeal schema; part of me must be transplanted into these objects in order for me to incorporate them into my body. This transplantation is, indeed, a material one, as I incorporate the space of everyday tools and objects into my own embodied space. But this transplantation is no less a psychic operation in that these bodily auxiliaries become such by virtue of the meaning that I invest in them.

For Merleau-Ponty, the composition of the body itself hinges on this question of meaning, and this meaning is, at every point, created rather than found. The construction of a corporeal schema is, he suggests, a way of trying to direct oneself toward that meaning, and it often requires the body to supplement its given materiality with auxiliaries: "Sometimes, finally, the meaning aimed at cannot be achieved by the body's natural means; it must then build itself an instrument, and it projects thereby around itself a cultural world" (Merleau-Ponty, 1962, p. 146). We see here that what a body might be, and what a body might be able to become as it moves through the world, is, for Merleau-Ponty, almost limitless. Body parts are not objects, but potentialities, and the body itself is, he writes, "a nexus of living meanings, not the law for a certain number of covariant terms" (p. 151). This does not mean that we have the capacity to create any kind of body we choose or that we can make material any kind of phantasmatic embodiment merely by willing it so. It does mean, however, that a phantasmatic body part cannot be considered *not-body* simply by virtue of its nonmateriality.

Merleau-Ponty uses the example of the phantom limb phenomenon to demonstrate not merely the ways in which the physiological and the psychic are inextricably linked but also the impoverishment of these categories for understanding embodiment. It is not strictly correct, he asserts, to consider the phantom limb as a wholly psychic appendage divorced from the realm of physiology, since the felt sense of a phantom limb is not qualitatively different than the felt sense of a "real" one. "The phantom arm," he writes, "is not a representation of the arm, but the ambivalent presence of an arm" (Merleau-Ponty, 1962, p. 81).

What might it mean to speak of an "ambivalent presence" of a body part or parts? It is not only that the phantasmatic and the material are inextricably intertwined; phenomenologically speaking, there exists no bright line between them.[2] Indeed, to suggest that one's felt sense can register a body that is, in part, ambivalently present is to challenge the assumption that a "felt sense" of the body is able to affirm one's certainty about the materiality of that body. What is felt about the body is both something more and something less than materiality. The corporeal schema that results from my proprioceptive engagements with the world is not merely a mental map of bodily materiality; it is what, through making the body available to the subject, constructs the body itself. The relation between the corporeal schema and the parts of which it is comprised is not a strictly indexical one, because a body part's position within the corporeal schema is determined by the psychic energy invested in that part rather than its morphological configurations. This principle is illustrated by Merleau-Ponty's discussion of anosognosia, in which a person fails to acknowledge or recognize parts of her or his own body. An anosognostic might perceive his or her own arm as "a long cold snake" (Merleau-Ponty, 1962, p. 76), or recognize this limb as an arm but conclude that it must belong to someone else. The limb in question is ambivalently present; the arm is materially "there" but has become excluded from the anosognostic's corporeal schema in such a way as to render it "not there." The certainty that a "felt sense" seems to promise is not a sense of materiality, but a sense of "mine-ness" or "own-ness." The materiality of the anosognostic's arm is not in dispute, even to the anosognostic himself; it is a sense of mine-ness that is lacking. Conversely, the presence of the phantom limb is a function of the mine-ness that inheres in it – not of its materiality.

If the materiality of the body promises a certainty or a truth, it is a truth that must be constantly created rather than finally or simply found. That creation arises from an ongoing series of acts, of physical and psychic exchanges with the world that are sometimes unconscious and sometimes volitional. To see body parts as potentialities rather than objects is to radically rethink both what it means to be a body and what it means to be a body in the world.

FLESH AND BODILY BORDERS

Upon first consideration, nothing would appear to be more internal to, or phenomenologically closer to, the subject than his or her bodily sensations. However, the body schema is not "biologically given," but must be built up over time into the assemblage that we eventually come to recognize as a whole, if only provisionally so. And this process is never complete or final; the postural model exists less as a stable thing through space and time and more as a series of different models. Thus, our sense of the body schema, the postural model of the body, is a sedimented effect without a stable referent or predictable content, since it may be different in form and shape, moment to moment, with each new iteration. Paul Schilder describes the body image as "in some way always the sum of the body images of the community according to the various relations in the community" and even insists that the body schema "belongs" to the world more than it belongs to the individual whose body it surveys – such is its instability and referential resistance.[3]

The phenomenological experience of embodiment, the concatenation of my perceptions that form a relation between my body and its world, can make external distinctions between body and world, between inside and outside of the self, difficult to discern. Merleau-Ponty designates that region of being that is comprised of the intertwined layers of body and world as "flesh." Merleau-Ponty describes perception as a productive activity and insists that my perception is not properly thought of as a survey of the world or its objects, but is, rather, the mode through which I make meaning not only of the world but also of myself. Perception is not only what brings the world to me; it is what actively forms me in my engagement with the world. Merleau-Ponty's description of the productive capacities of perception has two consequences for thinking of bodies as amalgams of inside and outside. First, it allows us to understand perception as forming a permeable border between the body and the world, a sensate envelope that functions to mediate between body and world. Second, it helps to elucidate the ways in which the activity of perception is the work of relation, where relation is finally what produces a body. Both the activity of perception and the body that perceives depend on a certain indeterminacy, an in-between-ness, for their coherence. The objects delivered by any perception are only legible in the context of their relation to their ground and to the location of the embodied perceiver; perception is, finally, a movement between the perceiving and perceived. Similarly, the body itself is brought into legibility at the border of its contact with the world, both in a material sense (through the bounding envelope of the skin) and in a less concrete way (through the relationship of the particularity of my body to the cultural context of bodies in general). Ultimately, the equivocal nature of perception and of the body extends to their relation with one another: Merleau-Ponty comes to posit perception not just as a capacity of the body but *as the body itself*, as an extension of the body, in that sensation – and thus the discreteness of the category of either world or body – happens at the sensate border, the edge. In the case of the body, this sensate border or edge is the skin.

Merleau-Ponty's notion of the world as a prolongation of the body establishes a relation between self and world that is not a barrier, but a sensate border. He suggests that perception itself *is* that sensate border, thus establishing a model in which perception is something akin to a skin:

> But my perception of the world feels it has an exterior; I feel at the surface of my visible being that my volubility dies away, that I become flesh, and that at the extremity of this inertia that was me there is something else, or rather another who is not a thing. He then is seated nowhere.
>
> *(Merleau-Ponty and Lefort, 1968, p. 61)*[4]

Through my interactions with the world, I "become flesh," and my acts of seeing, speaking, and even being are my "carnal relation with the flesh of the world." It is a transmission, an exchange across the border of what I perceive (the perception that both emanates from me and *is* me) toward that other who is only vaguely locatable as outside of my perception. That other is outside of me, is not-me, but is crucial for my sense of self, my project of becoming flesh. I become flesh in feeling the press of myself out toward the world and feeling the presence of the other for whom I, too, am an object or not quite an object just outside of the reach of her or his perception. This would seem to ally flesh with the invisible, in that I become flesh only in relation to that which is outside of my perception as I push against the surface of what is outside of me and other than me. I become flesh only at the very edge of my perception, and can do so only under the press of the invisible and imperceptible outside that, it would seem, forms the border of that flesh. My body is visible and able to be apprehended like any object, but my flesh is not; it is bounded by my perception and extends proprioceptively into the world.

The other enables me to become my own flesh through her location outside of my zone of perception, but she also constitutes my flesh through her perception of my body. This produces an objective body that, when wedded to my phenomenological body, constitutes my flesh. My body as seen by another is an objective fact, but my body as I feel and experience it is a phenomenological entity. The relation between these two bodies is not indexical; the one need not map onto the other. Merleau-Ponty describes the relation between the objective body and the phenomenological body as a doubling and redoubling in which "the objective body and the phenomenal body turn about one another and encroach upon one another" (Merleau-Ponty and Lefort, 1968, p. 117). This encroachment occasions a "dehiscence" that "opens my body in two, and because between my body looked at and my body looking, my body touched and my body touching, there is overlapping or encroachment, so that we must say that the things pass into us as well as we into the things" (p. 123). My relation to my own body and to the world around it is thus enabled by a reciprocity between myself and the other. Because I see and am seen, touch and am touched, "the world and I are within one another" (p. 123). This folding of self into world is possible through the reciprocal relation between myself and the other; my body becomes for another, and the body of the other simultaneously becomes for me. The body is for itself, and it is for others; it is both seeing and it is seen, it is sensible and sentient, and the enfolded relation and movement between these two halves constitute "flesh."

We have now explored the ways in which a bodily sense of self is created from both proprioception and perception, from contact between its outermost edge and the world. However, our external proprioceptive sense of the body is not our only means of feeling and inhabiting the body; the body is also experienced in a more solitary mode, as a kind of interiority. Experiencing the body as an interiority is a quite different kind of phenomenological event from proprioception and external perception, though I will argue that even a bodily feeling of utter isolation is no less a kind of relation between self and world. How can the body come to be felt as an interiority, as a place into which we can retract from the world, and what consequences does this have for gendered and raced embodiment?

"THIS ANONYMOUS LIFE": BODILY INTERIORITY

Among the many psychological case studies that Merleau-Ponty discusses in the *Phenomenology of Perception* is the case of a girl whose mother has warned her away from the man with whom she is in love. Forbidden to see the object of her desire, the girl loses the power of speech. Merleau-Ponty dwells upon this phenomenon at some length, and is concerned to show that the girl" loss of voice is something other than a simple refusal of speech in the sense that her voice is not present and refused or turned away from; instead she is "literally without a voice," severed from it, he will later suggest, "as certain insects sever one of their own legs" (Merleau-Ponty, 1962, p. 163). We are offered this simile, suggesting affinity between the voice and an insect's leg, the means by which the insect moves through the world. The image of the insect's dismemberment finds its startling counterpoint in the girl's voice, which we now understand not quite as something she has lost, but as something from which she is cut off. Possession of the voice thereby transfers from the girl to the world, and the figuration offers the voice as lodged and left in the world, sacrificed for the sake of retreat. And the simile offers a still more astonishing comparison: The insect, despite the loss of something as vital as a limb, continues to move and to live. Likewise the girl, despite the loss of something as vital as a voice, continues to live. She lives housed in the "anonymous life" of her body, suggesting that the experiential interiority of the body is even more essential to life than the voice.

The girl's is not a "deliberate or voluntary silence," but rather the result of a qualitative change in her ability to relate to her body and a corresponding change in her body's ability to relate to the world. This change is an act that the girl performs at the same time that it is something less than voluntary, taking place, he tells us, "at a *lower* level than that of will" (Merleau-Ponty, 1962, p. 163). Merleau-Ponty describes the way this liminal withholding, this withdrawal from life, *dissolves* time, relying on a distinction, elaborated upon elsewhere in the *Phenomenology*, between personal and impersonal time:

> In the case of the girl just discussed, the move towards the future, towards the living present or towards the past, the power of learning, of maturing, of entering into communication

with others, have become, as it were, arrested in a bodily symptom, existence is tied up and the body has become "the place where life hides away." For the patient, nothing further happens, nothing assumes meaning and form in life, or more precisely there occurs only a recurrent and always identical "now," life flows back on itself and history is dissolved in natural time.

(Merleau-Ponty, 1962, p. 190)

Though this reads in part as a description of feminine hysteria, the conversion of a psychic suffering that is in some sense unspeakable into a bodily symptom, Merleau-Ponty's account differs from classic Freudian hysteria in two respects. First, if the female body in cases of hysteria becomes the conduit for the transmission of affect, functioning *as* speech, then the relationship between body and speech here is precisely reversed, where affect and the ability for communication become submerged in the opacity of the body. Second, as Merleau-Ponty continues to describe the body that results from this change, the gender of that body shifts, moving from the third person feminine – the girl – to the third person masculine – the patient – to the revelation of first person – "my body." He goes on to suggest that this cloistering of the self inside the body is not only a mark of pathology but is a capacity of any body, of any gender:

> Even when normal and even when involved in situations with other people, the subject, in so far as he has a body, retains at every moment the power to withdraw from it. At the very moment when I live in the world, when I am given over to my plans, my occupations, my friends, my memories, I can close my eyes, lie down, listen to the blood pulsating in my ears, lose myself in some pleasure or pain, and shut myself up in this anonymous life which subtends my personal one.
>
> *(Merleau-Ponty, 1962, pp. 164–165)*

It seems at first as if Merleau-Ponty is suggesting that the maternal prohibition has broken some vital relation between the girl and the world, that an externally imposed isolation has corroded her ties to life. It soon becomes clear, however, that something more complicated has occurred. After suggesting that this capacity of bodily withdrawal characterizes a subject whose mourning has impoverished her world, he then suggests that this state of being, or this state of barely being, is temporally and spatially coincident with "normal" bodily being. The power to burrow into the body in order to escape from the press and threat of "situations with other people" is a power that every body, or at least the body of every "normal" subject, retains. And it is not only that "normal" life can accommodate or tolerate these moments but that there is a pleasure that attends to this shuttering of self into the body. He continues:

> But precisely because my body can shut itself off from the world, it is also what opens me out upon the world and places me in a situation there. The momentum of existence towards others, towards the future, towards the world can be restored as a river unfreezes.
>
> *(Merleau-Ponty, 1962, pp. 164–165)*

It is important to note how this opening toward the world occurs, how this ice-locked river suddenly cracks apart. For it is not only that my body is a thing that, at some moments, is capable of being immersed in the world and, at other moments, chooses to withdraw from it. This is certainly true, but Merleau-Ponty wants to stress that these are not independent and unrelated modes of being. At all times, the body retains the power to put itself into relations with the world and with others or to withdraw from them. The body's capacity for openness *is the same* as its capacity for withdrawal into apparent solipsism; this is the fulcrum of its being. When Merleau-Ponty writes elsewhere that "[m]y body is the pivot of the world" (1962, p. 82), he is pointing to this movement, the systole and diastole of bodily being.

This retraction or withdrawal is best understood as itself a relational activity. Merleau-Ponty begins the section of *Phenomenology of Perception* titled "The Body in Its Sexual Being" by asking: "Let us try to see how a thing or a being begins to exist for us through desire or love" (1962, p. 154). This at first seems only to preface a discussion of the ways in which the object of desire comes to exist, which does indeed follow. But by the end of the section, it becomes clear that "the thing or being which begins to exist for us through desire" is also, extraordinarily enough, the body itself.

When the body says no – to speech, or to food, or to interactions with others – when the body refuses the world and burrows into itself, it retracts from its own particularity as surely as it retracts from the external world. Instead of delivering to the self an identity that might be fortified and amplified by solitude, this inward turn is, quite the opposite, a draining away of life from the self. The retreat from the world transforms bodily life into "anonymous life," in which the pulse hums beneath the skin and is amplified in the ears, and the body's functions persist, maintaining a life that exists beneath any sense of self. This mode of existence, "which runs through me, yet does so independently of me, is only the barest raw material of a genuine presence in the world." The self can be regained only when the body "opens itself to others or to the past, when it opens the way to co-existence and once more (in the active sense) acquires significance beyond itself" (Merleau-Ponty, 1962, p. 165). The ability to relate to others, the capacity to have a world, has, then, as its necessary condition its converse, the ability to sub- merge oneself in the "anonymous life" of the body. The anonymity of the life in and of the body is mediated in part; it is not just anonymous life but *"this* anonymous life," and the self must be able to take hold of it enough to become engulfed in it. Instead of requiring the self to be in full possession of the body in order to encounter the world, Merleau-Ponty advances quite a different notion: In order to engage with the wider world, the self must be able to become lost to itself in the opaque thickness of the body.

RACE AND INSULARITY

Fanon's writing in *Black Skin, White Masks* is closely engaged with psychoanalysis and with the phenomenologies of Merleau-Ponty and Sartre. Though much divides these ways of thinking about the body and subjectivity, what Fanon leads us to in each is the zone of indeterminacy in bodily being that both of these traditions suggest is necessary in order for subjectivity and relation to exist. This bodily sense of location, a "zone of nonbeing" as Fanon will term it, is precisely what is denied the man of color through his relations with the white colonizer. It is also the necessary location of resistance: "There is a zone of nonbeing, an extraordinarily sterile and arid region, an utterly naked declivity where an authentic upheaval can be born" (Fanon, 1967, p. 8). Thus we see subjectivity, paradoxically, finding its point of germination in the "sterile and arid region[s]" of the body, though this is neither a body only incidentally overlaid with its race and its gender, nor a body that exists in some fantastic space without them, but a body whose access to even its most decidedly material and ostensibly "universal" aspects is shaped by its racialization and its gendering.

In the introduction to *Black Skin, White Masks*, Fanon discusses the situation of a colonized man arriving in France and describes the particular psychological attitude toward the traversal of national borders: "[T]here is a psychological phenomenon that consists in the belief that the world will open to the extent that frontiers are broken down" (1967, p. 21). Fanon asserts that this belief is at root an error and that the colonized subject's faith in transcending a physical barrier between nations, between the colonizer and the colonized other, is a fantasy that is insufficiently attentive to the internalization of those barriers, the mimetic relation between the physical structures of colonialism and the psychic structures that they produce.

One of those structures is the body schema, which Fanon describes in strikingly Merleau-Pontian terms:

> The body is surrounded by an atmosphere of uncertainty. I know that if I want to smoke, I shall have to reach out my right arm and take the pack of cigarettes lying at the other end of the table. The matches, however, are in the drawer on the left, and I shall have to lean back slightly. And all these movements are made not out of habit but out of implicit knowledge. A slow composition of my self as a body in the middle of a spatial and temporal world – such seems to be the schema. It does not impose itself on me; it is, rather, a definitive structuring of the self and of the world – definitive because it creates a real dialectic between my body and the world.
>
> *(Fanon, 1967, pp. 110–111)*

The body schema creates a "dialectic" between the body and the world. It has been suggested that this is an impossible structure, for if relation is what produces a body, then the body itself cannot be one of the relata. But this structure – my body creating itself through its interactions with the world – is only untenably paradoxical if we understand the body as an indivisible substance.[5] What Fanon's text shows us is that the body is not, in this way, singular, but consists of different regions of being interleaved with one another. We see this most clearly when aspects of the body begin to crumble, which Fanon describes as the effect of the white man's gaze on the body of the man of color:

> Below the corporeal schema, I had sketched a historico-racial schema. The elements that I used had been provided for me not by "residual sensations and perceptions primarily of a tactile, vestibular, kinesthetic, and visual character," but by the other, the white man, who had woven me out of a thousand details, anecdotes, stories. I thought that what I had in hand was to construct a physiological self, to balance space, to localize sensations, and here I was called on for more [...] Assailed at various points, the corporeal schema crumbled, its place taken by a racial epidermal schema. In the train, it was no longer a question of being aware of my body in the third person but in a triple person. I was given not one but two, three places.
>
> *(Fanon, 1967, pp. 111–112)*

The "various points" at which Fanon's body is assailed are located along axes of race and gender. He is "sealed into that crushing objecthood" and "abraded into nonbeing" (Fanon, 1967, p. 109) through the scene of interpellation that takes place on the train, the child who exclaims "Mama, look, a Negro!" an interpellation that will cast him as triply conscious of being racialized while simultaneously denying him gender: His being seen as Black prevents him from being seen as a man. Indeed, normative manhood is characterized by a certain anonymity, a social designation confirmed by the company of other men, an ability to meld into the throng of other men: "All I wanted was to be a man among other men. [...] I wanted to be a man, nothing but a man" (pp. 112–113). This very anonymity is shown to be a prerogative of racially unmarked manhood, which only white men may enjoy. Race in this instance works precisely to block recourse to this anonymity, an anonymity that Fanon shows us to be allocated through relations of social power.

Consciousness of the body in this way, Fanon will suggest (along with Sartre), is "solely a negating activity" and lends the body an "unfamiliar weight" (Fanon, 1967, p. 110). Fanon's description exceeds Sartre's (1995), however, in his description of the effects of the racist gaze; the man of color is lent a new consciousness that *takes the place* of an anonymous relationship to his own body, just as the historico-racial schema displaces and takes the place of his corporeal schema. What is foreclosed with this movement is the body's interiority, and the body that Fanon describes is primarily characterized by its lack of interiority, which is thereby shown to be a cultural achievement rather than a naturally given attribute of the body. The body Fanon describes is *all* surface: "Where shall I hide? [...] My body was given back to me sprawled out, distorted, recolored [...] Where shall I find shelter from now on?" (pp. 113–114), this last suggesting that even the possibility of imagining a future springs from an anonymous bodily interiority, its loss constricting time itself.

The body that is delivered back to Fanon through the lens of the world is transformed into the place where life *cannot* hide away, whose capacity for holding and hiding an anonymous life becomes irretrievably diminished to the extent that the Black man "cannot take pleasure in his insularity" (Fanon, 1967, p. 51). It is not just the body in its visibility that is targeted by the racism projected at it, and that projects it in turn, a body marked by otherness that is forced into relentlessly surveyed objecthood, but the body in its innermost interiority, a region often posited as beyond the reach of the poisonous effects of an objectifying gaze. Fanon and Merleau-Ponty both insist that anonymity is not just a retreat into the occasional luxury of unsurveyed privacy; it is the foundation of our lives as social beings, and the condition of relation itself, surprising as that may seem. In order to belong to the world, Merleau-Ponty suggests, I must exist as an anonymous being for the other, and he or she for me:

> My life must have a significance which I do not constitute; there must strictly speaking be an intersubjectivity; each one of us must be both anonymous in the sense of absolutely individual, and anonymous in the sense of absolutely general. Our being in the world, is the concrete bearer of this double anonymity.
>
> *(Merleau-Ponty, 1962, p. 448)*

I want to conclude by suggesting that Fanon and Merleau-Ponty's figurations of bodily interiority can offer promising directions for theories of social construction. We have seen in Merleau-Ponty a description of how one kind of gendered self, faced with a prohibiting power, might retreat into the interiority of the body, and we have seen in Fanon a further explication of the conditions of that retreat, where a differently gendered and raced self, faced with a more intense and more diffuse prohibiting power, finds access to that interiority foreclosed. I want to assert that there are important implications for thinking all kinds of gendered and raced subjectivities and that these psychic and bodily topographies can help us understand gender theory to refer not only to what is read on or done with the surface of bodies, but as a means by which we might ask whether and how bodily interiority is achieved and what kinds of liberations or sufferings are occasioned by that achievement or its failure.

One of the questions that gender theory teaches us to ask is: Of what does bodily being consist? An answer gestured to here might be: Of an outside and an inside in complex embrace-regions of the body that we easily have or are and deeper regions of the body that are not quite wholly recognizable to us or even as us. Bodily interiority thus functions as a way to withdraw from a form of social constitution that would constitute us simply as exterior and exposed surfaces for the play of social power.

It suggests that our very capacity to withdraw or to retreat – to decide, in effect, the spatial and temporal coordinates of that exposure – is also conditioned by matters of gender and race and differently. If the body is "the place where life hides away," then understanding this interiority can help us come to know, and perhaps finally retrieve, the life that hides there, the life that cannot find a way to hide there, and the life that stays only hidden there.

NOTES

1 I refer here to Lacan's notion of the undifferentiated state of the infantile body. Lacan posits bodily coherence as a cultural achievement rather than a natural state, though the process by which the *hommelette* achieves his anticipatory bodily coherence is visual rather than tactile.
2 For a reading of the body's parts as symbolic, imaginary, and material objects, there is no better source than Judith Butler's *Bodies That Matter*. Butler's aim there is "to rethink the physical and the psychical" as categorical descriptors of gendered embodiment (Butler, 1995, p. 65), and my own (Salamon, 2004) account of the equivocal nature of bodily inhabitation and perception is deeply informed by that text.
3 For a more thorough account of Schilder's theorization of the body schema, see my (2004) "The Bodily Ego and the Contested Domain of the Material."
4 This quotation and those that follow come from Merleau-Ponty's posthumously published work *The Visible and the Invisible* (1968), in which he develops a theory of "flesh." He uses this concept to completely dismantle the distinction between object and subject, between materiality and ideality, between the visible and the invisible. "Flesh" is emphatically *not* meant to describe what is material in opposition to what is immaterial but designates, rather, the join between them.
5 I am indebted to David Hoy for helping me think about theorizations of the body within the phenomenological tradition, especially the paradox and possibility of embodiment.

REFERENCES

Butler, J. (1995). *Bodies that matter*. New York: Routledge.

Fanon, F. (1967). *Black skin, White masks*. New York: Grove.

Lacan, J. (1982). The mirror stage as formative of the function of the I as revealed in psychoanalytic experience. In *Ecrits: A selection* (Alan Sheridan, Trans.) (pp. 1–7). New York: Norton.

Merleau-Ponty, M. (1962). *Phenomenology of perception* (Colin Smith, Trans.). London: Routledge.

Merleau-Ponty, M., & Lefort, C. (1968). *The visible and the invisible: Followed by working notes*. Evanston, IL: Northwestern University Press.

Salamon, G. (2004). The bodily ego and the contested domain of the material. *Differences: A Journal of Feminist Cultural Studies, 15*(5), 95–122.

Sartre, J.-P. (1995). *Being and nothingness* (Hazel E. Barnes, Trans.). New York: Washington Square.

Schilder, P. (1950). *The image and approval of the human body: Studies in the constructive energies of the psyche*. New York: International Universities.

CHAPTER 11

FANON, MERLEAU-PONTY, AND THE DIFFERENCE OF PHENOMENOLOGY

Jeremy Weate

A striking passage from James Baldwin's essay, *The Fire Next Time*, serves as a framing introduction of sorts for this chapter. He writes:

> but people who cannot suffer can never grow up, can never discover who they are. That man who is forced each day to snatch his manhood, his identity, out of the fire of human cruelty that rages to destroy it knows, if he survives his effort, and even if he does not survive it, something about himself and human life that no school on earth – and, indeed, no church – can teach. He achieves his own authority, and that is unshakeable. This is because, in order to save his life, he is forced to look beneath appearances, to take nothing for granted, to hear the meaning behind the words. If one is continually surviving the worst that life can bring, one eventually ceases to be controlled by a fear of what life can bring; whatever it brings must be borne.
>
> *(p. 376)*

One of the most abiding criticisms of phenomenology in both latent and manifest form in recent philosophical discourse is that it must install itself on the basis of the repression of difference. Phenomenology across its authors is assumed to involve a fundamental ground or unity which engenders meaningful activity in the world. That which appears, the phenomenon, is violated by metaphysical over-generalization, "Sameness" or "presence" in the hands of phenomenologists, according to their critics, and this whether the epistemic frame is transcendental or somatic.[1]

The problem with such criticism is that it encourages a non-experiential notion of thought. Metaphysics or ontology then becomes a matter for "thinking," to which any experiential or lived dimension would be derivative or secondary. In the eighties, this reductionism developed a semiological-textual armature, chiefly through the influence of deconstruction in the States. What is interesting in the post-structuralist approach to "thinking difference" is that its relation to lived experience is never entirely disavowed. As with Heidegger and Levinas in earlier years, phenomenology is suppressed or sublated in the development of theory, but never entirely rejected. We remain unclear about the relations between the body, experience, and thought (Dillon, 1995).

No wonder then that philosophy has been slow to participate in the burgeoning field of "race studies," and its various offshoots, including the more recent development of "whiteness" as a category of academic critique.[2] I will argue that whilst there *are* problems lurking in the assumptions phenomenology makes about its ground, these problems are not fatal to its future. As recent feminist thinkers have discovered, on the contrary, an encounter with phenomenology, particularly the thought of Maurice Merleau-Ponty, is *needed* today in order to re-establish a relation between lived experience and thought (Grosz, 1994; Weiss, 1999). In order to challenge a universalist approach to phenomenology and open up a philosophy of race, I shall display one of the profoundest critiques of phenomenology offered this century, that of Frantz Fanon in his paper *The Lived Experience of the Black*. It has been said that Fanon is not "a terribly sophisticated phenomenologist" – well, I am not sure

DOI: 10.4324/9781003037132-11

whether sophistication ought to be a virtue of this discipline.[3] As I shall show, in fact, Fanon's critique of phenomenology quickly exposes the core of its problematic relation to difference. Fanon's text therefore, in my view, provides a corrective to phenomenology, at the same time as showing how the theorization of lived experience that is its source can reveal the key issues at work between agency, history, and the world, and perhaps most fundamentally, the possibilities for justice.

PHENOMENOLOGY, THE DIFFERENCE OF EXPERIENCE, AND HISTORICAL FREEDOM

Fanon's most significant philosophical influence is often taken to be the existential phenomenology of Sartre. In particular, the connection has often been made that Fanon's thought is closely connected to issues of authenticity and bad-faith and the power of being-for-others.[4] Whilst Sartre's shadow is undoubtedly cast across many pages of a text such as *Black Skin, White Masks*, it is important to register that Fanon was also engaged in a dialogue with Merleau-Ponty.[5] I will claim that Merleau-Ponty's inclusive notion of "world" is both the point of criticism for Fanon and the source of the construction of his ideal of "disalienation."[6] Only by looking at the implicit dialogue between Sartre and Merleau-Ponty that Fanon enacts will we be able to comprehend Fanon's politics of difference. As Fanon's method in *Black Skin, White Masks* is in part phenomenological, an excursus into the chapter entitled *The Lived Experience of the Black*, and an examination of the final chapter, *En guise de conclusion*, will lead to a radical phenomenology of difference. It will also lead to a reformulated genealogy of political ideals, grounded in a phenomenology of the body.

It is not difficult to show how *The Lived Experience of the Black* involves a dialogue with Merleau-Ponty. The most obvious references are given in the first few pages of the text, with Fanon's substitution of Merleau-Ponty's notion of "corporeal schema" (*schéma corporel*) first of all for the "schéma historico-racial" and secondly in terms of the "schéma épidermique racial." Put briefly, the corporeal schema in Merleau-Ponty's work refers to the body's agency and its work in relating to and disclosing the historical world. At all stages in his oeuvre, Merleau-Ponty espouses a pre-dualistic ontology which affirms the reproductive synergy between body and world. He writes,

> We grasp external space through our bodily situation. A "corporeal or postural schema" gives us at every moment a global, practical, and implicit notion of the relation between our body and things, of our hold on them. A system of possible movements, or "motor projects," radiates from us to our environment. Our body is not in space like things; it inhabits or haunts space. It applies itself to space like a hand to an instrument, and when we wish to move about we do not move the body as we move an object. We transport it without instruments as if by magic, since it is ours and because through it we have direct access to space. For us the body [...] is our expression in the world, the visible form of our intentions.
>
> *(1964, p. 5)*

The corporeal schema lies *between* the body and the world, as that which engenders communication between one and the other. This does not imply an exchange between two independently subsisting entities suspended from temporality. Rather, this communication, which Merleau-Ponty elsewhere describes as "more ancient than thought" ("plus vieille que la pensée") (1962/1990, p. 254/294) is the moment where body and world re-order each other according to a "perpetual contribution" (1962, p. 254) of reciprocal transfer. Being "embedded" within a cultural-historical horizon therefore means, in Merleau-Pontyan terms, that that horizon itself is open to be altered, transformed, or disrupted. For example, no-one could separate the history of the guitar from its players. Somebody comes along, "learns" the guitar, and manipulates it as never before, and the history of guitar music is altered. With fingers and stance, their body communicates with the guitar through a pre-thetic schema that opens up the parameters of possibility (and therefore the history) of the instrument,[7] at the same time as transforming the player's life. Moreover, even those who will not change the history of guitar music themselves are liable to be "altered" as their practice develops and music communicates itself through their increasingly expressive being.

Ultimately, Merleau-Ponty's concept of the corporeal schema reveals the relation between agency, freedom, and temporality. For Merleau-Ponty, the corporeal capacity of the body allows for a "communication" with the expressive patternings of the cultural traditions to which it belongs or has attached itself. Within the interplay between body and world prior to intellectual representation, the possibility of the creative inflection between both engenders a corporealized conception of freedom. The body is "free" to the extent that it can participate in the transformation of its expressive horizons. As with the guitar player, this conception of freedom entails a fundamental relation to the historical: Being free involves the body's capacity through expression to transfigure (and be transfigured by) what is given as history. In this way, Merleau-Ponty's notion of the corporeal schema leads implicitly to a conception of history as characterized essentially by *difference*. Each moment of a culture's transfer across time through the agency of bodies is at the same time the site of its own differentiation. Moreover, there is therefore no "originary" moment to any culture: Every culture that attempts to assert its sameness across time has to repress the difference at work in its origin in every present. Although there is some ambiguity in Merleau-Ponty's thought here, it is on the whole the case that he posits this relation between agency and historical freedom as a condition of *habituation*. In other words, it is a matter of habit and inhabitation that we perpetually contribute to the differentiation of our historical world (our "habitus"), from one moment's action to the next.

We are now in a position to begin to explain Fanon's substitution of terms. In *The Lived Experience of the Black*, Fanon's opening argument is that a phenomenology of Blackness cannot be understood in the context of the "Black among his own" (Fanon, 2001, p. 185). It is only in the encounter with whiteness and more specifically the white imagination that an analysis of the experience of skin difference, of being the Black other, can be undertaken. For Fanon at home in the Antillean setting of Martinique, the coercion and internalization of racial inferiority could not be encountered as a form of experience. Before entering the "white world," Fanon was content with "an intellectual comprehension of these tensions" (p. 185). It was only after Fanon moved to Paris that he began to be aware of the pre-intellectualist dynamics of the interracial encounter. With the first explicit reference to Merleau-Ponty's terminology, Fanon writes, "In the white world the man of color faces difficulties in the elaboration of his bodily schema" (Fanon, 2001, p. 185).

Fanon proceeds to explicate Merleau-Ponty's notion of corporeal schema in the following paragraph. He ends the paragraph with the summary statement,

> A slow construction of my self as a body in the midst of a spatial and temporal world, such seems to be the schema. It is not imposed on me; rather, it is a definitive structuring of the self and the world – definitive because in this way an effective dialectic is settled between my body and the world.
>
> *(2001, p. 185)*

Fanon clearly concurs initially with Merleau-Ponty's insight that the self and the world are constructed through the work of the *schéma corporel*. However, his detour through phenomenology is adopted in order to theorize the interracial encounter of Black bodies in the west. It immediately becomes clear that in this case Merleau-Ponty's terminology is inadequate:

> Below the corporeal schema I created a historico-racial one. The elements that I used were provided to me not by "residual sensations and perceptions primarily of a tactile, vestibular, kinesthetic, and visual order," but by the other, the White, who has woven me out of a thousand details, anecdotes and stories.
>
> *(Fanon, 2001, p. 185)*

The move announced here against the primordial unity of the perceived world in Merleau-Ponty's phenomenology is dramatic. Fanon is suggesting that Merleau-Ponty's conception of the corporeal schema, hitherto the iterative locus of the reciprocal emergence of self and world, is undercut or undermined in the case of the Black subject in Europe. Rather than ascribing to an inclusive conception of the field of corporeal communication, Fanon points to a fundamental asymmetry between Blacks and whites and their active relation to "the world" in Europe. In the interracial encounter, the white is able to participate in the schematization of the world, whilst the Black may not, for his skin-difference closes down the possibility of free agency. A white *mythos* inserts itself between the Black body and its self-image, becoming the "elements used" in a reflexive understanding of Black subjectivity. In contesting the terms of Merleau-Ponty's account of bodily freedom, Fanon provides a genealogy of the existential *unfreedom* of the Black body in the racialized encounter. His account in *The Lived Experience of the Black* operates as a non-linear narrative, a scrambled descent into hell with ever more entrenched levels of alienation and the Black body-in-pain in operation. Fanon introduces his piece as "the fragments put together by another self." I shall now highlight aspects of the schizoid path of this descent.

Fanon sets up the historico-racial schema by way of a simple narrative which recurs as a fragmented refrain throughout the rest of the essay. It is the experience of a white child saying to his mother on a train, "Tiens, un nègre!" ("Look, a Negro!") This is the overture to alienation for the Black subject. To begin, the experience is taken lightly. "Look, a Negro!" It was true. I was amused" (Fanon, 2001, p. 185). This amusement is annulled as the child continues badgering his mother, this time adding to the expression of the gaze a component of fear. The fear of the child is read as the outcome of all that Fanon's skin represents. The child is no longer merely pointing to the skin difference as a form of naive wonder at a rare site – the curiosity of seeing (perhaps for the first time close up) a Black human being. The child, this allegedly pre-coding type, has in actual fact already imbibed various presuppositions beyond the simple physicality of skin difference. That is, the Black skin is already operating as a kind of metonym for the child, representing a specific imaginary-historical construction of otherness.

> I could not be amused anymore because I already knew of the legends, the stories, history, and especially, the *historicity* I learned from Jaspers. Then the corporeal schema collapsed, assailed at various points, yielding to a racial-epidermal schema.
>
> *(Fanon, 2001, p. 185)*

The ontological violation of the train episode is therefore given a more dramatic context because of the gaze being expressed by a *child*. The power of the gaze described resides in its demonstration that racist attitudes in Europe have permeated to the level of the "innocent." More significantly still, the careful reader will have noted that this last passage marks a subtle but important slippage, from the "historico-racial" schema to the "racial-epidermal schema." The passage from the corporeal schema to the "historico-racial" schema is intended to reveal that Merleau-Ponty's claim in favor of free historical agency on the part of able-bodied beings *tout court* is false. How then is this further passage from the historico-racial to the racial-epidermal schema to be understood?

In my view, the slippage is Fanon's attempt to provide a *genealogy* of racial essentialism. To begin with, his analysis closely resembles the Sartrean model for alienation:

> I existed in triplicate: I was occupying space. I moved toward the other ... and the evanescent other, hostile yet not opaque, transparent, absent, disappeared. Nausea ...
>
> *(Fanon, 2001, p. 185)*

Here Fanon reproduces Sartre's threefold model of the subject in relation to others. The subject is first of all an outlook upon the world, the locus of perception, a *pour soi*. In encountering the other, the subject is forced, however, to acknowledge a view of itself from the outside, as a contingent difference within the world, as an "other." The subject therefore becomes aware of its "being-for-others." This tension between a subjective and an objective account of the subject's embodiment must be resolved, for as it stands, the two views are opposed. As is well known, for Sartre, this resolution, the dream of a *for itself in-itself* is a futile one.[8] The "double consciousness" schism between being experienced as an other in relation to one's own interior experience can only lead to the unresolved *third* modality of nausea and abjection. The "occupation of space" therefore refers to the moment of being-for-others, when the body begins to lose its internally constituted freedom and is reduced to a lump presence through exteriorisation. Fanon's response, that of "moving towards the other," is the response of refusing the abjection of physical reductionism by attempting to adopt the constitutive agency of the other – hence the *movement* towards the other. The other's rejection then appears in the form of a non-recognition, a fading-away. The Black subject can neither accept an internally derived body-image nor the exterior view, at the same time as being refused the final possibility of adopting the exterior view as a form of agency in-itself. The resulting despair and sickness are not left alone however, for there is still the existential framework of a caricatured history:

> I was all at once responsible for my body, for my race, for my ancestors. I ran an objective gaze over myself, discovering my blackness, my ethnic characteristics; and then I was deafened by cannibalism, intellectual deficiency, fetishism, racial defects, slave-ships, and above all, above all else, "Sho good banania."
>
> *(Fanon, 2001, pp. 185–186)*

The gaze of the child is the domino-effect, which, with the experience of nausea, leads to a questioning of bodily freedom and the paralysis of agency. Instead of the body being located in the present of a "communication more ancient than thought," of being the site of a possible inflection of the cultural givens of bodily patternings, the Black "subject" experiences his own skin as the metonym for a parodic primitivism. In contrast to an autonomous relation to the reproductive inflection of history which Merleau-Ponty's corporeal schema suggests, history is cast upon the Black subject in the moment of despair as a being-for-others. Black skin is indissolubly connected to a history constructed by a white imaginary. The Black subject finds himself no longer in the present of possible transformation, but thrown back into a past that was never his own. Fanon writes, "The Negro, however sincere, is the slave of the past" (1986, p. 225). Fanon therefore is showing that he is in strong agreement with Merleau-Ponty's insight that freedom is the freedom to inflect the world, and to enter into a corporeal dialogue with historical grounds. But Fanon's point is that this freedom is expressed to the Black subject in the form of a *denial*. As Fanon's analysis of his own experience shows, the politics of exclusion embodied in the child's gaze disables the corporeal schema. This disabling is at the same time an alienation of the subject from the possibility of historical freedom in the present.

It is at this juncture that we can understand more fully the grounds for the slippage between the historico-racial schema and the epidermal schema. The former moment marks the inauguration of being *pour soi* succumbing to the European framework of being for others. The body-image of the Black subject is spliced asunder by historical means: An autonomously constructed self-image is thwarted by a fantastical parody of history. The entrance into Europe of Black subjects is at the same time a movement into an all-encompassing frame of historical reference that Black agency can do little to resist. The second moment, that of the *racial epidermal* schema, occupies a later stage in psycho-somatic disintegration and alienation. Instead of remaining an *historical* ascription of identity (albeit a false one supplied by a white mythos), the schema becomes "naturalized" as a *condition* of skin. The epidermal marks the stage where historical construction and contingency is effaced and replaced with the facticity of flesh. The color of skin now appears to be intrinsically significant. With the outset of epidermalization, we are at the edge of being-for-others sedimenting into an essence, a "fact" of Blackness. Fanon is therefore demonstrating that essentialism is a discourse derived from a perversive repression of history. By marking the two stages of the "historico-racial" and then the "racial epidermal," he is therefore contesting the view that essentialism, and in particular Black essentialism, is grounded in a biological problematic. For Fanon, the essentialization of Blackness is the product of a concealed perversion of history. It is only once this concealment is consolidated (through epidermalization) that questions concerning the *biological* ground of race arise. The distinction he makes between two stages of schematization or epistemic enframing therefore allows biologistic discourses around race to be seen as phenomena derivative upon a prior perversion of history that is subsequently concealed.

Although it may sound initially a strange suggestion, in the midst of Fanon's painful genealogy of alienation and essentialism, I find it hard to resist detecting the emergent dynamics of hope. In a similar manner to Foucault's investigations into the birth of disciplinarity in modernity being at once implacable *and* contingent, Fanon's narrative of alienation marks the path of what has been done and can therefore be *undone*. As I understand it, the function of a genealogical history is to expose the ideology of historical logic and necessity as the reified legitimation of force. If a genealogical undercurrent to Fanon's text gathers plausibility, then its facility is to expose the processes of Black alienation in order to prepare the ground for their *unraveling*. Fanon's hope then is that there is no necessity or inevitability in the corporeal schema ceding to the racial-epidermal schema. However, within *The Lived Experience of the Black*, this subterranean movement of resistance is masked to an extent by Fanon's desire to remain faithful to the profound sense of hopeless alienation at work in the Black existential situation.

For instance, later in the essay, this sentiment is expressed succinctly in two words, "Too late" (Fanon, 2001, p. 190). From this mournful shibboleth everything that pertains to Fanon's analysis of existential dread unfolds. The Black subject enters the arena of interpersonal encounters in the colonial situation with his or her history already constructed and given. The already given history, the parodic primitivism most powerfully represented by cannibalism, is the form of the denial of ascribing historical agency to the Black subject. "Everything has been foreseen, discovered, proven, taken advantage of. My nervous

hands rein in nothing; the vein is exhausted. Too late!" (p. 190) Given a temporal expression, nausea renders impossible the simplest bodily gesture. Heidegger's elementary criteria
for being-in-the-world, the categories of being "ready-to-hand" (*Vor-handen*) and "present-
at-hand" (*Zu-handen*) are denied. At the brink of the decomposition of self and world, all
Fanon's hands can do is shake. The limit point of this incapacitated alienation comes when
Fanon finally acquiesces to the onslaught of the alienating gaze and *internalizes it*. At two
points in his essay Fanon describes this moment with acute force,

> On that day, disoriented and incapable of being outside with the other, the White who
> unmercifully imprisoned me, I took myself far away, very far away indeed from my being-
> there, thus making myself an object.
>
> *(p. 186)*

> I sit down at the fire and I discover my livery.
>
> *(p. 94)*

Here, the white imaginary perspective intrudes to the extent that it becomes a self-inflicted
inferiorization. Again however, in the midst of despair, the flower of hope appears. For
Fanon is clear that the Black subject is not merely an unwilling victim in the procession
towards incapacitated alienation. There is then a *complicity* at work in the reification of a
parodic and inferiorized Black body-image. As Fanon writes later in the *Black Skin, White
Masks*, "I have ceaselessly striven to show the Negro man that in a sense he makes himself
abnormal" (1986, p. 225). The Black subject mimics the white gaze, and in a panopticon-
like manner, the white other no longer needs to be there.

THE BODY QUESTIONING

Fanon's analysis of Black *Erlebnis* under colonialism and imperialism clearly deeply problematizes orthodox phenomenology, and in particular the thought of Merleau-Ponty. The
equality that Merleau-Ponty assumed exists across all able-bodied beings is nullified and
rendered naïve by the Black experience. In *The Lived Experience of the Black*, Fanon pushes
this critique further, in the direction of problematizing a more fundamental category of
western thought – ontology itself:

> When one has admitted once and for all that ontology leaves existence aside, one sees why
> it does not allow for understanding the being of the Black. It is not a question of the Black
> being black anymore, but rather of his being black opposite the White.
>
> *(2001, p. 184)*

For Fanon, the encounter between "being" and difference leads to the dehiscence of ontology itself. Fanon repeats the Levinasian move here of construing ontology as the field of
the Same. [9] Ontology is therefore revealed as a strategy of legitimation for the repression
of autonomous difference. More particularly, for Fanon, ontology conceals the work of the
white mythos in *constructing* the image of Blackness which Black people in his view have
subsequently adopted in a reflexive comprehension of "black being."

Undoubtedly, Fanon is correct in asserting the violence wrought by ontology and its
phenomenological variant in the repression and concealment of intrinsic difference. It is
less certain however that any subsequent appeals to either a specific form of embodied
experience or to hope can do without them. What is required is less a rejection of ontology and phenomenology outright and more a critique of the means to which they have
been put. My argument is then that any assertion of the *difference* of Black lived experience

cannot be undertaken without recourse to the terms of a phenomenological ontology. This is partially acknowledged in the conclusion to *Black Skin, White Masks*, where Fanon writes, "I am a part of Being to the degree that I go beyond it" (1986, p. 229). Far from a phenomenological ontology necessarily demarcating (however unconsciously) the community of being that excludes or represses difference, the demand is that ontology itself is rethought (the implicit suggestion of Fanon here) as *differential*. Ontology would therefore mark the boundary of the same and the other. In an older terminology, ontology is re-cast as involving *transcendence within immanence*.[10] In this way "being" as a unified ontological category can no longer cash out in epistemological terms as the a priori given conditionals for experience. The phenomenon is not disclosed on the basis of the assumption of a unified transcendental ground. As we shall see, on the contrary, being is deferred and reconstituted as the form of the ideal, and the conditions of possibility for experience are pluralized. Within the present, ontology would always therefore involve difference – the interplay of immanence and transcendence. What alternatives are there to this solution? If a phenomenological ontology were delegitimated by the experience of difference, difference itself would be rendered impossible to thinking – nothing would be available to thought (save perhaps different strategies of immanence or different forms of will to power). The phenomenon of difference must be therefore understood as that which defers (and deters) being. But this argument moves far too quickly. What needs to be accounted for first of all in any phenomenological ontology of difference is the possibility of maintaining the difference of lived experience.

One of the sharpest commentators on the differences of experience that result from different forms of embodiment is James Baldwin. In a short essay called "Stranger in the Village" (1985), he recounts his experiences staying in a Swiss village. Towards the end of the piece, he considers the hypothetical differences between himself and the villagers in terms of varying interpretations of a work of architecture:

> The cathedral at Chartres, I have said, says something to the people of this village which it cannot say to me; but it is important to understand that this cathedral says something to me which it cannot say to them. Perhaps they are struck by the power of the spires, the glory of the windows; but they have known God, after all, longer than I have known him, and in a different way, and I am terrified by the slippery bottomless well to be found in the crypt, down which heretics were hurled to death, and by the obscene, inescapable gargoyles jutting out of the stone and seeming to say that God and the devil can never be divorced.
>
> *(1985, p. 89)*

Although the cathedral is situated within a common temporal horizon between villagers and Baldwin, the difference of embodiment divides the way in which it is revealed to both as an experiential/imaginary construct. Hence, a common horizon of terms fragments into different worlds of experience. In this way, everything that reveals itself in the world is liable to double readings across embodied difference (of race, class, gender, sexuality, etc.). Works of art, places, stories, traditions are all liable to be fragmented by contestive interpretations. As these counter-interpretations themselves are revealed in the face of the normative view, they therefore tend to reflect the forces of exclusion back to the subject of the experience. In this way, counter-interpretations repeat the pain of marginality. As Fanon writes, on the last page of *The Lived Experience of the Black*,

> Impossible to go to the movies without running into myself. I wait for myself. At the interval, and right before the movie starts, I wait for myself. Those in front of me look at me, spy on me, wait for me. A Negro groom is going to appear. My heart turns my head.
>
> *(2001, p. 200)*

With these experiences of difference and the "pain of interpretations" in mind, we are now in a position to work through the problem of expressing a desire for a community of being without violating difference. In *The Lived Experience of the Black*, Fanon expresses this desire as follows:

> All I wanted was to be a man among other men. I had wanted to arrive smooth and young in a world that was ours, that together we would have erected.
>
> *(2001, p. 186)*

For Fanon, this redemption from the gaze is articulated in terms of a transformative historicality, outlined forcefully in the final chapter of *Black Skin, White Masks*, "En guise de conclusion." Freedom for Fanon is first of all freedom from the weight of the past,

> The problem considered here is one of time. Those Negroes and white men will be disalienated who refuse to let themselves be sealed away in the materialized Tower of the Past.
>
> *(1986, p. 226)*

Instead of being mesmerized by the past, the present is attended to as the site of possible transformation and disalienation. The weight of history has therefore to be dismissed. "I will not make myself the man of any past. I do not want to exalt the past at the expense of my present and of my future" (Fanon, 1986, p. 226). The only past that is legitimate for the purposes of freedom is a *universal* past. "I am a man, and what I have to recapture is the whole past of the world" (1986, p. 226). In a series of passionate pronouncements, Fanon reiterates this desire for an unburdened universality, grounded in the present of agency:

> I am not a prisoner of history. I should not seek there for the meaning of my destiny.
> In the world through which I travel, I am endlessly creating myself.
> I am not the slave of the Slavery that dehumanized my ancestors.
> I am my own foundation.
>
> *(1986, pp. 229–231)*

Here then, Fanon argues that the present is the site of a potential rupture of what is given to have occurred: The unbearable *weight* of historical being. Fanon's redemption from the past involves not responding or *reacting* to it. Freedom for Fanon involves the active inflection of the "now," rather than a reactive valorization or reproduction of what has been given. History, as the framework of cultural origins (and therefore projections), is denied.

In these terms, it is not possible to avoid parallels with the account of the relations between history, agency, and freedom found in Merleau-Ponty's *Phenomenology of Perception*, in particular with the latter's notion of a pre-personal communication between the body and its habitus opening up the moment of freedom and the denial of fixed historical origins. Fanon transcends a locked Sartrean dialectical logic by relativizing history within the terms of an active present. Fanon's "endless recreation of himself," his existence as his own foundation, are the echo of Merleau-Ponty's "resumption at every moment" of the "perpetual contribution of his bodily being" (1962, p. 254). In both philosophers, rather than a mere moment within the dialectical process, freedom is a function of the present, as the site of a possible transformation of the given. In such a manner, the linearity of the past is broken, and the future is opened to difference, the difference of a transcendence of the same, participating in being by going beyond it.

There is however an important, if subtle, difference between the two versions of historical freedom. For Merleau-Ponty, as we have seen, the possibility of active inflection in and of the present is given with the ease of a "perpetual contribution." It would seem that the present is the site of rupture of the given's linearity, and that this rupture is guaranteed merely by the motility of the agent, as a matter of habit. In contrast, Fanon's freedom from the past involves a great deal more effort and resolve. For Fanon, transformation of the present requires something like a critical resistance to the dominating episteme – an active denial of the mythos that intervenes in the formation of body-images. Without that, Black subjectivity in particular is threatened with the weight of a past which disavows and disables the possibility of transforming the present. Once again, this weight cannot simply be off-loaded or deflected through a sort of ontological judo – the structures of complicity and internalization must be negotiated and worked through as stages on the way to autonomously grounded differentiation. In contrast, the lack of a critical resistance amongst those who approximate to the norm in Europe (white, male, straight, able-bodied) results in a complicit reproduction of the framework that privileges them through the ease of their actions. In this light, Merleau-Ponty's reflections on the body's relation to freedom risk being blind to the aporias of difference. Fanon's critique of phenomenology teaches us that the universal is the end of the struggle, not that which precedes it. *Black Skin, White Masks* ends with the most solemn of vows to a vigilance of the corporeal,

> My final prayer:
>
> O my body, make of me always a man who questions!
>
> *(1986, p. 232)*

PHENOMENOLOGICAL ONTOLOGY, DIFFERENTLY

As a result of my presentation of the encounter between Merleau-Ponty and Fanon, the phenomenological ontology of difference introduced above can now be clarified. Being, operating as a unified given (Merleau-Ponty's "one single world"), is incompatible with an agonistic hermeneutics engendered by bodily difference. As a temporo-historical horizon, being conventionally discloses difference only through the disjunctive movement of *time*, not through the difference of bodies.[11] Thus, in the case of Baldwin's cathedral, there would be no way of accounting for differences in the way the building is experienced or imagined, or rather, any such explanation would not be respected as of philosophical merit. Against this, through the characterization of ontology under development, each present becomes differentiated by different forms of embodiment, as the phenomena disclosed in that present are in turn revealed differently according to corporeal variation. Through our bodies, we belong to relatively different worlds, with different forms of visibility and invisibility, history and value being thereby disclosed. The merging of these worlds through encounters of difference leads inevitably to contested comprehensions of the phenomenon. Being therefore must, in order to maintain this phenomenological plurality and not *repress* it, re-situate itself as a *spatio-temporal* horizon, or rather as the ideal. What is, is what is to come. As Fanon says, we are indeed a part of being to the degree that we go beyond it. Being, as the possibility of (comm)unity, becomes the form of the ideal. Moreover, precisely because it cannot be given and does not function as the *a priori*, being is therefore an *ethical* ideal – it is the ideal of a community that is yet to exist and yet *ought* to exist, as the fulfillment of transcendence within immanence. In contrast, the extent to which a unified world is imposed as the episteme of the present marks the extent to which difference itself will be violated. The ethics of community is therefore the inverse of the repression of difference. In order to maintain this difference (and strive for community), it behooves us as participants in difference to be mindful of the ever-present possibility of a conflict of interpretations. Although the potentials of the present for inflectional agency have been stressed until now, it must be stated that this community has an inescapably *futural* dimension. The project of a community of difference, between those who have nothing in common, is a project that comes *after* experience. Community is unveiled *a posteriori*. It is only therefore possible to affirm a community that is forever "yet to come."[12] Any community of being is therefore a project, an openly processual entity forever cast into the future as ongoing work.

How can we begin to work towards this community of being? On what basis can *communication* between different beings begin? In what way does this analysis bear upon relations between others in the present of agency? If the imaginary framework of being-for-others (most sharply represented by Fanon's child on the train) is refused, what is now to take its place across difference? Here, I can offer no more than a suggestion, an allusion to what may turn out to be a "new humanism": We communicate with and move towards the other by dint of recognizing both their capacity and our own for *suffering*.[13] Fanon's *The Lived Experience of the Black* exemplifies this first step; as a testimony to affliction and psychic fragmentation it communicates the desire for community across difference. At the limit, although the other may look different, speak a language we do not understand, participate in rituals and practice that obey a different rationality to our own, regard the objects and artifacts in our world through a somatic lens that we cannot comprehend – we move toward each other through a common sentience and a shared capacity to suffer. In this sense, the grounds for hope lie where cultural juxtaposition is at its most vehement: In the contemporary metropolis. Richard Sennett ends his magisterial work on the fleshy history of the western city in this way,

> Lurking in the civic problems of a multi-cultural city is the moral difficulty of arousing sympathy for those who are Other. And this can only occur, I believe, by understanding why bodily pain requires a place in which it can be acknowledged, and in which its transcendent origins become visible. Such pain has a trajectory in human experience. It disorients and makes incomplete the self, defeats the desire for coherence; the body accepting pain is ready to become a civic body, sensible to the pain of another person, pains present together on the street, at last endurable – even though, in a diverse world, each person cannot explain what he or she is feeling, who he or she is, to the other.
>
> *(1994, p. 376)*

In this chapter I have argued that Merleau-Ponty's phenomenology of the body risks privileging a relation between freedom, agency, and historicality that ultimately violates the embodiment of difference such as that interposed by race. Fanon's *The Lived Experience of the Black* and the example from Baldwin display forcefully how difference denies the possibility of an already given community and commonality between human subjects. However, as I have argued throughout, Fanon's critique does not by necessity condemn Merleau-Ponty's phenomenology to a violent ontology of the Same. Rather, Fanon's critique has been used to begin to develop an ontology of difference that lies as the hidden soil of Merleau-Ponty's text. Despite Fanon's strong reservations over the legitimacy of "ontology," I have argued that only on its terms can emancipatory strategies be thought through. The "communication more ancient than thought" of the *Phenomenology of Perception* in particular provides the most powerful and resourceful way of thinking embodied free agency grounded in the difference of the present. Only on the basis of a conceptual schema itself present in Merleau-Ponty's work can Fanon's critique result in a productive phenomenology of difference which repositions community as the Ideal, the deferred universal, and not the given.[14] As I have suggested, the work towards this community begins by allowing for the communication of pain across difference in this present. Thus, a critical awareness of embodied differences between the subject and the horizons of its being does not seek to denounce or renounce justice, community, and a "new humanism" for the sake of irreducibility or a voluntaristic will-to-power. Rather, the phenomenologists' dream of uncovering a pre-thetic community is shown finally to be the goal of those who seek with vigilance to question their bodies in the present.

NOTES

1 Among the key critical texts are Levinas' "Meaning and Sense" (1996), Heidegger's "My Way to Phenomenology" (1972), and of course Derrida's early reading of Husserl (1973).

2 The two key authors inaugurating this are Toni Morrison, specifically her text *Playing in the Dark: Whiteness and the Literary Imagination* (1992) and the work of David Roediger.

3 Macey's impoverished comprehension of phenomenology leaves him searching for a biographical explanation as to why Fanon adopted its framework (1999, p. 10).

4 This is the tendency of Lewis R. Gordon's interpretation. See his book, *Fanon and the Crisis of European Man* (1995).

5 Gordon's book acknowledges the influence of Merleau-Ponty on Fanon without developing the nature of the dialogue in depth (1995, p. 14). Also, in his essay "Fanon's Body of Black Experience" (in Lewis, 1996). Ronald A. T. Judy spends the first page discussing Markmann's problematic translation of the fifth chapter's title, including mentioning Bernasconi's tracing of *l'expérience vécue* to Merleau-Ponty's translation of *Erlebnis* as a prelude to relating Fanon's text to Hegel's concept of experience.

6 Merleau-Ponty writes, "we must learn to find the communication between one consciousness and another in one and the same world. In reality, the other is not shut up inside my perspective of the world, because this perspective itself has no definite limits, because it slips spontaneously into the other's, and because both are brought together in the one single world in which we all participate as anonymous subjects of perception" (1962, p. 253).

7 Contenders along the way include Charlie Christian, Wes Montgomery, Django Reinhardt, Jimi Hendrix, and Derek Bailey.

8 In *Being and Nothingness*, Sartre writes, "Everything happens therefore as if the in-itself and the for-itself were presented in a state of disintegration in relation to an ideal synthesis. Not that the integration has ever *taken place* but on the contrary precisely because it is always indicated and always impossible" (1958, p. 623).

9 Levinas writes, "Western philosophy has most often been an ontology: a reduction of the other to the same by interposition of a middle and neutral term that ensures the comprehension of being" (1969, p. 43).

10 This argument for a reformulation of ontology embracing difference is developed at length in my PhD thesis (Weate, 1998).

11 This is in broad terms Heidegger's characterization of the relation between Being or the *Es gibt* and difference (1972).

12 Through different means, I concur finally with a Derridean logic.

13 See Robert Bernasconi, "Casting the Slough: Fanon's New Humanism for a New Humanity" in *Fanon: A Critical Reader*. As an alternative to a humanism engendered by internal violence (the view subsequently favoured by Fanon), what is being suggested here is a humanism grounded in injustice and the body-in-pain of the other.

14 Here, I must echo Lewis Gordon's cautionary note in *Fanon and the Crisis of European Man*, "it is not our intent to continue the long tradition of treating the thoughts of black philosophers as derivative of white ones" (1995, p. 14). I have only sought to show necessary *parallels* in the opening towards strategies of emancipation, not lines of causality.

REFERENCES

Baldwin, J. (1985). *The price of the ticket*. London: St. Martin's Press.

Bernasconi, R. (1996). Casting the slough: Fanon's new humanism for a new humanity. In L. R. Gordon, R. T. White, & T. D. Sharpley-Whiting (Eds.), *Fanon: A critical reader* (pp. 113–121). Malden, MA: Wiley.

Derrida, J. (1973). *Speech and phenomena*. Evanston, IL: Northwestern University Press.

Dillon, M. C. (1995). *Semiological reductionism: A critique of the deconstructionist movement in postmodern thought*. New York, NY: State University of New York Press.

Fanon, F. (1986). *Black skin, White masks*. London: Pluto Press.

Fanon, F. (2001). The lived experience of the Black. In R. Bernasconi (Ed.), *Race*, (pp. 184–202). Malden, MA: Wiley-Blackwell.

Gordon, L. R. (1995). *Fanon and the crisis of European man*. New York: Routledge.

Grosz, E. (1994). *Volatile bodies*. Bloomington, IN: Indiana University Press.

Heidegger, M. (1972). My way to phenomenology. In *On time and being* (J. Stambaugh, Trans.) (pp. 74–82). New York: Harper and Row.

Judy, R. A. T. (1996). Fanon's body of Black experience. In L. R. Gordon, R. T. White, & T. D. Sharpley-Whiting (Eds.), *Fanon: A critical reader* (pp. 53–73). Oxford: Wiley.

Lévinas, E. (1969). *Totality and infinity: An essay on exteriority* (A. Lingis, Trans.). Pittsburgh, PA: Duquesne University Press.

Levinas, E. (1996). Meaning and sense. In A. Peperzak, A. Critchley, & R. Bernasconi (Eds.), *Emmanuel Levinas: Basic philosophical writings*. Bloomington, IN: Indiana University Press.

Macey, D. (1999). Fanon, phenomenology, race. *Radical Philosophy*, *95*, 8–14.

Merleau-Ponty, M. (1962). *Phenomenology of perception*. London: Routledge & Kegan Paul.

Merleau-Ponty, M. (1964). An unpublished text by Maurice Merleau-Ponty: A prospectus of his work. In James M. Edie (Ed.), *The primacy of perception* (pp. 3–11). Evanston, IL: Northwestern University Press.

Morrison, T. (1992). *Playing in the dark: Whiteness and the literary imagination*. Cambridge, MA: Harvard University Press.

Sartre, J.-P. (1958). *Being and nothingness: An essay on phenomenological ontology* (Hazel E. Barnes, Trans.). London: Methuen.

Sennett, R. (1994). *Flesh and stone: The body and the city in western civilization*. London: Faber & Faber.

Weate, J. (1998). *Phenomenology and difference: The body, architecture and race*. PhD thesis, University of Warwick.

Weiss, G. (1999). *Body images: Embodiment as intercorporeality*. London & New York: Routledge.

PART IV
Temporality and Racism

CHAPTER 12

TOO LATE

Fanon, the Dismembered Past, and a Phenomenology of Racialized Time[1]

Alia Al-Saji

INTRODUCTION: RACISM, COLONIALISM, AND TIME

In the introduction to *Black Skin, White Masks*, Frantz Fanon notes the temporal architecture of the work and of the problem he is broaching:

> The architecture of this work is rooted in the temporal. Every human problem must be considered from the standpoint of time. Ideally, the present will always contribute to the building of the future. And this future is not the future of the cosmos but rather the future of my century, my country, my existence.[2]
>
> *(Fanon, 1967, pp. 12–13; Fanon, 1952, p. 14)*

This is not an abstract future, for, as Fanon emphasizes, "[i]n no way is it up to me to prepare the world that will follow me. I belong irreducibly to my time. And it is for my own time that I should live" (1967, p. 13; 1952, p. 13, translation revised).

In this essay, I think of racialized experience in temporal terms. This means exploring both how racialization is lived temporally and how racism and colonialism structure our experiences and ontologies of time. As such, it requires attending to the ways in which colonialism and racism manage, skew, divide, and even reconfigure time. Racism and colonialism are temporal formations, as well as being geographical, economic, social, and imaginary ones. They manage not only territories and bodies, but also histories, pasts, and futures. They shape time not only by differentially molding the field of possibilities of the present, but also through colonial reconfigurations and constructions of the past. Indeed, I argue that it is in part through the colonial remaking of the past that racism structures our sense of possibility, framing the phenomenological field of the present and attempting to delimit the future.

Attending to the temporal dimensions of racialization raises the problem of method. To take racism seriously is to understand its *structuring* – and not merely accessory or additive – role in differentially molding lived experiences of time. In particular, if racism is reflected not only in economic, social, and political conditions, but also structures lived experience, then anomalies and breakdowns in experience cannot be studied as purely individual afflictions in racial societies. As Fanon notes, "anomalies of affect" are normal in racist societies (1967, pp. 10, 191; 1952, pp. 10, 185). The study of the ways in which racism is lived – of the "aberrations of affect" (1967, p. 8; 1952, p. 8), embodiment, agency, and temporality that accompany it – raises the question of how psychopathology may crystallize social pathology, and of how phenomenological method can do justice to racialized experience. How can phenomenology see more than individual anomaly, or psychopathology, in order to critically uncover and diagnose social pathology – and "sociogeny" (1967, p. 11; 1952, p. 11)? If colonization and its aftermaths touch our psyches and affect our bodily selves,[3]

DOI: 10.4324/9781003037132-12

then, in societies built on the legacies of colonialism, slavery, or settlement, both racializing and racialized subjects will experience alienation, albeit in structurally different ways. The imbrication of the individual and the social in psychopathology presents challenges to any phenomenological study of racialized experience. Here phenomenology must attend not only to intersubjective and first-person constitution of meaning, but to social structures and historical and material conditions that may appear, at first sight, to lie beyond the scope of its description.[4] Just as a pure phenomenology may try to put these conditions in brackets, its failure to do so will reveal their affective weight and (de-)structuring power – the ways in which the social-historical has become ontological and in which psychopathology is symptomatic of this ontology of colonization. This means that phenomenologists will need to be not only *critical* – extending the scope of the phenomenological reduction to the naturalization of social oppression – and *interdisciplinary*, drawing on histories of colonialism and slavery to recognize their intransigence and, often covert, rephrasing in present experience, but also *decolonizing* in their method.[5]

I turn to Fanon and in particular *Black Skin, White Masks*, in order to analyze the temporal structures of racialized experience – what I am calling *racialized time*. I focus on Fanon for several reasons. Fanon proposes *Black Skin, White Masks* as a "clinical study" of racialization (1967, p. 12; 1952, p. 12) and a form of "sociodiagnostic," aimed at making "disalienation" possible (1967, p. 11; 1952, p. 11). In so doing, he joins phenomenology with decolonized psychiatry and anti-racist activism, at once grounding phenomenology in the social and adjusting its purpose.[6] In the chapter on the lived experience of the Black ("l'expérience vécue du Noir"), Fanon presents a first-person phenomenological account of how it feels to become racialized – to discover one's race. More than a description of a series of effects, the chapter unfolds a process of racialization that is affectively charged, embodied, vacillating, and ambivalent. The reader is asked to live with Fanon through the fragmentation of bodily affectivity and deferral of agency as the circles of racialization tighten.[7] While his account is often read in terms of embodiment and space, and while temporality remains implicit in his narrative (despite his references to time in the book), Fanon provides the signposts to understand the experience temporally. This is supported, I argue, by the structuring role that the past plays in the lived experience of racialization – a role that Fanon abbreviates in his reference to a "historico-racial schema" in the phenomenology he offers. In this essay, I take up Fanon's references to time and elaborate the work done by the past, in particular, in structuring racialized time.

We should be mindful from the start that what Fanon offers is *one* experience of racialization; the experience he describes is neither definitive nor exhaustive. Beyond it lies a multiplicity of racialized experiences, and Fanon acknowledges the limitations of his positionality – a Martiniquan, living under French colonialism and departmentalization (1967, p. 14; 1952, p. 14), a doctor, living in the memory and wake of slavery – and of his sensibility – socially and intellectually engaged. Black experience is "ambiguous," heterogeneous, and multiple, notes Fanon (1967, p. 136; 1952, p. 133). Certainly, Fanon's account is that of a Black man, and Black women are mostly unheard in the book. But as I read *Black Skin, White Masks*, its aim is also to draw out structural overlaps with other racialized experiences, while remaining cognizant of differences. Indeed, Fanon sees phenomenology as providing a method precisely for this; rather than collecting facts and behavior, he notes, it allows the understanding of a few concrete experiences in their structuring meanings (1967, pp. 168–169; 1952, p. 164, citing Jaspers). Significantly, it is when Fanon combines phenomenology and social critique that *Black Skin, White Masks* is most successful in my view. In the chapter on the lived experience of the Black, Fanon captures, I contend, a fragmenting tendency of racialization, its retrospective colonization of the past, that allows us to glimpse its temporal logic.

RACIALIZATION, EMBODIMENT, AND SOCIAL IMAGINARY

What is meant by racialization? In *Black Skin, White Masks*, Fanon shows how racialization is not only a process by which the identities of self and other are constituted (an "othering" process *à la* Jean-Paul Sartre); it is a socially pathological *othering* with important structural features. This othering involves a projective mechanism by which what is undesirable in the self is projected onto the other; the result is a negative mirroring whereby the other is constituted as that which this self is *not*, or does not take itself to be.[8] "Black," "native," and "Arab" are oppositionally (yet differentially) constructed as that *other*, which "white" identity disavows. In this othering, difference is no longer relational. Difference becomes *Manichean* and exclusionary – a masked difference, wherein colonized subjects serve as the *foil* for what "modern European" identity takes itself to be. What allows this difference to be seen as a feature of the world, and racializing operations to remain hidden from view, is the way in which race is perceived as belonging to sensory features of the body (such as skin color). Racialization hence relies on the naturalization of projected and oppositional difference to the perceived body of the racialized subject.

Racialization not only structures the ways in which bodies are represented and perceived, it configures our affective, perceptual, and cognitive maps, the imaginary warp and weft of our lives. Racialization describes the ways in which colonialism and white supremacy divide bodies politically, economically, spatially, and socially in order to exploit and dominate them.[9] Racialization comprises, then, the historical, social, economic, epistemological, and affective processes – the (de-)structuring violence and colonizing formations – by which races are constructed, seen, and, when interiorized or "epidermalized," lived. The power of Fanon's account of racism is twofold, in my view, for he is interested both in the *naturalization* of race, its constitution in relation to perceived bodily markers[10] that come to unconsciously stand in for race, and in its *rationalization*, the ways in which racism takes itself to originate as a mere reaction to the racialized other. What Fanon reveals is that constructions of race in the social imaginary have more to do with drawing lines of domination and privilege than with the concrete racialized and colonized lives who are its ostensible objects.[11] There is an ignorance to racism that is not merely accidental, but that sustains its operations – a forgetting which actively hides racializing mechanisms and misconstrues its objects. Racism is ambivalent, structurally relying on an "epistemology of ignorance" (to use a term from Charles Mills, 2007).[12] As Fanon notes, "[t]he European knows and he does not know" (1967, p. 199; 1952, p. 192) – both at the same time.

Racism is both recalcitrant and mobile. Its recalcitrance relies on an ability to adapt to its social time and place, taking on the guise of prevailing norms – becoming ambient or atmospheric.[13] Yet racism also covers over this rephrasing; it represses the histories and operations of power which constitute it and instead scapegoats or blames its victims (1967, p. 194; 1952, p. 188). More precisely, what is disavowed in the process of racialization is not some ahistorical essence; rather, the very guilt and corrosive de-structuring, which colonization brings about, is blamed on its *colonized others* – what Fanon refers to elsewhere as the "racial redistribution of guilt" (1967, p. 103; 1952, p. 101, translation altered). Racialized bodies are, at once, the material and affective labor, the disposable and consumed lives that colonization exploits – the "fertilizer" that nourishes colonialism, says Fanon, recalling Aimé Césaire (1967, p. 216; 1952, p. 209) – and they are the scapegoats upon which the *need* for colonization and its constitutive violence are projected.

It is important to remember that the racial imaginary to which Fanon refers – the imaginary mapping of racial dichotomies, hierarchies, and exclusions along lines of othering – is differentially shared by subjects living in a racial society. While Fanon describes it as a kind of "collective unconscious," he argues, against Jung, that "[it] is cultural, which means acquired" (1967, p. 188; 1952, p. 182). This imaginary persists as unreflected habit or acquisition, or as Fanon notes, *as cultural imposition* (1967, p. 191; 1952, p. 185). This imaginary constellation, this cultural view of the world, is acquired through childhood education, scholarly manuals, language, media, comic books, stories, films, and images.[14] As a result, particular ways of imagining, thinking, and perceiving become normative. It is for this reason that Fanon calls the racial imaginary "white." This is not to imply that it is restricted to phenotypically white subjects but rather that it upholds a social mapping of ways of being where habitually "white" forms of perceiving and being are privileged as normatively desirable for all subjects. Significantly, this account allows for racial imaginaries to be both historically dynamic and multiple, to differ for different racial societies as well as within each society. What is defining of a racial imaginary is *how* it draws borders that attempt to stabilize social categories of othering and manage racial formations; even as those borders shift, in policing who is included/excluded, the othering mechanism remains in force. Racial imaginaries are not coherent wholes; there is fragmentation with differential temporalities at play. That it draws borders means that within a racial imaginary a certain splitting takes place; "two frames of reference" come into effect (1967, p. 110; 1952, p. 108). These frames not only define different subject-positions along racial lines, but also differentially configure the kinds of past and fields of possibility available to subjects, as we will see below.

Since a racial imaginary is split according to "two frames of reference" – just as a racial world is a divided world – the pathological effects and affects of racialization are felt by both racializing and racialized bodies, albeit in structurally different ways. I have described the pathologies of racializing ways of being and seeing in a previous paper (Al-Saji, 2014); here my focus will be experiences of becoming racialized – that is, experiences in which racialization is felt and *en-fleshed*, or, to use Fanon's tactile term, "epidermalized" (Fanon, 1967, p. 11; Fanon, 1952, p. 11). This is not necessarily the experience of every person of color in racial societies. As Fanon notes, it is possible, however paradoxically, to live in the Antilles without "discovering" one's Blackness; one enacts and identifies with normatively white ways of being, while one's race is not explicitly brought into question. Racism remains implicit. However, an encounter with a racializing gaze transforms this state of affairs, for this gaze interpolates the Black subject by identifying him with his skin color and positioning him within a racialized frame of reference (bound to a colonized and enslaved Black past). This makes racism explicit in ways that are consciously and affectively lived (though not, as yet, necessarily reflectively worked-through). What is experienced is bodily transfiguration or transubstantiation – or, to use Fanon's terms, "tearing out *[arrachement]*" (1952, p. 110), disjointing, dismemberment, and disassembly (1952, p. 111). Looking closer at Fanon's phenomenological narrative in *Black Skin, White Masks*, I will argue that a temporal transformation or fragmentation is also at stake.

"Tiens, un nègre! [Look, a Negro!]" (1967, p. 109; 1952, p. 107). It is beginning with these words that Fanon recounts his experience of the racializing gaze. This gaze, we discover, is that of a child on a train, directed at Fanon as he is traveling through France. Prior to this racializing encounter, Fanon tells us, one might have lived one's body unreflectively, with movements and gestures implicitly known. Fanon refers this lived embodiment to a body schema [*schéma corporel*], tacitly structuring one's relation to the world. In a seemingly Merleau-Pontian vein, he describes this as a "slow composition of my *self* as a body [within] a spatial and temporal world" (1967, p. 111; 1952, p. 109, translation corrected) – an optimal (and implicitly white) sensory coordination. But Fanon's account diverges point-edly from Merleau-Ponty's *Phenomenology of Perception*, for Fanon notes that another schema already underlies the body schema and coexists in tension with it. This is the unconscious racial imaginary, the map of enduring and structuring racism that orients perception and delimits embodiment in a racial society – and this already at the pre-reflective level. Fanon calls this a "historico-racial schema." While its elements, he says, had been provided for me "by the other, the white man, who had woven me out of a thousand details, anecdotes, stories" (1967, p. 111; 1952, p. 109), Fanon emphasizes its historicity (1967, p. 112; 1952, p. 109). This schema, in other words, has to do with the past.

Although the racializing gaze does not create this schema (racism pre-existed the encounter on the train and made it possible, after all), this gaze displaces Fanon's posi-tionality in that schema and relates him explicitly to a Black past. Whereas prior to his interpolation as Black, Fanon could imagine all "civilizational" history as his own, he was now limited to those historical elements that made up a stereotyped Black past. Thus, he says, "my eardrums were bursting with cannibalism, mental retardation, fetishism, racial taints, slave-traders, and above all, above all 'Y a bon banania.'"[15] Affectively and palpably lived in this way, the historico-racial schema undermines the (idealized Merleau-Pontian) body schema. As Fanon notes, "assailed at various points, the body schema crumbled, giv-ing way to a racial epidermal schema" (1967, p. 112; 1952, p. 110, translation corrected). This final schema is that of the naturalization of race to one's lived body. Race is no longer simply a historical construction or a concept, but is lived as sensations of one's body, and specifically for Fanon, of one's skin; more so, these sensings – tearing, spasming, dismem-bering, wearing out – make one racialized, or epidermalize, flesh.[16] History, in other words, has been naturalized. The past is no longer lived at a distance, as past, but is experienced as an overdetermining and proximate, stuck and sticky, dimension of the present. To under-stand this, I look more closely at the historico-racial schema, before asking after the tempo-ral experience at stake in the crumbling of racialized bodies that Fanon describes.

THE HISTORICO-RACIAL SCHEMA, OR THE COLONIZATION OF THE PAST

How does the historico-racial schema erode and fragment racialized embodiment? Although we may at first be tempted to understand this disruption as the effect of the historico-racial schema becoming conscious – the dissonance created when racism becomes explicit – this consciousness does not sufficiently account for the feeling of *belonging* to a stereotyped Black past that Fanon describes (a belonging that does not entail uncritical acceptance). More so, it does not account for the ontological weight, fixity, or obduracy with which this past is felt to bear on the present – the way it glues or bogs us down.[17] What is required, in order to answer this question, is an understanding of how the historico-racial schema constitutes a racial past within which it places the racialized subject, at once displacing other pasts. More specifically, we need to ask how the past itself is colonized and racialized.

In attempting to explain how "[t]he black man has no ontological resistance in the eyes of the white man," how he lacks a sense of existence, Fanon notes:

Overnight the Negro has been given two frames of reference within which he has had to place himself. His metaphysics, or less pretentiously, his customs and the sources on which

they were based, were abolished because they were in contradiction with a civilization that
he did not know and that imposed itself on him.

(1967, p. 110; 1952, p. 108, translation revised)

Racialization takes place, in other words, not only in the present but also at the level of the
past. There is a form of othering within the past that splits it into "two frames of reference,"
dichotomously constructed. While the dominant frame is that of white "civilizational" history, the second frame positions colonized and racialized peoples as foils to this history, as
swept up in it without contributing to it. We would lose the tension and complexity within
this past were we to understand one of the frames as representative of an authentic Black
past. Fanon's point is that colonization of the past occludes other pasts, even attempting to
efface and rewrite them.

    While Fanon tries not to dwell on the past (precisely because of the affective loss and
disempowerment it engenders), Latin American decolonial thinker, Aníbal Quijano (2000),
probes the transformation that takes place at the level of the past in colonialism and racism. Quijano describes the colonial construction of time, a construction that is also a constitution and molding, since it has economic, social, and political dimensions, as well as
representational and imaginary ones.[18] His concern is to explain how a Eurocentric civilizational history and modernity were formed. He discerns three processes, which I can only
sketch briefly here: (1) The expropriation of the cultural discoveries of colonized peoples
as positive acquisitions of colonialism; (2) the elision and repression of pre-colonial pasts,
construed as empty, pre-historical, or primitive lands; and (3) the re-inscription of a linear
timeline in which colonized peoples are relocated as perpetually past to European cultures
that are seen as modern, futurally directed, and open (Quijano, 2000, pp. 541, 552). What
were coexistent cultures, and simultaneous temporalities, in the colonial encounter become
temporally distributed as successive moments along a linear civilizational time. While
Europe and its settler states are seen as the "mirror of the future" of humanity and seat
of modernity, colonized peoples are projected backward as past (Quijano, 2007, p. 176).[19]

    In my reading, this past with which we, colonized peoples, are identified is no longer
our past[20] – for the pre-colonial past has been occluded, and the time of colonized reaction and resistance has been flattened, disjointed, caricatured.[21] Rather, the past to which
we are colonially tethered is a past of stereotyped remnants, isolated fragments, and
violent distortions extrapolated back from one's alienated and stagnant state under colonialism. This is hence a *closed* past, incapable of development on its own terms and cut
off from invention and the creation of alternate possibility. This is a past, moreover, that
serves to retrospectively justify the need for colonial domination and paternalism, the
"white man's burden." Linear colonial history thus, paradoxically, assumes a duality of
times ("two frames of reference" as Fanon said): the *closed* and perpetual past, in which
colonized peoples are stuck, is subordinated to the *open* time of Eurocentric modernity
– which is understood to have been "autoproduced" (or, at least, to have arisen out of a
Greece already belonging to Europe) (Quijano, 2000, p. 552). Yet, the economy of theft
upon which European modernity was built – its debt to colonial expansion and slavery
– is rendered invisible in this duality of open and closed times, eliding the violence that
consumed lives and impoverished and stagnated cultures. Here, the closed past of the
colonized forms an ahistorical or prehistorical time, irrelevant to the present; it is empty
landscape or material resource, awaiting colonial impetus to infuse meaning. But obfus-
cated, too, is how the *open time* of Western modernity, "white destiny" to use Fanon's
words (1967, p. 10; 1952, p. 10), is an aspirational, teleological schema without issue, built
on exploitation, racialized debilitation, and Black death. (I argue in section four that this

schema repeats but does not create, since the possibilities it maps are exhausted, lacking leeway and mobility, an ankylosed colonial time.)

Quijano's account is complex, but it is important to note that he is describing more than a representational or psychological process (although he is also describing this). The colonization of time, which he describes, is a cultural, economic, political, and material molding that was part of Iberian, French, and Anglo-Saxon colonialism, the effects of which endure in the racial societies that issue from them. In a certain sense, the power of this representation of history comes from the ways it has actualized and justified itself in intersubjective and cultural existence – assimilating peoples through what Quijano calls "a long period of the colonization of cognitive perspectives, modes of producing and giving meaning, the results of material existence, the imaginary, the universe of intersubjective relations with the world: in short, the culture" (Quijano, 2000, p. 541). The colonized, in other words, were forced to learn the dominant culture in ways that reproduced modes of domination and justified them (recalling Fanon's notion of cultural imposition) – although this "internalization" was not without bodily resistances and spasms (see section four). The closed past, with which colonized and racialized peoples are identified, is *instituted* and *inhabited*; it is a lifeworld of habitualities and not merely a representation. This past has taken on reality; it has *been made* through the very processes of colonization and ongoing racialization and by means of the distortions and reactions they produce.

I mean to point to how the construction of a colonial past (in its "two frames of reference," open and closed) is underwritten by ongoing colonial violence that is much more than representational. But the ontological weight and epistemic flatness of this past also rely on hiding the violence that its institution requires. Forgotten is material and cultural dismemberment, where land, bodies, and air are exploited as empty resource and consumed as fodder – their possibilities foreclosed to make real (and univocal) colonial time – and meaning-making.

Thus, the ontological complexity of our pasts as colonized peoples – with their impositions, elisions, and resistances, their depths of foreclosed possibility – is *dismembered* and reduced to the flatness of a self-contained and in-itself colonial past.[22] It becomes the past of a (decontextualized) people, solely attributed to them in forgetfulness of both colonialism and their resistance to it.[23] As through a selective and distorting mirror, one recognizes elements of the past: Singular traits generalized, reactions to racism taken out of context, protective rigidity, violence and anger stereotyped.[24] This sense of recognition – the vexed and painful belonging to an alienating and alienated past – means that this past cannot simply be shrugged away, or its closure easily re-imagined.[25] We are stuck in, and weighed down by, this past. It is felt in the possibilities we, colonized subjects, have for living the present; it is lived in racialized ways of being in time. This brings us back to Fanon.

"TOO LATE": RACIALIZED WAYS OF BEING IN TIME

What if, rephrasing Du Bois' question "how does it feel to be a problem?" (Du Bois, 2007, p. 7), one were to ask Fanon: How does it feel to be racialized? The answer I think would come along these lines:

> Too late [*Trop tard*]. Everything is anticipated, thought out, demonstrated, made the most of [*Tout est prévu, trouvé, prouvé, exploité*]. My trembling hands take hold of nothing; the vein has been mined out [*le gisement est épuisé*]. Too late! But once again I want to understand.
> *(Fanon, 1967, p. 121; Fanon, 1952, p. 118)*

And then the response from the perspective of the racializing other and white time: "You come too late, much too late. There will always be a world – a white world – between you and us" (1967, p. 122; 1952, p. 119).[26] But what does it mean to feel that one has come too late to a world?

Possibility

This feeling of lateness cannot merely be understood in terms of the pre-existence of the world, a pre-existence which characterizes the phenomenological experience of a world.[27] The feeling of coming to a world that was *always already there*, that contains meanings sedimented through other lives, gives the sense of that world as "intersubjective" and real. But this intersubjective world is not perceived as a completed reality; it is felt to be inexhaustible and only incompletely given, open to the creation of new possibility. This is not the world of exhausted and used-up possibilities that Fanon describes. In order to understand the feeling of arriving "too late," which Fanon expresses, I take up Matthew Ratcliffe's (2012) suggestion of exploring the distinct structuring of possibility at stake in different experience. But I want to do so without assuming the normativity of relationality – specifically of Black–white reciprocity – in the constitution of this world; that is, I wish to eschew taking intersubjective coexistence (with whiteness) for granted, since it is questionable how much this can be realized in an anti-Black world. Indeed, I argue that Fanon does not express a sense of limited or truncated possibility, but a different configuration of the field of possibility: *Structured by lateness*. Racialization, on my account, would also be about managing and mediating the configuration of possibility – a mediation in which the colonial past plays a structuring role. (Thus, while Fanon refers to a "white" world and "white" others, it is important to eschew taking these as normative touch-stones, unproblematized or ideal referents, in reading his phenomenology – and to remember their "affective ankylosis," a concept I return to below.)

The world that Fanon experiences is one where everything has been foreseen and discovered; all appears to be given. It is not that this world lacks possibility, but that the field of possibilities has already been defined in relation to other (white) body schemas. More so, white subjects have already used up these possibilities, worn them out, and eroded them; they have moved on and left the *ruins of possibility* behind. As Fanon notes earlier in the same chapter, the white other is "absent, has disappeared" (1967, p. 112; 1952, p. 110, translation revised). Indeed, this other is always ahead of Fanon, oriented toward an unlocalizable and vanishingly general futurity that cannot be caught up with. This positions Fanon as anachronistic. But, more importantly, it means that the encounter with the white other is a *missed encounter*, that there is no coexistence in a lived present upon which reciprocity could be built. What Fanon experiences is temporal non-relationality or disjuncture.

Hence, Fanon perceives a field of possibility structured according to the past and exhausted possibles of an absent other. As past, these possibilities lose their contingency and virtuality; they become factical and necessary, the routes to their realization fixed. More precisely, the field of possibility loses its playfulness and imaginary variability.[28] Though Fanon may sometimes be able to take up the structured possibilities already defined, and follow through their realization according to the routes deposited by the other (to the degree that this is permitted a Black body in an anti-Black world), he does not see them as allowing variation, as being able to be worked out *differently*. The structure of possibility allows *repetition* but neither invention, variation, nor leeway; it is a *closed map*. Without leeway to take them up, possibilities are not genuinely felt as *mine*, on Fanon's account, and this explains his description of the white world as an indifferent and cold world (1967, p. 113; 1952, p. 111). This goes deeper than saying that the moral values and norms of the world are defined by a dominant group to which I do not belong. Fanon's description extends, I think, to the practical significances of things, to the organization of lived space, and to our affective landscape. For he implies that the perceptual and practical norms of the white world call for a virtual (white) subject capable of living and acting according to them, one whose body schema provides a system of possible actions that can take up these norms dextrously in responding to the beckoning of the world – that can coordinate movements and sensations to bring the future "optimally" into grasp.[29] Crucially, this white body schema is conditioned by an *ankylosed* affectivity, actively indifferent to racialized suffering, quickly moving on and forgetting slavery and colonialism. The racialized subject is delayed in regards to this virtual (absent but posited-as-real) subject, structurally incapable of catching up.

This means that the openness of a "white world," or Eurocentric modernity, is a deceptive aspirational schema, a treadmill where colonized subjects are structurally destined to fall, to be tripped up.[30] Indeed, we find ourselves, again and again, in a persistent past – a fragmentary past of shifting stereotypes that continually slips away under our feet, so that we lack the traction to make a difference in the field of possibility of the present. Portrayed as a "time before time," the time of the colonized is split off – shears away – from the linear civilizational (white) time that is supposed to flow into the living present and have a future.[31] This perpetual deferral of possibility, the lack of traction or coevalness, results, in Fanon's words, not merely in a feeling of inferiority, but in depersonalization and "a feeling of nonexistence" (1967, p. 139; 1952, p. 135). This recalls the racialized subject's lack of "ontological resistance" (1967, p. 110; 1952, p. 108), and brings us back to the role of the past. For the past is a *dimension* that structures existence – in the sense of being *that according to which* we perceive, sense, and act; it is with the past, by taking it up, reconfiguring it, and playing on its relations, that we can act in the present. Whether instituted dimension, memory, or unconscious habituality, this past is a resource for agency. But when it is a colonized past that mediates our relation to the world, this dimensionality is *dismembered, de-structured*. While colonial ways of being are dug out, as grooves and ruts, and mapped as "objective" possibilities of the world, colonized ways of being and resistance are submerged and foreclosed as possibilities, their routes to realization blocked. I think that this foreclosure of possibility can help us understand how the colonization of the past is also temporal fragmentation and *de-structuration*[32] – or, to think with Saidiya Hartman, *dis-membering*.[33]

Taking seriously the *de-structuring* violence that colonialism and slavery wrought means also understanding how this violence *structures* the societies, of wealth and predatory accumulation that issue from them. The lines of possibility mapped out in a "white world" are, hence, inseparable from the exploitation, impoverishment, and mining out – and from "the weight of cannons and swords"[34] – that exhaust colonized and racialized peoples, wear us down, and delay entry into "development." What Fanon says of hunger is telling: "It is utopian to expect the black man or the Arab to exert the effort of embedding abstract values in their *Weltanschauung* when they have barely enough food to survive [*alors qu'ils mangent à peine à leur faim*]" (1967, p. 95; 1952, pp. 92–93). Because, he adds, they "lack the possibility [*n'en ont pas la possibilité*]" (1967, p. 95; 1952, p. 93). There are several levels to this foreclosure of possibility. On the one hand, it is the *dimension* of conceptual thinking that is foreclosed and not this or that concept, and this blockage is part of colonial domination (psychological and material). While hunger is an obstacle to abstract thinking, Fanon's point is deeper: Colonization turns the bodies of the colonized into instruments against them – kept barely alive while being digested and used up, "walking manure [*un fumier ambulant*]" he says, citing Césaire (Fanon, 1952, p. 95; Césaire, 2017, p. 114). They are sapped of the energy and time for thinking and revolt. On the other hand, we need to remember the economy of theft, of exhausted life and land, that was needed to free up abstract thinking; abstract thinking requires the labor of others, often forced, to institute the material conditions that allow some bodies to disengage from the needs of survival. The affects of colonized hunger may need *alternative forms of thinking*, creating concepts from the affective texture of lived experience (as I think Fanon is doing in *Black Skin, White Masks*). This needs to hold together sustenance and invention, material-vital conditions and ontology – but also to invent sociality and ways of living and dying, on one's own terms, from the reconfigured ruin of foreclosed and dead possibilities.[35]

This reading of possibility may shed light on Fanon's claim that "every ontology is rendered unrealizable [*irréalisable*] in a colonized and civilized society" (1967, p. 109; 1952, p. 107, translation corrected). Foreclosed possibility can be understood as those dimensions – systems of reference – that colonialism tries to abolish when it institutes the two frames of reference of colonial time (monumental colonial and caricatural colonized) as the only lines of possibility that can count in the map of the real. Its routes to realization suspended, colonized possibility is put in abeyance and cut off from the present.[36] Here, I think of possibility as de-structured, but not destroyed; its temporality dismembered, not erased.[37] The irreparability of colonial wounds, the breach of the Middle Passage, the ruptures of slavery and colonialism mean that there is no going back to an intact past, where such possibility can be recuperated sound and whole; it remains in the past subjunctive of "what could have been," a tense wherein the pain of dismemberment continues to be heard.[38] Could foreclosed and dismembered possibility be felt in racialized affect, sensibility, and spasm? I turn to this question at the end of the essay, after carefully distinguishing them from the *ankylosis* of colonial/white affectivity.

Affective Ankylosis

In rehearsing the ways in which racism responds – repeatedly, adaptively, and intransigently – to attempts to argue against it, Fanon writes:

> You come too late, much too late. There will always be a world – a white world – between you and us ... This impossibility for the [white] other to liquidate [*liquider*] the past once and for all. In the face of this affective ankylosis [*ankylose affective*] of the white, it is understandable that I could have made up my mind to utter my Negro cry [*mon cri nègre*]. Little by little, putting out pseudopodia here and there, I secreted a race.
>
> *(Fanon, 1967, p. 122; Fanon, 1952, p. 119, translation revised)*

This ankylosed past refers back to a story told by Fanon one page earlier: "A dog lies down on the grave of his master and starves to death. We had to wait for Janet to demonstrate that the aforesaid dog, in contrast to man, simply lacked the capacity to liquidate [*liquider*] the past" (1967, p. 121; 1952, p. 118). For Fanon, this ankylosis explains, at least in part, the non-relationality of the "white world" that keeps racialized subjects in abeyance or postponement.

It is worth dwelling on the concept of "affective ankylosis [*ankylose affective*]."[39] It is one of the more puzzling socio-diagnostic neologisms Fanon invents. *Ankylosis* should be read in medical, anatomical, and metaphorical senses at once. It describes a condition where joints become fused and coalesce (fusion that is bony or fibrous), so that articulations are restricted, and movement is limited or no longer possible between them. Fanon associates *affective ankylosis* with an inability to liquidate the past – playing on the sense of *"liquider"* as both liquidating and making fluid. While this might make us think that what he advocates is an abolition of the past (and Fanon's discomfort with the past sometimes moves in this direction), I think that it is important to remember that what he is talking about on these pages is colonial nostalgia and the recalcitrance of racism (a "white world"). Colonialism has *already* tried to abolish pre-colonial cultures and colonized ways of being, dismembering their links to the present; abolishing the past as that which registers and remembers colonization (in its *longue durée*) would, yet again, exculpate colonialism and naturalize the stagnancy of the colonized.

Fanon is clear that what is ankylosed is colonial or white affectivity – a "white world" – that holds racialized subjects in abeyance through fused and immovable articulations of time (which foreclose and redraw the map of realizable possibility). What are fixated on are the "beneficial" effects of colonialism, hagiography, and monumental history, and the backwardness of the colonized that justifies colonization (the two frames of reference, above). But ankylosis is not simply a question of fixity; as an organic pathology, ankylosis diagnoses a past that coalesces and adheres, repeatedly over time, but that may also numb, inflame, or become gangrenous.[40] Indeed, in "Racisme et culture," Fanon shows how the *longue durée* of racism has to do with an intransigence that is adaptive – repeating itself under the guise of prevailing ambient norms; *that according to which* we are othered changes, but othering remains in place.[41] More than just fusion or ossification, ankylosis points to repetition, consolidation, and festering – to an organic pathology of colonial (white) life. The temporal schema of ankylosis highlights both the recalcitrance and insensitivity, or disregard, that structure colonial affectivity. (And it can be contrasted to the *sensitivity* of colonized affect, below.) This *colonial* ankylosed past needs liquidation or liquification. I understand this to mean that the colonial past (with its two frames of reference) needs to be made fluid: To be reconfigured, re-articulated, and felt differently. More deeply, it needs *lysis* and not just fluidity;[42] it needs to be dissolved in its structuring of the past, and not simply questioned in this or that representation or stereotype.

What makes the colonial past – the historico-racial schema – ankylosed? I think that there are at least three features that can help us understand this, extending my analysis in section three: (1) The colonial compartmentalization and dichotomous mapping of lives, cultures, and times produces a fragmentation of the past into, on the one hand, isolated events selectively memorialized, and on the other hand, "empty" spans or gaps when nothing of import is supposed to have happened (where colonized resistance, suffering, and agency are made invisible). (2) This fragmentation is paradoxically accompanied by a flattening of time. What were multiply intertwined, complex, and contentious pasts are unwoven, simplified, dismembered, and re-ordered in a linear and uniform time. Simultaneity is made into the historical succession of datable and demarcated epochs. (3) It should be noted that this linear time relies on a particular temporal orientation, whereby futurity is ontologically privileged over pastness. Emptily projected into an abstract future, white subjectivity can absent itself from coexistence in the present (1967, p. 112; 1952, p. 110). Indeed, the linearization of time depends on a mode of active and skewed forgetting that relegates the past to the bygone and the ineffective. Forget, we are told, and move on (except for those memorable events of colonial history that are worth memorializing in the present). While the past is a tissue woven of memory and forgetting, and though forgetting can be a productive condition for habit formation and sedimentation, the kind of forgetting I am describing operates according to a differential economy that disavows the weight and agency of the past, at once fossilizing it. What is elided is the continuing role that the past

– unconsciously, habitually, in memory, and through institutions – plays in the present: The past as a dimension according to which we live the present, a dimension that submerges us, bogs us down, or buoys us up.

To recognize the dimensional role of the past is to understand its ontological and affective weight and the harm its ankylosis effects in the structure of possibility of the present. As an ankylosed dimension, the colonial past is closed to reconfiguration or reinterpretation in the present, to "liquidation" as Fanon says. The possibilities of this past appear fixed, "in the sense in which a chemical solution is fixed by a dye" (1967, p. 109; 1952, p. 107); there is little leeway for new possibility to be inscribed, or invented, in this past. What the ankylosed past lacks is the ability to be reconfigured, worked through, and made sense of differently. It does not *hesitate*; it lacks imaginary and creative leeway. It is important to note that affective ankylosis is *a pathology of colonialism and whiteness*. Here, I correct a misreading by recent readers of Fanon, who have projected ankylosis onto racialized subjects – thereby equating the colonized with that which colonialism seeks to make of us.[43] While the ankylosed colonial past puts racialized and colonized subjects in abeyance, our response is not that of numb affect, repetition, or immobilization. Indeed, according to Fanon, colonized reaction is one of sensitivity and spasming.

Racialized Sensitivity and the Burning, Dismembered Past

What is an ankylosed past for whiteness and colonialism is a dismembered, de-structured, and "burning past [*passé cuisant*]" for the colonized. Fanon uses this evocative term in "Le 'syndrome nord africain'" to describe the past that Maghribans living in France feel as chronic and unlocalizable pain (Fanon, 2006, p. 12). This recalls *Black Skin, White Masks*: "all this whiteness that burns me [*me calcine*]" (1967, p. 114; 1952, p. 111). Here, the very sensibility of racialized flesh registers the weight of colonial duration – immanently woven into its texture through tactile, pain, and kinaesthetic sensings – and responds to the de-structuring violence, the "absolute wound" of colonization (1967, p. 97; 1952, p. 94, translation corrected). Racialized flesh is "susceptible" (1952, p. 114), Fanon says, "sensitive" (1967, p. 120; 1952, p. 117) – hypersensible and prickly. Significantly, tactile sensings that burn, tear apart, dissect, dismember are not localized on one part of a coordinated body schema (as would be assumed in a Merleau-Pontian phenomenology). This sensitivity extends all over, through skin and folds, giving that through which a racial-epidermal body is formed.

Caught between perpetual past and dismembered possibility, the interval in which colonized subjects live is affectively overloaded, sensitive, and "tetanised." Fanon diagnoses "affective tetanisation" as the useless spasming of the muscles of the colonized. "*Tétanisation affective*" is used by Fanon in medical and metaphorical senses inseparably (1952, p. 110). While a simple reading of *tetanisation* equates it to the rapid or hyper-stimulation of muscles whereby successive contractions fuse together, it is possible to deepen this by recalling Fanon's characterization of colonialism as pathogen, toxicity, and infection. If colonization is *tetanus*, then it is a (bacterial) infection that penetrates colonized flesh through colonial wounds, generating toxins. It leads to spasms that may look externally like paralysis but that hide, in their depth, intense activity and (appropriate) sensitivity to the violence, toxicity, and hostility of the white world.

In *Damnés de la terre*, Fanon notes how the colonized are treated as "quasi-mineral background [*un cadre quasi minéral*]" (2002, p. 53), material resource on a par with land, water, desert, or as he says in "Le 'syndrome nord africain,'" the Arab is like "stone [*pierre*]"

(Fanon, 2006, p. 21). While it may be tempting to understand this as a form of ankylosis, we need to remember the difference between affect and imposition that continues to structure colonized experience. Tetanisation, facial and muscular spasms may, in their repetitiveness and movement in place, resemble ossification, but the affective experience of spasm holds, as both Dariek Scott (2010) and Fred Moten (2018) have argued, a potential for activity and reservoir of power. Ankylosis, on my account, is what colonialism is and projects onto the colonized; auto-protective spasms, muscular contraction, and tension are the colonized, lived and oneiric, reactions to this imposition. In appearance both resemble paralysis, but the two phenomena are affectively and phenomenologically distinct (in what they do and how they feel, in their tactile and kinaesthetic dimensions). While such muscular contractions and ticks were constructed in colonial psychiatry to be symptomatic of Arab inactivity and "paresse," Fanon diagnoses their inner trembling and hesitation as movement in place, that remembers, refuses, and waits.

The past with its colonial impositions and foreclosed depths of possibility is felt in these sensings, spasms, and tension without teleology or utility. Suspended in an unrealizable time (outside of linear time), the interval of racialized sensitivity is that of refusal and waiting.[44] It *remembers* the affects of slavery and colonialism, the weight of their recursive and snowballing durations. But it *refuses* the ankylosed prosthesis of pastness with which colonialism tries to replace this affect, to supplant and give the illusion of wholeness to the dismembered past of the colonized.[45] It refuses the push to move on, to catch up to a "white destiny."[46] But what of *waiting*? Waiting ("en attente") can be a search for an opening towards another, as yet unrealized, reconfigured past and re-imagined time.[47] But before this reconfiguration, the interval needs to be felt. When flesh refuses the touch of the white world and the prosthesis of a colonial past, it *spasms* in response. I would like to think of spasms as ways of *dwelling with* the wounds of colonization and slavery – in their duration and material memory. Waiting would be a modality of affective dwelling. I think of this as the concrete form of sensitivity that Fanon proposes, of pushing out affective pseudopodia in response to the ankylosis of the white world: "if I had to define myself, I would say that I wait; I interrogate the surroundings, I interpret everything in terms of what I discover, I become sensitive [*sensitif*]" (1967, p. 120; 1952, p. 117) This waiting is not measured in terms of a timeline, of immediacy or simultaneity with colonial time. It involves, rather, inventing one's *own time*, one's own ways of mourning, dreaming, living, and dying. Foreclosed and hungry possibility may act here as an affective fulcrum, the hesitation or leeway within the past for this invention to occur – not to be brought back to life, but to permit the leap to another dimension of possibility as yet unrealizable and unforeseen.

NOTES

1 The revisions on this paper stem from several conversations I have had since the first publication of "Too Late" in 2013. My thanks to Linda Martín Alcoff, Amy Allen, Mickaella Perina, Falguni Sheth, Jan Slaby, and George Yancy. I also wish to acknowledge the support of the Social Sciences and Humanities Research Council of Canada for this research.

2 Since I often re-translate Fanon's *Peau noire, masques blancs* (1952), I cite the pagination from both the Markmann translation (1967) and the French original.

3 See Kelly Oliver, *The Colonization of Psychic Space: A Psychoanalytic Social Theory of Oppression* (Minneapolis: University of Minnesota Press, 2004).

4 For ways of using phenomenology to critically understand racialization, in addition to Frantz Fanon and Jean-Paul Sartre, see Linda Martín Alcoff (2006) and Robert Bernasconi

(2012). Significantly, phenomenology is no longer simply a "pure" method for these authors, but productively combines with decolonized psychiatry (Fanon), a hermeneutics of horizons (Alcoff), and historical studies of racism (Bernasconi).

5 "Neutrality" with respect to colonialism is built on a turning-away from acknowledging it, and reinforces the colonial status quo.

6 For more on Fanon's decolonized or revolutionary psychiatry, see Françoise Vergès (1996) and Hussein Bulhan (1999). See also Fanon (2001).

7 See Fanon (1967, p. 112; 1952, pp. 109–110).

8 See Fanon (1967, p. 191; 1952, p. 185). Such undesirability is, of course, itself constituted in the collective unconscious for Fanon.

9 This is what Falguni Sheth (2009) calls technologies of race. As I will show in this essay, this racial mapping is also temporal.

10 Perceptibility is constituted within a colonial horizon, wherein visible, audible, and other signs of "race" are overdetermined (phenotype, skin color, facial features, but also mannerism, accent, cultural-religious dress, and practice).

11 See Robert Bernasconi (2012).

12 José Medina (2013) argues that this is "active ignorance." Ann Laura Stoler (2011) calls this "colonial aphasia."

13 For the way in which racism becomes "atmospheric," see Fanon's "Racisme et culture" (2006, p. 40).

14 "[I]l y a une constellation de données, une série de propositions qui lentement, sournoisement, à la faveur des écrits, des journaux, de l'éducation, des livres scolaires, des affiches, du cinéma, de la radio, pénètrent un individu – en constituant la vision du monde de la collectivité à laquelle il appartient" (Fanon, 1952, p. 150). See also Fanon (1952, pp. 25, 143–144) and (1967, pp. 28, 146). For more on the concept of social imaginary, see Medina (2013, p. 68).

15 Fanon (1952, p. 110); I have re-translated this passage using Macey (2012, p. 164). The French phrase "Y a bon banania," which Fanon employs, is difficult to translate. It recalls to the French reader a well-known brand of cocoa drink mix that uses in its advertising and on its tin the caricature of a grinning Black man (supposed to represent a Senegalese *tirailleur*, a colonial infantry soldier). But it also replaces the "correct" French of "c'est bon" with "y a bon" – amplifying the racialization of the Senegalese soldier by making him speak "*petit-nègre*," racializing through visible, audible, and linguistic dimensions.

16 The fragmentation of the past is *accompanied* by a fragmentation of flesh, so that we may wonder how the sequential ordering of schemas that Fanon gives could be maintained, given what I would characterize as the non-linear temporality of his phenomenology. I am thinking *flesh* with Hortense Spillers (1987), in tension with Merleau-Ponty. Elsewhere, I question whether the optimally coordinated and seamless (Merleau-Pontian) body schema, with which Fanon begins his narrative, was not but an idealized "white" origin story, or "white destiny" (Fanon, 1967, p. 10; Fanon, 1952, p. 10); rather than describing how bodies are primarily experienced, it would be a vexed and unattainable norm.

17 Fanon says "engluer," see *Peau noire, masques blancs* (1952, pp. 32; 224). I delve into this "gluey" or sticky past more deeply in Al-Saji (2019).

18 Drawing on Quijano, Alejandro Vallega calls this "the coloniality of time" (2014, p. 100).

19 Johannes Fabian (1983) calls this denial of coevalness to other cultures "allochronism."

20 I think of colonialism as enduring and continuing, under different guise, not only in settler colonial states but also in countries that have formally decolonized. Colonialism endures economically, militarily, materially, and culturally. In my case, for Iraq, to use the term "formerly colonized" would be to obscure the reality of rephrased colonization over a *longue durée* and its weight in the present.

21 A note on my voice as *diasporic Iraqi*. As I move in this essay from *Black Skin, White Masks* to colonization and back – as the circles of colonization wind tighter, through pastness and possibility – I shift to using "we" when referring to colonized and racialized subjectivities. This is to stem a tendency to eschew, or disidentify with, colonized non-being for diasporic subjects and to forget the colonial roots of current (U.S. and "western") imperial wars and

"foreign" policy. I want to insist on the continuation, repetition, and reconfiguration of colonization, not only in the Americas but globally. But I do not want to imply a homogenous identity. Quijano's and Fanon's philosophies cover a multiplicity of shifting and overlapping positionalities. Quijano's starting point is Latin America. *Black Skin, White Masks* moves between *Blackness* (distinguishing but sometimes blurring Antillean, African, and African-American), *colonization* (Algeria, Madagascar, Vietnam), and different *racializations* (Arab). But this is not to ignore the different mappings of racisms, and the rupture that anti-Blackness institutes in being.

22 I am indebted for the concept of the "dismembered past" to Saidiya Hartman's *Scenes of Subjection: Terror, Slavery, and Self-Making in Nineteenth-Century America* (1997, pp. 11; 72–77).

23 Yet this is not without resistance and agential reaction, nor is it simply in the image that colonial culture projects, as I argue in section four. In his critique of Quijano, Vallega notes that colonization should be understood to have an outside (2014, p. 129).

24 To give an example from Fanon's *L'an V de la révolution algérienne*: When some Algerian women return to veiling under French colonialism, this is seen by colonizers as part of the inherent closure and backwardness of that culture. The complex uses of and motivations for veiling are thus elided, whether as an expression of cultural or national resistance (2001, p. 29), a protective reaction against the violence of French colonizers, or a cover for smuggling weapons for the FLN (2001, pp. 44–45) – to name but a few motivations.

25 Fanon evokes this sense of recognition several times in *Black Skin, White Masks*, most poignantly when he describes watching a film in the cinema and waiting for *himself* to appear on the screen (1967, p. 140; 1952, p. 138). Fanon also mentions this "hint of recognition" in an example contrasting the reception of a Tarzan film in the Antilles and in Europe (1967, pp. 152–153; 1952, p. 150). See Al-Saji, "Glued to the Image" (2019).

26 In his prescient reading, Homi Bhabha takes up this phrase to develop a concept of "postcolonial belatedness" (1994, p. 237) that interrupts the time of modernity. My account diverges both in my use of phenomenology and in the desire to dwell in and wait with this time-lag, without as yet making it productive. This hesitant reading tries to feel the lived weight of racialized lateness.

27 As Oliver points out, Fanon's sense of arriving "too late" differs from the Sartrean notion of being thrown into a world that is not of one's own making but in which one can nevertheless make meaning (2004, p. 15). She proposes "double alienation" as an alternative.

28 To borrow from María Lugones (1996) and her non-agonistic concept of playfulness.

29 Here I draw on and rephrase Merleau-Ponty's *Phenomenology of Perception* (2012, p. 261; 1945, p. 298).

30 See David Marriott, 2013.

31 "Time before time" comes from Maurice Merleau-Ponty's *The Visible and the Invisible* (1968, p. 243; 1964, p. 292).

32 For Fanon's concept of colonization as "*destructuration*," see Fanon (1952, pp. 92, 94).

33 See Hartman (1997, pp. 11, 77). Hartman is herself drawing on "re-memory" from Toni Morrison's *Beloved* (2004). Dismemberment in slavery and colonialism can also be thought with Spillers as "high crimes against the *flesh*": "That [socio-political order of the New World], with its human sequence written in blood, *represents* for its African and indigenous peoples, a scene of *actual* mutilation, dismemberment, and exile" (1987, p. 67; original italics). Relatedly, I note that both Hartman and Fanon speak of "amputation," albeit in different directions. While I believe that Markmann's translation of Fanon (1967) may overstate the use of this term as an ableist metaphor, it is important to remember the pain and wounding of *amputating*, hamstringing, and mutilating the body that Fanon is encoding in his writing. "Amputation," then, is a difficult term that needs to be parsed and to which I return in another work.

34 Says Fanon in "Racisme et culture" (2006, p. 42).

35 The power of the affect of hunger in slavery, not only for food, but for kin, memory, love, and intersubjective touch can be read in Morrison (2004). Also see Weheylie (2014). I add the affect of mourning here – to be able to take time to mourn, without having to move on. In

this vein, we should remember the ways in which French colonialism instituted restrictions in Madagascar on Malagasy death rituals.

36 Conceptually, the possible and the real go together (while the virtual and actual are a different pairing). This means that in "inventorying the real," we cannot stay on the surface. We need to excavate dimensions of possibility that have been torn apart and submerged.

37 Fanon's "Racisme et culture" allows us to understand how the de-structuration of colonized systems of reference is not erasure but breaking, sacking, crushing – indeed, "agonie continue" (2006, pp. 41–42).

38 See Saidiya Hartman's "Venus in Two Acts" (2008, p. 11).

39 Here I want to deepen an analysis that I began in Al-Saji (2014), where I understood ankylosis as constitutive of racist, "racializing affect" (pp. 140–142).

40 This recalls Aimé Césaire's description of colonialism as gangrene and rot (1955, pp. 12; 31).

41 Fanon, "Racisme et culture" (2006, p. 40).

42 See Fanon (1967, p. 10; 1952, p. 10) and Moten (2018, pp. 221–222).

43 Cf. Christopher Chamberlin (2018) and Shiloh Whitney (2018).

44 For a different thinking of the interval in Fanon, see Kara Keeling (2003).

45 I am reading Fanon here with Saidiya Hartman.

46 See Helen Ngo, in this volume.

47 See Fanon (2002, p. 54).

REFERENCES

Al-Saji, A. (2014). A phenomenology of hesitation: Interrupting racializing habits of seeing. In E. Lee (Ed.), *Living alterities: Phenomenology, embodiment, and race*. Albany, NY: State University of New York Press.

Al-Saji, A. (2019). Glued to the image: A critical phenomenology of racialization through works of art. *The Journal of Aesthetics and Art Criticism, 77*(4), 475–488.

Alcoff, L. M. (2006). *Visible identities: Race, gender, and the self*. Oxford: Oxford University Press.

Bernasconi, R. (2012). Crossed lines in the racialization process: Race as a border concept. *Research in Phenomenology, 42*, 206–228.

Bhabha, H. K. (1994). *The location of culture*. London and New York: Routledge.

Bulhan, H. A. (1999). Revolutionary psychiatry of Fanon. In N. C. Gibson (Ed.), *Rethinking Fanon* (pp. 141–175). Amherst, NY: Humanity Books.

Césaire, A. (1955 [1950]). *Discours sur le colonialisme, 5ième édition*. Paris: Présence Africaine.

Césaire, A. (2017). *Cahier d'un retour au pays natal, a bilingual edition* (N. Gregson Davis, Trans.). Durham, NC: Duke University Press.

Chamberlin, C. (2018). Affective Ankylosis and the body in Fanon and Capécia. *Studies in Gender and Sexuality, 19*(2), 120–132.

Du Bois, W. E. B. (2007). *The souls of Black folk* (Brent Hayes Edwards, Ed.). Oxford: Oxford University Press. (Original work published 1903)

Fabian, J. (1983). *Time and the other: How anthropology makes its object*. New York: Columbia University Press.

Fanon, F. (1952). *Peau noire, masques blancs*. Paris: Éditions du Seuil.

Fanon, F. (1967). *Black skin, White masks* (Charles Lam Markmann, Trans.). New York: Grove Press. (Original work published 1952)

Fanon, F. (2001). *L'an V de la révolution algérienne*. Paris: La Découverte. (Original work published 1959)

Fanon, F. (2002). *Les damnés de la terre*. Paris: La Découverte.

Fanon, F. (2006). *Pour la révolution africaine*. Paris: La Découverte.

Hartman, S. (1997). *Scenes of subjection: Terror, slavery, and self-making in nineteenth-century America.* Oxford: Oxford University Press.

Hartman, S. (2008). Venus in two acts. *Small Axe, 26,* 12.2.

Keeling, K. (2003). In the interval: Frantz Fanon and the "problems" of visual representation. *Qui Parle, 13*(2), 91–117.

Lugones, M. (1996). Playfulness, "World"-traveling, and loving perception. In A. Garry & M. Pearsall (Eds.), *Women, knowledge and reality: Explorations in feminist philosophy* (pp. 419–433). London and New York: Routledge.

Macey, D. (2012 [2000]). *Frantz Fanon: A biography.* London: Verso.

Marriott, D. (2013). Waiting to fall. *The New Centennial Review, 13*(3), 163–240.

Medina, J. (2013). *The epistemology of resistance: Gender and racial oppression, epistemic injustice, and resistant imaginations.* Oxford: Oxford University Press.

Merleau-Ponty, M. (1945). *Phénoménologie de la perception.* Paris: Gallimard.

Merleau-Ponty, M. (1964). *Le visible et l'invisible,* ed. C. Lefort. Paris: Gallimard.

Merleau-Ponty, M. (1968). *The visible and the invisible* (A. Lingis, Trans.). Evanston, IL: Northwestern University Press. (Original work published 1964)

Merleau-Ponty, M. (2012). *Phenomenology of perception* (Donald A. Landes, Trans.). London and New York: Routledge. (Original work published 1945)

Mills, C. W. (2007). White ignorance. In S. Sullivan & N. Tuana (Eds.), *Race and epistemologies of ignorance* (pp. 11–38). Albany, NY: State University of New York Press.

Morrison, T. (2004). *Beloved.* New York: Vintage Books. (Original work published 1987)

Moten, F. (2018). *The universal machine.* Durham, NC: Duke University Press.

Oliver, K. (2004). *The colonization of psychic space: A psychoanalytic social theory of oppression.* Minneapolis, MN: University of Minnesota Press.

Quijano, A. (2000). Coloniality of power, eurocentrism, and Latin America. *Nepantla: Views from the South, 1*(3), 533–580.

Quijano, A. (2007). Coloniality and modernity/rationality. *Cultural Studies, 22*(2–3), 168–178.

Ratcliffe, M. (2012). Phenomenology as a form of empathy. *Inquiry, 55*(5), 473–495.

Scott, D. (2010). *Extravagant abjection: Blackness, power, and sexuality in African American literary imagination.* New York: New York University Press.

Sheth, F. (2009). *Toward a political philosophy of race.* Albany, NY: SUNY Press.

Spillers, H. J. (1987). Mama's baby, Papa's maybe: An American grammar book. *Diacritics, 17*(2), 64–81.

Stoler, A. L. (2011). Colonial Aphasia: Race and disabled histories in France. *Public Culture, 23*(1), 121–156.

Vallega, A. (2014). *Latin American philosophy from identity to radical exteriority.* Bloomington, IN: Indiana University Press.

Vergès, F. (1996). To cure and to free: The Fanonian project of "Decolonized Psychiatry." In L. R. Gordon, T. D. Sharpley-Whiting, & R. T. White (Eds.), *Fanon: A Critical Reader* (pp. 85–99). Malden, MA: Blackwell Publishers.

Weheliye, A. G. (2014). *Habeas Viscus: Racializing assemblages, biopolitics, and Black feminist theories of the human.* Durham, NC: Duke University Press.

Whitney, S. (2018). Affective intentionality and affective injustice: Merleau-Ponty and Fanon on the body schema as a theory of affect. *The Southern Journal of Philosophy, 56*(4), 488–515.

CHAPTER 13

FROM "GET OVER IT" TO "TEAR IT DOWN"

Racialized Temporalities, "White Time," and Temporal Contestations[1]

Helen Ngo

In the introduction to *Black Skin, White Masks*, Fanon writes: "The architecture of this work is rooted in the temporal. Every human problem must be considered from the standpoint of time" (Fanon, 1967, pp. 12–13). This chapter offers an exploration of racialized and colonized temporalities, drawing inspiration from Fanon's account of racialized "lateness," as elaborated by Alia Al-Saji (2013). Together, their analyses offer a springboard from which I consider how racialized[2] and white bodies are differentially temporalized, with the racialized body predetermined by, and tethered to, the past. Such temporalization serves not only to anachronize the racialized body, but also to close off its projective possibilities for being or becoming otherwise. Drawing on Charles Mills' (2007; 2014) accounts of "white ignorance" and "white time," I then examine how racialization relies on a forgetting or a disavowal and leaving behind of its own process. The result, I argue, is to render whiteness and white bodies as temporally present and even futural in their orientation, free from the vestiges of racism's history and free to adopt any number of stances on its continuing legacy. It is against this setting that I argue exhortations to "get over it" – whenever charges of racism are leveled in the public domain by racialized subjects – are not only dangerous in their denial of racism, but also disingenuous in the way they purport to move beyond a racially divided world, when in fact this very gesture serves to reinscribe differential racialized temporalities. Further, looking to typical responses in the contestations over public commemorations of events and figures within "white time" (for example, calls to tear down the monuments of colonialism and slavery), I examine how these responses cast the deep attachments and temporal "untetheredness" of whiteness in a different light.

THE RACIALIZED BODY STUCK IN AND TO THE PAST

In her article, "Too Late: Racialized Time and the Closure of the Past," Al-Saji (2013) examines some of the temporal dimensions of racism, tracing the ways in which processes of racialization and colonization differentially mark the racialized/colonized subject and body, tethering it to a temporal past. Fanon provides the starting point for this analysis, with his vivid account of the lived experience of Black embodiment in *Black Skin, White Masks*. In his psychoanalytic and phenomenological account, Fanon offers a striking analysis of racism as it not only becomes interiorized but "epidermalized" – or in phenomenological terms, lived and inhabited bodily. As I have previously argued, body schema disintegration in the face of racism's steady onslaught serves as a key and recurring theme in Fanon's text, such that racialized embodiment becomes marked by a kind of body schema fragmentation (Ngo, 2017, p. 68). An example of this is found in Fanon's

DOI: 10.4324/9781003037132-13

account of experiencing his body as temporally disjointed, and specifically, always "too late": "Too late. Everything is anticipated, thought out, demonstrated, made the most of. My trembling hands take hold of nothing; the vein has been mined out. Too late!" (Fanon, 1967, p. 121). Thus, Fanon's Black body is not only hermeneutically "overdetermined" in being overladen with racist meaning and inscription, but also temporally *predetermined* – he arrives on the scene always too late in relation to the place already carved out and waiting for him. Hence: "I cannot go to a film without seeing myself. I wait for me. The people in the theater are watching me, examining me, waiting for me. A Negro groom is going to appear" (1967, p. 140).

For Al-Saji, this "too late" marks a distinctly temporal fragmentation, whereby despite Fanon's self-described futural orientation, his "will to find a meaning in things" (Fanon, 1967, p. 109), Fanon finds himself ineluctably chained down to the past. She writes:

> this (racializing) gaze displaces Fanon's positionality in that schema and relates him explic-
> itly to a black past. Whereas prior to his interpolation as black, Fanon could imagine all
> "civilizational" history as his own, he was now limited to those historical elements that
> made up a stereotyped black past. Thus, he says, "I was battered down by tom toms, can-
> nibalism, intellectual deficiency, fetishism, racial defects, slave-ships, and above all else,
> above all: "Sho' good eatin" ["*Y'a bon banania*"].
>
> *(Al-Saji, 2013, p. 5)*

Importantly, it is not just that Fanon's identity (as represented, as constructed) is affixed to that of the past, it is that – and here we pay attention to the distinctly phenomenological register of his analysis – he has to *live it*. Phenomenology, with its inquiry into the structures of consciousness from the internal vantage point of its lived experience, foregrounds the *bodily* dimension of phenomenal experience after Merleau-Ponty shows us how the body not only frames perceptual and conscious experience, but makes it possible at all (Merleau-Ponty, 2012, p. 93). Experientially, the Black past becomes Fanon's lived present, with race "no longer simply a historical construction or a concept, but [it] comes to be lived as a property of one's body, and specifically for Fanon, of one's skin" (Al-Saji, 2013, p. 5). It is in this sense that we can understand Fanon's claim in the concluding pages to *Black Skin, White Masks*, that "The Negro [*le Noir*], however sincere, is the slave of the past" (1967, p. 225) – even as he, only pages later, resolves to push through, and move beyond this temporal entrapment: "[But] I do not have the right to allow myself to be mired in what the past has determined ... I am not the slave of the Slavery that dehumanized my ancestors" (p. 230). This tug back and forth, this negotiation toward freedom via the oppressive weight of history's racism presents itself throughout Fanon's text in various ways, expressing a fundamental tension whose origin is the hermeneutic overdetermination and temporal predetermination of the Black subject in white, colonial society.

We see time and again how racialized and colonized bodies are weighed down by this temporal framing. In the case of Indigenous peoples, not only are they invariably tied to mythical and primitive pasts in public imaginaries, the process of colonization itself (and specifically, settler colonization) relies on this temporalization for its justification. As Eve Tuck and Rubén Gaztambide-Fernández have argued, "Settler colonialism requires the construction of non-white peoples as less than or not-quite civilized, an *earlier* expression of human civilization" (2013, p. 74, my emphasis). It is this casting of Indigenous peoples as temporally prior to "civilization" that justifies the project of settler colonialism – a project that "destroys to replace" (Wolfe, 2006, p. 388) – since on this view, the settler colonial project could be seen in the Australian context, as elsewhere,[3] to be merely ushering along the "dying race" to its inevitable fate (Boucher and Russell, 2015, p. 17). Indeed, it is in reply and in defiance to this presumed fate that Australian Aboriginal artist Vernon Ah Kee's iconic t-shirt design, with the words "still here" boldly and plainly emblazoned across the center, can be read.

In the case of racialized non-Indigenous bodies, this temporalization occurs most frequently through the commonplace plumbing of origins; the unasked "What is your ethnic or racial identity?" most commonly finds expression as "Where are you from?", "Where are you from *originally*?", "What is your cultural *background* or *heritage*?" – questions framed always in terms of origin, beginnings, and of times past.[4] Sara Ahmed, for example, writes:

> Strangers always get asked the question, "Where are you from?" and if this question does not lead to an answer that explains what is suspicious, then they are asked where their parents are from, or even asked questions that go further "back" until the "what" that is suspicious is revealed.
>
> *(2006, p. 142)*

So prevalent is this questioning of racial origins of non-whites in the Australian context that comedians such as Michael Hing relished in the turning of tables when the dual citizenship crisis took hold of Federal Parliament in 2017–2018, a crisis which saw a string of sitting members of Parliament disqualified due to a little-known and little-used section of the Constitution. As Hing commented, "Suddenly … questions about white people's ancestry are all the rage!"[5] Of course, this habitually selective plumbing of racial origins is, as Toula Nicolacopoulos and George Vassilacopoulos point out, deeply bound with white Australia's unconfronted status as the colonial occupier – and its persistent failure to ask *itself* the question of its (colonial) origins:

> True heirs to this tradition of power and self-denial, white Australians are today still refusing to become free. In our two centuries-long refusal to hear the words – "I come from here. Where do you come from?" – that the sovereign being of the Indigenous peoples poses to us, we have taken the Western occupier's mentality to a new, possibly ultimate, level … Suffering what we describe as "onto-pathology," white Australia has become dependent upon "the perpetual-foreigners-within," those migrants in relation to whom the so-called "old Australians" assert their imagined difference.
>
> *(2014, pp. 13–14)*

Sandwiched between "old inhabitants" and "new migrants," white Australia nonetheless manages to maneuver both its colonized and racialized others into the past, reserving for itself (as we will see) a sense of "youthful" presence and possibility.

Returning to our register of the phenomenologically lived body, we can observe that such weighing down of racialized bodies to the past manifests also in a certain temporalized, bodily orientation. That is, racialized bodies are not only "stuck" in the past but are also dispositionally oriented toward it. Ahmed, for example, writing on the contrast between the (racialized) stranger and whites whose bodies are more "at home" in a post-9/11 world, notes:

> [For whites, there] is no question posed about their origin. The stranger's genealogy is always suspect. The stranger becomes a stranger because of some *trace* of a dubious origin. Having the "right" passport makes no difference if you have the wrong body or name.
>
> *(2006, p. 141, emphasis original)*

She continues:

> Those who get stopped are, perhaps, *moved in a different way*. I have suggested that my name slows me down ... For the body recognized as "could be Muslim" the experience begins with discomfort: spaces we occupy do not "extend" the surfaces of our bodies. But our actions anticipate more. Having been singled out in the line, at the borders, we become defensive and thus assume a defensive posture as we "wait" for the line of racism to take our rights of passage away. *If we inherit the failure of things to be habitual, then we might also acquire a tendency to look behind us.*
>
> (p. 142, emphasis original)

While Ahmed is here concerned with the spatial extension of the racialized body, and its mobility and motility through social spaces, we can note that there is also a temporal dimension to this mode of embodiment insofar as such racialized bodies become oriented to look *behind*. This is to say, the navigation of a racialized world in which one is cast in the terms of the past generates on the part of the racialized subject, a habitual looking back – a looking back which contrasts and competes with the *projective* intentionality of the lived body, as phenomenologically described. Heidegger's *dasein* for example, although arguably disembodied, is distinctly futural in its temporality. Through its being-toward-death, *dasein* is temporally oriented toward the "not-yet," the "constantly still outstanding" (Heidegger, 2008, p. 286),[6] such that, as Anne O'Byrne argues, even the question of *dasein's* historicity – figured through the phenomenon of its natality – is "quickly subsume[d] ... under the futural thrust of being-toward-death that (Heidegger) establishes as Dasein's" (O'Byrne, 2010, p. 17). Of course, Heidegger's analysis unfolds on the register of the ontological, which for him is to be kept distinct from the ontic, but as O'Byrne further points out, the stability of this distinction is not one that commentators (or even Heidegger himself) can assure (pp. 17–19). For the purposes of our analysis, the tension generated from this racialized looking-behind, when set against the projective possibilities that are supposedly proper to existential being, echoes the tension at the heart of Fanon's reach for freedom in a world that insists on his mummification. It is a tension we can hear, both in its temporal register and beyond, when Aboriginal (Munanjahli) and South Sea Islander woman Chelsea Watego (formerly Chelsea Bond) asks in a letter to her children, "How does one thrive in a world that wishes us dead?" (Bond, 2020, p. 6). And yet, as Fanon writes, "The future should be an edifice supported by *living* men" (1967, p. 13, my emphasis).[7]

THE CLOSED PAST, THE ANIMATING PAST

It is important to register at this point that the past with which we have thus far been concerned is what Al-Saji calls a "closed past" (2013, p. 6). That is, the past to which colonized subjects are tethered is not necessarily a past that is recognizable to them; it is not *their* past. She writes:

> On my reading, the past with which colonized peoples are identified is no longer their past, *for the precolonial past has been repressed*; rather, it is a past of stereotyped remnants, isolated fragments and colonized distortions extrapolated back from their oppressed and alienated state under colonialism. *This is hence a closed past, incapable of development on its own terms and cut off from the creativity that gives rise to an open future.*
>
> (2013, p. 6, emphasis added)

On the one hand, these colonized distortions raise important questions around perspective, authorship, and ownership in relation to the past. But in addition to this, what the notion of a "closed past" points to is the differential conceptions of time that can underwrite racialized mobilizations of it. In the phenomenological tradition, time as properly conceived is not some detached "object of ... knowledge, but rather a dimension of our being" (Merleau-Ponty, 2012, p. 438) Time is lived time, both experienced and animating. Elaborating Husserl's account of inner time-consciousness, Merleau-Ponty writes that "Time is not a line, but rather a network of intentionalities" (p. 440), although in his later work he criticizes Husserl for not going far enough with this account of temporal intentionality.[8] Importantly for our purposes, the past, on this phenomenological reading, is never fully closed over or sealed off, but rather is carried along in the twin moves Husserl describes as "retention" and "protention." Whereas retention names the lingering or retaining of that which has just passed or been fulfilled, protention names the (futural) anticipation of what is not yet fulfilled (Dimitriu, 2013, p. 213), or what might never come to be fulfilled. Together with a third phenomenon, "primal impression" (the "now-point" of the present), protention and retention account for the structural unity of any temporal experience. A past in this sense, then, is never sealed off because traces of it retain into the present, but equally important, from the perspective of the past-*as*-present (the past when it was present), it also protends some futural horizon.[9] Each past imagines, if you will, certain possibilities. And while Merleau-Ponty in his later work on time goes further in filling out the picture of the past (through what Al-Saji elsewhere calls "the backward movement of institution" [2009, p. 217], the idea that new meanings can be generated for the past), what's useful for our purposes is to note the way that the past, even on the more minimal Husserlian construction, is still always anticipating possible futures.

Fanon's, however, is a closed past; he recounts multiply throughout the chapter how the white gaze "fixes" him, "in the sense in which a chemical solution is fixed by a dye" (1967, p. 109). He is left with no room – no space, but also no time – in which to move. Consequently, this is not a past that Fanon can take up, a past with which he can meaningfully engage, or a past he can elaborate. As Al-Saji notes, "the field of possibility loses its playfulness and imaginary variability ... The structure of possibility allows repetition but not creation or variation; it is a closed map" (2013, p. 8). This distinction – between the *closed* past imposed upon colonized bodies, and the open past we find in phenomenological accounts – explains the seeming incongruence between Fanon's descriptions of being weighed down by the past, against other autoethnographic accounts of the past as grounding and generative, as we sometimes find in the narratives of colonized and racialized peoples. Aboriginal (Koenpul) scholar Aileen Moreton-Robinson, for example, speaks of Indigenous subjectivity and belonging, and the way it is uniquely constituted by an enduring "ontological relationship" to country – a relationship which derives from the Dreaming (Moreton-Robinson, 2015, p. 11).[10] As she writes, the activities, movements, and legacies of ancestral beings of the Dreaming

> also established the Aboriginal ways of life: a moral code for its social institutions and patterns of activity. Ancestral beings provided the rules for what can and cannot be done through both good and bad behaviour.
>
> *(2015, p. 12)*

The rendering of the past we get here differs markedly from that of the racializing closed past described by Fanon, since Moreton-Robinson in this chapter is describing Indigenous belonging on its own terms. Here, the past is one that roots Indigenous being, such that one can be dislocated, but "through cultural protocols and the commonality of our ontological relationship ... [still] be in place but away from our home country" (Moreton-Robinson, 2015, p. 13). Not only does this past secure one's orientation to place and to others in the present, it also provides the foundation upon which activity, social relations, and moral behavior can be forged and guided. This is a past that infuses and animates the present, a past that is generative of new forms of life (what Merleau-Ponty might call the "instituting past") – it is not the closed past that Fanon describes, a past saturated, and in which possibilities for genuine creativity are exhausted. That past is a past without its own future. Fanon's closed time – describing racialized temporality as configured from within a white world – is what Merleau-Ponty calls "constituted time," a time which is not really time at all.[11]

RACIALIZED FORGETTING

If racialized and colonized bodies are temporalized with specific reference to a closed and saturated past, then we might ask how the process of racialization itself is temporally figured. In her reading of Fanon, Al-Saji argues that what is original to his account is its move beyond racialization as a process of othering (in the Sartrean vein) to show that it entails a twin movement of naturalization and rationalization. That is, if the othering that takes place in the process of racialization is an oppositional and hierarchical one, a "negative mirroring" onto the racialized body (Al-Saji, 2013, p. 3), then what sustains this hierarchy is a naturalization of perceived racial difference – such that these differences are taken to be "natural" rather than socially or historically constituted. But such a naturalization can only be effected via a racialized forgetting, which Al-Saji argues, "is not merely accidental, but that sustains [racism's] operations – a forgetting which actively hides racializing mechanisms and misconstrues its objects" (p. 4). Charles Mills, of course, has written extensively on the question of "white ignorance" as an epistemological condition for the maintenance of the system of racism. For him, white ignorance can manifest as a refusal to recognize racism's history, a denial which is made possible by a "management of memory" (Mills, 2007, p. 28) – in other words, a forgetting. I propose that this forgetting can also be viewed temporally, such that white ignorance entails not just a deliberate unknowing or not-knowing, but also a leaving behind and moving on.

We see this time and again when public controversies involving charges of racism are deflected with a plea to innocence – or ignorance – of specific racist histories. For example, when mainstream Australian newspaper *The Herald Sun* published the Sambo-styled caricature of Serena Williams following the dramatic events of the 2018 US Open Women's Final, cartoonist Mark Knight saw fit to defend against charges of racism by claiming that he had "absolutely no knowledge of those cartoons, or that period" (*ABC News*, September 11, 2018).[12] For a professional cartoonist (lauded by his own news agency as "Australia's finest cartoonist") to claim no knowledge of one of the twentieth century's most iconic genres of cartooning – deploying visual tropes that were not unfamiliar to Australian audiences (Corbould, 2018)[13] – this exhibits more than a curious lack of familiarity with one's own profession, it exhibits a quintessential white ignorance and white forgetting. Knight's further attempts to de-historicize the cartoon is telling:

> This whole business that I'm some sort of racist calling on ... racial cartoons from the past, it's just made up, it's not there. The cartoon was about her behaviour on the day and having this massive tantrum and that's all it really ... what it was.
>
> (ABC News, *September 11, 2018*)

Here we see the once again familiar move to decouple representations from their racist histories, to recast them as *singular* instantiations. What statements such as these attempt is a forgetting of racist histories, even though those histories do not seem to "forget" their racialized subjects. When Knight insists that he "drew her as she was" (*ABC News*, September 11, 2018), which apparently means with over-exaggerated lips, nose, and buttocks,[14] we see Fanon's account of naturalization and rationalization at work: Williams' facial and bodily features "naturally" elicited this pictorial response from Knight, and therefore can be rationalized as not-racist, since they apparently did not provide commentary on her race.

But in addition to the forgetting of racist histories, this episode and its defense also speak to whites' ability to move on from the past (especially an unsavory racist past), to untether themselves from it, and to not have to claim these pasts as their own – much less reckon with them. This is arguably why it took some 40 years after its end to formally apologize for the Stolen Generations affair (in which mixed-raced Indigenous children were forcibly removed from their families to be raised as white); former Australian Prime Minister John Howard's insistence that he would not apologize because these were not *his* misdeeds, not *his* generation's responsibility, puts the temporal orientation of whiteness on full display (Davies, 2008).[15] This is the same temporal disposition, I argue, that underwrites efforts to move "beyond race," as is the case when people claim to be color-blind ("I don't see races, I don't see color, I see people"), or purport to live in a post-racial society.[16] As critical race theorist David Theo Goldberg has argued, post-racialism entails a "denial of denial: there is no guilt because there is nothing recognizable to be guilty about, least of all the guilt itself" (2015, p. 49). Such pronouncements are consistent with racism's own keenness to forget – even erase – its own history, to move on and "get over it."

"WHITE TIME," WHITE FUTURITY, AND UNTETHERED WHITE TEMPORALITY

If racism sustains itself through an ongoing process of forgetting, then what of white temporality? What are its hallmarks? In a first sense, as Charles Mills observes in, "White Time: The Chronic Injustice of Ideal Theory," "the theology and related temporal mensuration of the West continue to shape our basic categories" (Mills, 2014, p. 30). Here he cites anthropologist Jack Goody, who remarks upon the way in which our internationally standardized time is grounded in and around the birth and death of Jesus Christ, relegating other markers and organizations of time (such as the Islamic Hegira, or the Hebrew and Chinese new years) to the periphery of our time consciousness.[17] More than this however, Mills notes that

> The White settler state … "sets the historical chronometer" at zero, to signal that before its arrival, no history has taken place, no real passage of time, since a time in which no history passes is a time that has not really itself passed. Insofar as humans are distinguished from animals by their ability to make history, to master time and turn it to their ends, the inability to attain this level raises questions about one's (full) humanity. The capacity to utilize time becomes racialized.
>
> *(2014, p. 31)*

In other words, white history and white activity (conquest, foundings of nation-states, and so forth) are positioned as the very origination of time, rendering what came before as not-time in any historically meaningful sense. On this view, Australia was not just "founded" on the basis of *terra nullius*, but also *tempus nullius* – uninhabited time, time not utilized or made use of, time that therefore does not register as such. The collapsing of some 60,000 years of Aboriginal history in Australia to the realm of "pre-history" provides a compelling example of this, a point recently underscored in the protest staged by nine-year-old white schoolgirl, Harper Nielsen. In a move that attracted widespread news attention, Nielsen refused to stand for the ritual school singing of the national anthem on the basis that the lyric "for we are *young* and free" disregards or even erases the depth of Aboriginal history in this land (Nielsen, 2018).

But a second sense in which whiteness is differentially temporalized can be elucidated from our preceding phenomenological analysis. If, following my reading of Ahmed, the temporality of racialized being can be mapped out onto the realm of bodily spatiality, then we might ask what kind of temporality white bodily spatiality and disposition engenders. The preceding analysis of racialized forgetting and white ignorance seems to discount the possibility that white temporality is retrospectively oriented, at least not in the sense of a Fanonian closed past. In contrast to that past, we might then posit whiteness as temporally present, or even futurally directed. This would concur with observations made by both Mills and Al-Saji, with the latter citing Latin American sociologist Anibal Quijano's argument that colonialism "[reinscribes] a linear timeline in which colonized peoples are relocated as perpetually past to European cultures that are seen as modern and futurally open" (Al-Saji, 2013, p. 6). A spatial correlate to this temporally futural disposition, I would argue, can be found in Shannon Sullivan's concept of ontological expansiveness, which she defines in this way:

> [a]s ontologically expansive, white people tend to act and think as if all spaces – whether geographical, psychical, linguistic, economic, spiritual, bodily, or otherwise – are or should be available for them to move in and out of as they wish.
>
> *(Sullivan, 2006, p. 10)*

As I have previously noted, this concept of ontological expansiveness translates the "I can" of phenomenological embodiment into a racially patterned world, and in doing so, follows the analysis that Iris Marion Young offers with respect to female embodiment (Ngo, 2017, p. 80). And as both Young and I show, this "I can" serves to ground intentional action; it is futurally directed in the sense of enabling further possibilities (Ngo, 2017, p. 119; Young, 2005, pp. 36–37). Sullivan's 'white ontological expansiveness," therefore, can on the one hand be read to describe the futurity of white embodiment.

I think we could go further, however, since after all, "white ontological expansiveness" describes the ability to move through *all spaces*, just as the phenomenological "I can" entails a kind of spatial extension and motility in a multitude of directions. Transposing this to a temporal frame, I would argue that white embodiment is not only futurally oriented, but also free to take up the present and past as it wishes, and in the manner of its own choosing. We see this in the various expressions of white nostalgia – past-era dress-up parties, period films, or "old-time" music genre revivals – where whites can recreate the vestiges of times gone without having to navigate the racial complexities therein, without having to work through racially complicated relationships to those pasts. Note that this is not the same as being *bound* to the past, since its taking up expresses a re-animation, a re-enlivening that brings those pasts forward and casts them anew. Moreover, what characterizes this relation is one of voluntariness (although I use the term loosely). Thus, while the likes of (cartoonist) Mark Knight can afford not to know their history, other whites of course, do take these racist histories seriously. However, even when there is this effort to own and reckon with such pasts, given the underlying temporalization of whiteness as untethered to the past and futurally oriented, such efforts get cast as benevolence, as marks of "good allyship" or "good civic membership." This is not to discount the necessity of such a historical reckoning, nor to diminish their sincerity or effort, but rather to point out the way the burdens of the past are differentially distributed and borne.

"GET OVER IT," "TEAR IT DOWN": PUBLIC COMMEMORATIONS AND TEMPORAL CONTESTATIONS

What, then, do we make of the familiar call to "get over it" when racism is brought to attention? At the same time, how can we understand the growing calls – via movements such as "Rhodes Must Fall" and "Black Lives Matter" – to tear down the monuments of colonialism, slavery, and Western imperialism? In this final section I will bring the preceding analyses to bear on the contestations around the annual commemoration of "Australia Day," followed by a revisiting of white temporality via a consideration of the felling of commemorative statues, and the responses they have generated.

In recent years, there has been a renewed groundswell of criticism and challenge to the country's national day of celebration on the basis that its chosen date, 26 January, which marks the declaration of British sovereignty on the land of the Gadigal people of the Eora nations,[18] is deeply offensive to the Aboriginal peoples, communities, and history of this land. As Aboriginal (Tanganekald, Meintangk-Boandik) legal scholar Irene Watson asks with respect to the anniversary: "Why celebrate this violent colonial history of genocide? Who does this?" (Watson, 2018). While such objections are not new – Indigenous peoples have been marking the "Day of Mourning" since 1938 – recent years have seen a growing consciousness among non-Indigenous Australians, with "Invasion Day" protests attracting up to 60,000 participants in major cities (Knaus and Wahlquist, 2018), local government councils moving citizenship ceremonies away from that day, as well as broad-based "Change the Date"[19] campaigns across the arts and media.[20] Predictably, such public moves have generated a sizeable backlash from the wider Australian community, with successive Prime Ministers, political leaders, and public organizations doubling down on the suitability of this date and this celebration, emphasizing need for "national unity" and "coming together."[21] In less restrained corners of public debate, some have responded with a quintessentially Australian "get over it," a collective eye-roll to the tired questions of First Nations justice that will not go away.

This exhortation, to "get over" the historical harms of colonialism, strikes as an interesting one from the perspective of racialized temporality. On the one hand, it exhibits a diminishing of the violence that colonialism has visited upon Indigenous communities and people, as Aboriginal (Darumbal) and South Sea Islander journalist Amy McQuire notes: "On this day, First Nations peoples mourn the loss of land, of their children, of their wages, of their remains. They mourn the loss of control over their own future" (McQuire, 2014). But more than this, the calls to "get over" this racist history and to move beyond it also exhibits, I argue, a denial of the fact that this is how and where colonized bodies are made to dwell. As I have sought to show in this chapter, in addition to the continued material, political, and legal injustices of colonialism, the processes of colonization and racialization have also differentially temporalized colonized and racialized bodies, pegging them to the (closed) past. The call to "get over it," then, amounts not just to a denial about racism's ongoing presence, but also a disingenuity about the different temporal structures of racialized and white embodiment – that is to say, a disingenuity about the deeper existential structures that shape white and racialized/colonized being respectively.

On the other hand, the call not to dwell on such past injustices is characteristic of white temporality and of the process of racialization itself; recall here, the analysis of racialized forgetting. Such forgetting is both willful and selective, as Aboriginal (Yorta Yorta) rapper Adam Briggs astutely noted, in relation to the heated public debates around Australia/Invasion Day:

> They tell us to "get over it, forget it and move on!" Move on? Well, Gallipoli was about 100 years ago, so let's f—ing move on from that too. But no – that's "Aussie spirit."
>
> *(Northover, 2018)*

Briggs' invocation of ANZAC day (which commemorates the battle of Gallipoli in World War I) is particularly striking in the context of this discussion, given the public holiday is commemorated with the phrase, "Lest We Forget."[22] Other commentators have remarked upon the curious emotional attachment Australia Day adherents seem to exhibit for 26 January as *the* date for commemoration (citing respect for history and tradition), given this "tradition" was formally established only as recently as 1994. These, I suggest, offer us cues to think further about the nature of white temporality, particularly with its attachments to the historical narratives within "white time." For example, how does the fashioning of a national self-image and self-identity through historical commemorations of Australia Day, ANZAC Day, and so forth, point to a different mode of relating to the white past?

Globally, contests around the felling of statues – which gained traction during "Rhodes Must Fall" in South Africa (2015) and the reinvigoration of "Black Lives Matter" in the US (2020), with both campaigns inspiring movements internationally – speak directly to this question. These movements, and the public debates they have initiated, offer a window into the different ways that whiteness, too, can become temporally fixated on a particular self-image and past. The moral and political panic seen in response to the removal, tearing down, defacing, annotating, and re-presentation of various monuments (Cecil Rhodes, Edward Colston, James Cook, Robert E. Lee, among others[23]), points to a different kind of temporal "stuckness." For example, conservative mainstream commentators' inevitable appeals to the "un-rewritability" of history exhibit an unmoving fidelity to a version of the past that, as many have pointed out, is already actively and selectively written. But this fidelity, and the refusal to engage in a rethinking and re-evaluation of those pasts (as per the demands of political activists[24]), suggest that whites too can become temporally wedded to certain pasts, and the narratives and self-identity they generate. This explains the sense of threat felt when these histories do come under challenge; when the statues do come tumbling down.[25] For example, in 2017 the then Australian Prime Minister Malcolm Turnbull responded to the painting of slogans "change the date" and "no pride in genocide" at the base of a Captain Cook statue, by describing them as "a deeply disturbing and totalitarian campaign to not just challenge our history but to deny it and obliterate it" (Mayers, 2017). In the same year, US President Donald Trump responded to a protest for the removal of a Gen. Robert E. Lee statue, stating: "Sad to see the history and culture of our great country being ripped apart" (Keneally, 2017). Given this, it might seem too quick to describe white temporality as untethered, per my earlier claim, since such examples appear to show the deep attachment of white subjectivity to the past, and its rootedness in it. Nonetheless, I argue that while such examples complicate our understanding of white temporality, they do not displace the foregoing analysis, since they speak to the ability of whites to decide which (self-defining) pasts to hold fast to, and which ones to let go (as well as *when* to let go).

That is to say, it is a holding fast, not a holding *over*; relationships to the past remain of white people's making and remaking. This is therefore a different mode of relating to the past than we find in Fanon's account of racialized and colonized temporality.

If anything, what the above suggests is that the temporal "untetheredness" of whiteness as described earlier, which constitutes a salient feature of white embodiment on the phenomenological register, is itself nested within and accountable to the narrative of "white time" as described by Mills. Insofar as white embodiment remains free from any one temporal frame, this temporal "freedom" nonetheless unfolds against a horizon of meaning, histories, and habits that have come to constitute whiteness. Among these, as we saw in Mills' account of "white time," include the designation of whites as history-makers and utilizers (indeed, masters) of time; the temporal untetheredness of whiteness thus is tempered by the conceptualization of agency embedded within "white time" as well as the historical markers of that agency. White temporality might be untethered in the sense of being unbound, but this is not to say that it is ahistorical – indeed, it is the historical production of whiteness as neutral, agential, and expansive, that allow it to act as if it were temporally untethered, in contrast to racialized temporality.

CONCLUSION

Fanon's foregrounding of the temporalization of the Black lived experience offers us a rich and innovative starting point from which to think through the various dimensions of racialized and white embodiment, as well as the different ways temporality figures in contestations around racism, history, and commemoration in the public domain. In this chapter, I have sought to elaborate and expand the account of racialized temporality found in Fanon's work, fleshing out his claims of the overdetermining and predetermining weight of the past on racialized subjects. Reconnecting this with the phenomenological tradition of embodiment (one of the several traditions informing Fanon's own thought), I have tried to articulate the bodily expressions of this racialized temporality, and in doing so, have contrasted this with an examination of white temporality, "white time," and the different relations to the past it makes possible. As Fanon recognized, the question of temporality, while not one of obvious political concern, tells us something important about the deep structures of our embodied orientations and encounters in a racially organized world, and about how racism itself is effected and sustained. Moreover, for Fanon, it is only through a reckoning with and moving beyond the weight of the past that the process of disalienation (of which the book is centrally concerned[26]) can truly get under way, that one might "initiate the cycle of my freedom" (1967, p. 231).

NOTES

1 This chapter is based on an article that originally appeared as Ngo, H., 2019, "'Get Over It'? Racialized Temporalities and Bodily Orientations in Time," *Journal of Intercultural Studies*, *40*(2), pp. 239–253. I thank the editors of this volume for the opportunity to revisit and revise that work, and I thank George Yancy for his feedback on the article and for his invitation to think further about the nature of white temporality (as explored in the final section of this chapter).

2 For the sake of readability, throughout the chapter I will often use the term "racialized" to include "colonized," however in doing so I do not claim that they are coterminous or

interchangeable terms. I use the term "racialized" given that processes of colonization are indelibly linked to and motivated by racialization – even though I acknowledge that Indigenous peoples are impacted in specific and different ways to non-Indigenous racialized subjects. At times I revert to the term "colonized" when considering the specific case of colonialism.

3 In the North American context, Charles Mills writes: "Two hundred years after Locke, closing the temporal bracket so to speak, Native Americans would be depicted as a 'dying race,' a people who, unable to use the time, located not on the White time-track but in a prehistoric other time, 'a futureless past,' were in any case almost out of time, scheduled for extinction" (Mills, 2007, p. 31).

4 It might be objected that the question finds this form as a way of avoiding the more direct (and more obtuse) form, "What race are you?" – but I would disagree. While I accept that there is some observance of the social etiquette of not naming race directly, I find it significant and telling that the question morphs from present tense ("What race *are* you?") to a question of past and of origin.

5 This comes from a video produced for The Feed (SBS Viceland). The longer commentary goes as follows: "and for as *long* as I can remember, white people have loved asking me where I am from. Every cab ride, every barbeque, every first date ... [cut to montage] Until Now. The tables have turned motherf—kers! Suddenly we find out about s.44 of the Australian Constitution ... and questions about white people's ancestry are all the rage!" Available from: https://www.smh.com.au/video/video-entertainment/video-comedy/a-m essage-from-australians-who-look-a-bit-foreign-20170815-4x5uh.html [Accessed September 29, 2018].

6 Heidegger writes elsewhere: "It is essential to the basic constitution of Dasein that there is *constantly something still be settled*" (Heidegger, 2008, p. 279, emphasis original).

7 I further note, regarding Fanon's reference to living *men* (*l'homme existant*), Al-Saji's comment: "Certainly, Fanon's account is that of a black man; and black women are mostly unheard in the book" (Al-Saji, p. 3).

8 As Al-Saji explains in a different article, the later Merleau-Ponty more critically rethinks the Husserlian presentation of the present as a "now-point," as well as the past characterized in terms of retentional intentionality. For Merleau-Ponty in *The Visible and the Invisible*, the "internal interdependence" of the past and the present is not sufficiently captured by this concept of retention and thus fails to adequately account for the passing of the present into the past, except by way of external interjection. This means that the past is not "recognized as internally necessary," and there remains in this account of retentional intentionality, a seriality and rectilinearity that Husserl is not able to overcome (Al-Saji, 2009, pp. 210–215).

9 Dimitriu further explains Husserlian protention thus: "When we hear a melody, we will always protend further notes of the music. What exactly these notes will be depends entirely on the particular situation in which we are embedded. Nothing changes, however, the fact that we will protend a new note" (Dimitriu, 2013, p. 214).

10 This also marks a point where Moreton-Robinson draws exception from Fanon's characterization of the colonized subject (which unfolds in the Martinican and Algerian contexts), although on the question of colonized temporality I think they would agree.

11 Merleau-Ponty writes: "Time must not merely be, it must come about; time is never completely constituted. Constituted time – the series of possible relations according to the before and the after – is not time itself, it is merely the final registering of time, and it is the result of time's *passage*, which objective thought always presupposes but never manages to grasp ... Constituted time is a milieu that is distinct from myself and that is immobile where nothing passes by and where nothing happens. There must be another time, a true time, where I learn what passage or transition is in itself" (Merleau-Ponty, 2012, p. 438).

12 Video interview with Mark Knight excerpted here: "Serena Williams: Cartoonist Mark Knight defends depiction of US Open tantrum amid accusations of racism," *ABC News*, September 11, 2018. Available from: http://www.abc.net.au/news/2018-09-11/cartoon ist-mark-knight-defends-serena-williams-depiction/10230044 [Accessed September 28, 2018]. Text transcribed by me.

In the face of the controversy, newspaper *The Herald Sun* then defiantly reprinted the cartoon on its front page, supposedly in defence of satire against a "PC world gone mad." Available from: http://www.abc.net.au/news/2018-09-19/mark-knight-cartoon-of-serena-williams/ 10281910 [Accessed September 28, 2018].

13 Corbould points to an article by Richard Waterhouse which explores the Australian reception of this genre: "Minstrel show and vaudeville house: The Australian popular stage, 1838–1914."

14 A comment from cartoonist Darren Bell (of King Features) provides an interesting counterpoint to the caricaturing of Black people in the US: "If you're tempted to make their lips look like airbags, or to make their nose take up half their faces, you're being lazy. Especially when, as in the case of Serena, her lips and her nose aren't especially large … If you look at Serena and you're inclined to exaggerate her nose and her lips, odds are that is why they stand out to you. And if you're not purposely trying to tap into those 100-year-old stereotypes, then as a professional, you're supposed to be aware of that impulse and put it in check. I go through that thought process when I draw anyone" (Bell, cited in Cavna, 2018).

15 Per Prime Minister John Howard: "I do not believe, as a matter of principle, that one generation can accept responsibility for the acts of an earlier generation. I don't accept that as a matter of principle" (Davies, 2008).

16 This conviction of "color-blindness," unsurprisingly, was evident in defences of Knight's cartoon depiction of Serena Williams, with *Herald Sun* editor stating "It had nothing to do with gender or race, this was about a bad sport being mocked." The naturalization of racial difference was also evident in fellow cartoonist Paul Zanetti's remarks: "All he has done as cartoonists do is tell the truth. All he did was depict her in satirical manner." ("Herald Sun backs Mark Knight's cartoon on Serena Williams," *Herald Sun*, September 12, 2018.) Available from: https://www.heraldsun.com.au/news/victoria/herald-sun-backs-mark-knights-cartoon-on-serena-williams/news-story/30c877e3937a510d64609d89ac521d9f [Accessed September 28, 2018].

17 Goody writes: "The very calculation of time in the past, and in the present too, has been appropriated by the west. The dates on which history depends are measured before and after the birth of Christ (BC and AD, or BCE and CE to be more politically correct). The recognition of other eras, relating to the Hegira, to the Hebrew or to the Chinese New Year, is relegated to the margins of historical scholarship and of international usage" (cited in Mills 2014, p. 30).

18 Otherwise known as Sydney Cove. I note that the date marks this declaration and the raising of the Union Jack flag, rather than the landing of the First Fleet, as widely assumed (this took place a week earlier in Botany Bay). I further note that this event follows Lt. James Cook's earlier declaration of British possession of the island of Bedanug (renamed "Possession Island") in August 1770.

19 I note that contestations around Australia Day celebrations do not boil down to merely a question of date. Many, such as Indigenous writer and scholar Tony Birch, have questioned the legitimacy of a national celebration at all, in the face of Australia's continued injustices against its First Nations peoples (Birch, 2018).

20 As two examples, *The Saturday Paper* mounted a "Change the Date" campaign in 2017, and national youth radio broadcaster Triple J moving their iconic "Hottest 100" countdown away from 26 January as an acknowledgement of the insensitivity of celebration on this day.

21 The National Australia Day Council, for example, champions the day as a day "for all Australians, no matter where our personal stories began, [to] reflect on being Australian, celebrate contemporary Australia and recognize our history." Available from: https://www.sbs.com.au/news/australia-day-explained-why-it-s-really-held-on-26-january -and-the-push-to-change-the-date [Accessed October 2, 2018].

22 McQuire makes a similar point: "Australians may want us to 'get over it,' to stop being so 'sensitive.' But then, why do we still set aside a day of remembrance on ANZAC day to commemorate those who risked their lives at war? And why don't we acknowledge the brave Aboriginal fighters who sacrificed everything in the frontier wars?" (McQuire, 2014).

23 For some examples, see https://time.com/5850135/edward-colston-statue-slave-trader-protests/, https://www.nationalgeographic.com/history/2020/07/toppling-statues-is-firs t-step-toward-ending-confederate-myths/, https://mymodernmet.com/light-projections-robert-e-lee-memorial/ https://www.nytimes.com/2020/06/10/us/christopher-columbus-statue-boston-richmond.html [Accessed August 20, 2020].

24 For example, "Rhodes Must Fall" organizer Simukai Chigudu states in an interview: "People would say, 'You're shutting down debate,' and we would say, 'No, actually, we're opening up debate. We're the ones who are saying that we need to debate Rhodes' legacy." Available from: https://www.newstatesman.com/politics/uk/2020/06/rhodes-must-fall-oxford-sl avery-statue-oxford-university-oriel-black-lives-matter [Accessed August 20, 2020].

25 Of course, more than the statues themselves are at stake here; they stand in for a broader reclaiming of public, cultural, and political domains. For example as Chigudu notes: "The Rhodes Must Fall campaign in South Africa generated this sense of energy and urgency, a sense that we could start to challenge our institution to take a much more self-critical look at questions of representation, of curriculum, and how we mark public space, including colo-nial iconography." Available from: https://www.newstatesman.com/politics/uk/2020/06/rhodes-must-fall-oxford-slavery-statue-oxford-university-oriel-black-lives-matter [Accessed August 20, 2020].

26 *Black Skin, White Masks (Peau noire, masques blancs)* was originally entitled *Un essai pour la désal-iénation des noirs.*

REFERENCES

Ahmed, S. (2006). *Queer phenomenology: Orientations, objects, others.* Durham, NC: Duke University Press.

Al-Saji, A. (2009). An absence that counts in the world: Merleau-Ponty's later philosophy of time in Light of Bernet's "Einleitung." *Journal of the British Society for Phenomenology, 40*(2), 207–227.

Al-Saji, A. (2013). Too late: Racialized time and the closure of the past. *Insights, 6*(5), 2–13.

Birch, T. (2018). A change of date will do nothing to shake Australia from Its colonial-settler triumphalism. *Indigenous X*, 21 January. Available from: https://indigenousx.com.au/tony -birch-a-   change-of-date-will-do-nothing-to-shake-australia-from-its-colonial-settler-triu mphalism/ #.WmVjdjPZWEc [Accessed January 23, 2018].

Bond, C. (2020). Dear Ancestor. In A. Whittaker (Ed.), *Fire Front: First Nations poetry and power today* (pp. 3–8). Brisbane, Australia: University of Queensland Press.

Boucher, L., & Russell, L. (2015). *Settler colonial governance in nineteenth-century Victoria.* Cocos (Keeling) Islands: ANU Press.

Cavna, M. (2018). A racist Serena Williams cartoon went viral. Here's how to caricature her the right way. *The Washington Post*, 13 September. Available from: https://www.washingtonpost. com/ news/comic-riffs/wp/2018/09/13/a-racist-serena-williams-cartoon-went-viral-heres-how-to-caricature-her-the-right-way/?utm_term=.31cd153117b5 [Accessed September 28, 2018].

Corbould, C. (2018). The Herald Sun's Serena Williams cartoon draws on a long and damaging history of racist caricature. *The Conversation*, 11 September. Available from: https://theconv ersation.com/the-herald-suns-serena-williams-cartoon-draws-on-a-long-and-   damaging-h istory-of-racist-caricature-102982 [Accessed September 28, 2018].

Davies, A. (2008). Nothing to say sorry for: Howard. *The Sydney Morning Herald*, 12 March. Available from: https://www.smh.com.au/national/nothing-to-say-sorry-for-howard-2008 0312-gds4t6.html [Accessed September 29, 2018].

Dimitriu, C. (2013). The protention-retention asymmetry in Husserl's conception of time consciousness. *Praxis Filosófica, 37*, 209–229.

Fanon, F. (1967). *Black skin, White masks* (L. Markmann, Trans.). London: Grove Press.

Goldberg, D. T. (2015). *Are we all postracial yet?* Malden, MA: Polity Press.

Heidegger, M. (2008). *Being and time* (Macquarie and Robinson, Trans.). New York: Harper & Row.

Keneally, M. (2017, August 17). Trump says culture being "ripped apart" by Confederate memorial removals. *ABC News.* Available from: https://abcnews.go.com/Politics/trump-ca lls-removal-confederate-memorials-sad/story?id=49271200

Knaus, C., & Wahlquist, C. (2018). "Abolish Australia Day": Invasion day marches draw tens of thousands of protesters. *The Guardian*, 26 January. Available from: https://www.theguard ian.com/australia-news/2018/jan/26/abolish-australia-day-invasion-day-marches-draw-te ns-of- thousands-of-protesters [Accessed October 2, 2018].

Mayers, L. (2017, August 25).Australia Day: Malcolm Turnbull condemns Captain Cook Statuevandalism as "cowardly." *ABC News, Australia.* Available from:https://www.abc.net.au/ news/2017-08-26/australia-day-argument-intensifies-as-vandals-hit-captain-cook/8845064

McQuire, A. (2014). Australia Day: Indigenous people are told to "Get Over It." It's impossible. *The Guardian*, 27 January. Available from: https://www.theguardian.com/commentisfre e/2014/jan/27/australia-day-indigenous-people-are-told-to-get-over-it-its-impossible [Accessed October 2, 2018].

Merleau-Ponty, M. (2012). *Phenomenology of perception.* New York: Routledge.

Mills, C. (2007). White ignorance. In N. Tuana and S. Sullivan (Eds.), *Race and epistemologies of ignorance* (pp. 11–38). Albany, NY: State University of New York Press.

Mills, C. (2014). White time: The chronic injustice of ideal theory. *Du Bois Review: Social Science Research on Race, 11*(1), 27–42.

Moreton-Robinson, A. (2015). *The white possessive: Property, power, and indigenous sovereignty.* Minneapolis, MN: University of Minnesota Press.

Ngo, H. (2017). *The habits of racism: A phenomenology of racism and racialized embodiment.* Lanham, MD: Lexington Books.

Nicolacopoulos, T., & Vassilacopoulos, G. (2014). *Indigenous sovereignty and the being of the occupier: Manifesto for a white Australian philosophy of origins.* Melbourne, VIC: re.press.

Nielsen, H. (2018). Why I won't stand for the national anthem. *The Saturday Paper*, 22 September. Available from: https://www.thesaturdaypaper.com.au/opinion/topic/2018/09/22/why-i- wont- stand-the-national-anthem/15375384006891 [Accessed September 29, 2018].

Northover, K. (2018). Let's get over Gallipoli too: Briggs on Australia Day and the spirit of oppression. *The Sydney Morning Herald*, 12 January. Available from: https://www.smh.com.au/ entertainment/lunch-with-briggs-its-a-new-conversation-20180111-h0gt7q.html [Accessed October 3, 2018].

O'Byrne, A. (2010). *Natality and finitude.* Bloomington, IN: Indiana University Press.

Sullivan, S. (2006). *Revealing Whiteness: The unconscious habits of racial privilege.* Bloomington, IN: Indiana University Press.

Tuck, E., & Gaztambide-Fernández, R. (2013). Curriculum, replacement, and settler futurity. *Journal of Curriculum Theorizing, 29*(1), 72–89.

Waterhouse, R. (1989). Minstrel show and vaudeville house: The Australian popular stage, 1838–1914. *Australian Historical Studies, 23*(93), 366–385.

Watson, I. (2018). Why celebrate on the day that marks crimes of colonialism and genocide? *Indigenous X*, 25 January. Available from: https://indigenousx.com.au/irene-watson-why- celebrate-on-the-day-that-marks-crimes-of-colonialism-and-genocide/#.W6m5eS1L3q0 [Accessed October 4, 2018].

Wolfe, P. (2006). Settler colonialism and the elimination of the Native. *Journal of Genocide Research, 8*(4), 387–409.

Young, I. (2005). Throwing like a girl: A phenomenology of feminine body comportment, motility, and spatiality. In I. Young (Ed.), *On female body experience: "Throwing like a girl" and other essays* (pp. 27–45). New York: Oxford University Press.

CHAPTER 14

TO DWELL FOR THE POSTCOLONIAL

Grant Farred

INTRODUCTION

In the preface to Fanon's *The Wretched of the Earth*, Sartre states that "Everyone can think what he likes, provided however that he thinks" (1961/2004, p. lvii). Later, in the same text, Fanon writes: "Perhaps everything needs to be started over again" (Fanon, 1961/2004, p. 56).

It is doubtful that either Jean-Paul Sartre or Frantz Fanon would have understood himself as operating under the Heideggerian injunction, but that is precisely what they are doing. In Alain Badiou's (2000) estimation, offered in *The Clamor of Being*, Martin Heidegger is the philosopher of the twentieth century. Heidegger holds this status for Badiou because of his attention to temporality and thinking. Sartre, it would seem, does not only understand the importance of thinking but it constitutes for him a prerequisite for participation in the political: "Everyone can think what he likes, provided however that he thinks." For Heidegger, however, thinking, if it takes place, is almost indistinguishable from truth, so Sartre's demand – "provided however that he thinks" – would strike Heidegger as a serious inability. For Heidegger, to think is to grasp the truth, or, to come to truth through thinking, or, to know truth as thinking. In Heideggerian terms, Sartre's tolerance, articulated as the conditional (the provisional), "provided," reveals itself as a grievous mistake: the forming of an opinion is not thinking.

According to Rüdiger Safranski (2002), one of Heidegger's biographers, and to Heidegger himself, nothing matters quite as much as beginning, a truism if there ever was one, at the beginning. "Philosophizing," Heidegger was known to assert, "ultimately means nothing other than being a beginner" (Heidegger, cited in Safranski, 2002, p. 1). Thinking from the beginning is an invitation – the most direct form of address, a challenge, a call to thinking – that Fanon issues to the postcolonial in *The Wretched of the Earth*. Fanon's invitation, however, is seldom heard, and even less frequently taken up. But there can be no doubt about its clarity: "Perhaps everything needs to be started over again." Not simply "started over again," but "everything" – which means that nothing can be excluded, beginning with the postcolonial itself because that is the site of Fanon's greatest resonance – must be made a matter for consideration. As Heidegger says about the "Old German words *thing* and *ding*," so the postcolonial must, now under the sign of the beginning, "become the name for an affair or a matter of pertinence" (1971, p. 4) because the Fanonian articulation of the word "postcolonial" is now being returned to itself, remanded to a "first" thinking that is not a first thinking but a call for a thinking of how *The Wretched of the Earth* starts (a) thinking of the postcolonial.

All that Fanon fought for in *The Wretched of the Earth*, struggled for in *Black Skin, White Masks*, the radical political imagining that saturates his work, the philosophical imperative that shapes it insistently, those struggles for which he gave his life, "everything," must be assigned a propositional "pertinence." Not least of all, in this act of starting everything again, is the importance of recognizing the interrogative Frantz Fanon issues himself and

DOI: 10.4324/9781003037132-14

those who engage him: Thinking Frantz Fanon must begin again, it is a project that must be started over. That is because of the all-inclusive "perhaps." In the Fanonian articulation there is inscribed in "perhaps" a political charge that exceeds the propositional, an excess that returns, upon different terms, to the beginning. To the beginning, a beginning, that both is and is not overdetermined by the moment – either the historic significance of the fiftieth anniversary of the publication of *The Wretched of the Earth* or the condition of the extant postcolonial. Thinking, the postcolonial of (started, inaugurated by) *The Wretched of the Earth* in this instance, is only possible if it accepts as its primary condition, its proper first name, (the) "perhaps."

The "perhaps" requires the reluctant eschewing of the propositional, that which offers itself, however tentatively, as an answer, in favor of the suppositional, that which begins with only the proviso – the provisional. In the suppositional, it is possible that things might be so but, also, that they might not. It is in this way that the suppositional – "perhaps" – allows for the opening into thinking by assigning, to everyone, the designation beginner. If everyone is a beginner, then everyone might begin to think the postcolonial from the position of a shared suppositional; a suppositional, it should be added, that cannot ever be fully disarticulated from the propositional. Or, to invoke Sartre's phrasing in philosophical terms recalibrated by Heidegger and Fanon's work, "Everyone can think what he likes" as long as she or he begins with "perhaps." The signal possibility that the "perhaps" of *The Wretched of the Earth* offers is, poorly phrased (in terms of how Heidegger thinks the concept in *Being and Time*), temporality.

However, reductive as such a gesture might be, the Fanonian "perhaps" makes possible a thinking of the postcolonial that begins not with its end (a discourse all too familiar to us), or from its having ended (in abjection, in failure), but as *The Wretched of the Earth*'s thinking a "starting over again."

Fanon's phrasing is succinct, but clear. This is not a new beginning, itself always only a putative possibility, but a starting over again. Starting over again demands a working with, a working over, if you will, extant conditions. Starting over attends to what is but refuses the very (necessary) delimitations of what is. It is a difficult project, to start over again, iterated already in the acknowledgement – starting over "again" – that such an imagining has a previous life (or lives) but there is, as Fanon and Heidegger both remind us, no sub-stitute for thinking again: Making the "perhaps" of *The Wretched of the Earth* a supposition of pertinence. Heidegger, more than Fanon, is concerned with what is lost in the overuse of terms so that starting over again for him recognizes that "true meaning falls easily into oblivion in favor of foreground meanings" (Heidegger, 1971, p. 179). However, Heidegger also understands both the retrievability – the recovery, the making audible again – of the "true meaning" and the kind of interrogation that is needed to achieve it: "its primal call does not thereby become incapable of speech; it merely falls silent" (p. 179). In *The Wretched of the Earth* it is, of course, not the postcolonial that has "fallen silent"; it is, rather, that the "perhaps" was never (fully) heard. Its suppositionality (and its propositionality) was not only superseded by the romance of the postcolonial – the promise of "starting over" after colonialism, which is in truth a starting, is the only "starting over" imaginable, despite Fanon's warnings and cautions in *The Wretched of the Earth*. More pertinently, the "perhaps" was rendered inaudible, without any possibility of being heard, let alone taken up as a pro-ject for thought, a project already audible, ominously so, in *The Wretched of the Earth*. After all, Fanon warns, "We must not expect the nation to produce new men" (1961/2004, p. 229), a declarative inaudible except as a command to thinking – at the very least, a call for the interrogative, an explication for why there will be no "new men." If the "new nation" cannot be "expected" to "produce new men," then this shortcoming constitutes a serious flaw in itself – considering Fanon's attention to constructing a new political consciousness, a new thinking of the anti-colonial Self, in *The Wretched of the Earth*. At the very least, then, because of this, the "new nation" must "produce" a thinking about itself, a thinking about how it thinks, or fails to think about what it is not thinking about.

If the "nation" cannot produce "new men," that is, a thinking disjoined from its colonial(ist) antecedent, then it is not, in Heidegger's terms, a nation fit for dwelling. This is a project, dwelling, that girds *The Wretched of the Earth*. The postcolonial nation of *The Wretched of the Earth* is not, in Heideggerian terms, a building – broadly understood as the making, the constructing, the making possible of, that "space" – in which the postcolonial can dwell, or in which the postcolonial can be. As Heidegger understands, it is no small thing to dwell. For Heidegger to dwell means to be

> set at peace, means to remain at peace within the free, the preserve, the free sphere that safeguards each thing in its nature. *The fundamental character of dwelling is this sparing and pre-serving.* It pervades dwelling in its whole range. That range soon reveals itself to us as soon as we reflect that human beings consist in dwelling and, indeed, dwelling in the sense of the stay of mortals on the earth.
>
> *(Heidegger, 1971, p. 149,l emphasis original)*

In the most fundamental Heideggerian terms possible, dwelling is nothing less than Being. That is, dwelling is everything because "human being consists in dwelling" (1971, p. 149). These are the terms on which *The Wretched of the Earth* must be approached: As Fanon's struggle to build the postcolonial as house for dwelling. That is the house that *The Wretched of the Earth* seeks to build, that is the house that thinking must now undertake, again (perhaps even over and over again), to build. Because building does not always, or necessarily, produce a dwelling – that in which the "fundamental character" of Being, *Dasein*, can be revealed, in which postcolonial Being can be "spared and preserved," it is dwelling that must be the first order of postcolonial business. The call for a dwelling for postcolonialism is, in this Heideggerian way, the work that thinking must undertake; this is what the Fanonian "perhaps" makes audible. It is the making of a dwelling that must be sought for, built, in the act of "starting over again." If the postcolonial dwelling is yet to be built, if the house in which postcoloniality can be has not yet been constructed, then it becomes imperative to understand that thinking postcolonialism as that which is yet to be thought is the task that *The Wretched of the Earth* sets.

TO DWELL FOR THE POSTCOLONIAL

> Enough will have been gained if dwelling and building have become *worthy of questioning* and thus have remained *worthy of thought*.
>
> *(Heidegger, 1971, p. 154; original emphasis)*

> The Third World must not be content to define itself in relation to values which preceded it.
>
> *(Fanon, 1961/2004, p. 55)*

The political imperative for Fanon, to make the nation after colonialism, translates as an address to the Heideggerian question: How to make a building in which the postcolonial can dwell? It is a question audible in so fundamental a biopolitical register as to be almost Agambenian: How to spare and preserve life? In Giorgio Agamben's (1998) terms, of course, the terms would be read as "*zoe*" and "*bios*" – bare life and political life. These are, needless to say, critical issues, issues that have preoccupied postcolonial scholars for at least three generations now.

From the very beginning, however, Fanon's attention is both on the fundamental – which we might understand as the ongoing political struggle against, inter alia, inequity – and the inaugural. That is, with the beginning, that which understands its own precariousness, that which refuses the known – "The Third World must not be content to …" (Fanon, 1961/2004, p. 55). However, salient as his refusal of the dialectic is in this instance, much of Fanon's thinking is prone to precisely this mode of thinking. Nowhere is Fanon's dialectical materialism more evident than in the opening essay of *The Wretched of the Earth*, "On Violence." "The basic confrontation," he writes,

> which seemed to be colonialism versus anticolonialism, indeed capitalism versus socialism, is already losing its importance. What matters today, the issue which blocks the horizon, is the need for a redistribution of wealth.
>
> *(Fanon, 1961/2004, p. 55)*

Here Fanon's thinking moves, rapidly, from the dialectic to what might seem like a synthetic call – for the "redistribution of wealth" – but it ends, in truth, with nothing but a declarative that spawns a further dialectic: "Humanity will have to address the question [of redistribution], no matter how devastating the consequences might be" (Fanon, 1961/2004, p. 55).

It is because of Fanon's proclivity for the dialectical and the declarative, however, that his brief turn from the former reveals the significance of the "perhaps." In starting over, even if only for a moment, there can be no vitalization of the dialectic, itself issued, true to Fanonian form, as the declarative, albeit a far more tentative one than is at first apparent: "The Third World must not be content to define itself in relation to values which preceded it" (Fanon, 1961/2004, p. 55). A double break is articulated here: (1) from the culture of the colonizer, itself, of course, an impossible sundering, and (2) contra Fanon's celebration of the colonized's culture, the implicit recognition that there can be no (easy) hearkening to pre-coloniality. It is out of this aporia, the declarative that is grounded in nothing so much as uncertainty, that Fanon confronts at once the limits and the advantages of the dialectic. The dialectic derives its force from the oppositional; it provides something that can be argued against as well as struggled for. This, of course, is also its limit because every position must be measured, measure itself, against its antithesis. In its own way, the dialectic works, for all its gainsaying, primarily through the force of mediation.

If the dialectic is suspended, the question inherent in Fanon's articulation persists: To which "values" will the postcolonial turn having recognized that it now operates under the terms of the double break? That neither the immediate nor the distant past will suffice as models of thought? It is here that the "perhaps" comes into its own and it does so neither as the propositional nor the suppositional, but as a sovereign "starting over." The question that *The Wretched of the Earth* poses is one that Fanon cannot answer. He is vague, generic, unhelpfully categorical in addressing his own interrogative: "underdeveloped countries must endeavor to focus on their very own values as well as methods and style specific to them" (Fanon, 1961/2004, p. 55). The only force that sustains Fanon's critique of "values" is his repeated turn to thinking from the beginning; or, thinking as that act that marks the beginning of the postcolonial. Fanon's skepticism about the "new," his insistence on the insufficiency of the transition of political power from the colonizer to the colonized, persists: "The country finds itself under new management, but in actual fact everything has to be started over from scratch, everything has to be rethought" (Fanon, 1961/2004, p. 56). The refrain of "starting over" is constant, buttressed in this instance by the determination that "everything has to be rethought."

The Wretched of the Earth, for all Fanon's commitment to the redistribution of wealth and resources, reveals itself as a work struggling, sometimes despite itself, even sometimes, it seems, unknown to itself, with the Manicheanism of the Cold War. That is, *The Wretched of the Earth* cannot, in its most philosophical moments (when thinking, not the political declarative, prevails), countenance either socialism or capitalism. Of course, Fanon has far greater regard for socialism, but *The Wretched of the Earth* is a struggle for what Heidegger names, elusively, the "unconcealedness of what is already there" (1971, p. 171). We might even name Fanon's grasping for "values," although it seems that it is something else that he is reaching for, a desire for a postcolonial *élan vital* – a more vital mode of postcolonial life, one in which a Heideggerian dwelling might be discerned. That is, where the "primal call" of the dwelling cannot only be heard, but where there is the intent to "remain at peace within the free, the preserve, the free sphere that safeguards each thing in its nature." In this postcolonial dwelling, life is not only spared or preserved, it thrives; life knows no other mode except *élan vital*.

We do not think of Martin Heidegger as a radical environmentalist, and rightly so. There might, however, in "Building Dwelling Thinking" be reason to pause, albeit briefly, and consider him as such. In his poetic discussion of the "simple oneness of the four," "earth and sky, divinities and mortals," Heidegger argues: "Saving the earth does master the earth and does not subjugate it, which is merely one step from spoliation" (1971, p. 151). Much as it is incumbent, in Heidegger's terms, upon "mortals" to desist from seeking to "master the earth" or "subjugating" it in order to avoid "spoliation," so Fanon warns against another form of political "spoliation." Heidegger's injunction bears directly upon Fanon's understanding of how the new nation will conduct its politics: "Achieving power in the name of a narrow-minded nationalism, in the name of race" (Fanon, 1961/2004, p. 109). "Saving" (or liberating or preserving life) the colonized from colonialism must not, as it were, mutate into subjugation through "narrow-minded nationalism"; "spoliation" is intolerable, under whatever guise it takes, "race" or any other. If Heidegger can be dubbed a momentary radical environmentalist, then Fanon stands as an environmentalist of the postcolonial variety: That figure of the political committed to, as Heidegger (1971, p. 153) might have it, to "*understanding* the nature of the thing," he who tends to the "thing," he who cares for the earth, he who seeks to preserve the nation as indivisible from – because it is indivisible from – the sacrosanctness of the "four." The "nature of the thing," of anything, of all things, must be not only properly understood but grasped in their relationship to other things; the radical environmentalist seeks to protect not only the earth but humanity's relationship to every other thing that surrounds it, that inhabits it.

Fanon, in the ideological grappling, the ideological commitments, the political struggle that animates *The Wretched of the Earth*, makes it a text of such philosophical pertinence that it is at one with Heidegger's sensibility. Fanon's "values" is nothing but a tentative naming for "something more." Fanon rejects capitalism, is cautious about committing himself totally to the socialist project, because he senses – even if he cannot name it properly and he cannot name it properly because what he senses has, as yet, no name, because it has no name does not, however, undermine the sensory pull of "something more" – that the (re-)thinking will make something more available. What is is not enough. The new management, the new nation, is not enough; that is why there can be no "new man." It is for this immediate reason that "everything needs to be started again." For once there need be no hesitation in joining the Fanonian declarative: If what is is not enough, there is nothing to do but start again. In this instance we can dispense, if only here, dispense with the "perhaps."

Herein lies the Heideggerian challenge. How to "gather," Heidegger's term for the drawing together of things, for the drawing things into and out of themselves, drawing beyond the thing itself (gathering "expresses something that does not belong to it" [1971, p. 153]), the "unconcealed" postcolonial into itself? How to, as Heidegger might insist, "presence" the "unconcealed?" How to reveal the postcolonial to itself? To "unconceal" is akin to how Heidegger explains what it takes to "save." Both of these "really mean to set something free into its own presencing" (1971, p. 150). It is the possibility for "presencing" that converts the building into a dwelling. (It is this way that building is always subservient to, in the service of, dwelling. Building inclines toward that very "something that does not belong to it." Dwelling, as form of withholding, must give itself to building in order for building to become dwelling: Dwelling is the "expression" of what building is not.) For Heidegger, however, thinking the relationship of building to dwelling is a difficult process. While he insists that "not every building is a dwelling," he also has considerable regard for the act of building. So much so that he acknowledges that "all building is in itself a dwelling" (p. 149). That is not to say, and if so only secondarily, that there is no undertaking of building that is not premised on the possibility of dwelling. Rather, it is to understand that it is the desire for dwelling that motivates "all building." Dwelling comes before building. More poetically phrased, the "nature of building is letting dwell" (p. 160). The intent of the building, that in which the building is conceived, to "let dwell." Building is never, should never be, only to build; it must already be a dwelling before it is a building. Thinking the postcolonial as a dwelling precedes, for Fanon, the act of building the nation. At the core of dwelling is thinking; the act of building is not so much, though it is that too, instrumentalist – to make the nation – as it is the manifestation, the "presencing," of the thinking of dwelling.

Dwelling not only precedes building, but there can be building without the intent to dwell. Building cannot be undertaken without the Heideggerian imperative that is also, implicitly, a philosophical and political challenge: "*Only if we are capable of dwelling, only then can we build*" (1971, p. 160, emphasis original). Under these conditions, there must be no building that is not, before itself, thought as a dwelling. Is the nation where no new men are possible a building in which the postcolonial can dwell? Does it not, because it is only a building, already prohibit dwelling? If the building can no longer be dwelled in, if the thinking that made the building a dwelling has not been preserved, what is there to do but to start over and think again? What is there to do but start over and build a dwelling through thinking? If there is no presencing of dwelling, if there is no presencing in the dwelling, the building cannot stand. The "primal call" that is dwelling is only audible in, and because of, the thinking: "We are attempting to trace in thought the nature of dwelling" (p. 161). There is no way to understand the relationship between building and dwelling, a relationship Heidegger traces with his customary divergences (we think building and dwelling with each other, as complementary, as one preceding the other, as mutually constitutive), except through thought. We can only come to know dwelling if we "trace" it through thought; if we understand that we must first commit ourselves to think before it will even be possible to approach dwelling.

And we must think dwelling, we must follow the trace, wherever it may lead us, because dwelling is Being. It is for this reason that Heidegger finds it so inexplicable that, for others, "dwelling is not experienced as man's being; dwelling is never thought of as the basic character of human being" (1971, p. 161). If there is no dwelling in which the postcolonial is "experienced as man's being," in which dwelling is thought of as the "basic character" of the postcolonial, can the postcolonial be said to have started already? Where is the trace of thought in the postcolonial? How can the postcolonial be if not in the thinking, a thinking that accepts – as the necessary beginning – dwelling as "man's being?" We must "think for the sake of dwelling" (p. 161). In order to dwell we must think. If this is the condition of thought, then the question provoked – we might even say directly posed – by this Heidegger essay is one capable of rearticulating the principle that girds "Building Dwelling Thinking," a naming that is already an ascension, a hierarchy that moves from "building" to "thinking," is a pertinent one: If we dwell because we think, can we think without dwelling? Is the trace of dwelling inscribed in (all) thinking? Is all thinking directed toward dwelling? So that we might dwell in thought, dwell because of thought?

PERHAPS

O, call back yesterday, *bid time return*!
(Shakespeare, King Richard II., Act iii. Sc. 2, emphasis added)

Where is the "presencing" of the postcolonial to be glimpsed if not in the Fanonian "perhaps?" It is the possibility for postcolonial "presencing" that Fanon, in these speculative, almost disjunctive moments, senses in *The Wretched of the Earth*. It is being, Fanon senses, that might be found – might be dwelling – in the "perhaps"; it is something of this magnitude that Fanon senses lies before him. "Presencing" makes of the postcolonial a dwelling, it makes the building of the nation into a dwelling; "presencing" is "unconcealed" in the act of "starting over." The postcolonial dwelling lies before Fanon, waiting – demanding – only to be thought, requiring only a thinking against the building, a thinking against the building that is not enough. Neither "presencing" nor "man's being" is easily accessible for Heidegger. The word he uses, as we know by now, is "unconcealed": it requires that "presencing" or "man's being" be taken out of concealment. It is only possible to dwell if the building is built with dwelling in mind; if the building is built as a dwelling, not as a building.

The (postcolonial) nation against which *The Wretched of the Earth* struggles was constructed as a building. It is a nation that did not think of how to think a dwelling. Or, more laboriously phrased, the new nation did not think of how to build itself as a dwelling. (Fanon's distinction between the two modes of thinking – the nation – is critical here: "National consciousness, which is not nationalism, is alone capable of giving us an international dimension" [Fanon, 1961/2004, p. 179]). "Nationalism" did not seek to understand the kind of unconcealment that makes "national consciousness" possible because it is itself nothing less than an obdurate form of concealment; or, in Heidegger's terms, it would be very difficult to find a "trace of thought" in nationalism. Because it tends so obstinately toward itself, because it has no conception of how to think – how to approach – unconcealment, it cannot not see, it cannot know, in both the colloquial and the Heideggerian sense, what lies before it.

If it seems at times, entirely plausibly, that Fanon's distinction between "nationalism" and "national consciousness" is a precarious, less than rigorously thought attempt to enforce difference, then it is philosophically spared because of what he senses. That is, it is unconcealment toward which he reaches in *The Wretched of the Earth*. Whatever the conceptual limitations that mark Fanon's delineation of "national consciousness," however closely it veers toward "nationalism," whatever the amount of clarification required in order that the terms might be more easily disarticulated, there can be no doubt that Fanon understands the following: "National consciousness" is that mode of being that expresses something that does not belong to it. Or, more importantly for our purposes, it "expresses" – it gathers us away from nationalism, so to speak – something that does not *yet* belong to it. That is to say, there is "something" in Fanon's insistence upon the distinction that gathers us away from "narrow-minded nationalism" (1961/2004, p. 109), it alerts us to those who invoke "race" expediently. We must ask, and remember, with Heidegger: "What is that name which names what is called for? Surely the word 'thinking'" (Heidegger, 1971, p. 133). It is always necessary to "think" the "name" in whose name we are called to mobilize, to act; it is always necessary to "think" about what the "name calls for." There can be no way to take up the "name" "nationalism" except through thought. Fanon's thought as regards the distinction might lack in assiduousness, but in its rudimentary caution it understands that "nationalism" does not belong in the postcolonial. Nationalism is the name which must be resisted, however it dissembles, whatever name it assumes for the purpose of conducting its politics. It is in the name of this resistance that, contra Heidegger, it might be possible to bring together – to gather into our thinking – "historical and philosophical knowledge" (p. 136). They might be, "by an ancient doctrine … radically different from each other" (p. 136), but their occasional gathering together enables them to think efficaciously against "nationalism." "Historical and philosophical knowledge" might be made to dwell together against the building that is nationalism.

It is because Fanon knows the value, if you will, of "what is already there" that *The Wretched of the Earth* stands as a thinking about how to make the postcolonial presence itself. The presencing of the postcolonial is audible in the iteration "everything must be started over again." *The Wretched of the Earth* is the struggle to make manifest, or reveal, like the *Dasein* (or *Ereignis*) of Heidegger's *Being and Time*, "what is already there." It is for this reason that the structure of Fanon's argument in *The Wretched of the Earth* is salient. Fanon's work builds, as it were, from the question about values through his critique of technocracy (the inadequacy of "new management") where the refrain of "starting over" first manifests itself to the constative recognition – "Perhaps everything needs to be started over again" (1961/2004, p. 56).

"Perhaps" the postcolonial must be thought not in Shakespearean formulation, so redolent with nostalgia and loss, to "bid time return." "Perhaps" the unconcealedness of the postcolonial is the thinking of temporality that will not permit of the chronological – that which would ask for the "return" of the moment. Rather, the postcolonial must be thought as a Fanonian project: The "Third World's" refusal to follow relationally after, that is, the *eidos* that insists that the postcolonial can only come after the colonial. If Heidegger and Fanon's arguments are in any way instructive (and theirs are, in this regard, lofty sensibilities), then it is in their ability to explicate that the postcolonial has not yet passed. The postcolonial is what lies ahead, unconcealed, it is still to come, unconcealed, because it has not been thought. That is the project: To make a dwelling (fit) for the postcolonial, that dwelling in which it would be possible to be postcolonial.

Because there is as yet no dwelling for the postcolonial, it becomes possible to say that the postcolonial has not yet begun – "*Perhaps everything needs to be started again.*" That is, following Fanon, we were never postcolonial. There is, then, no better time to press the "perhaps" into both historical and philosophical duty because, fifty years after Fanon named the difficulties, we must ask, in his name: Is there any better occasion to start again, to think on how we might be postcolonial? "What is that name which names what is called for?" Heidegger's is a contorted phrasing, but it demands, at the very least, an account of the name – the "postcolonial" – and he asks what is it in Fanon's work that calls us? What does *The Wretched of the Earth* call for? In the name of what does it call us?

REFERENCES

Agamben, G. (1998). *Homo sacer: Sovereign power and bare life*. Stanford, CA: Stanford University Press.

Badiou, A. (2000). *Deleuze: The clamor of being*. Minneapolis, MN: University of Minnesota Press.

Fanon, F. (2004). *The wretched of the earth* (Richard Philcox, Trans.). New York: Grove Press. (Original work published 1961)

Heidegger, M. (1971). *Poetry, language, thought* (Albert Hofstadter, Trans.). New York: Harper & Row.

Safranski, R. (2002). *Martin Heidegger: Between good and evil* (Ewald Osers, Trans.). Cambridge, MA: Harvard University Press.

Sartre, J. P. (2004). Preface. In F. Fanon (Ed.), *The wretched of the earth* (Richard Philcox, Trans.) (pp. xliii–lxii). New York: Grove Press. (Original work published 1961)

PART V

Phenomenology after Fanon

CHAPTER 15

A PHENOMENOLOGY OF BIKO'S BLACK CONSCIOUSNESS

Lewis R. Gordon

Mabogo Samuel More (also known as Percy Mabogo More) has pointed out the philosophical importance of Steve Biko's thought in the areas of Africana existential philosophy and social and political philosophy. In the latter, Biko's thought is distinguished by his critique of liberalism and his discussions of the political and epistemic conditions for Black liberation. As for the former, much is offered from his readings of Hegel, Marx, Sartre, and Fanon, and Biko's own creative understanding of social identities formed by political practice, that is most acutely formulated in his theory of Black Consciousness. This gathering notion has generated discussion in terms of its existential dimensions in the work of Mabogo More and the resources of psychoanalysis and deconstruction in the writings of Rozena Maart. This short essay will add some thoughts on its phenomenological significance.

Why phenomenology? Phenomenology examines the formation of meaning as constituted by consciousness where the latter is relationally understood as always directed to a manifestation *of* something. That Black Consciousness refers to a form of *consciousness* already calls for a phenomenological analysis. Biko is explicit about its inclusiveness, that Black Consciousness is not premised upon biology or birth but social and political location. Under the brutal system of Apartheid in South Africa, whole categories of people were positioned below those who counted most –namely, whites. That system generated lower layers of subhuman existence ranging from Asians and Coloureds to Blacks. The Coloureds were designations for mixed offspring of Afrikaner (white South Africans of Dutch descent) and indigenous Blacks. The racial schema made British and indigenous Black offspring a problematic category. Among the Asians, the East Indian population was the largest, although Northeast Asians were also included below whites (except, at times, for the Japanese). As with American Apartheid, Jews complicated the schema, as they were generally seen as Eastern European and German Caucasian immigrants to the region. The South African Jewish story is complicated as there was also a group of descendants of Yemenite Jews who migrated there at least 1,000 years prior to the influx of Ashkenazi and small numbers of Sephardi during the last quarter of the nineteenth century. The work of Neil Roos has offered additional complications to the South African schema, since there were few white women (and in some communities none) among the Boers who eventually became the Afrikaners, which meant that the growth of their community had to be through sexual relationships with indigenous women. It is clear, argues Roos, that children who could "pass" made their way back into the Boer community and contributed to the line of contemporary whites, and those who could not assimilate fell into the world that became Coloureds. Among Biko's contributions is a generation of political mythos that both offered a critique of racial formation through actively *constructing* an expanded and new conception of one of its categories. For him, East Indians, Coloureds, and indigenous Blacks in South Africa all became *blacks*, a designation that reflected the reality of their political situation. Biko's addition offers a politically situated understanding of consciousness that lends itself at first to a Hegelian-affected model of racial relations and a

DOI: 10.4324/9781003037132-15

semiological and, ultimately, existential phenomenological model that suggests more than the Hegelian one. The Hegelian narrative, as articulated in his *Phenomenology of Spirit* and with some additional considerations in his *Philosophy of Right*, is familiar. The self is not a complete formation of itself but a dialectical unfolding of overcoming through which selves and correlated concepts of domination, bondage, and freedom emerge. The self, so to speak, is always struggling with its own fragmentation and incompleteness in relation to a world that resists it and through which other selves emerge through such struggles. A point of realization is the understanding that the self cannot be a self *by itself.* In transcendental terms, the only meaningful understanding of selfhood and freedom is that manifested in a world of others. The semiological addition points out that relations of meaning accompany such an unfolding, which manifest a fragile balance at each point of identification. The matrix of such a system is often binary, and it offers seductions in relation to each binary point. Consequently, much of the semiological discussion is about what happens between white and Black, which everyone occupies always at a point short of an ideal. Hence, whiteness by itself is never white enough except in relation to its distance from Blackness, which makes this domination also a form of dependency. Blackness is always too Black except in relation to its distance from itself, which means that one is always too Black in relation to white but never white enough. Coloured, Asian, and brown function as degrees of whiteness and Blackness. The slipperiness of these categories means a system of unceasing conflict, the subtext of which is a teleological whiteness. Biko's notion of Black Consciousness demands shifting such a telos. To aim at becoming Black undermines the legitimacy of whiteness, but it does so with an additional consideration. Whiteness, in spite of the historic and empirical reality of mixture (as pointed out by Roos and many other scholars in recent scholarship on white formation), works on a presumption of purity. Blackness, however, is a broad category that includes, as is the case in the New World from the Americas to North America – a mixture. Consequently, Biko was able to work with a range of peoples under the rubric of Blackness that ironically includes some of those listed under old racial designations as "white." The old racial designations supported absolute interpretations of such identities, but Biko argued for their permeability.

As a semiological notion, Black Consciousness is thus fluid. It becomes a term that can be understood as an identity of most people. It also brings under critical reflection the question of the formation of whiteness – there was not always, for instance, a Europe. That geopolitical notion emerged from the process that succeeded the expulsion of the Moors from the Iberian Peninsula in 1492 in the name of Christendom. The consequent unfolding of a political anthropology of hierarchical racial formation brought along with it the transformation of what was, in reality, the western peninsula of Asia into "Europe" as literally the home of white people, of Europeans. (I will leave aside the current political dynamics in the formation of a European Union in the face of the multiraciality of nearly all of these countries.) The Hegelian challenge returns here through the fragility of these relations by virtue of their dependence on dialectics of struggle for recognition. There was no reason for Christendom to have considered itself white, nor for Moorish Islam to have considered itself Black, except for the unique consequences that led to the formation of Europe as the place of whites and Africa as the place of Blacks. The Hegelian model affirms their mutual role in the formation of their modern identity. This point could be illustrated through the etymology of the word "race." The term has immediate roots in the French by way of the Italian word *razza*, which in turn suggests origins in Spain or Portugal through the term *raza*, which, according to Sebastian de Covarrubias in 1611, referred to "the caste of purebred horses, which are marked by a brand so that they can be recognized

... Raza in lineages is meant negatively, as in having some raza of Moor or Jew."[1] Yet, if we consider that Spain and Portugal were under Moorish (Afro-Arabic) rule for 800 years, a continued etymology suggests the Arabic word *ra's*, which is related to the Hebrew and Amharic words *rosh* and *ras* – head, beginning, or origin. One could push this history/genealogy further and go to the Coptic or to the ancient Egyptian/Kamitan considerations in the word *Ra*, as in the god Amon-Ra, which refers to the sun and, at times, the King of all gods, or is located in the origin stories of the gods. In short, the theme of origins, beginnings, and the rising sun, even when connected to animals such as horses and dogs, suggests the following narrative. The Moors introduced *ra's* into the Iberian Peninsula (Andalusia) to articulate origins and to differentiate even themselves from the Christian Germanic peoples (Visigoths) they conquered and colonized. By 1492, the by then hybrid (Germanic-Afro-Latin-Arabic) peoples who pushed out the Moors (mostly Afro-Arabic, but by this point probably Afro-Arabic-Latin-Germanic) in the name of Christendom used the term that by then became *raz* and eventually *razza* to designate the foreign darker peoples within a theologically oriented naturalistic episteme who, in a holy war, were pushed further southward back to the continent of Africa and into (as they imagined it) the Atlantic Ocean and the New World. Although both uses of the word and its mutation refer to foreigners, the indexical point is what has shifted in the transition from the Middle Ages to the Modern World. Where *ra's* may have once meant "I" and "we" who are from elsewhere, it became "they" who are not from here and who exemplified a deviation from a theological order in which being Christian located one in a normative and natural relationship with God. The discursive shift into what is often referred to as the "other" took shape. We see here the compatibility with the Hegelian model, since the term emerged, through struggle, to the effect of a mutual formation. But, as we will see, its slope was a slippery one, so its movement went beyond the threshold of "self" and "other."

At this point, a connection between Biko and Frantz Fanon might prove useful. In his critique of Hegel and the question of recognition, Fanon argued in *Black Skin, White Masks*, which he elaborated further in *The Wretched of the Earth*, that anti-Black racism structures Blacks outside of the dialectics of recognition and the ethical struggle of self and other. In effect, the semiological structure of oppositions pushes the poles to a continued extreme in racist situations. The result is a struggle *to enter* ethico-political relations, ironically to establish the self both as "self" and "other." The not-self-and-not-other is characterized by Fanon as "the zone of nonbeing" in his early work, and in his final one, it simply means to be the damned of the earth. For our purposes, this racialized schema below the Hegelian model, when mastery/Lordship and enslavement/bondsman have been issued as overcoming, demands an approach that addresses contradictions that are not of a dialectical kind. The call for Black *Consciousness* already demands addressing a "lived reality," as Fanon would say, a meaning-constituting point of view, but *one that has not been acknowledged as such*. In effect, it is the point of view from that which is not a point of view. The consequence is the retort: At least the other is an other. To become such initiates ethical relations.

To arrive at such a conclusion, additional phenomenological considerations are needed. One must not only take into account the lived-reality of consciousness, but also how reflection itself already situates a relationship with contingent forces in a dialectics of freedom. Put differently, the self is posed as the self through the realization of others, which means that a social framework for selfhood is that upon which even identity (an effort to recognize the self) relies. Linked to all this is the communicative dimension of every process of recognition. At the basic level of conscious life, which we share with other animals, this communication is primarily signification for activities at the level of signs, but the human being also lives at the level of meaning wrought with ambiguity, as Ernst Cassirer and Maurice Merleau-Ponty have argued. This other level is governed by symbols more than signs, of meanings more than signification. At this level, which is a fundamentally social level, the organization of meaning does not only affect life but also constructs new forms of life. Fanon characterized this phenomenon as sociogenesis. Biko explored in more detail its *political* dimensions.

Political phenomena are those governed by discursive opposition. To understand this, one should think about the etymological roots of politics in the *polis* or ancient city-state. Although the term is Greek in origin, the activity is much older. Walls to protect them surrounded ancient cities. This encirclement established a relationship between those within and those without, and in each instance different governing norms emerged. The relation to without is primarily one of war; this relationship within would dissolve the city, since it would be a civil war. It is not possible for people within the city to live without disagreement, however, which means that opposition, short of war (between states), is needed. The shift to the discursive, recognized in ancient times through to the present as "speech," initiated or produced new forms of relations, identities, and ways of life that became known as politics. The question asked by Fanon and Biko (and most modern revolutionaries, but especially so by African ones and their Diaspora) is the role of politics in the context of political formation. In other words, what should one do when the place of discursive opposition has been barred to some people? What should those who live in the city but are structurally outside of it do if they do not accept their place of being insiders who have been pushed outside? Their questions pose the possibility of politics for the sake of establishing political life. It is an activity that is paradoxical. They must do politics in order to establish politics, where politics is recognized according to norms that will always respond to them as illegitimate – as violent – by attempting to change what is already recognized as the discursive limits. Put differently, one group wants to claim benevolence to those whom they dominate, and the other must seize its freedom. Echoing Frederick Douglass, Biko writes:

> We must learn to accept that no group, however benevolent, can ever hand power to the vanquished on a plate. We must accept that the limits of tyrants are prescribed by the endurance of those whom they oppress ... The system concedes nothing without demand, for it formulates its very method of operation on the basis that the ignorant will learn to know, the child will grow into an adult and therefore demands will begin to be made. It gears itself to resist demands in whatever way it sees fit. When you refuse to make these demands and choose to come to a round table to beg for your deliverance, you are asking for the contempt of those who have power over you.
>
> *(Biko, 2002, p. 91)*

We see here, then, a conflict not simply between politics (in the city) and the nonpolitical (beyond the walls of the city), but also about the very notion of politics itself. There are those within the city who are structured as though outside of it, which means the city has to explain why discursive opposition with certain inhabitants is not the continuation of politics instead of the feared attack on social order. Biko's pseudonym "Frank Talk" situated this opposition in Apartheid South Africa: Why was the response to him, as the embodiment of speech, the brutal assertion of the state? His assassination was not simply one of a man but also an effort to suppress an activity and an idea, of political entities outside of the narrow framework of those defined by the state in terms with more political consequences than political activities. In other words, the Apartheid state was not only a war on people of color, it was also a war on politics.

Biko understood this. His genius included rendering politics *Black*. By fusing the Apartheid state's opposition to Blacks with its opposition to politics, he was able to pose a genuinely revolutionary question of social transformation. The question of *citizenship* instead of rule, as Mahmood Mamdani has formulated for the opposition, became a question, as well, that interrogated white legitimacy *in political terms*. I stress political terms here because of the bankruptcy the anti-Apartheid groups found in the assertion of *ethical* terms. Recall that the ethical already presupposed the self/other dialectic. Biko's (and Fanon's) challenge was to show that much had to have been in place for ethics to be the dominating factor. To assert the ethical, consequently, had the effect of presupposing the inherent justice of the political situation when it was circumstance itself that was being brought into question. The political conflict with ethics in this sense, then, is the reality that colonialism has left us with a situation that requires political intervention for ethical life. In Biko's words: "In time we shall be in a position to bestow upon South Africa the greatest gift possible – a more human face" (Biko, 2002, p. 98). What Biko also showed, however, is that such a structure and encomium render politics Black.

Black Consciousness is thus identical with political life, and those who are willing to take on the risk of politics in a context where a state has waged war on politics are, as their opposition mounts, Blackened by such a process. As a political concept, this makes the potential range of Black Consciousness wide enough to mean the collapse of the anti-democratic state. The moving symbol of this was the expansion of that consciousness in Apartheid South Africa and its spilling over into the international community with the consequence of a response that required more than the question of inclusion instead of the construction of *a different state*. The new state, as Fanon would no doubt argue, now faces *its* political struggles, and, as scholars such as Ashwin Desai, Richard Pithouse, and Nigel Gibson have shown, *the poors* have emerged as a new dimension of that struggle in the post-Apartheid government's effort to put the brakes on democratic expansion; a move from possible socialism and de facto liberalism to neoliberalism has brought with it renewed tension between citizenship and rule.

I would like to, at this point, explore further in phenomenological terms the significance of the gift of "a more human face." The phenomenological dimensions of politics are that discursive opposition requires communication that in turn requires intersubjectivity. There is, thus, a social dimension of political life, and much of the oppression has been an effort to bar social life and hence political life to certain groups of people. Phenomenology also demands that one examines consciousness as a lived, embodied reality, not as a floating abstraction. What this means is that consciousness must always be considered as indexical and in the flesh. Speech should not, from this perspective, be considered an expression of consciousness but instead as symbiotically related to the bodies by which, through which, and in which it is made manifest. In human beings, this phenomenon is manifested in our entire bodies, but it is most acutely so in our face and hands, our primary sites of signification, although the entire body is symbolic. It is no accident that oppression often takes the form of forcing its subjects downward, to look down, so their faces cannot be seen, and even where there is nothing they can do, their hands are often tied. In these instances, oppression is an effort to erase the face and eliminate the gesticulating capacity of hands; it is an effort to render a subject speechless. In anti-Black societies, to be Black is to be without a face. This is because only human beings (and presumed equals of human beings) have faces, and Blacks, in such societies, are not fully human beings. By raising the question of Black Consciousness, Biko also raises the question of Black *human beings*, which is considered a contradiction of terms in such societies. A conflict comes to the fore that is similar to the one on politics. Just as the state was shown to have been waging war on politics, and that politics was Black, so, too, one finds a war against the human being, and in it one against humanity, in which looking at the human being in Black face becomes crucial to looking at the human being *as a human being*. This requires transforming the relationship of I–it ("them blacks") to I–You (with Blacks) in which an "us" and a "we" could be considered *from the point of view of Blacks*. When "I" could see being "you," even when it is impossible for me to be identical with you, there is possibility of transparency even at the level of conflict. In effect, the movement is the ethical responsibility of a shared world.

The phenomenology of Black Consciousness suggests, then, that such a consciousness cannot properly function as a negative term of a prior positivity. Its link to the political is such that its opposition would have to be the chimera, appealed to in retreats to neutrality and blindness. Should we consider, for instance, the popular liberal model of cosmopolitanism? The conclusion will be that such claims hold subterranean endorsements of white normativity. This is because white consciousness is not properly a racial consciousness. It is that which does not require its relative term, which means, in effect, that it could simply assert itself, at least in political terms, as consciousness itself. The effect would be an affirmation of status quo conditions through an appeal to an ethics of the self: The cosmopolitanist fails to see, in other words, that politics is at work in the illusion of transcending particularity. To point this out to the cosmopolitanist would constitute an intrusion of the political in the dream world of ethical efficacy. It would mean to Blacken the cosmopolitan world, or, in the suggestive language of Biko's critique, to render it conscious of political reality, to begin its path into Black Consciousness.

We are living in the period of post-Apartheid in South Africa. That is a good thing. What is unfortunate is that the prize has come along with an aggressive assertion at a global level of the kinds of liberalism Biko criticized in *I Write What I Like*. The path of this development has been a world situation in which the war on politics has also returned as forces of destruction have pushed regimes more to the right. As the right-wing in liberal democracies and theocratic states has ascended, the dissolution of civil liberties has been such that political life is in even greater jeopardy. In this global order, Biko's thought has come full circle, where even liberalism finds itself in increasing need of political solutions to political problems and therein faces the possibility of its own Black and hopefully far less naïve Consciousness. As the South African example reveals, neoliberalism has meant the construction of procedural structures that enable, as Mamdani has argued, the shining example of a deracialized state in the sullied interests of a radically unequal and more rigorously racist civil society. In spite of the gripe and anxieties over the Black middle class and small exemplars of Black wealth, which is still more an exception than a rule, in the new South Africa, the fact remains that white South Africans can now benefit from white supremacy without shame in the global arena. The structures that now more rigorously subordinate groups of South Africans in poverty ("the poors") present themselves in ways that at first seem to make Biko's appeal to a *Black* Consciousness problematic. Nevertheless, the Blacks who now represent Blackness in the South African government are clearly not based on Biko's political designation, but the old South African racial designations. The fact remains that the liberalism they exemplify clearly also lacks the political understanding of Black Consciousness that he offered. In effect, they have taken the reins from the whites and have presented a more rigorous means of disarming the political voice of excluded populations.

Biko's critique of liberalism ultimately challenged appeals to blindness. If politics itself is what is at stake in the failure to address Blackness, then there is the ironic conclusion that the contemporary South African state is also an anti-Black one. The places for speech, for protest, avowed by the efforts of a liberal state in the African context, require challenging claims of homogeneity in African societies and the reflexive appeals to a communitarian consciousness. In effect, it means that sites of opposition must be protected, but such communities are genealogically linked to Biko's formulation of Blackness. In effect, the struggle of politics itself has returned. But at this moment, since it is an avowed liberal democracy in power, it now faces the contradictions of its claims. For its claims of transcending the pathologies of many of its neighbors rests on possessing what many of them lack. Some liberalization would be welcomed in central Africa, as Kwame Gyekye and Elias Bongmba have recently argued, but the contemporary South African situation is revealing that such an achievement, if wedded to neoliberal demands for state-level equality and a radically unequal, market-centered economy, brings liberalism in conflict with the political promise it was supposed to exemplify.

Biko did not consider Black Consciousness a fixed category. Whether as the poors or the Blacks, the political itself now faces global challenges that reveal the continued significance of Biko's foresight on the dialectics of its appearance. Freedom continues to demand a face.

NOTE

1 Sebastian de Covarrubias Orozsco, *Tesoro de la lengua* (1611), quoted in, and translated by, David Nirenberg (2007, p. 79).

BIBLIOGRAPHY

Biko, S. B. (2002). *I write what I like: Selected writings* (Ed. with a personal memoir by Aelred Stubbs, Preface by Desmond Tutu, Intro. by Malusi and Thoko Mpumlwana, Foreword by Lewis R. Gordon). Chicago, IL: University of Chicago Press.

Bongmba, E. K. (2006). *The dialectics of transformation in Africa*. New York: Palgrave Macmillan.

Comaroff, J. L., & Comaroff, J. (1991). *Of revelation and revolution (vol. 1): Christianity, colonialism, and consciousness in South Africa*. Chicago, IL: University of Chicago Press.

Comaroff, J. L., & Comaroff, J. (1997). *Of revelation and revolution (vol. 2): The dialectics of modernity on a South African frontier*. Chicago, IL: University of Chicago Press.

Desai, A. (2000a). *The poors of Chatsworth: Race, class and social movements in post-apartheid South Africa*. Durban, SA: Madiba Publishers.

Desai, A. (2000b). *South Africa: Still revolting*. Johannesburg: Impact Africa Publishing.

Desai, A. (2002). *We are the poors: Community struggles in post-apartheid South Africa*. New York: Monthly Review Press.

Dussel, E. (1995). *The invention of the Americas: Eclipse of "the Other" and the myth of modernity*, (Michael. D. Barber, Trans.). New York: Continuum.

Dussel, E. (2003). *Beyond philosophy: Ethics, history, marxism, and liberation theology* (E. Mendieta, Trans. & Ed.). Lanham, MD: Rowman and Littlefield.

Fanon, F. (1963). *The wretched of the Earth* (Constance Farrington, Trans.) (Jean-Paul Sartre, Introduction). New York: Grove Press.

Fanon, F. (1967). *Black skin, White masks* (Charles Lamm Markman, Trans.). New York: Grove Press.

Fanon, F. (2003). *Fanon: The postcolonial imagination*. Cambridge, UK: Polity Press.

Gibson, N. (Ed.). (2005). *Challenging hegemony: Social movements and the quest for a new humanism in post-apartheid South Africa*. Trenton, NJ: Africa World Press.

Gordon, J. A. (2007). The gift of double consciousness: Some obstacles to grasping the contributions of the colonized. In Nalini Persram (Ed.), *Postcolonialism and political theory* (pp. 143–161). Lanham, MD: Lexington Books.

Gordon, L. R. (2000). *Existentia Africana: Understanding Africana existential thought*. New York: Routledge.

Gordon, L. R. (2007). Problematic people and epistemic decolonization: Toward the postcolonial in Africana political thought. In Nalini Persram (Ed.), *Postcolonialism and political theory* (pp. 121–141). Lanham, MD: Lexington Books.

Gordon, L. R. (2008). *An introduction to Africana philosophy*. Cambridge, MA: Cambridge University Press.

Gyeke, K. (1995/1987). *An essay on African philosophical thought: The Akan conceptual scheme* (Rev. ed.). Philadelphia, PA: Temple University Press.

Gyekye, K. (1997). *Tradition and modernity, philosophical reflections on the African experience*. New York and Oxford: Oxford University Press.

Hegel, G. W. F. (1956). *The philosophy of history* (J. Sibree, Trans.; C. J. Friedrich, Introduction). New York: Dover Publications.

Hegel, G. W. F. (1967). *Philosophy of right* (T. M. Knox, Trans.). Oxford: Clarendon.

Hegel, G. W. F. (1979). *Phenomenology of spirit* (A. V. Miller, Trans.). Oxford: Oxford University Press. (Original work published 1807)

Hegel, G. W. F. (1989). *Hegel's science of logic* (A. V. Miller, Trans.). Amherst, NY: Humanity/Prometheus Books.

Maart, R. (1990). *Talk about it*. Stratford, ON: Williams-Wallace Publishers.

Maart, R. (2004). *Rosa's district six*. Toronto, ON: Tsar Publications.

Maart, R. (2006a). *The politics of consciousness, the consciousness of politics: When Black consciousness meets White consciousness, vol. 1, The interrogation of writing*. Guelph, ON: Awomandla Publishers.

Maart, R. (2006b). *The politics of consciousness, the consciousness of politics: When Black consciousness meets White consciousness, vol. 2, The research settings, the interrogation of speech and imagination*. Guelph, ON: Awomandla Publishers.

Mamdani, M. (1996). *Citizen and subject: Contemporary Africa and the legacy of late colonialism*. Princeton, NJ: Princeton University Press.

More, M. P. S. (2004a). Philosophy in South Africa under and after Apartheid. In Wiredu (Ed.), *A companion to African philosophy* (pp. 149–160). Malden, MA: Blackwell Publishers.

More, M. P. S. (2004b). Albert Luthuli, Steve Biko, and Nelson Mandela: The philosophical basis of their thought and practice. In Wiredu (Ed.), *A companion to African philosophy* (pp. 207–215). Malden, MA: Blackwell Publishers.

More, M. P. S. (2004c). Biko: Africana existentialist philosopher. *Alternation, 11*(1), 79–108.

Nirenberg, D. (2007). Race and the middle ages: The case of Spain and its Jews. In Margaret R. Greer, Walter D. Mignolo, & Maueen Quilligan (Eds.), *Rereading the Black legend: The discourses of religious and racial difference in the Renaissance empires* (pp. 71–87). Chicago, IL: University of Chicago Press.

Pithouse, R. (2006). *Asinamali: University struggles in post-Apartheid South Africa*. Trenton, NJ: Africa World Press.

Robinson, C. (2001). *An anthropology of Marxism*. Aldershot, UK: Ashgate.

Roos, N. (2005). *Ordinary springboks: White servicemen and social justice in South Africa, 1939–1961*. Aldershot, UK: Ashgate.

Van Sertima, I. (Ed.). (1992). *Golden age of the Moor*. New Brunswick, NJ: Transaction Publishers.

CHAPTER 16

A PHENOMENOLOGY OF WHITENESS[1]

Sara Ahmed

The field of critical whiteness studies is full of an almost habitual anxiety about what it means to take up the category of "whiteness" as a primary object of knowledge. Richard Dyer for instance admits to being disturbed by the very idea of what he calls white studies: "My blood runs cold at the thought that talking about whiteness could lead to the development of something called 'White Studies'" (1997, p. 10). Or as Fine, Weis, Powell, and Wong describe:

> we worry that in our desire to create spaces to speak, intellectually or empirically, about whiteness, we may have reified whiteness as a fixed category of experience; that we have allowed it to be treated as a monolith, in the singular, as an "essential something."
>
> *(1997, p. xi)*

Does speaking about whiteness allow it to become an "essential something"? If whiteness gains currency by being unnoticed, then what does it mean to notice whiteness? What does making the invisible marks of privilege more visible actually do? Could whiteness studies produce an attachment to whiteness by holding it in place as an object? Such questions are addressed by scholars not in order to suspend the project of whiteness studies, but to consider what it means for a project of critique to be complicit with its object.

We could say that any project that aims to dismantle or challenge the categories that are made invisible through privilege is bound to participate in the object of its critique. We might even expect such projects to fail, and be prepared to witness this failure as productive. And yet, we can get stuck in this position, endlessly caught up in describing what we are doing to whiteness, rather than what whiteness is doing. In this chapter I want to consider whiteness as a category of experience that disappears as a category through experience, and how this disappearance makes whiteness "worldly." To put this simply, what I offer here is a vocabulary for re-describing how whiteness becomes "worldly." Whiteness describes the very "what" that coheres as a world. My aim is not to bypass the risk of reifying the category of whiteness, but to re-locate that risk, so that it is not seen as originating with "our desire to create spaces to speak, intellectually or empirically to speak about whiteness" (Fine et al., 1997, p. xi), which is not in any way to dismiss this concern. We can consider how whiteness becomes worldly as an effect of reification. Reification is not then something we do to whiteness, but something whiteness does, or to be more precise, what allows whiteness to be done.

In this chapter, I re-pose the question of whiteness as a phenomenological issue, as a question of how whiteness is lived as a background to experience. In so doing, I will consider what "whiteness" does without assuming whiteness as an ontological given, but as that which has been received, or become given, over time. Whiteness could be described as an ongoing and unfinished history, which orientates bodies in specific directions, affecting how they "take up" space. In formulating my argument, I follow the work of Frantz Fanon, and also philosophers who have sought to offer a "phenomenology of race," such as David Macey (1999), Linda Martin Alcoff (1999), and Lewis R. Gordon (1995, 1999).[2] Within this literature, a starting point is the refutation of nominalism and the idea that race does

DOI: 10.4324/9781003037132-16

not exist, or is not real. Such philosophers would certainly accept that race is "invented" by science *as if it was* a property of bodies, or of groups. But they also show that it does not follow from such a critique that race does not exist. Phenomenology helps us to show how whiteness is an effect of racialization, which in turn shapes what it is that bodies "can do."

ORIENTATIONS

We can begin by considering how whiteness involves a form of orientation. If we start with the point of orientations, we find that orientations are about starting points. As Husserl describes in the second volume of *Ideas*:

> If we consider the characteristic way in which the Body presents itself and do the same for things, then we find the following situation: each Ego has its own domain of perceptual things and necessarily perceives the things in a certain orientation. The things appear and do so from this or that side, and in this mode of appearing is included irrevocably a relation to a here and its basic directions.
>
> *(1989, p. 166)*

Orientations are about how we begin, how we proceed from "here." Husserl relates the questions of "this or that side" to the point of "here," which he also describes as the zero-point of orientation, the point from which the world unfolds, and which makes what is "there" over "there." It is from this point that the differences between "this side" and "that side" matter. It is also only given that we are "here" at this point, that near and far are lived as relative markers of distance. Alfred Schutz and Thomas Luckmann also describe orientation as a question of one's starting point: "The place in which I find myself, my actual "here," is the starting point for my orientation in space" (1974, p. 36). The starting point for orientation is the point from which the world unfolds: The "here" of the body and the "where" of its dwelling. Given this, orientations are about the intimacy of bodies and their dwelling places.

If orientations are about how we begin from "here," then they are a point of unfolding. At what point does the world unfold? Or at what point does Husserl's world unfold? Let's start where he starts, in his first volume of *Ideas*, which is with the world as it is given "from the natural standpoint." Such a world is the world we are "in," where things take place around me, and are placed around me: "I am aware of a world, spread out in space endlessly" (1969, p. 101). Phenomenology asks us to be aware of the "what" that is "around." The world that is "around" has already taken certain shapes, as the very form of what is "more and less" familiar. As Husserl describes:

> For me real objects are there, definite, more or less familiar, agreeing with what is actually perceived without being themselves perceived or even intuitively present. I can let my attention wander from the writing-table I have just seen or observed, through the unseen portions of the room behind my back to the veranda into the garden, to the children in the summer house, and so forth, to all the objects concerning which I precisely "know" that they are there and yonder in my immediate co-perceived surroundings.
>
> *(1969, p. 101)*

The familiar world begins with the writing-table, which is in "the room." We can name this room as Husserl's study, as the room in which he writes. *It is from here that the world unfolds.* He begins with the writing-table, and then turns to other parts of this room, those which are, as it were, behind him. We are reminded that what he can see in the first place depends on which way he is facing. In Husserl's writing the familiar slides into the familial; the home is a family home as a residence that is inhabited by children. In a way, the children who are "yonder" point to what is made available through memory, or even habitual knowledge: They are sensed as being there, behind him, even if they are not seen by him at this moment in time. The family home provides, as it were, the background against which an object (the writing-table) appears in the present, in front of him. The family home is only ever *co-perceived*, and allows the philosopher to do his work.

By reading the objects that appear in Husserl's writing, we get a sense of how being directed towards some objects and not others involves a more general orientation towards the world. The direction you face is not simply casual: The fact that Husserl faces the writing-table is a sign of his occupation.[3] So Husserl's gaze might fall on the paper, which is on the table, given that he is sitting at the desk, the writing-table, and not at another kind of table, such as the kitchen table. Such other tables would not, perhaps, be the "right" kind of tables for the making of philosophy. The writing-table might be the table "for him," the one that would provide the right kind of horizontal surface for the philosopher. As Ann Banfield observes "Tables and chairs, things nearest to hand for the sedentary philosopher, who comes to occupy chairs of philosophy, are the furniture of that 'room of one's own' from which the real world is observed" (2000, p. 66). Tables are "near to hand," along with chairs, as the furniture that secures the very "place" of philosophy. The use of tables shows us the very orientation of philosophy in part by showing us what is proximate to the body of the philosopher, or "what" the philosopher comes into contact "with."

What you come into contact with is shaped by what you do: Bodies are orientated when they are occupied in time and space. Bodies are shaped by this contact with objects. What gets near is both shaped by what bodies do, and in turn affects what bodies can do. The nearness of the philosopher to his paper, his ink, and his table is not simply about "where" he does his work, and the spaces he inhabits, as if the "where" could be separated from "what" he does. The "what" that he does is what puts certain objects within reach, just as it keeps other things in the background. What comes into view, or what is within our horizon, is not a matter of what we find here or there, or even where we find ourselves, as we move here or there. What is reachable is determined precisely by orientations we have already taken. Or we could say that orientations are about the directions we take that put some things and not others in our reach.

WHITENESS AS AN ORIENTATION

How then does whiteness involve orientation? We can turn to Frantz Fanon's work, which directly addresses the question of the relation between phenomenology and race. Take the following description:

> And then the occasion arose when I had to meet the white man's eyes. An unfamiliar weight burdened me. The real world challenged my claims. In the white world the man of color encounters difficulties in the development of his bodily schema. Consciousness of the body is solely a negating activity. It is a third-person consciousness. The body is surrounded by an atmosphere of certain uncertainty. I know that if I want to smoke, I shall have to reach out my right arm and take the pack of cigarettes lying at the other end of the table. The matches, however, are in the drawer on the left, and I shall have to lean back slightly. And all these movements are made not out of habit, but out of implicit knowledge.
>
> *(Fanon, 1986, pp. 110–11)*

Fanon is describing what seems to be a casual scene. By speculating on what he would have to do if he wants to smoke, Fanon describes his body as ready for action. The feeling of desire, in this case, the desire to smoke, leads the body to reach towards "the other end of the table," in order to grasp an object. Such a performance is an orientation towards the future, insofar as the action is also the expression of a wish or intention. As Fanon suggests, bodies do this work, or they have this capacity to work, only given the familiarity of the world they inhabit: To put it simply, they know where to find things. "Doing things" depends not so much on intrinsic capacity, or even upon dispositions or habits, but on the ways in which the world is available as a space for action, a space where things "have a certain place" or are "in place." We do not have to think where to find such objects; our knowledge is implicit, and we reach towards them without hesitation. Losing things, for this reason, can lead to moments of existential crisis: We expect to find "it" there, as an expectation that directs an action, and if "it" is not there, we might even worry that we are losing our minds, along with our possessions. Objects extend bodies, for sure, but they also seem to measure the competence of bodies, and their capacity to "find their way."

And yet, Fanon implies that this scene is far from casual. Sure, he might find the cigarettes, and the matches, although as we can see, he does not simply happen upon them. This example is not really about a happening. It follows, after all, an extraordinary claim. The claim takes the form of an argument with phenomenology. As he puts it later on this page:

> Below the corporeal schema I had sketched out a historic-racial schema. The elements that I used had been provided for me not by "residual sensations and perceptions primarily of a tactile, vestibular, kinaesthetic, and visual character," but by the other, the white man, who had woven me out of a thousand details.
>
> *(Fanon, 1986, p. 111)*[4]

In other words, Fanon is suggesting that attending to the corporeal schema is not sufficient, as it is not made up of the right kind of elements. Where phenomenology attends to the tactile, vestibular, kinaesthetic, and visual character of embodied reality, Fanon asks us to think of the "historic-racial" schema which is "below it." In other words, the racial and historical dimensions are beneath the surface of the body described by phenomenology, which becomes, by virtue of its own orientation, a way of thinking the body that has surface appeal.

For the Black man, Fanon implies, we have to look beyond the surface. He writes:

> I could no longer laugh, because I already knew that there were legends, stories, history, and above all *historicity*, which I had learnt about from Jaspers. Then, assailed at various points, the corporeal scheme crumbled, *its place taken by the racial epidermal schema.*
>
> *(1986, p. 112, second emphasis mine)*

Clearly, then Fanon's example of what he would do if he wanted to smoke, which is an example of being orientated towards an object, is a description of a body-at-home, a body that extends into space through how it reaches towards objects that are already "in place." Being in place, or having a place, involves the intimacy of co-inhabiting spaces with other things.

Fanon's example shows the body *before* it is racialized or made Black by becoming the object of the hostile white gaze. In this sense, for Fanon, race "interrupts" the corporeal schema. Alternatively, we could say that "the corporeal schema" is already racialized; in other words, race does not just interrupt such a schema, but structures its mode of operation. The corporeal schema is of a "body-at-home." If the world is made white, then the body-at-home is one that can inhabit whiteness. As Fanon's work shows, after all, bodies are shaped by histories of colonialism, which makes the world "white," a world that is inherited, or which is already given before the point of an individual's arrival. This is the familiar world, the world of whiteness, as a world we know implicitly. Colonialism makes the world "white," which is of course a world "ready" for certain kinds of bodies, as a world that puts certain objects within their reach. Bodies remember such histories, even when we forget them. Such histories, we might say, surface on the body, or even shape how bodies surface (see Ahmed, 2004a). Race then does become a social as well as bodily given, or what we *receive* from others as an inheritance of this history.

It is useful to recall that inheritance is crucial to the Marxist conception of history. For Marx, although we "make history," this making is shaped by inheritance: "Human beings make their own history, but they do not make it arbitrarily in conditions chosen by themselves, but in conditions always-already given and inherited from the past" (cited in Balibar, 2002, p. 8). If the conditions in which we live are inherited from the past, they are "passed down" not only in blood or in genes, *but also through the work or labour of generations.* The "passing" of history is composed of social, as well as material, ways of organizing the world that shape the materials out of which life is made, and which shapes the very "matter" of bodies. If history is made "out of" what is passed down, as the conditions in which we live, then history is made out of what is given not only in the sense of that which is "always-already" there, *before our own arrival*, but in the active sense of the gift: History is a gift given.

Such an inheritance can be re-thought in terms of orientations: *We inherit the reachability of some objects*, those that are "given" to us, or at least made available to us, within the "what" that is around. I am not suggesting here that "whiteness" is one such "reachable object," but that whiteness is an orientation that puts certain things within reach. By objects, we would include not just physical objects, but also styles, capacities, aspirations, techniques, habits. In putting certain things in reach, a world acquires its shape; the white world is a world orientated "around" whiteness precisely at the point where whiteness disappears from view. This world too is "inherited" as a dwelling: It is a world shaped by colonial histories, which affect not simply how maps are drawn (as lines on the ground that direct action), but the kinds of orientations we have towards objects and others. Race becomes, in this model, a question of what is within reach, what is available to perceive and to do "things" with.

The world too is inherited as a dwelling. Whiteness might be what is "here," as a point from which the world unfolds, which is also the point of inheritance. If whiteness is inherited, then it is also reproduced. Whiteness gets reproduced by being seen as a form of positive residence: As if it was a property of persons, cultures, and places. Whiteness becomes, you could even say, "like itself," as a form of family resemblance. It is no accident that race has been understood through familial metaphors in the sense that "races" come to be seen as having "shared ancestry" (Fenton, 2003, p. 2). Race in this model "extends" the family form; other members of the race are "like a family," just as the family is defined in racial terms. The analogy works powerfully to produce a particular version of race *and* a particular version of family, predicated on "likeness," where likeness becomes a matter of "shared attributes." The primary trace of a familial connection is after all resemblance: We assume resemblance is a sign of a connection (although how that connection is described or explained involves different kinds of knowledge). So we might say "she looks like her sister," "she has her father's nose," and so on: The desire for likeness imagines bodies as having the same features, as if the gift of life is the giving of an attribute. The desire for connection generates likeness, at the same time as likeness is read as evidence of a connection. As Steve Fenton puts it, "People or places do not just possess cultures of shared ancestry; they elaborate these into the idea of a community founded upon these attributes" (2003, p. 3). We can make an even stronger claim: It is the idea of community as "being-in-common" that generates "shared attributes," which are then *retrospectively* taken up as evidence of community.

What does it mean for attributes to be shared? Whilst sharing is often described as participation in something (we share this or that thing, or we have this or that thing in common), and even as the joy of taking part, sharing also involves division, or the ownership of *parts*. To have a share in something is to be invested in the value of that thing. The word itself we might note comes from the Old English word *scearu*, which refers to cutting or division. So the word "share" which seems to point to commonality depends on both cutting and division, where things are cut up and distributed amongst others.

In everyday talk about such family connections, likeness is a sign of inheritance; *to look like a family is to "look alike."* I want to suggest another way of thinking about the relationship between inheritance and likeness: We inherit proximities (and hence orientations) as our point of entry into a familial space, as "a part" of a new generation. Such an inheritance in turn generates "likeness." This argument builds upon my claim in *The Cultural Politics of Emotion* (2004a), where I suggest that likeness is an *effect* of proximity or contact, which is then "taken up" as a sign of inheritance. Here, I would also argue that likeness is an effect of proximity, rather than its cause, with an additional claim: We inherit proximities, although this is an inheritance that can be refused and which does not fully determine a course of action. To suggest that we inherit proximities is also to point to how that past that is "behind" our arrival restricts as well as enables human action: If we are shaped by "what" we come into contact with, then we are also shaped by what we inherit, which delimits the objects that we might come into contact with.

I would not wish to dismiss the discourse of "family resemblance," but to offer a different account of its powerful function as a legislative device. One of the sayings that has always spoken to me is "like two peas in a pod." Anyone who has shelled peas would know, of course, that peas are not only alike and that seeing them as being alike is already to overlook some important differences. But it's the pod and not the peas that interests me here. This saying suggests for me that likeness is as an effect of *the proximity of shared residence.* This is not just an argument about nurture over nature (that the pod is a nurturing device), as this way of thinking relies on an overly simple logic of causality (the pod causes the peas). Rather the very proximity of pea to pea, as well the intimacy of the dwelling, which surrounds them like a skin, shapes the very form of the peas. Likeness is not then "in" the peas, let alone "in" the pod, but is an effect of their contiguity, of how they are touched by each other and envelop each other. Or if we say that the peas "share" the pod, then we can immediately see how the "pod" does not simply generate what is "shared" in the sense of what is in common, but also what gets divided or distributed into parts.

In the case of race, we would say that bodies come to be seen as "alike," as for instance "sharing whiteness" as a "characteristic," as an effect of such proximities, where certain "things" are already "in place." The familial is in a way like the "pod," as a shared space of dwelling, in which things are shaped by their proximity to other things. "The familial" is after all about "the familiar": This is the world we implicitly know, as a world that is organized in specific ways. It is the world Fanon speaks of when he describes the "implicit knowledge" we might have of "where things are," as a knowledge that is exercised by orientations towards objects. Objects are familiar, for sure, but familiarity is also about our capacity to use objects, how they are within reach as objects we do things with. To think of this implicit knowledge as inherited is to think about how we inherit a relation to place and to placement: At home, things are not done a certain way, but the domestic "puts things" in their place. Whiteness is inherited through the very placement of things.

HABIT WORLDS

Fanon talks about the "white world" by describing how it feels to inhabit that world "without" a white body. The world, we might say, extends the form of some bodies more than others, and such bodies in turn then feel at home in this world. We could even describe whiteness as a bad habit, which is what allows certain bodies to feel at home. We can explore here how public spaces take shape through the habitual actions of bodies, such that the contours of space could be described as habitual. I turn to the concept of habits to theorize not so much how bodies acquire their shape, but how spaces acquire the shape of the bodies that "inhabit" them. We could think about the "habit" in the "in-habit."

We need to examine not only how bodies become white, or fail to do so, but also how spaces can take on the very "qualities" that are given to such bodies. In a way, we can think about the habitual as a form of inheritance. It is not so much that we inherit habits, although we can do so: Rather the habitual can be thought of as a bodily and spatial form of inheritance. As Pierre Bourdieu (1977) shows us, we can link habits to what is unconscious, and routine, or what becomes "second nature."[5] To describe whiteness as a habit, as second nature, is to suggest that whiteness is what bodies do, where the body takes the shape of the action. Habits are not "exterior" to bodies, as things can be "put on" or "taken off." If habits are about what bodies do, in ways that are repeated, then they might also shape what bodies *can do*. For Merleau-Ponty, the habitual body is a body that acts in the world, where actions bring other things near. As he puts it:

> my body appears to me as an attitude directed towards a certain existing or possible task. And indeed its spatiality is not, like that of external objects or like that of "spatial sensations," a *spatiality of position*, but a *spatiality of situation*. If I stand in front of my desk and lean on it with both hands, only my hands are stressed and the whole of the body trails behind them like the tail of a comet. It is not that I am unaware of the whereabouts of my shoulder or back, but these are simply swallowed up in the position of my hands, and my whole posture can be read so to speak in the pressure they exert on the table.
>
> *(Merleau-Ponty, 2002, p. 115, emphasis original)*

Here, the directedness of the body towards an action (which we have discovered also means an orientation towards certain kinds of objects) is how the body "appears."[6] The body is "habitual" not only in the sense that it performs actions repeatedly, but in the sense that when it performs such actions, *it does not command attention*, apart from at the "surface" where it "encounters" an external object (such as the hands that lean on the desk or table, which feel the "stress" of the action). In other words, the body is habitual insofar as it "trails behind" in the performing of action, insofar as it does not pose "a problem" or an obstacle to the action, or is not "stressed" by "what" the action encounters. For Merleau-Ponty, the habitual body "does not get in the way of an action": It is *behind the action*.

I want to suggest here that whiteness could be understood as "the behind." If whiteness is behind an action, then it is reproduced precisely through not having our attention. White bodies are habitual insofar as they "trail behind" actions: They do not get "stressed" in their encounters with objects or others, as their whiteness "goes unnoticed." Whiteness would be what lags behind; white bodies do not have to face their whiteness; they are not orientated "towards" it, and this "not" is what allows whiteness to cohere, as that which bodies are orientated around. When bodies "lag behind" actions, they extend their reach (Merleau-Ponty, 2002, p. 166).

It becomes possible to talk about the whiteness of space given the very accumulation of such "points" of extension. Spaces acquire the "skin" of the bodies that inhabit them. What is important to note here is that it is not just bodies that are orientated. Spaces also take shape by being orientated around some bodies, more than others. We can also consider "institutions" as orientation devices, which take the shape of "what" resides within them. After all, institutions provide collective or public spaces. When we describe institutions as "being" white (institutional whiteness), we are pointing to how institutional spaces are shaped by the proximity of some bodies and not others: White bodies gather, and cohere to form the edges of such spaces. When I walk into university meetings, that is just what I encounter. Sometimes I get used to it. At one conference we organize, four Black feminists arrive. They all happen to walk into the room at the same time. Yes, we do notice such arrivals. The fact that we notice such arrivals tells us more about what is already in place than it does about "who" arrives. Someone says: "it is like walking into a sea of whiteness." This phrase comes up, and it hangs in the air. The speech act becomes an object, which gathers us around.

So yes, they walk into the room, and I notice that they were not there before, as a retro-spective reoccupation of a space that I already inhabited. I look around, and re-encounter the sea of whiteness. As many have argued, whiteness is invisible and unmarked, as the absent centre against which others appear only as deviants, or points of deviation (Dyer, 1997; Frankenberg, 1993). Whiteness is only invisible for those who inhabit it, or those who get so used to its inhabitance that they learn not to see it, even when they are not it (see Ahmed, 2004b). As Nirmal Puwar puts it in *Space Invaders* (2004) white bodies are somatic norms that make non-white bodies feel "out of place" within certain spaces, like strangers. Spaces are orientated "around" whiteness, insofar as whiteness is not seen. We do not face whiteness; it "trails behind" bodies, as what is assumed to be given. The effect of this "around whiteness" is the institutionalization of a certain "likeness" which makes non-white bodies feel uncomfortable, exposed, visible, different, when they take up this space.

The institutionalization of whiteness involves work: The institution comes to have a body as an effect of this work. It is important that we do not reify institutions by presum-ing they are simply given and that they decide what we do. Rather, institutions become given, as an effect of the repetition of decisions made over time, which shapes the surface of institutional spaces. Institutions involve the accumulation of past decisions about how to allocate resources, as well as "who" to recruit. Recruitment functions as a technology for the reproduction of whiteness. We can recall that Althusser's model of ideology is based on recruitment:

> ideology "acts" or "functions" in such a way that it "recruits" subjects among the individu-als (it recruits them all), or "transforms" the individuals into subjects (it transforms them all) by the very precise operation which I have called *interpellation* or hailing, and which can be imagined along the lines of the most commonplace everyday police (or other) hailing: "Hey you there."
>
> *(1971, p. 163, emphasis original)*

The subject is recruited by turning around, which immediately associates recruitment with following a direction, as the direction that takes the line of an address. To recruit can suggest both to renew and to restore. The act of recruitment, of bringing new bodies in, restores the body of the institution, which depends on gathering bodies to cohere as a body. Becoming a "part" of an institution, which we can consider the demand to share in it, or even have a share of it, hence requires not only that one inhabits its buildings but also that we follow its line: We might start by saying "we"; by mourning its failures and rejoicing in its successes; by reading the documents that circulate within it, creating vertical and horizontal lines of communication; by the chance encounters we have with those who share its grounds. To be recruited is not only to join but to sign up to a specific institution: To inhabit it *by turning around as a return of its address.*

Furthermore, recruitment creates the very ego ideal of the institution, what it imagines as the ideal that working "at" the institution means working towards or even what it imagines expresses its "character."[7] When we begin to think about the institutionalization of whiteness,[8] we are asking how whiteness becomes the ego ideal of an organization. As scholars in critical management studies have shown us, organizations "tend to recruit in their own image" (Singh, 2002). The "hey you" is not just addressed to anybody: Some bodies more than others are recruited, those that can inherit the "character" of the organization, by returning its image with a reflection that reflects back that image, what we could call a "good likeness." It is not just that there is a desire for whiteness that leads to white bodies getting in. Rather whiteness is what the institution is orientated "around," so that even bodies that might not appear white still have to inhabit whiteness, if they are to get "in."

Institutions too involve orientation devices which keep things in place. The affect of such placement could be described as a form of comfort. To be orientated, or to be at home in the world, is also to feel a certain comfort: We might only notice comfort as an affect when we lose it, when we become uncomfortable. The word "comfort" suggests well-being and satisfaction, but it can also suggest an ease and easiness. Comfort is about an encounter between more than one body, which is the promise of a "sinking" feeling. To be comfortable is to be so at ease with one's environment that it is hard to distinguish where one's body ends and the world begins. One fits, and by fitting, the surfaces of bodies disappear from view. White bodies are comfortable *as they inhabit spaces that extend their shape.* The bodies and spaces "point" towards each other, as a "point" that is not seen as it is also "the point" from which we see.

In other words, whiteness may function as a form of public comfort *by allowing bodies to extend into spaces that have already taken their shape.* Those spaces are lived as comfortable, as they allow bodies to fit in; the surfaces of social space are already impressed upon by the shape of such bodies. We can think of the chair beside the table. It might acquire its shape by the repetition of some bodies inhabiting it: We can almost see the shape of bodies as "impressions" on the surface. So spaces extend bodies and bodies extend spaces. The impressions of the surface function as traces of such extensions. The surfaces of social as well as bodily space "record" the repetition of acts, and the "passing by" of some and not others.

It can be problematic to describe whiteness as something we "pass through": Such an argument could make whiteness into something substantive, as if whiteness has an ontological force of its own, which compels us, and even "drives" action. It is important to remember that whiteness is not reducible to white skin, or even to "something" we can have or be, even if we pass through whiteness. When we talk about a "sea of whiteness" or "white space" we are talking about the repetition of the passing by of some bodies and not others, for sure. But non-white bodies do inhabit white spaces; we know this. Such bodies are made invisible when we see spaces as being white, at the same time as they become hyper-visible when they do not pass, which means they "stand out" and "stand apart," like the black sheep in the family home. You learn to fade in the background, but sometimes you can't or you don't. The moments when the body appears "out of place" are moments of political and personal trouble. As Nirmal Puwar (2004) shows us, when bodies arrive who seem "out of place" in such institutional worlds, we have a process of *disorientation*: People blink and look again. The proximity of such bodies makes familiar spaces seem strange: "People are 'thrown' because a whole world view is jolted" (Puwar, 2004, p. 43).

Bodies stand out when they are out of place. Such standing re-confirms the whiteness of the space. Whiteness is an effect of what coheres rather than the origin of coherence. The effect of repetition is not then simply about a body count: It is not simply a matter of how many bodies are "in." Rather what is repeated is a very style of embodiment, a way of inhabiting space, which claims space *by the accumulation of gestures of "sinking" into that space*. If whiteness allows bodies to move with comfort through space, and to inhabit the world as if it was home, then those bodies take up more space. This extension of white motility should not be confused with freedom. To move easily is not to move freely, and it is still a way of constraining what bodies do "do." Bodies that are not restricted by racism, or by other technologies for ensuring spaces are given to some rather than others, are bodies that don't have to come up against the limitations of this fantasy of mobility. Such bodies are both shaped by motility, *and may even take the shape of that motility*.

It is here that we can begin to complicate the relationship between motility and what I call "institutional lines." Some bodies, even those that pass as white, might still be "out of line" with the institutions they inhabit. After all, institutions are meeting points, but they are also where different "lines" intersect, where lines cross with other lines, to create and divide spaces. We can recall here the importance of "intersectionality" to Black feminist theory. Given that relationships of power "intersect," how we inhabit a given category depends on how we inhabit others (Brewer, 1993; Collins, 1998; Lorde, 1984; Smith, 1998). There are "points" in such intersections, as the "points" where lines meet. A body is such a meeting point. To follow one line (say whiteness) will not necessarily get you too many points, if you do not or cannot follow others. How you can move along institutional lines is affected by other lines that you follow. What happens in these "points" of intersection – whether we are knocked off course if we do not follow a given line – might not be determined before we arrive at that point, and might also depend on what else is behind us.

In a way, whiteness itself is a straightening device: Bodies disappear into the "sea of whiteness" when they "line up." This is not to make "the fit" between bodies and spaces natural: White bodies can line up, only if they pass, by approximating whiteness, by "being like." To say that all bodies have to pass as white is not to neutralize the difference between bodies. Whiteness is also a matter of what is behind, as a form of inheritance, which affects how bodies arrive in spaces and worlds. We accumulate behinds, just as what is behind is an effect of past accumulations. Some of us have more behind us than others at the very moment in which we arrive into the world. If you inherit class privilege, for instance, then you have more resources behind you, which can be converted into capital, into what can "propel" you forward and up. Becoming white as an institutional line is closely related to the vertical promise of class mobility: You can move up only by approximating the habitus of the white bourgeois body (see Skeggs, 2003). Moving "up," requires inhabiting such a body, or at least approximating its style, whilst your capacity to inhabit such a body depends upon what is behind you. Pointing to this loop between the "behind" and the "up" is another way of describing how hierarchies get reproduced over time.

We could say that bodies "move up" when their whiteness is not in dispute. And yet, whiteness does not always lag behind in the temporality of a life course. When someone's whiteness is in dispute, then they come under "stress," which in turn threatens bodily motility, or what the body "can do." We could consider, for instance, how Husserl's phenomenology seems to involve an ease of movement, of being able to occupy the space around the table. Perhaps we could also see this mobile body as a body that "can do" things, in terms of whiteness. This is not to locate such whiteness *in* the body of the philosopher. Husserl's biography might indeed help us here. For when Husserl's whiteness came into dispute, when he was read as being Jewish, he literally lost his chair: He temporarily lost the public recognition of his place as a philosopher.[9] It is no accident that such recognition is symbolically given through an item of furniture: To take up space is to be given an object, which allows the body to be occupied in a certain way. The philosopher must have his seat, after all. If we say that phenomenology is about whiteness, in the sense that it has been written from this "point of view," as a point that is "forgotten," then what phenomenology describes is not so much white bodies, but the ways in which bodies come to feel at home in spaces by being orientated in this way and that, where such bodies are not "points" of stress or what we can call stress points. To make this point very simply: Whiteness becomes a social and bodily orientation given that some bodies will be more at home in a world that is orientated around whiteness. If we began instead with disorientation, *with the body that loses its chair*, then the descriptions we offer will be quite different.

BEING NOT

We might say that Frantz Fanon begins with a body that has lost its chair. Rather than objects securing his place, his body becomes an object alongside other objects. The experience is one of nausea and the crisis of losing one's place in the world, as a loss of something that you have not been given. For the Black man, consciousness of the body is "third person consciousness" and the feeling is one of negation (Fanon, 1986, p. 110). To feel negated is to feel pressure upon your bodily surface; your body feels the pressure point as a restriction in what it can do. As Lewis Gordon suggests in his critique of Hegel, "White people are universal, it is said and Black people are not" (1999, p. 34). If to be human is to be white, then to be not white is to inhabit the negative: It is to be "not." The pressure of this "not" is another way of describing the social and existential realities of racism.

If Merleau-Ponty's model of the body in *Phenomenology of Perception* is about "motility," expressed in the hopefulness of the utterance, "I can," Fanon's phenomenology of the Black body would be better described in terms of the bodily and social experience of restriction, uncertainty, and blockage, or perhaps even in terms of the despair of the utterance, "I can not." The Black man, in becoming an object, no longer acts or extends himself; instead, he is amputated, losing his body (Fanon, 1986, p. 112). In a way, Merleau-Ponty describes the body as "successful," as being "able" to extend itself (through objects) in order to act on and in the world. Fanon helps us to expose this "success" not as a measure of competence, but as the bodily form of privilege: The ability to move through the world without losing one's way. To be Black in "the white world" is to turn back towards itself, to become an object, which means not only not being extended by the contours of the world, but being diminished as an effect of the bodily extensions of others.

For bodies that are not extended by the skin of the social, bodily movement is not so easy. Such bodies are stopped, where the stopping is an action that creates its own impressions. Who are you? Why are you here? What are you doing? Each question, when asked, is a kind of *stopping device*: You are stopped by being asked the question, just as asking the question requires you to be stopped. A phenomenology of "being stopped" might take us in a different direction than one which begins with motility, with a body that "can do" by flowing into space.

To stop involves many meanings: To cease, to end, and also to cut off, to arrest, to check, to prevent, to block, to obstruct, or to close. Black activism has shown us how policing involves a differential economy of stopping: Some bodies more than others are "stopped," by being the subject of the policeman's address. The "hey you" is not here addressed to the body that can inherit the ego ideal of an organization or who can be recruited to follow a given line but to the body who cannot be recruited, to the body that is "out of place" in this place. In other words, the "unrecruitable" body must still be "recruited" into this place, in part through the very repetition of the action of "being stopped" as a mode of address. The "stop and search" is, of course, a technology of racism, as we know. The stop and search does not always stop there: The search itself can be extended by practices of indefinite detention. Stopping is both a political economy, which is distributed unevenly between others, and an affective economy, which leaves its impressions, affecting those bodies that are subject to its address.

How does it feel to be stopped? Being stopped is not just stressful: It makes the "body" itself the "site" of social stress. Let me use a recent example of being stopped:

> I arrive in New York, clutching my British passport. I hand it over. He looks at me, and then looks at my passport. I know what questions will follow. "Where are you from?" My passport indicates my place of birth. "Britain," I say. I feel like adding, "can't you read. I was born in Salford" but I stop myself. He looks down at my passport, not at me. "Where is your father from?" It was the same last time I arrived in New York. It is the question I get asked now, which seems to locate what is suspect not in my body, but as that which has been passed down the family line, almost like a bad inheritance. "Pakistan," I say, slowly. "Do you have a Pakistani passport." No, I say. Eventually, he lets me through. The name "Ahmed," a Muslim name, slows me down. It blocks my passage, even if only temporarily. I get stuck, and then move on. When I fly out of New York later that week, I am held up again. This time it is a friendlier encounter. I find out I am now on the "no fly list," and they have to ring to get permission to let me through. It takes time, of course. "Don't worry," he says, "my mother is on it too." I feel some strange comradeship with his mother. I know what he is saying: he means "anyone" could be on this list, almost as if to say "even my mother," whose innocence of course would be beyond doubt. I know it's a way of saying, "it's not about you. Don't take it personally." It isn't about me of course. And yet it involves me. My name names me after all. It might not be personal, but nor is about "anyone." It is my name that slows me down.

For some bodies, the "passport" is an object that extends motility, and allows you to pass through borders. For others, such "passports" do not work in this way. Instead, they turn the gaze onto you, as a suspicious body, or even a "could be terrorist" (see Ahmed, 2004a). Movement for some involves blocking movement for others.[10] If the nationality of the passport does not seem to follow the line of the name, and such judgements exercise histories of normative thinking, then the body is suspect. We can see here that the experience of being "held up" is not simply a delay or postponement, followed by starting up, or moving on. Rather "being held up" shifts one's orientation; it turns one's attention back to oneself, as one's body does not "trail behind," but catches you out.

In the encounter I describe at the borders of New York City, I become a stranger, again, made strange by the name I have been given. In everyday language, a stranger would be anybody we do not know. When we don't recognize someone, then they are a stranger. In *Strange Encounters*, I suggested an alternative model: I suggest that we recognize some people *as* strangers, and that "some bodies" more than others are recognizable as strangers, as bodies that are "out of place" (Ahmed, 2000). The stranger has a place by being "out of place" at home. The technologies for telling the difference between friends and strangers suggest that this distinction is not only practical, but is transformed into an ethics, whereby the proximity of the stranger is seen to risk the very "life" of the family/ community and nation. Such proximity is required to institute the right to defense.

Not all those at the borders, such as tourists, migrants, or foreign nationals are recognized as strangers; some will seem more "at home" than others, some will pass through, with their passports extending physical motility into social mobility. There is no question posed about their origin. The stranger's genealogy in contrast is always suspect. The stranger becomes a stranger because of some trace of a dubious origin. Having the "right" passport makes no difference if you have the wrong body or name: And indeed, the stranger with the "right" passport might cause particular trouble, as the one who risks passing through, or passing by. The discourse of "stranger danger" reminds us that "danger" is often posited as originating from what is outside the community, or as coming from outsiders, those people who are not "at home," and who themselves have come from "somewhere elsewhere" (the "where" of this "elsewhere" always makes a difference). The politics of mobility, of who gets to move with ease across the lines that divide spaces can be re-described as the politics of who gets to be at home, who gets to inhabit spaces, as spaces that are inhabitable for some bodies and not others, insofar as they extend the surfaces of some bodies and not others.

Those who get stopped are *moved in a different way*. I have suggested that my name slows me down. A Muslim name. We might note that the name itself becomes a "bad inheritance." Names are passed down, we know, in different ways. I was given my father's name, as a name which extends the paternal line. But it is a name that connects me to my Pakistani side. We can see from this example that if we do inherit habits, we can also inherit what fails to become habitual: To inherit a Muslim name, in the West, is to inherit the impossibility of a body that can "trail behind," or even to inherit the impossibility of extending the body's reach. For the body recognized as "could be Muslim," the experience begins with discomfort: Spaces we occupy do not "extend" the surfaces of our bodies. But our actions anticipate more. Having been singled out in the line, at the borders, we become defensive; we assume a defensive posture, as we "wait" for the line of racism, to take our rights of passage away. If we inherit the failure of things to be habitual, then we might also acquire a tendency to look behind us.

To be not white is not to be extended by the spaces you inhabit. This is an uncomfortable feeling. Comfort is a feeling that tends not to be consciously felt, as I have suggested. You sink. When you don't sink, when you fidget and move around, then what is in the background becomes in front of you, as a world that is gathered in a specific way. Discomfort, in other words, allows things to move by bringing what is in the background, what gets over-looked, to life. In a way, the experience of not being white in a white world not only gives us a different viewing point, but it disorientates how things are arranged. This "not" does not always feel negative. Every experience I have had of pleasure and excitement about a world opening up has begun with such ordinary feelings of discomfort, of not quite fitting in a chair, of becoming unseated, of being left holding onto the ground. So yes, if we start with the body that loses its chair, the world we describe will be quite different.

CONCLUSION: ON ARRIVAL

The experience of negation, of being stopped or feeling out of place, or feeling uncomfortable, does not "stop" there. When the arrival of some bodies is noticed, when an arrival is noticeable, it generates disorientation in how things are arranged. But does this disorientation involve disorientating whiteness? Is arriving enough? Of course, our arrival did not just happen. It took collective work, and painstaking labor. For me, now, here, based as I am in higher education in Britain, I receive an alternative inheritance from this history of collective action, and I receive it every day, simply by walking on *this* ground, which has been cleared by such action. Our arrival at British universities was only possible given the history of Black activism, both in the UK and transnationally, which has cleared this ground.

And yet, we can arrive, and things can stay in place. Organizations can recover from disorientation, and they can use disorientation to recover. I am giving a paper about whiteness to a very white audience.[11] I can feel the discomfort, perhaps. It is hard to know sometimes whether feelings are in the room or are a matter of our orientation; the impressions we have of the room by virtue of the angle at which we are placed. I feel uncomfortable, let's say that. Someone struggles to ask a question. Basically he asks, "but you are a professor now. How does that fit?" The question can be re-phrased: "how can what you say about whiteness be true, given that *you* can become a professor?" The discomfort, we can see, exposes the very failure to fit.

The very fact of our arrival can be used as evidence that the whiteness of which we speak is no longer in place. I was appointed to teach "the race course," I reply. I am the only person of color employed on a full-time permanent basis in the department, I say. It becomes too personal. The argument is too much to sustain when your body is so exposed, when you feel so noticeable. I stop, and do not complete my answer to the question. When our appointments and promotion are taken up as signs of organizational commitment to equality and diversity, we are in trouble. Any success is read as a sign of an overcoming of institutional whiteness. "Look, you're here!" "Look, look!" Our talk about racism is read as a form of stubbornness, paranoia, or even melancholia, as if we are holding onto something (whiteness) that our arrival shows has already gone. Our talk about whiteness is read as a sign of ingratitude, of failing to be grateful for the hospitality we have received by virtue of our arrival. It is this very structural position of being the guest, or the stranger, the one who receives hospitality, which keeps us in certain places, even when you move up.[12] So, if you "move up," then you come to embody the social promise of diversity, which gives you a certain place. It is the very use of Black bodies as signs of diversity that confirms such whiteness, premised on a conversion of having to being: As if by having us, the organization can "be" diverse.

Diversity in this world becomes then a happy sign, a sign that racism has been overcome. In a research project into diversity work,[13] I encounter what I call "an institutional desire for good practice." This desire takes the form of an expectation that publicly funded research on race, diversity, and equality should be useful, and should provide techniques for achieving equality and challenging institutional racism. In actual terms, this involves a desire to hear "happy stories of diversity" rather than unhappy stories of racism. We write a report about how good practice and anti-racist tool kits are being used as technologies of concealment, displacing racism from public view. Anti-racism even becomes a new form of organizational pride. The response to our final report: Too much focus on racism, we need more evidence of good practice. The response to your work is symptomatic of what you critique. They don't even notice the irony. You have been funded to "show" their commitment to diversity and are expected to return their investment by giving evidence of its worth.

Within academic fields, I would argue, we can also witness this desire for happy stories of diversity, although the desire takes different form. When I give papers on whiteness, I am always asked about resistance, as a sign of how things can be otherwise. Some of these questions take the form of "what can white people do?" The sheer solipsism of this response must be challenged. We can recall Adrienne Rich's description of white solipsism: "to speak, imagine and think as if whiteness described the world" (1979: 299). To respond to accounts of institutional whiteness with the question "what can white people do?" is not only to return to the place of the white subject, but it is also to locate agency in this place. It is also to re-position the white subject as somewhere other than implicated in the critique.

Other questions do not re-center on the agency of white bodies, but just on the need for some kind of understanding of power that shows that things don't always hold, that shows the cracks, the movement, the instabilities and that appreciates how much things have changed, even whilst recognizing that there is much left to do. So one response to my considering of whiteness has been "is there any sense that resistance is possible in this account?" And, "if whiteness is a bad habit, what might it be replaced with?" You become obliged to give evidence of where things can be undone, to locate the point of undoing, somewhere or another, even if that location is not in the world, but in the very mode of your critique. What does it mean if we assume that critiques have to leave room for resistance, as room-making devices? This desire to make room is understandable – if the work of critique does not show that its object can be undone, or promise to undo its object, then what is the point of that critique? But this desire can also become an object for us to investigate. The desire for signs of resistance can also be a form for resistance to hearing about racism. If we want to know how things can be different *too quickly*, then we might not hear anything at all.

The desire for resistance is not the same as the desire for good practice. And yet, both desires can involve a defense against hearing about racism as an ongoing and unfinished history that we have yet to describe fully. We still need to describe how it is that the world of whiteness coheres as a world, even as we tend to the "stresses" in this coherence, and the uneven distribution of such stress. A phenomenology of whiteness helps us to notice institutional habits; it brings what is behind, what does not get seen as the background to social action, to the surface in a certain way. It does not teach us how to change those habits and that is partly the point. In not being promising, in refusing to promise anything, such an approach to whiteness can allow us to keep open the force of the critique. It is by showing how we are stuck, by attending to what is habitual and routine in "the what" of the world, that we can keep open the possibility of habit changes, without using that possibility to displace our attention to the present, and without simply wishing for new tricks.

NOTES

1 This chapter extends some of the arguments about racism and orientation offered in chapter 3, *Queer Phenomenology: Orientations, Objects, Others* (Ahmed, 2006).
2 Within this literature, a key influence is existentialism, and specifically Jean-Paul Sartre's concept of bad faith. See especially Gordon (1995) for an analysis of anti-Black racism as a form of bad faith. Gordon's work on Black existentialism also draws on Black writers such as Du Bois and Fanon, clearing the way for another articulation of the relation between philosophy, race, and racism.

3 The signs of occupation are also signs of gender. In other words, philosophy can be described as a gendered form of occupation, which is not to say that only men do philosophy, but rather that "doing philosophy" has historically been a masculine form of work. For an exploration of gender and orientation see Young (2005). See Butler (1997) for a discussion of why phenomenology is useful for feminism in its attention to bodily sedimentation.

4 This quote within the quote is drawn from Jean Lhermitte's *L'Image de notre Corps*.

5 For work that uses Bourdieu's concept of habitus to explore the racialized body see Wicker (1997), Hage (1998), and Puwar (2004).

6 It is worth noting here that the word "habit" comes from the Latin for condition, appearance, and dress.

7 We need to ask what happens when diversity becomes incorporated into the "ego ideal" of an organization. We could assume that if enough bodies who are non-white gather then the "in place" might be less secure; the organization might become less white. The very demand for bodies who are different, though, can still keep things in place. Diversity becomes something they "are," which means the organization can "have it" by being seen as taking "them" in.

8 For an analysis of the relationship between whiteness and institutional racism, see, "Declarations of Whiteness: The Non-Performativity of Anti-Racism," *borderlands* (Ahmed, 2004b).

9 Thanks to Imogen Tyler for encouraging me to think about the significance of Husserl's loss of a chair for my argument about whiteness, and to Mimi Sheller for her insights into the politics of mobility.

10 I develop this thesis on the "economies of movement" (how movement for some blocks the movement of others) in *The Cultural Politics of Emotion* (2004a). See also the Introduction to Ahmed, Castañeda, Fortier, and Sheller (2003), which critiques the ways in which mobility has been taken up within social and cultural theory.

11 I am very indebted here to Audre Lorde who described so well the dynamics of resistance to hearing the force of critique implicit in Black women's anger about racism. Lorde gives us accounts of her interactions with white academics at conferences to show the subtle and not so subtle mechanisms of defence against hearing Black women's arguments about racism (see 1984, pp. 124–126).

12 For papers on the continued marginalization of Black women in British higher education institutions see Mirza (2006) and Jones (2006).

13 I was involved in a project assessing the turn to diversity within the learning and skills sector (including adult and community learning, and further education), as well as higher education between 2004–2006. I was co-director of this project with Elaine Swan, and the project team included Shona Hunter, Sevgi Kilic, and Lewis Turner. My own study was based in higher education, and involved 20 interviews with diversity practitioners in Australia (Ahmed, 2007a) and the UK (Ahmed, 2007b).

REFERENCES

Ahmed, S. (2000). *Strange encounters: Embodied others in post-coloniality*. London: Routledge.

Ahmed, S., Castañeda, C., Fortier, A.-M., & Sheller, M. (2003). Introduction. In S. Ahmed, C. Castañeda, A.-M. Fortier, & M. Sheller (Eds.), *Uprooting/regroundings: Questions of home and migration* (pp. 1–19). New York, NY: Routledge.

Ahmed, S. (2004a). *The cultural politics of emotion*. Edinburgh: Edinburgh University Press.

Ahmed, S. (2004b). Declarations of whiteness: The non-performativity of anti-racism. *borderlands* 3(2). [http://www.borderlandsejournal.adelaide.edu.au/vol3no2_2004/ahmed_de clarations].

Ahmed, S. (2006). *Queer phenomenology: Orientations, objects, others*. Durham, NC: Duke University Press.

Ahmed, S. (2007a). The language of diversity. *Ethnic and Racial Studies, 30*(2), 235–256.

Ahmed, S. (2007b). "You end up doing the document rather than doing the doing": Race equality, diversity and the politics of documentation. *Ethnic and Racial Studies, 30*(4): 590–609.

Alcoff, L. (1999). Towards a phenomenology of racial embodiment. *Radical Philosophy, 95,* 15–26.

Althusser, L. (1971). *Lenin and philosophy and other essays* (Ben Brewster, Trans.). London: New Left Books.

Balibar, E. (2002). *Politics and the other scene.* London: Verso.

Banfield, A. (2000). *The phantom table: Woolf, Fry, Russell, and the epistemology of modernism.* New York: Cambridge University Press.

Bourdieu, P. (1977). *Outline of a theory of practice* (R. Nice, Trans.). Cambridge: Cambridge University Press.

Brewer, R. M. (1993). Theorizing race, class and gender: The new scholarship of Black feminist intellectuals and Black women's labor. In Stanlie M. James & Abena P. A. Busia (Eds.), *Theorizing Black feminisms: The visionary pragmatism of Black women* (pp. 13–30). London: Routledge.

Butler, J. (1997). *The psychic life of power: Theories in subjection.* Stanford, CA: Stanford University Press"

Collins, P. H. (1998). *Fighting words: Black women & the search for justice.* Minneapolis, MN: University of Minnesota Press.

Dyer, R. (1997). *White.* London: Routledge.

Fanon, F. (1986). *Black skin, White masks.* London: Pluto Press.

Fenton, S. (2003). *Ethnicity.* Cambridge: Cambridge University Press.

Fine, M., Weis, L., Powell, L., & Mun Wong, L. (Eds.). (1997). *Off-White: Readings on race, power and society.* New York: Routledge.

Frankenberg, R. (1993). *White women, race matters: The social construction of whiteness.* Minneapolis, MN: University of Minnesota Press.

Gordon, L. R. (1995). *Bad faith and antiblack racism.* Atlantic Highlands, NJ: Humanities Press.

Gordon, L. R. (1999). Fanon, philosophy, racism. In S. E. Babbitt & S. Cambell (Eds.), *Racism and philosophy* (pp. 32–49). Ithaca, NY: Cornell University Press.

Hage, G. (1998). *White nation: Fantasies of white supremacy in a multicultural society.* Annandale, PA: Pluto Press.

Husserl, E. (1969). *Ideas: General introduction to pure phenomenology* (W. R. Boyce Gibson, Trans.). London: George Allen and Unwin.

Husserl, E. (1989). *Ideas pertaining to a pure phenomenology and to a phenomenological philosophy* (Richard Rojcewicz & André Schuwer, Trans.). Dordrecht: Kluwer Academic Publishers.

Jones, C. (2006). Falling between the cracks: What diversity means for Black women in higher education. *Policy Futures in Education, 4*(2), 145–59.

Lorde, A. (1984). *Sister outsider: Essays and speeches.* Trumansburg: The Crossing Press.

Macey, D. (1999). Fanon, phenomenology, race. *Radical Philosophy, 95,* 8–14.

Merleau-Ponty, M. (2002). *The phenomenology of perception* (Colin Smith, Trans.). London: Routledge.

Mirza, H. (2006). Transcendence over diversity: Black women in the academy. *Policy Futures in Education, 4*(2), 101–13.

Puwar, N. (2004). *Space invaders: Race, gender, and bodies out of place.* Oxford: Berg.

Rich, A. (1979). *On lies, secrets and silence: Selected prose 1966–1978.* New York: W.W. Norton Company.

Schutz, A., & Luckmann, T. (1974). *The structure of the lifeworld* (Richard M. Zaner and H. Tristram Engelhardt, Trans.). London: Heinemann Educational Books.

Singh, V. (2002). *Managing diversity for strategic advantage.* London: Council for Excellence in Management and Leadership.

Skeggs, B. (2003). *Class, self, culture*. London: Routledge.

Smith, V. (1998). *Not just race, not just gender: Black feminist readings*. New York: Routledge.

Wicker, H.-R. (1997). From complex culture to cultural complexity. In Pnina Werbner & Tariq Modood (Eds.), *Debating cultural hybridity: Multicultural identities and the politics of anti-racism* (pp. 29–45). London: Zed Books.

Young, I. M. (2005). *The female body experience*. Oxford: Oxford University Press.

CHAPTER 17

AFRICANA PHENOMENOLOGY

Its Philosophical Implications

Paget Henry

Given some of the exclusive claims on reason that the West has made, it has been difficult to see clearly the rationality of non-Western peoples. This eclipsing of the rationality of non-Western peoples, particularly people of African descent, has made problematic the status of theory in fields such as Africana Studies. Quite often, it is assumed that developments in this field will take the form of case studies that will help to confirm or disconfirm theories and methodologies produced by the West. In other words, nothing new of theoretical importance is expected to emerge from the growth of Africana Studies. Indeed even some Africana scholars have associated theory and rational linear thought with white males. This is certainly not how I see Africana Studies. My disagreement with this view is confirmed with every new development in the growing field of Africana philosophy. Here the theoretical side of Africana Studies becomes particularly evident, given the nature of philosophical practices. In this chapter, I examine the case of Africana phenomenology, an emerging subfield within the larger discursive terrain of Africana philosophy. Like the larger terrain of which it is a part, Africana phenomenology is not very well known because it too has been forced to exist in the non-rational and a-theoretical shadow cast over it by Western philosophy in general, and Western phenomenology in particular. Thus our aim in this chapter is twofold: the first is to bring the field of Africana phenomenology clearly into view by outlining its contours, problems, and theorists. In particular, I will focus on the contributions of W. E. B. DuBois, Frantz Fanon, and Lewis Gordon. Second, I will explore the philosophical implications of the emergence of Africana phenomenology as a subfield of Africana philosophy. These, I will argue, point to a metaphysical distinctness that can only be adequately engaged by a more comparative approach to philosophy.

CULTURE AND PHENOMENOLOGY

By phenomenology, I mean the discursive practice through which self-reflective descriptions of the constituting activities of consciousness are produced after the "natural attitude" of everyday life has been bracketed by some ego-displacing technique. An Africana phenomenology would thus be the self-reflective descriptions of the constituting activities of the consciousness of Africana peoples, after the natural attitudes of Africana egos have been displaced by de-centering techniques practiced in these cultures. This thematizing of the specificity of Africana phenomenology raises two important theoretical questions: the relationship of phenomenology to specific cultures and disciplines. In relation to the first of these, the notion of a distinct Africana phenomenology very explicitly suggests a cultural dimension to this enterprise. This cultural approach to phenomenology is an unusual one, as it culturally conditions the certainty of self-reflective knowledge and raises very explicitly the need to do phenomenology from a comparative cultural perspective. This I shall argue

DOI: 10.4324/9781003037132-17

is one of the important theoretical consequences that have accompanied the emergence of Africana phenomenology from its history of invisibility.

With regard to our second theoretical question, the self-reflective core of phenomenology suggests that as an epistemic practice it is not peculiar to philosophy as a discipline. Rather, it is an activity that can be initiated from inside any knowledge-producing human discipline. It is also important to note that all human disciplines, including the logical and empirical practices of philosophy, produce knowledge in the natural attitude. Like philosophy, the other disciplines can all interrupt their everyday practices and engage the transcendental or knowledge-constitutive ground that supports their more routine practices. However, the distance to this ground varies between disciplines and is determined largely by qualitative differences in creative and knowledge-producing codes. But in spite of these differences, it is the existence of this shared ground that explains why phenomenological philosophy has been able to reach the transcendental spaces of other discourses, and in the West has been enriched by Edmund Husserl's reflections on the foundations of mathematics. In the case of Africana phenomenology, it is the reflections of creative writers and race theorists that have been particularly enriching.

This problem of culture and phenomenology has in part been concealed by the ways in which reason and culture have been brought together in the identity of European phenomenology. In its classic formulations by Descartes, Kant, Hegel, and Husserl, European phenomenology was seen as the self-reflective practice that disclosed the latent movements of a universal reason, which was also the prime constituting force operating within the core of the European subject. Consequently, it was the phenomenology of this subject that would for the first time make manifest these latent activities of universal reason. The crucial significance of this reason as a constituting force was the perceived universality of its categories, positings, claims – in short, its self – and knowledge – producing capabilities. In its fully realized state, Husserl saw reason as "the form of a universal philosophy which grows through consistent apodictic insight and supplies its own norms through an apodictic method" (1970, p. 16).

However, this possibility of a universal reason was, quite paradoxically, limited to a very specific cultural particularity: the cultural particularity of Europe. This particularization of universal reason was at the same time the universalizing of the European subject as its science, and phenomenology would give reason a fully realized vision of itself. In this peculiar configuration, Europe acquired a monopoly that made it co-extensive with the geography of reason. This geography is well known to us from the works of Hegel, Kant, Husserl, and Weber. For Husserl, the development of European phenomenology was tied to the question of whether or not "European humanity bears within itself an absolute idea, rather than being merely an empirical anthropological type like 'China' or 'India'" (1970, p. 16).

To grasp the reality and presence of Africana phenomenology, this imperial geography and its exclusive relationship between reason and European culture has to be pulled apart. Without such a clearing, it will be impossible to perceive or even imagine the reality of an Africana phenomenology. In preparing the ground for such new phenomenological possibilities, a number of additional factors will also have to be reconsidered. Here I will briefly mention three: (1) the occasion for self-reflection; (2) the path into the practice of self-reflection; and (3) the role played by knowledge produced in the natural attitude in our constructions and reconstructions of the transcendental domain.

In the history of Western philosophy, the occasion for phenomenological reflection has consistently been the problem of rationality and the consequences of rational/scientific knowledge production. Thus the dialectical logic of Hegel's phenomenology was an attempt to keep the creative and explanatory agency of Spirit as an integral part of the changing discursive spaces produced by the rise of the natural sciences (1967). In Husserl, the occasion for self-reflection was the crisis produced by the positivistically reduced notions of rationality and humanity that accompanied the rise of mathematics and the natural sciences (1970). Habermas has formulated this reduction as the colonization of the Western life-world by its systems of technical and instrumental rationality (1987, p. 322). It is only in its existential and grammatological variants that these problems of the rational cogito have been replaced by those of the desiring and the signifying subjects. In Sartre, the occasion for self-reflection is the bad faith that the European subject has consistently brought to the knowing situation and the capacity that bad faith has given it to mobilize reason in the service of unreason and untruth (1956, pp. 47–67). In Derrida, the occasion for self-reflection has been Western philosophy's practice (including its phenomenology) of restricting the nature and scope of writing, in relation to speaking and thinking, to a fraction of what it really is (1976, pp. 6–26). Derrida's grammatology has as its goal the rescuing of writing from a metaphysically imposed obscurity, similar to Husserlian phenomenology's goal of rescuing a more fully realized concept of reason from its positivistically imposed obscurity.

These variations within the overall telos of rationality that has governed the self-image of European phenomenology are important for raising the question of other occasions for self- reflection that are outside of this rational horizon. These possibilities are important for us, as I will argue that the governing telos of Africana phenomenology has been racial liberation and the problems of racial domination from which it springs. In our examinations of DuBois, Fanon, and Gordon, we will see how variations on the problem of racial liberation displace the problem of rationality as the source of occasions for self-reflection.

The second and closely related set of variations necessary for a clear seeing of Africana phenomenology are those variations that have occurred in the paths to self-reflection. In Descartes, it was the method of radical doubting (1960, pp. 7–22). In Hegel, it was the practice of spiritual and theological meditation (1971). In Husserl, self-reflection was practiced through the phenomenological reduction (1975, pp. 5–20). In Sartre, it was through existential analysis (1956, pp. 557–575), and in Derrida it took the form of reflection of the creativity of the systems of writing in which the subject was embedded (1976, pp. 75–93). What do these variations in methods of producing self-reflective knowledge mean for some of the universal claims made by European phenomenology? Are these the only methods of producing self-reflective knowledge? I will argue that these variations problematize these universal claims, and that Africana phenomenology further complicates the situation by adding yet another method: that of poetics.

The third and final point that I want to make in preparing the ground for an Africana phenomenology is the relations between the everyday ethical/practical projects of phenomenologies (rescuing reason, writing, or racial equality) and our constructions and ongoing reconstructions of the transcendental domain. These constructions and reconstructions seem to be profoundly influenced by the nature of these world-oriented projects. Thus Kant's logical reconstruction of this domain was clearly shaped by his interest in clarifying the foundations of the natural sciences. Hegel's spiritual reading was inseparable from his interests in clarifying the foundations and validity of the spiritual and theological discourses. Husserl's goal of making the transcendental domain the pre-suppositionless and rigorously formulated foundation of all discourses was clearly related to his interest in clarifying the status of the processes of idealization that constitute the foundations of mathematics. Finally, Derrida's semiotic vision of the transcendental domain is also inseparable from his project of clarifying the foundations of writing. These examples point to a circle of mutual influencing between the world-oriented projects of phenomenologies and their corresponding views of what is foundational or transcendental for knowledge production. But such a pattern of influence points to a historicizing of the transcendental domain that would limit any absolute claims for Spirit, logic, pre-suppositionless idealization, or arche-writing. In all of these accounts of the transcendental domain, there has been a clear tendency to extend their foundational reach beyond what this circle of mutual influence would suggest. In Africana phenomenology, this tendency has been distinctly weaker and could be related to the differences in the telos and nature of its ethical/practical project.

With these three points in place, our conception of phenomenology should now be a more open and flexible one. This flexibility extends to its relations with cultures, historical processes, disciplines, ethical/practical projects, occasions for self-reflection, and methods of self-reflection. On the horizon of such a comparative conception of this subfield of philosophies around the world, the reality and possibility of an Africana phenomenology can be clearly seen.

AFRICANA PHENOMENOLOGY

In the tradition of Africana phenomenology, the occasion for self-reflection has not been the positivistic reduction of rationality and the mechanized caricature of the European subject that it threatens to produce. Rather, the occasion for reflection has been the racist negating of the humanity of Africans and the caricature of "the negro" that it has produced. Unlike European phenomenology, these Africana reflections have been interested in clarifying the systemic error producing foundations of the European humanities and social sciences that have had to legitimate and make appear as correct this racist reduction of African humanity. The positivistic reduction of European humanity and the racist reduction of African humanity are opposite sides of the coin of modern Western capitalism. The mechanical caricature is a part of the upper and rational side of itself that Western capitalism likes to affirm. The racist caricature of "the Negro" is a creation of the "underside" of this mechanized capitalism, a part of its irrational shadow that it cannot affirm but must project onto others that it perceives as its opposite. The sociological setting for the production of the caricature of "the negro" was not the Habermasian internal colonization of a life-world by its own systems of technical and instrumental reason. Rather this setting was the external colonization of one life-world (the African) by another (the European). This process of imperial domination by a society of a different race and a different culture shattered the traditional socio-cultural worlds of pre-colonial Africa. It racialized identities that were predominantly spiritual and physically captured, enslaved, and exported millions of Africans for economic exploitation on plantations in the Western hemisphere. In short, it was in this context of colonial conquest that Africans became part of "the underside of modernity" (Dussel, 1996) or what Husserl earlier referred to as "the Europeanization of all other civilizations" (1970, p. 16).

The implosive impact of this Europeanization on the life-worlds of African societies can be quickly indicated by some of its classic representations in literature. In continental Africa, Chinua Achebe's novel, *Things Fall Apart*, has become one of the classic metaphors for the shattering impact of European colonization. In the Caribbean, a novel that holds a corresponding symbolic status is George Lamming's, *In the Castle of My Skin*. Here the impact of racialization, or what Fanon will call negrification, is much greater than in Achebe's novel. The African has ceased to be a Yoruba or Akan and has become a "black," a "negro" or a "nigger." In Afro-America, Richard Wright's *Black Boy* or Ralf Ellison's *Invisible Man* would be corresponding works. In both of these novels, the process of racialization (niggerization) is even more extreme than in the case of Lamming. Thus the terrain of self-reflection in the Africana world has been a rather burnt-out, exploded, and blackened one, very different from the technological dystopia of Aldous Huxley's *Brave New World* or George Orwell's *1984*.

In spite of this broken and blackened nature of the terrain of Africana self-reflection, it is still very much a human world with hope and genius. This hope has been one of its classic expressions by another Afro-Caribbean writer, Derek Walcott. He writes:

> break a vase and the love that reassembles the fragments is stronger than the love which took its symmetry for granted when it was whole. The glue that fits the pieces is the sealing of its original shape. It is such a love that reassembles our African and Asiatic fragments, the cracked heirlooms whose restoration shows its white scars.
>
> *(Walcott, 1993, p. 9)*

This blackened imploding of the pre-colonial African consciousness and its loving reconstruction are two important poles defining the world of Africana phenomenology.

DUBOIS AND AFRICANA PHENOMENOLOGY

Although the roots of Africana self-reflection are to be found in Africa, the pattern of development of the field is such that it is best to start with the reflections of the period of enslavement and its aftermath. These periods produced the writings of eighteenth- and nineteenth-century ex-slaves such as Olaudah Equiano, Ottobah Cugoano, Frederick Douglass, Harriet Jacobs, Mary Prince, and David Walker. In the twentieth century, self-reflective Africana writing continued in the works of Edward Blyden, Antenor Firmin, Marcus Garvey, Ida B. Wells, W. E. B. DuBois, Alain Locke, Frantz Fanon, Wilson Harris, Sylvia Wynter, Lewis Gordon, and many others. Of these writers, the first to outline a comprehensive phenomenology of Africana self-consciousness was DuBois, whose life and work spanned the late nineteenth and the first half of the twentieth century.

In his work *The Autobiography*, DuBois tells us that he entered Harvard with the goal of pursuing a career in philosophy. The courses he took exposed him to the thought of the American pragmatists, particularly William James and Josiah Royce, and the engagements of the school with Hegel's philosophy (Zamir, 1995, pp. 113–133). This was the context in which the young DuBois encountered Hegel's phenomenology. When we consider the latter's impact on C. L. R. James, Rene Menil (founding member of Legitime defense), Frantz Fanon, and Wilson Harris, it is probably the European phenomenology that has had the most influence on Africana phenomenology. Hegel's phenomenology is a classic example of what Habermas calls a general interpretation as opposed to a general theory (1971, pp. 246–273). The former is a generalized narrative of self-development that is directed at a subject and must therefore have an "addressee." General theories are aimed at objects rather than subjects. The application of a general interpretation thus becomes a process of self-application – one must literally try on the theory and respond to the experienced sense of fit. In other words, general interpretations require the explicit thematizing of the responses of specific subjects to their discursive offerings. In the case of general theories, application takes the form of an externally imposed subsumption that requires experimental evaluation rather than confirmation from an addressee. As a general interpretation, the application of Hegel's phenomenology to the self-consciousness of the Africana subject can only be judged appropriate by the sense of fit this subject reports. The changes that DuBois made in Hegel's phenomenology derived from the experience of an imperfect fit.

For the young DuBois, the Africana subject was a culturally distinct, and hence non-European, site of original meanings, discourses, and experiences. Consequently, to make himself the addressee of Hegel's phenomenology, DuBois's engagements with it had to be different from those of European or Euro-American philosophers. As Hegel's primary addressees, the latter could very easily test it by putting themselves in the role of the self-consciousness that had reached the stage of the master. Further, they could identify with the earlier stages in this process of self-development, as they were drawn directly from European history. Because the self-consciousness of the Africana subject is not the primary addressee of Hegel's phenomenology, self-application cannot produce the same results. Further, DuBois cannot identify with either the earlier or later stages in Hegel's general interpretation, as they are not drawn from the history of the Africana subject. Thus what DuBois will take from Hegel is how to view the racialized Africana subject and its possibilities for recovery from the standpoint of the self- and world-constituting activities of its consciousness. In short, it is the general phenomenological approach of grasping self and world from the perspective of a constituting consciousness that DuBois takes from Hegel. However, unlike Hegel, DuBois will not make an absolute onto-epistemic commitment to this perspective.

For Hegel, the self-development of the European subject was not a smooth, unitary process of growth. Rather it was an upward movement that was marked by splits, doublings, and self/other binaries that resulted in premature exclusions and negations that would have to be overcome in subsequent stages. Thus in the paragraphs that open the section on "Lordship and Bondage" in *The Phenomenology of Mind*, Hegel writes extensively about the doubling or duplication that arises from the fact that self-consciousness exists not only for itself, but also for another self-consciousness. In other words, it is the fact that self-consciousness must be both for itself and for another that produces its "double meanings" (Hegel, 1967, p. 229). Here too we find another significant influence that Hegel had on DuBois's phenomenology.

The first attempt of the young DuBois to bring the Africana subject into an engagement with Hegel's phenomenology was his 1890 Harvard commencement address: "Jefferson Davis as Representative of Civilization." There, clearly in the role of the slave, DuBois presents the Africana subject as "the Submissive Man" who is "at once the check and complement of the Teutonic Strong Man" (Levering-Lewis, 1995, p. 19). With this different metaphor of Africana selfhood, the young DuBois is here making a significant departure from Hegel on the basis of the different phenomenological history of the Africana subject. The "Submissive Man" is both check and complement to the European subject because not even to the latter's mind is it given to recognize the whole truth of human ontogenesis (p. 19). Such a vision of the totality can only emerge from conversations in which the contributions of all civilizations are acknowledged and their complementarity recognized. With this concept of a global complementarity between cultures, DuBois breaks with the conflating of Europe and the universal that was such an integral part of Hegel's phenomenology. This break in turn sets the stage for the positions that DuBois will take in his important essay, "The Conservation of Races," and for the way in which he will engage Hegel in *The Souls of Black Folks*.

DOUBLE CONSCIOUSNESS AND
DUBOISIAN PHENOMENOLOGY

In the opening essay of *Souls*, "Of Our Spiritual Strivings," DuBois outlines his theory of double consciousness which constitutes the core of his phenomenology. The double consciousness of which he speaks in this essay is not just the result of the Africana subject having also to exist before another self-consciousness. Its life in Africa made existing for another self-consciousness an already familiar reality for this subject, and quite possibly the Hegelian form of double consciousness. DuBoisian double consciousness results from the Africana subject having to exist for a self-consciousness that racialized itself as white. In the dialectic of racial recognition that takes place between the two, it is not the humanity but the Blackness of the Africana subject that confirms the whiteness of the Teutonic "Strong Man." As a result, the racialization of the African as Black produced a very different form of doubling than in the case of Hegel's non-racialized master or slave.

For DuBois, this racialization of identities and supporting institutional orders were not leftovers from the traditional past but integral parts of the modern world order of European capitalism. It was as integral as the processes of commodification, colonization, rationalization, and secularization that Marx, Weber, and Durkheim were to the rise of Western capitalism. The growth of processes of racialization throughout the formative and mature periods of Western capitalism is evident in its expanding discourses on the hierarchies of races and the increasingly global reach of its institutions of white supremacy.

In DuBois's view, the impact of these processes of racialization on both the psyche and the transcendental consciousness of the Africana subject was the creating of new divisions within them – divisions that were different from Hegelian forms of doubling. With regard to the psyche, the new division was created by the shattering and contesting of the "We" or the collective identity of the Africana subject. It was shattered by the caricature image of "the negro" as the polar opposite of "the white" that existed and continues to exist in the mind of the European and the Euro-American. This stereotyped image of the African in the white mind was given some of its clearest expressions in the "blackface" that whites would put on when they played "negroes" on the vaudeville stage. It was the institutionalizing of this absolute racial distance between whites and Blacks that shattered and contested the pre-colonial collective identities of the Akan, Hausa, Yoruba, Fon, and other African ethnic groups. DuBoisian double consciousness is a phenomenological account of the self-consciousness of these African subjects whose "We" had been shattered and challenged by this process of negrification.

DuBois represented the double life-world created by racialization through the metaphor of the veil. Thus he spoke of life within and outside of the veil. This concept/metaphor is another important descriptive term in DuBois's phenomenology. In *Darkwater*, DuBois gave us a hint as to how he had adjusted to life behind the veil. He retreated into a "tower above the loud complaining of the human sea" (DuBois, 1999, p. 17), from where he would attempt to grasp and engage the world intellectually. This is one possible existential response to the involuntary presence of this racial veil. This response reminds us of George Lamming's retreat into "The Castle of My Skin," taking with him only the tools of the creative writer. Tower and castle are here important symbols of the response of Africana subjects to the double life-world created by the veil. In *Souls*, DuBois mentions the responses of other Africana subjects that were not so

fiercely sunny: their youth shrunk into tasteless sycophancy, or into silent hatred of the pale
world about them and mocking distrust of everything white, or wasted itself in a bitter cry,
why did God make me an outcast and a stranger in my own house.

(1969, p. 16)

It is these less sunny psyches that will be the focus of Fanon's phenomenology. Thus along
with the images of tower and castle, sycophancy, waste, stranger, and outcast are also
important descriptive terms of Africana self-consciousness before the veil of the racial
other.

The specifics of this dilemma of the racial veil are such that it really has no counterpart in any of the stages of Hegel's phenomenology of European self-consciousness.
Zamir's (1994) suggestion that Africana double consciousness can be seen as a case of
Hegel's "unhappy consciousness" does not really work. The divided Hegelian subject
moves between a desire for an "I" that is autonomous and self-constituting, and the need
for confirmation and recognition from the other. These are some of the existential dilemmas that the Africana subject would have experienced before its racialization. In the phase
of the former's development that Hegel referred to as "the unhappy consciousness," this
divided subject has moved beyond the terms of the master-slave relationship to explore stoic
and skeptical responses to its inner divisions. What Hegel calls the "double-consciousness"
(1967, p. 251) of this unhappy subject stems from an awareness of itself as "changeable" at
the same time that it is also "consciousness of unchangeableness" (p. 252). As the latter, it
must seek to liberate itself from its changeable existence but is unable to reach the life of the
unchangeable. This is the particular "dualizing of self-consciousness" that constitutes the
dilemmas of the unhappy consciousness.

As a racialized subject, the Africana individual remains very much within the terms
of the master-slave relationship. Consequently, the above dualizing is not the source of the
two poles between which the Africana subject oscillates. This subject moves not between
a changeable "I" and an unchangeable "Other" but between two "We"s. Behind this particular experience of "twoness" is the earlier noted phenomenon of the external colonization of one life-world by another and the contempt and pity it produced. The self-reflections
of the DuBoisian subject cannot avoid engagements with this specific type of twoness. He/
she must encounter questions such as, "what, after all, am I? Am I an American or am I a
Negro? Can I be both? Or, is it my duty to cease to be a Negro as soon as possible and to be
an American?" (Levering-Lewis, 1995, p. 24). One feels here the clashing of two racialized
and hence irreconcilable collective identities. This is not the dilemma of Hegel's unhappy
consciousness.

In addition to the splitting of the Africana psyche, DuBoisian double consciousness also refers to a similar splitting of the transcendental consciousness of this racialized subject. The internalizing of the caricature of "the negro" also produced significant
changes in the categoric structure of the transcendental domain of the Africana subject.
This complex set of categoric changes DuBois summed up under the label of "second
sight" (1969, p. 16), which is a new or second way of seeing self and world. Second sight
is the ability of the racialized Africana subject to see him/herself as a "negro," that is,
through the eyes of the white other. It is new in the sense that it was not a capability that
pre-colonial Africans had. This new half of the double vision of the Africana subject
suggests that first sight is the ability to see one's self through one's own eyes. The categoric changes in the organization of the transcendental domain that are associated with
double consciousness derive from the complex and changing dynamics that developed
between first and second sight.

To the extent that second sight, the ability to see one's self as a "negro" replaced first sight, it constituted a major obstacle to any genuine Africana self-consciousness. Tied to the European or Euro-American life-worlds, second sight yielded the Africana subject "no true self-consciousness, but only lets him see himself through the revelation of the other world" (DuBois, 1969, p. 16). In other words, this exclusive form of second sight is in reality a categoric form of self-blindness, a deformation, a detour rather than a positive phase in the development of Africana self-consciousness. This "negro" detour will only take the Africana subject down a blind alley. It is a classic case of false consciousness that will only take this subject away from its self. This struggle to see through the darkness of second sight is the categoric dilemma of Africana self-consciousness as disclosed by DuBois's phenomenology. This dilemma of second sight affected Africana knowledge production as profoundly as those of the tower, the outcast, or the stranger affected self-production.

THE ETHICAL/PRACTICAL PROJECT OF DUBOIS'S PHENOMENOLOGY

As in the case of Hegel or Husserl, DuBois's phenomenology was intricately linked to an ethical/practical project. This was a project of racial equality that included the deniggerization of Africana identities and the full recognition of the humanity of Africana peoples and also of their cultural contributions to the shared problems of human ontogenesis. We saw glimpses of this project in the Jefferson Davis address. We will now develop it more fully by drawing primarily from *Souls*, *The History of the Suppression of the Slave Trade*, and *The Philadelphia Negro*. This ethical dimension of DuBois's phenomenology is quite distinct and constitutes another area of a clear break with Hegel. DuBois's project of racial equality displaces the Hegelian one of keeping the vision of Spirit a part of the rational world of the European subject. I will develop this distinctness of the DuBoisian project around three crucial points: (1) DuBois's potentiated second sight; (2) his poeticist style of self-reflection; and (3) his commitment to racial and cultural equality.

The categoric transformation represented by second sight was very much a double-edged sword. On one side it guards against the achieving of true self-consciousness by Africana subjects, and on the other it can give the latter very special access and insight into the dehumanizing "will to power" of the European imperial subject. This peculiar insight, which I am calling potentiated second sight, is a crucial link between the transcendental and the ethical dimensions of DuBois's phenomenology. The potentiating of second sight is always a latent possibility in the racialized and divided self-consciousness of the Africana subject. This possibility can be activated in two basic ways: first through the recovery of a significant measure of first sight, that is, the ability to see one's self as an African as opposed to "the negro" that the white mind was constantly producing and projecting. This ability to see one's self as an African will depend upon one's ability to creatively uproot the "blackface" stereotype, and to reconstruct self and world within the creative codes of African discourses and symbols. To the extent that an individual or group is able to do this, they will have an alternative space from which to see through and critique the imposed "negro" stereotype. The Rastafarians are a good example of this first way of potentiating second sight.

The second is clearly the finding of an independent point of self-elevation such as DuBois's tower or George Lamming's castle. From such a point, there must be the cultivating of an informed and critical "I" that is capable of distancing itself from the caricature of "the negro" so that it is able to see clearly the latter's formation, its white psychosocial significance, and also its dissolution. The cultivation of such an "I" would then become either a new form of first sight or some form of third sight. Whichever it is, in conjunction with the ability to see one's self as an African, two very potent bases outside of the psychic terrain of "the negro" identity will have been established. Together they are not only able to see through and implode the imposed stereotype, but also to provide great insight into the psyche of the creators and perpetrators of this tragic farce. In the wide distances between the capabilities of the recovered African/tower identity and those of the "blackface" stereotype, the Africana subject had a living and reflectively accessible measure of the inhumanity of the Western imperial self. Lewis Gordon captures well the ironic dimensions of potentiated second sight when he notes that it emerges in the subject who has become aware of the lived contradiction of this deception, and who like Fanon is therefore able to announce "the absence of his interiority from the point of view of his interiority" (1995a, p. 33). It is from the reflective immediacy of the decaying carcass of "the negro" that the critiques of potentiated second sight derive their ethical/moral power, pinpoint accuracy, and razor-sharp quality.

In DuBois, our first glimpses of such critiques are to be found in his early short story, "A Vacation Unique." In this story, DuBois's hero, Cuffy, invites his Harvard classmate to disguise himself as a "negro" and to come and see the world from this point of view. Cuffy says to his classmate: "outside of mind you may study mind, and outside of matter by reason of the fourth dimension of color you may have a striking view of the intestines of the fourth great civilization" (Zamir, 1995, p. 223). In other words, what the classmate will get is an intestinal view of American civilization, of the hunger that drives it to dominate and racialize. This intestinal view of the white imperial self is repeated in *Darkwater*, in another of DuBois's classic statements of what I have called potentiated second sight. In the chapter "The Souls of White Folks," he writes:

> of them I am singularly clairvoyant. I see in and through them. I view them from unusual points of vantage. Not as foreigner do I come, for I am native, not foreign, bone of their thought and flesh of their language ... Rather I see these souls undressed and from the back and side. I see the workings of their entrails. I know their thoughts and they know that I know.
>
> *(DuBois, 1999, p. 17)*

How did DuBois know? By shining the light of his potentiated second sight on the creators of the "blackface" caricature that he has killed. To confirm that DuBois is not the only Africana subject in possession of this special faculty of second sight, we need only think of Cugoano, Douglass, Garvey, Fanon, Malcolm X, or Angela Davis. But it was DuBois who first gave it a systematic formulation, and as such it constitutes one of the distinguishing features of the ethical/practical project of his phenomenology.

The second distinctive feature of this project is DuBois's poeticist style of self-reflection. As noted earlier, all phenomenologies employ some technique of bracketing the natural attitude in order to reach the constituting movements of consciousness through what Husserl called "the self-evidence of original activity" (Derrida, 1989, p. 163). The immediately evident self- and world-constituting activities of the Africana self were grasped by DuBois poetically, and explored more fully through the writing of novels and short stories. Thus in his approaches to consciousness DuBois used what we can call a poeticist reduction in contrast to the spirituo-theological and phenomenological reductions of Hegel and Husserl. Further, in *Souls*, DuBois also made use of music to supplement his poeticist techniques of bracketing the everyday world. However, here again, DuBois made no absolute onto-epistemic commitment to his poetics in spite of its vital role in gaining him access to the original or founding activity of the Africana self. He always used it in conjunction with other discourses, particularly history and sociology as both supplement and check.

DuBois's bracketing of the natural attitude and the everyday world was specific to his poetics. In his historical and sociological writings he returns quite easily to the everyday world. The dominance of intentional approaches that mark his poetics is reversed in these writings, where it takes second place to what we can call "extentional" approaches. As we will see, this shifting back and forth between intentional and extentional approaches is one important difference between the phenomenologies of DuBois and Gordon. Thus the knowing subject in DuBois changed identity and discipline as it wrote its many works. Earlier we noted that for DuBois it was not given to any one culture to see the whole truth. Similarly, it was not given to any one discipline or mode of the knowing subject to see the whole truth. The partiality of vision that DuBois saw as basic to all human cultures, he extended *a fortiori* to the disciplines and to the various modes that the knowing subject can adopt, including the poetic mode. Just as the "Submissive Man" must check and comple- ment the "Strong Man," so must poetics check and complement sociology and history, as well as being itself checked and complemented by them. Although DuBois never explicitly thematized the principles by which he was able to bring these different disciplines and modes of the subject together to produce that powerful discursive synthesis that I have called his socio-historical poetics, they are the primary keys to the metaphysical founda- tions of his thought. We will return to these foundations later. Here it must suffice to note that the poeticist element in this synthesis gave DuBois his distinctive path to the process of self-reflection and thus access to the original activity of the Africana consciousness.

The third and final factor in this account of the ethical/practical dimension of DuBois's phenomenology is its clear commitment to projects of cultural and racial equal- ity. In this commitment we see the love that reassembles the broken fragments of the vase of which Derek Walcott spoke. The racial hierarchies, the class inequalities, and the cari- caturing of identities produced by the coming into being of Western capitalism have given rise to human tragedies of major proportions. In both social and political terms, DuBois responded very thoughtfully and passionately to the devastating circumstances that these tragic outcomes created for Africana peoples. However, over the course of his long life these responses change a lot. In *The Philadelphia Negro*, DuBois outlined a program of limited assimilation, led by a Black elite, to deal specifically with the problem of racial as opposed to class inequality. In *Black Reconstruction*, DuBois discovers and explores the potential of the self-organizing capabilities of the African American masses as a key part of the solution to the problem of racial inequality. In *Dusk of Dawn*, DuBois explores an ethnic enclave strategy that calls for a period of separate economic and political organizing before inte- grating into the larger social mainstream. With his departure for Ghana towards the end of his life, it is possible to argue that DuBois had given up on changing the racial order of America. But in spite of these changes in his sociopolitical responses to the racializing processes of Western capitalism, his ethical responses to the human crises that it produced never wavered.

This unwavering ethical stance is most elegantly stated in the "final word" that closes *The Philadelphia Negro*. There DuBois links the problem of racial inequality directly to that question of questions: "after all who are men? Is every featherless biped to be counted a man and brother? Are all races and types to be joint heirs of the new earth that men have striven to raise in thirty centuries or more?" (1996, pp. 385–356). DuBois tells us that Western civilization has answered these questions in the negative on the basis of a widening but still very limited and exclusionary conception of humanity. After speaking about the conditional admittance of groups like the Celts and the Asians, DuBois turns to the case of the Africans. He writes:

> but with the Negroes of Africa we come to a full stop, and in its heart the civilized world with one accord denies that these come within the pale of nineteenth century humanity. This feeling, widespread and deep-seated, is, in America, the vastest of the Negro problems.
>
> *(p. 387)*

Here is DuBois, the poet, closing with potentiated second sight a major sociological work.

This, in brief outline, is DuBois's phenomenology of Africana self-consciousness. The Submissive Man, the tower, the veil, double consciousness, second sight, the love that puts the Submissive Man back together again are some of its distinguishing features. The double consciousness of which DuBois speaks cannot be adequately viewed as one of the stages of Hegel's phenomenology. Rather it is the theorizing of a period of imperial/racial domination in the self-consciousness of the Africana subject that is absent from the life of Hegel's European subject. Thus, when Shamoon Zamir asks:

> How is it then that DuBois can read Hegel quite so critically, before he has begun to read Marx, without (as far as is known) a knowledge of Kierkegaard, well before Alexandre Kojéve and Sartre's commentaries on the Phenomenology, and very much against the grain of the readings of Hegel common in nineteenth century America?
>
> *(1995, p. 117)*

I think that in addition to DuBois's genius, the answer is to be found in the uniqueness of this period of Black racialization that DuBois's phenomenology had to theorize. Although by no means complete within itself, this phenomenology revealed in its inner structure the paradigmatic form that other Africana phenomenologies, such as those of Fanon and Gordon would take. They all share with DuBois this distinguishing notion of double consciousness, different aspects of which they will thematize and develop.

FANON AND AFRICANA PHENOMENOLOGY

If DuBois contributed the first important chapter to an explicitly thematized phenomenology of Africana self-consciousness, then the second was clearly written by the Martinican psychoanalyst and revolutionary, Frantz Fanon. His major contribution to this particular subfield of Africana philosophy is the more detailed and incisive psycho-existential analysis of this historical phase of double consciousness identified by DuBois. In this effort, Fanon's achievements in *Black Skin, White Masks* remain unsurpassed. There is no finer or more detailed account of the state of racial double consciousness.

As self-consciousness, the human being was for Fanon "motion toward the world and toward his like. A movement of aggression, which leads to enslavement or to conquest; a movement of love, a gift of the self, the ultimate stage of what by common accord is called ethical orientation" (1967, p. 41). It is Fanon's view that every human consciousness has the capacity for these two kinds of movements. Further, it is the job of the phenomenologist and the psychologist to grasp in their originality and immediacy the specific meanings and the guiding telos of these two sets of creative movements that are inherent in human consciousness. This self-creative telos of individual human consciousness, Fanon comprehends as its "ontogeny" (p. 13). Thus the primary goal of his phenomenology is an account of the crisis confronting the ontogenesis of the Africana subject as a result of the historical phase of double consciousness that it is going through. In short, like DuBois, this crisis constitutes Fanon's occasion for self-reflection, the contradictory condition that motivates his journey inward.

However, again like DuBois, Fanon makes no absolute epistemic commitments to this ontogenic approach as a whole or to its specific philosophical and psychoanalytic dimensions. Indeed, given the socio-historical origins of this phase of double consciousness, Fanon insisted that "ontology cannot explain the being of the black man" (1967, p. 110). Consequently, ontogeny must be supplemented by sociogeny. In other words, the self-constituting powers of the Africana consciousness must be dialectically supplemented and checked by the formative powers of socio- cultural orders.

Within this onto-/socio-genic approach, Fanon further refines his path to the practice of self-reflection by rising the ontogenic question of how should "the psychic modality" of human consciousness be studied? Fanon identifies two distinct approaches to self-reflective knowledge within the overall framework of his ontogenic project. The first, which is on the "philosophical level" (Fanon, 1967, p. 23), aims at the immediate grasping of the human subject through intuitive accounts of its basic needs and its movements toward the world. These intuitive accounts will always be incomplete and provisional, but at the same time very necessary. Hence, this philosophical approach requires that one should "strive unremittingly for a concrete and ever new understanding of man" (p. 22). In developing these intuitive accounts Fanon made use of both a poetic and a Sartrean inflected phenomenological reduction. As in the case of DuBois, much of the power of Fanon's writing comes from his ability to incorporate poetic insights into his socio-historical and psychological writings. Indeed Fanon's text is unimaginable without the self-reflective knowledge produced within the frameworks of these two epistemic reductions. Thus an important part of making Fanon's phenomenology more visible would be to make more explicit the ways in which he combined the use of these poetic and phenomenological reductions.

The second approach to self-reflection that Fanon identified was psychoanalytic. In contrast to the concrete orientation of the first or philosophical one, this approach first constructs what Habermas would call a general interpretation of the development of the human subject, and then attempts to grasp the concrete individual in terms of its deviations from this model. The use of this psychoanalytic model led to Fanon's engagements with Freud, Jung, Adler, and Lacan. In other words, Fanon will supplement and check his more concrete and philosophical approach to self-reflection with this more abstract and psychoanalytic one. As in the case above with poetry and phenomenology, the links that Fanon establishes between the psychoanalytic and the philosophical are themselves original, creative movements of Fanon's consciousness toward the world that he did not explicitly thematize, but they hold the keys to the distinct metaphysical foundations upon which his thought rests. It is this complex and synthetic methodology that informs Fanon's phenomenology. Its psychoanalytic dimensions separate it from DuBois's. However, both are interested in the "psychopathological and philosophical explanation of the state of being a Negro" (Fanon, 1967, p. 15).

DOUBLE CONSCIOUSNESS AND FANONIAN PHENOMENOLOGY

What is the state of being a "negro"? It is a state of enforced negrification in which colonized Africana peoples lost their earlier cultural identities and became identified by the color of their skin. The outer form of this state is the substituting of an epidermal identity in the place of a cultural one. The inner content of this outer transformation is the socio-historical reality of being forced to live as the unconscious, liminal shadow, the repressed and undesirable side of the imperial European subject that had racialized its identity as white. The caricature of "the negro" is first and foremost for Fanon a dark projection that is basic to the cathartic and scapegoating mechanisms of the European psyche. This projective mechanism Fanon describes as follows: "in the degree to which I find in myself something unheard-of, something reprehensible, only one solution remains for me: to get rid of it, to ascribe its origins to someone else" (1967, p. 190). The stereotype of "the negro" is a discursive crystallization of the contents of an "inordinately black hollow" in the European psyche that it must externalize and experience as belonging to someone else. Thus for Fanon, in the West, "the Negro has one function: that of symbolizing the lower emotions, the baser inclinations, the dark side of the soul" (p. 190). This is the meaning of negrifica-tion, the state of being a "negro."

Because the African is not a "negro," negrification as a form of racialization produced what Fanon called a psycho-existential deviation, an aberration of affect in the psyche of Africana peoples. Such a deviation arises in the psyche of a people when "an inferi-ority complex has been created by the death and burial of its local cultural originality" (Fanon, 1967, p. 18). In the case of Africana peoples, this deviation is the opening up of that racial fissure in their sense of a "We" that DuBois described as double consciousness. Fanon writes: "the black man has two dimensions. One with his fellows, the other with the white man" (p. 17). However, these two sets of relations are not always of equal weight. As negrification takes hold, the second set begins to transform the first. In its being for another Africana self-consciousness, the negrified African will be profoundly influenced by the relationship with the white other. Self-evaluation will take the form: I am better of or worse than another "negro" depending on whether I am whiter or more Europeanized. This detouring of all intersubjective relations through white norms and evaluations is a major disturbance in the interactive relations of the Africana subject that follows from its "two dimensions."

For Fanon, this "self-division" and its consequences are the keys to the state of being a "negro." His approach to this internal division is to examine carefully its distorting impact on the relations of "the negro" with others, both Black and white. Fanon begins his analysis of the disruptive impact of this double consciousness with an examination of "the negro's" attitude toward his own and the colonizer's languages. Here Fanon shows that the distort-ing impact of double consciousness is the negrified subject's desire to present him/herself as a master of the languages of Europe. Before the white other, this display of linguistic mas-tery is a bid for recognition and a demonstration of the degree to which he/she has rejected the African past. Before the Black other, the same display may be an attempt to gain recog-nition for how far that individual has succeeded in Europeanizing his/her existence. The underlying disturbance in self-other relations that these attitudes to language reveal is the following: that the racialized African "will be proportionately whiter – that is, he will come closer to being a real human being – in direct ratio to his mastery of the French language" (Fanon, 1967, p. 18). In the midst of this disturbance we can hear the DuBoisian questions: "What, after all, am I?" Am I a French person or am I a 'Negro?' Can I be both?" Fanon could have made the same point using religion, music, philosophy, dance, or literature as the sociogenic reality behind these psycho-existential deviations.

However, this general account of the double consciousness of the negrified Africana subject was not the primary goal of Fanon's phenomenology. Rather, it was the exploration of two specific possibilities within this broader disturbance in Africana self-other relations. The first was the tragic possibility of "the negro" who deals with his/her negrification by attempting to conceal it behind "white masks." Fanon develops this possibility through examinations of cases of Blacks who must have white lovers. In such cases, Fanon recognizes a self-negating desire in the Black to be white, which for him represents the extreme point of self-alienation in "the state of being a Negro." Fanon also makes it clear that not all racialized Africana subjects are in such extreme states of alienation. But nonetheless, he wants to point out their existence and examine them in detail.

The second possibility within the broader disturbance in Africana self-other relations that Fanon takes up is indeed quite different. It is the agonizing possibility of an Africana subject working his/her way out of "the state of being a Negro." It is here that the awakening of potentiated second sight makes its appearance in Fanon. What is the lived experience of the racialized Africana subject who is awakening from the nightmare and false consciousness of his/her negrification? This is the question to which Fanon brought the combined powers of his distinct phenomenological methodology. It is here that we can see the breathtaking moments in which the poetic and phenomenological reductions are brought together produce self-reflective knowledge of the most profound nature.

The early awakenings of the negrified Africana subject are marked by the experience of not being able to affirm a self of one's own choosing in the presence of the institutionally empowered stereotype of "the negro" that the white psyche must externalize and project onto another. Thus it is the experience of walking a tightrope located between the opposing but unequal egocentric pulls of these two sources of Africana selfhood. This is what Fanon meant when he said that "the black man has no ontological resistance in the eyes of the white man" (1967, p. 110). Normatively empowered by institutionalization, the image of the Black in the white mind overpowers the self-image of the awakening Africana subject. This is the source of the power and weight of ordinary second sight. It is against this weight, and in spite of its ontological power that the awakening Africana subject must fight to regain first sight and potentiated second sight, explode the caricature of "the negro," and affirm an identity of his/her own choosing. Adding to the pain and terror of this struggle is the fact that below the tightrope on which the Africana subject is walking is "the zone of non-being." To fail is to experience a collapse of one's ego and a fall into nothingness. It is the stumbling and falling of this awakening subject on the edge of non-being, the experiences of going out of and coming back into ego-being that Fanon's phenomenology describes so powerfully.

This description begins with an archeological view of some of the organizing schemas that structure the consciousness of the Africana subject. At the most basic level we find an intentional schema that consists of the motions of this subject toward the world that Fanon earlier described as being basic to human beings. He then goes on to describe a corporeal or bodily schema that is also an integral part of the Africana self-image. On the third layer, Fanon identifies an epidermal or historico-racial schema that is yet another important part of the identity of the Africana subject. These are the key frameworks that ground and shape the identity of our awakening man or woman. In the mind of this subject, joy and recognition should accompany his/her motions toward the other and the world. His/her bodily schema is the basis of a "physiological self" that balances one in space, localizes sensations, and makes one physically attractive to the other. His/her historico-racial schema was either African, African American, Afro-Caribbean, or Afro-Latin American.

Fanon gives us several examples of the implosive ego collapse that the awakening Africana self has experienced before the institutionalized power of the white gaze. Echoing the youthful DuBois's experience of racial stigmatization by a white playmate, Fanon uses the case of a young child to illustrate the power and content of the white gaze: "Mama, see the Negro! I am frightened." Behind this fright was a very different set of intentional, bodily, and historico-racial schemas that challenges those of the Africana subject in the early phases of denegrification. The resulting clash between these negrifying and denegrifying perspectives Fanon describes as follows: "Assailed at various points, the corporeal scheme crumbled, its place taken by the epidermal schema. In the train it was no longer a question of being aware of my body in the third person but in a triple person" (1967, p. 112). In other words, this encounter with the white other was experienced as "an amputation, an excision, a hemorrhage" (p. 112).

If this awakening subject is to achieve denegrification and potentiated second sight, such amputations and falls into the zone of non-being must be endured and overcome. In the zone of non-being, "an authentic upheaval can be born," that is, new images of self, new projects for bringing one's self back into ego-being can be undertaken. This push for rebirth is strong, defiant, almost compulsive. Through this agency Fanon's awakening subject takes the broken pieces of his/her selfhood and refashions them into a new project of being in the world. One new project explored by Fanon is the possibility of asserting one's self "as a BLACK MAN" (emphasis original). However, like the earlier project, this one could also go down in defeat. In the event of such an outcome, one must return to the zone of non-being with faith in its self-creating powers. Out of it will come other possibilities such as asserting one's self as a rational or scholarly person, as in the case of DuBois, or as an irrational seer, the very embodiment of unreason. These new projects of selfhood Fanon sees as dialectical possibilities that are open to the awakening Black subject if he/she is "able to accomplish this descent into a real hell" (1967, p. 10). In short, phenomenologically speaking, the zone of non-being is a valuable resource for the subject who is working his/her way out negrification and the double consciousness that it produces.

THE ETHICAL/PRACTICAL DIMENSIONS

Important as the above inner struggles against negrification are, they cannot by themselves overthrow the institutionalized power of white racism. As we've seen, this racism was for Fanon both onto- and socio-genic in nature. It was not the truth of negrification that defeated this struggling subject but the social power that came with its institutionalization. This sociological dimension had to be defeated through revolutionary struggles of the type that Fanon described so powerfully in *The Wretched of the Earth*. Thus as in the case of DuBois, Fanon's phenomenology is intricately linked to an ethical/practical project. This project has several distinguishing features such as its ethic of love or its commitment to national independence. For reasons of space, I will discuss only the ethic of love.

The ethical dimensions of Fanon's phenomenology have been given their most systematic treatment by Nelson Maldonado-Torres. The originality of his treatment is the elucidating of the place of love in Fanon's ethics. Maldonado-Torres's key to locating the site of Fanonian love is a masterful "phenomenology of the cry" (2002, p. 173) in Fanon's work. He shows that when examined in this way, the cry leads us to the loving responses of which Fanon's awakening subject is sometimes capable. These responses echo very loudly the love that reassembles broken vases of which Walcott spoke.

For Maldonado-Torres, the cry is "the revelation of someone who has been forgotten or wronged" (2002, p. 173). It is the audible sigh that sometimes follows a train of defeated attempts at self-affirmation. But as Maldonado-Torres shows, the cry in Fanon is much more than this plea for self-preservation. It is also "a call for the Other" (p. 179). It is this sociality in the cry of Fanon's awakening Africana subject that is the source of its moving ethical power. In other words, even though this subject will often find him/herself on the edge of non-being, it is still possible to rise above pure self-interest to cry for and reach out to others who are in similar or worse states of negrification. Thus it is no surprise that Fanon begins and ends *Black Skin, White Masks* with such strong affirmations of his belief in the possibilities of love. This in brief is Fanon's contribution to Africana phenomenology.

LEWIS GORDON AND AFRICANA PHENOMOLOGY

If the first two chapters in an explicit Africana phenomenology were written by DuBois and Fanon, then the third has been written by Lewis Gordon. His chapter makes several important contributions to this sub-field of Africana philosophy that both engage and carry forward the work of DuBois and Fanon. The way in which Gordon engages Fanon can be clearly seen in his *Fanon and the Crisis of European Man* (1995b), and his engagements with DuBois in his *Existentia Africana* (2000). These engagements make it unmistakably clear that Gordon's occasion for self-reflection is also the racialization of Africana self-consciousness within the projective and exploitative structures of modern European capitalism. Here, for reasons of space, I will take up only two of the important contributions that Gordon has made to the sub-field of Africana phenomenology. The first of these is the greater systematization that he has brought to this area of Africana thought. The second is his phenomenological analysis of "the state of being a Negro" in the postcolonial/post-segregation era, in other words, an era in which the institutional power of white projects of negrification have been significantly weakened as a result of the anti-colonial and anti-racist struggles of the 1960s. Let us begin with the first of these two important contributions.

Gordon makes clear very early the nature of his method of study. He refers to it as "descriptive ontology or what is sometimes called existential phenomenology" (Levering-Lewis, 1995, p. 5). This is the methodology by which Gordon brackets the everyday world and enters on his own path to the practice of self-reflection. Gordon's path inward to the study of consciousness has been shaped by strong influences from Sartre and Husserl, as well as his own practice of creative writing. Gordon brings these three reflective streams together to forge a path to the study of consciousness that is original and distinct, and thus different from the paths used by DuBois or Fanon. Gordon's distinctness stems from the stronger Husserlian influences on this area of his thought than is the case with DuBois or Fanon. These influences account for the clear presence of reflections that are done within what Husserl called the phenomenological reduction, and the absence of the psychoanalytic strategies that are so strong in Fanon. Further distinguishing Gordon's self-reflective path is the fact that the influences of his poetics are not as strong as they are in the cases of DuBois and Fanon. However, Gordon and Fanon share strong Sartrean influences on their strategies of self-reflection. In short, to understand how Gordon sees the world when puts on his phenomenological glasses, we need to understand these factors shaping the curve of their lenses.

Although Gordon and Fanon share strong Sartrean influences, they manifest themselves very differently in their reflective approaches to the study of Africana self-consciousness. Like Sartre, Gordon makes a sharper distinction between ego and consciousness than either Fanon or DuBois. It is consciousness rather than the ego that is the primary focus of Gordon's analysis. This is an important difference with Fanon, who, as psycho-analyst, focused more on the ego. This accounts for the more philosophical as opposed to the psychological orientation of Gordon's work. It also accounts for why Gordon's con-tributions include the greater systematizing of the philosophical foundations of Africana phenomenology.

With his focus on consciousness, Gordon's definition of the human reality to be stud-ied is different from Fanon's. Rather than motion towards the world, which would reflect the desires of the ego as consciousness, Gordon defines the core of human reality as free-dom. As freedom, we are not determined by any law or necessity from within or without. We are free to choose our existence with nothing to legitimate or guarantee it other than our choice. Consequently, we are primarily responsible for who we are and what we will become.

However, according to Sartre and Gordon, phenomenological reflection reveals that the experiencing of ourselves as freedom produces disturbing feelings of anguish, of being nothing and hence an intense desire to be something definite. Thus we often evade this anguished freedom by fleeing into the facticity and determinateness of a closed ego. This ego could be structured around being a doctor, a lawyer, a philosopher, or a parent. As any of these forms of ego-being, I now experience myself as something that is definite enough to negate the nothingness and anguish of my freedom. This "effort to hide from responsibil-ity for ourselves as freedom" (Levering-Lewis, 1995, p. 8) is what both Sartre and Gordon meant by bad faith. In bad faith, "I flee a displeasing truth for pleasing falsehood. I must convince myself that a falsehood is in fact true" (p. 8). In short, to be in bad faith is to lie to ourselves and believe the lie.

As Fanon's ego produced a shadow, so too does Gordon's. However, although the pro-jecting of these shadows is crucial to their accounts of "the state of being a Negro," it is important to note the significant differences in the origins of these shadows. Fanon's is psychological and engages the Freudian concept of an unconscious, while Gordon's is philosophical and has its roots in the dialectic between being and nothingness as it affects the formation of human consciousness and freedom. It is the discursive use of the notion of bad faith to thematize this dialectic that enables Gordon to systematize the philosophical as opposed to the psychological foundations of Africana phenomenology.

In Gordon's case, it is the ontogenic tensions produced by the lie that separates the ego from its anguished shadow that produces the need for mechanisms of projective catharsis rather than the ego's need to repress its "lower emotions." But in both cases, self-reflection has produced portraits of the human subject as a site of agency that has to project a shadow while at the same time denying that it is doing so. And in both, this is directly linked to the production and persistence of what Gordon calls anti-Black racism. This racism is for Gordon a bad faith attempt "to deny the blackness within" (anguished freedom) by projecting it onto the Black skins of Africana peoples while asserting an ego that is struc-tured around whiteness. This is the manner in which Gordon has more clearly systema-tized the links between phenomenological philosophy and the racialization of Africana self-consciousness.

In addition to thematizing and systematizing the dynamics of bad faith that remained implicit in Fanon, Gordon has also taken up the challenge of making more phenomeno-logically consistent the linking of ontogenic dynamics, such as those of bad faith, with the sociogenic ones (e.g., institutions) that come together to produce oppressive social realities like anti-Black racism. Consequently, like Alfred Schutz, Gordon needs a phenomenology of the social world in addition to that of individual self-consciousness. But the ethical/

practical project of transformation to which Gordon's phenomenology is linked is not the one of rescuing rationality from its positivistic capture that Schutz shared with Husserl. Rather, with DuBois and Fanon, Gordon's ethical/practical project is one of denegrification and racial equality. Consequently, he needs both a theory and a praxis that will allow him to link the strategic demands of dismantling racist social structures to the intentional activity of the transcendental domain as disclosed by phenomenology.

In effecting this synthesis, Gordon achieves greater phenomenological consistency than DuBois or Fanon. The distinctness of Gordon's synthesis is that it grasps institutions in terms of bad faith rather than their historical materiality as established social structures. From the perspective of bad faith, Gordon sees institutions as social practices that limit freedom or encourage the evading of freedom. These limits are conceptualized by Gordon as a continuum of relations that range from choices to options. "Actional" choices that are institutionally recognized or supported are instances of the social affirmation of one's freedom. At the other end of the continuum are options. Options are "calcified" situations in which institutions are not only separated from the intentional streams of meaning out of which they arose, but at the same time severely restrict the set of choices they make available to individuals (2005). Thus it is in terms of options and choices that Gordon thematizes the problems of class and racial inequality. Three responses of individuals and groups to these differences in options and choices are of particular interest to Gordon. These are theodicean justifications by elites with actional choices, implosivity by groups who are without them, and revolution. The first two are for Gordon bad faith responses and are important for his intentional reading of institutions. Thus it is through the use of the notion of bad faith on both the ontogenic and sociogenic levels that Gordon is able to achieve a greater degree of phenomenological consistency.

As noted earlier, Gordon's second important contribution to Africana phenomenology is his analysis of the persistence of anti-Black racism in the post-colonial/post-segregation era. In our examination of Fanon, we saw that negrification and anti-Black racism, though having their roots in psycho-existential shadow of the white ego, derived a lot of their power and persistence from social processes of institutionalization. One of the primary marks of the post-colonial/post-segregation era has been the removal of many of the institutional supports that reinforced the stereotype of "the Negro." Indeed it is possible to argue that in the present era, there remain three crucial areas of American society that continue to provide institutional support for anti-Black racism: the practice of residential segregation, law enforcement, and the entertainment value of anti-Black stereotype in mass media. This is a very different world from that of Fanon's or DuBois's. Can anti-Black racism persist within such a weakened institutional order? The significant contribution of Gordon's important book, *Bad Faith and Anti-Black Racism*, is its detailed answer to this question.

Gordon's answer is a definite yes. This answer in the affirmative is based primarily on the persistence of strong projective needs arising from the bad faith practices of white subjects that are still externalized onto Black bodies. In other words, unless whites find new scapegoats or more good faith ways of facing the anguish of their freedom, they will continue to see Africana peoples through the eyes of that unacceptable anguish. This distorted seeing will persist in spite of the removal of its institutional props. This persistence means that Africana peoples are still being racialized and its accompanying processes of double consciousness still being reproduced. For Gordon the strongest indicator of this is the phenomenon of "black anti-blackness" which he analyzes as a manifestation of double consciousness. His analysis of Black anti-Blackness is a brilliant updating of CLR James's classic summary statement of this peculiar phenomenon in, *The Black Jacobins*: "'why do you ill-treat your mule in that?' asked a colonist of a carter. 'But when I do not work, I am beaten, when he does not work, I beat him – he is my Negro'" (James, 1989, p. 15).

OTHER CONTRIBUTIONS

In addition to DuBois, Fanon, and Gordon, other important contributions to an Africana phenomenology have been made by Sylvia Wynter, Wilson Harris, Rene Menil, Charles Long, Nelson Maldonado-Torres, James Bryant, and myself which I can only mention briefly. My own contribution has been to open up the chapter on African existential thought before the start of colonization, slavery, negrification, and Europeanization (Henry, 2000, pp. 144–166). Bryant's contribution has been a careful phenomenological analysis of the transformation of pre-colonial African religious identities to Afro-Christian ones as a response to negrification. Long's contribution has been a phenomenology of the rituals and ceremonies of African American religious life. As we've already seen, Maldonado-Torres's contribution has been in the area of phenomenology and ethics. Harris's contribution is a detailed exploration of the creative potential of the zone of non-being or what he calls "the void." Rene Menil's contribution has been a Hegelian inflected phenomenological account of the internalizing of the stereotype of "the Negro." Finally, Wynter's contribution has been a historicizing and semioticizing of the transcendental domain that can be usefully compared to the work of the German philosopher, Karl-Otto Apel. Wynter introduces these changes through her important concepts of knowledge-constitutive goals and liminal categories. These contributions together with those of DuBois, Fanon, and Gordon give us a fairly comprehensive picture of the phenomenological dimensions of Africana thought.

PHILOSOPHICAL IMPLICATIONS OF AFRICANA PHENOMENOLOGY

We began our analysis of Africana phenomenology with a clearing of the cultural terrain needed to make this philosophy visible. In particular, this clearing was directed at some of the exclusive claims that had been established between rationality and European phenomenology, as well as the establishing of flexible variations in three crucial areas of phenomenological philosophy: the occasion for self-reflection, the path to self-reflection, and the ethical/practical projects of phenomenologies. Now that we have outlined Africana phenomenology in the space of this clearing, it should be evident that it is a discourse that has been conditioned by and draws on a specific set of lived experiences and the cultural traditions of Africa and Europe. In this sense it is quite different from Western phenomenology.

What are we to make of the differences between these two philosophical discourses? Are they of a similar nature to the differences within each of them? Are the rational and allegedly universal structures of Western phenomenology such that they can incorporate Africana philosophy as a particular case without significant philosophical remainders? From the nature of the variations in cultural contexts, occasions for self-reflection, paths to reflection, and ethical/practical projects, I think it should be clear that neither of these phenomenologies could absorb the other as a case without significant theoretical loss. The variations just referred to are not quantitative but qualitative in nature. Thus in spite of important areas of overlap and convergence, these qualitative differences have created significant degrees of incommensurability between the creative and discursive codes of these two phenomenologies. The resulting divergences are such that they limit the universal claims of both, creating epistemic breaks that can only be engaged/resolved through conversation and comparative analysis.

From the philosophical standpoint, these incommensurate or unassimilable differences are primarily the result of metaphysical differences in the a priori foundations pre-supposed by the knowledge producing practices of these two phenomenologies. I am aware that Western philosophy is currently going through what Habermas and others have called a "post-metaphysical" phase. Does this mean that Africana philosophy is also going through a similar phase? I don't think so. The metaphysical foundations of Africana philosophy have never included the absolute claims for reason that have been at the center of the transcendental foundations of Western philosophy. In the Africana tradition, reason has always had to share the metaphysical stage with poetics and historical action. Indeed, in its post-metaphysical phase – a phase in which it is scaling down its claims for reason – Western philosophy may move closer to some of the fundamental metaphysical positions of Africana philosophy.

What is most striking about Habermas's post-metaphysical arguments is that, like Derrida's attempts to deconstruct Western metaphysics, they are profoundly metaphysical. Habermas uses the term metaphysical to designate the thinking of philosophical idealism from Plato through Plotinus to Kant, Fichte, Schelling, and Hegel. On the other hand, he sees late medieval nominalism, modern empiricism, neo-pragmatism, and post-structuralism as anti-metaphysical philosophies (Habermas, 1992, p. 29). What I see both of these groups sharing is the necessity of going beyond "physics" the moment that they step out of specific exercises of knowledge production to assess the onto-epistemic significance of those exercises. Thus empiricists cannot on the basis of empirical practices rule out or establish their priority over intuitive or other non-empirical modes of knowing. To establish such as claim, the empiricist must move beyond his/her specific knowledge producing practice and by means of logic, rhetoric, future projections of knowledge accumulation, etc., make the argument for priority, or foundational status. It is these questions of discourse-constitutive priorities regarding explanatory factors (Spirit, matter, class, race), disciplines, methodologies, conceptions of the human being, and ethical/ practical projects that constitute the ineliminable metaphysical elements in all discourses. They are shared by Habermas's metaphysical and anti-metaphysical groups of philosophers. These pre-theoretical or discourse-constitutive choices are inescapable, and their justification or non-justification takes us into the realm of metaphysics.

When we direct our focus at the discourse-constitutive foundations of DuBois's thought, we can observe the presence of a familiar set of competing explanatory factors, disciplines, methodologies, conceptions of the human being as we find in Hegel or Husserl. What we do not find is a similar prioritizing or systematizing of these discourse-constitutive fundamentals in relation to reason or Spirit. DuBois appears to enclose these fundamentals within a very different set of epistemic norms although he never really took the time to specify them. Consequently, there has been a lot of debate about this particular dimension of DuBois's thought. Cornel West interprets this refusal to specify as a pragmatist evasion of epistemology (1989, pp. 138–140). Robert Gooding-Williams objects strongly to this reading of DuBois's refusal (1991–1992, pp. 517–542).

Within this unspecified DuBoisian framework, reason and Spirit are two of the fundamentals rather than the supreme principle of prioritizing and systematizing. Earlier, we noted that DuBois did not make as strong an onto-epistemic commitment to the paradigm of consciousness as either Hegel or Husserl. The same was true of his attitude toward the method of poetics as well as those of history and sociology. In his important essay, "Sociology Hesitant," DuBois argues for the possibilities of doing sociology from the perspectives of both a free and an externally determined subject. At the same time he makes no arguments for continuity between the two positions or for a fixed, pre-theoretical hierarchical arrangement between them. One leaves this essay with the feeling that he is equally happy with both. I think that DuBois's attitude to all of these discourse- constitutive fundamentals that he organizes and uses can be best compared to the attitude of a jazz musician to his/her improvisations. They are all real epistemic offerings; they possess creative potential, but they are partial and limited formations that could not only be done differently, but also need to be checked and complemented. Thus most, if not all, of DuBois pre-theoretical orderings of selected fundamentals are provisional, variable, in need of complements, and therefore change significantly in his different texts. This is the metaphysical position that we confront in DuBois's works. Thus, there appears to be an improvisational aesthetic norm guiding the metaphysical orderings that make DuBoisian knowledge production possible.

In the case of Fanon, we can observe a similarly relaxed and improvisational attitude toward the problems of prioritizing and systematizing discourse-constitutive fundamentals. This attitude is evident in his often-quoted remark: "I leave methods to the botanists and the mathematicians" (Fanon, 1967, p. 12). Without clear specification, Fanon employs poetics, existential philosophy, and psychoanalysis to define his path to consciousness. In this strategy, we saw that Fanon embraced the concrete intuitive method of existential philosophy as well as the more abstract method of a general interpretation used by psychoanalysis. Further, we saw that this multi-layered ontogenic discourse was implicitly linked to a sociogenic base.

Methodologically speaking, this sociogenic base comes more fully into view in *The Wretched of the Earth*, where the focus of Fanon's phenomenological analyses is not so much individual as it is national consciousness. Thematized in primarily Marxist terms, the relationships between the sociogenic and the phenomenological factors constituting the national consciousness of the colonized in revolt are configured differently. These and other breaks in the composition and ordering of discourse-constitutive fundamentals between this work and *Black Skin, White Masks*, remind us of similar breaks between major works by DuBois. The great metaphysical secret of *The Wretched of the Earth* is its almost seamless synthesis of existential phenomenology, transcendental phenomenology, psychoanalysis, Afro-Caribbean poetics, Marxist political economy, and Africana colonial history. How these different discourses were brought together, whence the "tidalectical" flows between them, or the occasions for shifting from one to the other? Of these creative and synthetic strategies Fanon does not really speak. He leaves us completely on our own, and at the mercy of our own creative and synthetic capabilities.

Although not quite as improvisational as DuBois, none of these priorities in factors of explanation, methods, and disciplines were made explicit, or the creative strategies by which they were synthesized carefully outlined. Thus the internal structure of Fanon's psychosocial poetics remains as much a mystery as DuBois's socio-historical poetics. However, in spite of these outward signs of disorder, Fanon's discourses display remarkable coherence and unmatched explanatory power. To account for this, I suggest a set of improvisational metaphysical principles that are quite similar to those of DuBois.

In the case of Gordon, where we find the greatest concern with the pre-theoretical systematization of discourse-constitutive fundamentals, the presence of this improvisational metaphysics is clearly evident. Indeed in Gordon's case the connection to jazz is direct as it appears in his work and through the fact that he is a jazz drummer. As we've seen, Gordon has established a clear priority of consciousness over the ego, the intentional over the extentional, and the free over the externally determined subject. However, at the same time, there is no absolute commitment to the paradigm of consciousness that matches Husserl's or even the early Sartre. Rather what we find is a similar improvisational attitude toward this particular piece of discursive systematization. The difference between Gordon and DuBois or Fanon is not to be found in their attitudes toward specific systematic orderings, but in the fact that DuBois and Fanon had more of these improvised orderings going at the same time. Gordon has fewer, has worked out the philosophical ones more systematically, but his attitude toward them is not final but improvisational. This distinct metaphysical position that we can observe in Gordon, Fanon, and DuBois was not evident in either the African or Afro-Christian phases of Africana philosophy. Rather, it emerged in the period that elsewhere I have called poeticist/historicist. This double designation was a way of representing the compound and synthetic nature of this phase of Africana thought. However, I did not really develop the provisional and improvisational nature of the creative codes that guided the formation of these compound syntheses.

If indeed this still-to-be-thematized set of improvisational codes are the keys to the metaphysical foundations of this specific phase of Africana phenomenology, then it should be clear why it cannot be incorporated into Western phenomenology without significant philosophical loss. When more fully thematized, it is very likely to be an original metaphysics that reflects the experiences of Africana peoples and the distinct knowledge producing practices that were developed under the world-shattering conditions of racialization and colonization. Its spirit is very different from that of Euro-American pragmatism or of mainstream European philosophy. If I had to give this metaphysics a more conventional name it would be creative realism, as what it assumes to be ultimately real is the creative act in its spontaneous movements rather than any of its specific creations. This is the creative code, the compositional principle of Africana metaphysics that makes it impossible for its phenomenology to be absorbed by the rationalism of Western phenomenology. Within the context of this improvisational metaphysics, the process of de-centering reason that Western metaphysics is presently going through could hardly be viewed as a post-metaphysical event. Rather it would very likely be seen as just one of many contrapuntal movements or complementary reversals that must take place among discursive formations. Such movements must take place as the capacity to disclose the whole truth is not given to any single discursive formation.

CONCLUSION

In the foregoing analyses, I have emphasized the differences between Africana and Western phenomenologies. These differences were both thematic, such as the issue of racialization, and metaphysical as indicated by the different rules guiding the prioritizing and systematizing of discourse-constitutive fundamentals. However, the broader comparative framework employed gave some indication of a number of areas of similarity.

The question that now arises from this clearer outlining of Africana phenomenology is the following: in what from the Africana perspective is a post-imperial as opposed to a post-metaphysical age, and how are these two phenomenologies to relate to each other? Clearly the next phases in these phenomenologies are not going to be identical. The cultural and racial differences will in all probability continue to be important sources of difference.

What will the post-"negro" phase of Africana phenomenology be like? What will it bring
to the philosophical table in the place of double consciousness, second sight, white masks,
and an improvisational metaphysics? What will follow the "post-metaphysical" phase of
Western phenomenology? What will it bring to the philosophical table in the place of its
earlier claims for a universal reason? Is there a systematic relation between the post-imperial and the "post-metaphysical" phases of these two phenomenologies?

These important questions can only be adequately answered by developing new and
more innovative modes of comparative philosophical analysis that do not attempt to subsume culturally distinct philosophies under the categories of another. Rather, these new
modes of comparative analysis should seek to create bridges, partial points or areas of
complementary convergence, meta-philosophical discourses, and communicative groups
between these culturally distinct philosophies. The need for such modes of comparative
analysis is one of the important consequences that follow from this clearer recognition of
Africana phenomenology.

REFERENCES

Derrida, J. (1976). *Of grammatology.* Baltimore, MD: Johns Hopkins University Press.
Derrida, J. (1989). *Edmund Husserl's the origins of geometry.* Lincoln, NE: University of Nebraska
    Press.
Descartes, R. (1960). *Meditations on first philosophy.* Indianapolis, IN: Bobbs-Merrill Publishing.
DuBois, W. E. B. (1969). *The souls of Black folk.* New York: Fawcett Publications.
DuBois, W. E. B. (1996). *The Philadelphia Negro.* Philadelphia, PA: University of Pennsylvania
    Press.
DuBois, W. E. B. (1999). *Darkwater.* New York: Dover Publications.
Dussel, E. (1996). *The underside of modernity.* Atlantic Highlands, NJ: Humanities Press.
Fanon, F. (1967). *Black skin, White masks.* New York: Grove Press.
Gooding-Williams, R. (1991–92). Evading narrative myth, evading prophetic pragmatism:
    Cornel West's *The American evasion of philosophy. The Massachusetts Review, 32*(4), 517–542.
Gordon, L. (1995a). *Bad faith and anti-black racism.* Atlantic Highlands, NJ: Humanities Press.
Gordon, L. (1995b). *Fanon and the crisis of European man.* New York: Routledge.
Gordon, L. (2000). *Existentia Africana.* New York: Routledge.
Gordon, L. (2005). Fanon and development: A philosophical look. *Africa Development, 29*(1),
    71–94.
Habermas, J. (1971). *Knowledge and human interests.* Boston, MA: Beacon Press.
Habermas, J. (1971). *The early theological writings.* Philadelphia, PA: University of Pennsylvania
    Press.
Habermas, J. (1987). *The theory of communicative action.* Boston, MA: Beacon Press.
Habermas, J. (1992). *Postmetaphysical thinking.* Cambridge: MIT Press.
Hegel, G. (1967). *The phenomenology of mind.* New York: Harper & Row.
Henry, P. (2000). *Caliban's reason.* New York: Routledge.
Husserl, E. (1970). *The crisis of European sciences and transcendental phenomenology.* Evanston, IL:
    Northwestern University Press.
Husserl, E. (1975). *Ideas.* New York: Collier Books.
James, C. L. R. (1989). *The Black Jacobins.* New York: Vintage Books.
Levering-Lewis, D. (1995). *WEB DuBois: A reader.* New York: Henry Holt & Co.

Maldonado-Torres, N. (2002). *Thinking from the limits of being: Levinas, Fanon, Dussel and the cry of ethical revolt* [Unpublished doctoral dissertation]. Brown University.
Sartre, J.-P. (1956). *Being and nothingness.* New York: Philosophical Library.
Walcott, D. (1993). *The Antilles.* New York: Farrar, Strauss, Giroux.
West, C. (1989). *The American evasion of philosophy.* Madison, WI: University of Wisconsin Press.
Zamir, S. (1995). *Dark voices.* Chicago, IL: University of Chicago Press.

INDEX

Achebe, C., *Things Fall Apart* 250
activism 3, 34, 35, 178; anti-Apartheid 2;
    Black 240, 242; mental health and 24
Adams, P. 80
Adler, A. 52, 101–102, 103, 104
affective ankylosis 186–188
"affective tetanisation" 188–189
African National Congress 4
Africana phenomenology 14–15, 16,
    247, 248, 270; Dubois' contribution to
    255–258; European phenomenology and
    248–249; Fanon's contribution to 258–259;
    Gordon's contribution to 263–266;
    philosophical implications of 266–269;
    self-reflection 250, 251
Afro-Pessimism 15–16
Agamben, G. 211–212
agency 13, 69, 163, 164, 170, 172, 178
agitation 37, 38
Ahmed, S. 14, 196, 197, 201; *The Cultural
    Politics of Emotion* 234; *Strange Encounters* 241
Alcoff, L. M. 140, 229
Algeria 8, 23, 27, 30, 33, 49, 65; French
    drama 24; *see also* Blida-Joinville
    Psychiatric Hospital; North Africans
Algiers school 28, 29, 31, 32, 33, 37
alienation 3, 9, 23, 24, 26, 27, 32, 49, 53, 67,
    68, 101, 104, 166, 167; concrete existence
    105; madness and 54; mental illness and
    31; *see also* disalienation
Allport, 82
Al-Saji, A. 13, 195, 198, 199, 201; "Too Late:
    Racialized Time and the Closure of the
    Past" 194
alter-ego 51, 53
ankylosis 186–187, 188, 189
anonymity 160, 161
anosognosia 154
anthropology 143
anti-Black racism 14, 105, 225; embodiment
    and 114; in Gordon's phenomenology
    265–266; objectification and 114–115;
    stereotypes and 114–115; symbolization
    and 114
anti-Blackness 10, 15
anti-Semitism 105
Apartheid 2, 3, 4, 14, 81, 111, 112, 221
artistic creation 74
Asseleh, S. 34, 37

attitude(s) 90, 91, 97; action and 91; bad faith
    93–94; in *Black Skin, White Masks* 92–96;
    sociogeny 91
Australia 200, 201; settler colonialism and
    195–196
Ayme, J. 34
Azoulay, J. 29, 30, 43n14; "Introduction
    to Sexuality Disorders Among North
    Africans" 30

bad faith 93–94, 96, 163; "of the world" 1
Badiou, A., *The Clamor of Being* 209
Baldwin, J. 6, 12, 171, 172; *The Fire Next Time*
    162; "Stranger in the Village" 169
Battle of Algiers 40–41
behaviorism 50
Being 91; difference and 169
being-for-others 166, 172
being-in-the-world 11, 66, 115, 121, 132, 168
being-toward-death 197
Bernasconi, R. 5, 9, 10
Bhabha, H. 24, 37, 73
Biko, S. 3, 14, 81, 221, 222, 223, 224–225, 226
Bird-Pollan, S. 24
Black Consciousness 2, 3, 10, 14, 16, 119, 221,
    222, 223; politics and 225–226
Black experience 10
Black Lives Matter 203
Black people 5; lived experience 11
Black Skin, White Masks 2–3, 8–15, 17n2,
    25–26, 29, 37–38, 48–49, 55–56, 65,
    73–74, 97, 128, 140–141, 151, 158–159,
    163, 168, 170, 177–178, 195; attitude(s)
    92–96; corporeality in 119, 120; critique
    of psychoanalysis 103–104; critique
    of psychological literature 101–102;
    dialectical structure 100; disalienation in
    105–106; embodiment in 111, 121–122; "*le
    Nègre*" 100–101; "*le Noir*" 100; method in
    92–96; myths about the black man 104,
    105; as phenomenology of mind 9, 67–68,
    69–70; postcoloniality in 4; progressive
    structure 101–102, 103; psychopolitics in
    7; racialization in 179, 180–181; social
    psychotherapy in 103; women in 105
Blackness 11, 14, 15, 16, 95, 180, 222;
    corporeal schema and 133, 144; "fact of"
    66, 69; historico-racial schema 11, 144,
    145–146; "*Nègre*" 51, 52; perception and